Everywhere I Ne... Wanted To Go

The man gently handed me what looked like a playing card face down. I turned it over to carefully absorb its message:

"True freedom is very close; it's just on the other side of your walls."

This is the story of what happened next.

www.personirresponsible.com

To respect the anonymity of my fellow travellers, I have changed their names, except when to do so would fundamentally destroy the point. I have also altered various personal details so that those individuals may continue to pootle along without fear of judgement or identification.

This story is told from the best of my knowledge and recollection, relying on the diary I kept and from the daydreams that kept my mind active as I trundled along. Any mistakes I make are mine. All mine.

MICHAELMAS TERM

Getting to grips with the basics of life and frequently answering the question:

"Aren't you scared?"

"Home"

The average British bathroom is about two and a half metres long and just shy of two metres wide. Or one may prefer a more succinct: $4.3m^2$. I do not suppose such banal knowledge will ever furnish the winning point at a pub quiz, no matter how grungy the local establishment may be. Other observations can be surmised too: the typical English bathroom usually contains a full-sized bathtub, a hand basin under which a small vanity unit might reside, and, naturally, but also peculiarly, the toilet. On the one hand, it makes sense from a plumbing perspective, but yet, from a hygiene perspective, surely not? Perhaps though, that is not a thought one needs to dwell upon for long.

The last bathroom I loosely called mine had crammed-in modern furniture: its tub was white, plastic and purchased from your common or garden builders' merchants. It had a bulbous edge, allowing me to swivel around to hang my legs comfortably over the side; pressing my neck against the cold, white tiles, my dripping feet creating a watery trip hazard for later. Oddly, the taps had been installed at the wrong end so there was no lumbar-appeasing slant at the head of the bath. Still, it was sufficiently deep to permit flotation – just. Best of all, it came with ample hot water, keeping me sufficiently temperate as I squandered time, marinated, or, on very rare occasions, propitiated aching muscles. Mostly, I used it for its primary purpose: to cleanse. With oodles of childish bubbles, *obviously*.

Until this very moment of my final soak, I had been living in a honey-coloured limestone worker's cottage on the edge of the magnificent Cotswolds. The bathroom was an extension tacked on to the side of the house. It was the only room with two straight walls. The back one seemed to have been accommodated from I know not what, perhaps an old pigsty. That wall was excessively thick, more than one metre deep, with a single frosted window set hard at the outer periphery. The sill had been appointed as a terracotta-tiled altar for my bathroom candles, decorations and ablution accoutrements. A thinner wall would have allowed better space to contort oneself into clothing but in Merrie England cottages were practically fortified, robbing their future inhabitants of gratuitous towelling manoeuvres.

Exiting the bathroom, one faced the stable door, which was the only entrance to the abode. On the left, a bland swing door, behind which was tucked a tiny utility room. It had once been dominated by the washing machine. There was just enough floor space to cram the cat's two litter trays beneath the wall-mounted boiler that the door's edge barely swerved past. A room so compact that hard hats and elbow-padding, let alone the full hazmat suit, ought to have been a compulsory requirement.

Opposite this futility room stood the doorway to the poky living room, previously bedecked with rugs strewn haphazardly across wooden floorboards. One had to take a small step down, past two slightly wonky windows obscured by plastic privacy-screen – there to protect the incumbent from neighbourly inquisitiveness. The lounge ceiling was held aloft by low slung, fat oak beams and made cosy by an inglenook fire. The fireside still gripped old, rusting steel handles with knobbly hooks bedded into the red, crumbling brickwork. The opposing door was overly-painted, antique and squat: forcing all but the vertically compressed to duck when exiting the living chamber. From there, one could either lunge upstairs via an uneven, curved stairwell or bow right into the kitchen.

Two good sized rooms lay upstairs, one formerly my office, the other my bedroom. Each had a single square window, but only the office offered a view of any merit: the village green with predictable lonesome oak and park bench. The cat could usually be seen basking on one of the two broad sills; occasionally 'akking' at a bird in the distance, but more often snoozing, paws akimbo. It was not the outlook that had me sold on the cottage, but the mesmerising magnolia wattle and daub panelling gently bulging between the blackened beams that separated the upstairs rooms.

There was no ceiling, just a typical high-pitched, and very slender roof. Its thatch had long since been disposed of and replaced with slate. One could hear the scrapings of woodpigeons' claws as they tottered back and forth across the weathered stone in the mornings. In typical Cotswold cottage fashion, the residence was humid in the summer; damp and chilly in the winter, but it was oh-so-quaint, *daahling*, in the estate agents' pictures. It took little to become a homely place where too many hot chocolates laden with squirty cream in front of the log fire had me piling on thigh pounds in sufficient readiness for a nuclear winter of indeterminate duration.

It was there that I happened upon the news that over two thousand, five-hundred local authority latrines across the nation had permanently shut their lids following the Covid era of 2020 to 2021. Just another casualty of a policy of austerity which had already chomped and ground down anything that was convenient for the so-called 'Great Unwashed', who are the very same group of people that politicians will refer to as 'hardworking families up and down the country' during an election year. That peculiar brand of people who have everyday bodily functions, and who might, just might, wish to venture out of their homes once in a while for no other reason than to go and see how the other half are mortgaged.

"Britain's going down the toilet!" exclaimed not a single one of my friends because they really are not inclined to make idiomatic pronouncements of the lavatorial kind. They, largely being of the British contingent, merely tutted and then found something else to whinge about. Regardless, it did make me ponder: if Britain is really going down the toilet, shouldn't someone go out there and find it? They could then bung in wodges of loo-roll to plug it, which in turn, would swamp the area with rejuvenating freshwater and all would be lushly reborn. Or, we could ask the ever-changing incumbent Prime Minister to just twiddle with the national stopcock. And, if such acts of heroism were there for the taking, why should that act be reserved for a cape-crusader type wearing skin-tight underwear outside of his brightly-coloured leggings? Why couldn't it be an overweight, middle-aged, singleton divorcee, accompanied by a similarly middle-aged, and prematurely grey, immigrant cat as a wingman? Why not? Why not indeed!

****

I remember the day he announced, "We should buy one of those and travel around Europe." He gestured towards a glossy black vehicle. It was many summers ago now, I was twenty-something, closer to thirty but still full of vitality, burning ambition and wanderlust. That year we'd hired a smallish motorhome in Germany, zipping across Austria to Hungary, and then back again.

He did all the driving although I had acquired a driver's licence a few years prior. Despite it all, I simply could not placate the creeping terror around cars that held my psyche hostage. Oddly, as these things tend to be, I have always been perfectly content as a passenger, regardless of the conditions of the highways, the country, or the maniac holding the steering wheel.

I loved the freedom of the road, and this motorhome promised adventures of the marital kind. I recollect that the bathroom stall was tiny, containing a yellowy-beige all-in-one unit that had been purposely moulded to fit the space, not unlike one in an aeroplane. Both of us had great reluctance about using the loo, because neither of us wanted the responsibility of emptying it later. "Men's work!" I may well have decried in order to abdicate from that particular household chore. I imagine that, in the end, we did use it but I do not recall any of those details. This is not a book about memorable poos in forgettable places; well, bar one unfortunate incident.

Yet, I still remember his remark so vividly and concisely: "We should buy one of those and travel around Europe." He was gesturing towards the aforementioned van as my brain, despite recognising all the words, failed to adequately decode his utterance.

Never before had I declared a van 'sexy', but there was something undeniably sleek about the contour of this vehicle. It was a look that set it apart from all other run-of-the-mill traders' vans. It is now ubiquitous, but at the time, it was the head-turning catwalk model of small trucks, something to be admired and envied.

Until the early 2000s, vans had largely been bulky, boxy or angular, and were usually obnoxiously in the way or at least trying to be. Especially the white ones. 'White Van Driver' had become notoriously indifferent to almost all common driving courtesies. Owners were perceived to be tabloid-reading, Burger King-devouring, hand-gesturing menaces of the local highways and byways. When outside of the van, they swanned about with arms of contrasting depths of tan, low-slung cargo pants or middle-aged, man-jeans exposing several inches of crack, barely covered by a grubby, ill-fitting t-shirt.

Then along came the Trafic to bring a smidgen of sophistication to the arena. Prior to these, the only vans that I had registered were the Tampax Vans. They were actually more tampon-shaped in my womanly opinion and absolutely no one ever called them Piaggios. They might be the only vans of distinction that any layperson might ever recall, and I still had to Google the proper name of them for the purposes of writing this book - so rare they are these days, and so novel they were in those days.

"What?!?" I retorted.

"We should buy a Trafic and tour across Europe. It'd be fun." repeated the man known then as my husband.

I took a few puffs of my cigarette, contemplated the idea and then retorted, "I think divorce would be more fun!" in my most pontifying English accent.

****

The average internal spec of a bog-standard traders' van, I learned, is not radically different from that of an average English bathroom. Unless one opts for a long wheelbase van. In that case, one soon discovers that parking one's mobile toilet, which also includes one's living room, kitchen, office and bedroom, in the local supermarket is considerably more complicated than parking an ordinarily-sized car. To think I used to find the notion of reverse-parking my Nissan Juke into a piddly little bay at the local Tesco utterly petrifying!

Vans are unwieldy to drive. Modern vans have modern amenities but this particular one, although similarly aged as my car, was short on benefits. Absent were the heated seats, effective air-conditioning, built-in reversing camera, Bluetooth technology enabling hands-free driving, and integrated Satnav. I relinquished all these comforts and replaced them with an elongated white van from the Citroën family, complete with portable toilet, pre-existing dents and squeaky seats. Within seconds of purchasing it my friend and I, naturally, dubbed it The Shitron.

Like my car, it had six gears but the shift stick was more onerous to orchestrate. The handbrake was on the right, a long way down the side of the driver's seat. I could barely release it and get the van moving at the same time without profound cursing. Ergonomically speaking, it was quite unsuitable for a woman of average height. Likewise, in typical sexist arrangement, there was only one mirror behind the sun shields: the one on the left. Such inconsiderate thinking thwarts any searches for facial displeasures while waiting on red lights.

A previous owner, wisely, had installed a reversing camera, but the radio transmission could only be detected by bats. The most monumental design flaw, if not outright vehicular crime, was reserved for the cup holder – singular. Infuriatingly, it only has sufficient circumference for a slimline espresso container. The average reusable mini-flask has to be stowed carefully on the seat beside the driver, propped up by a handbag and other paraphernalia, then further reinforced by a fervent prayer followed up with a threat that it must not topple, or else!

Still, I bought the van, not so much for its Citroën qualities, its mileage or number of 'careful lady owners', but because I was enamoured by the Scandi-style design of the living quarters. The long, light tongue and groove pine contrasted beautifully against pristine white block cupboards. The kitchenette consisted of a small 12v metallic effect refrigerator, a two ringed gas stove and a tiny sink unit.

Opposite, sat a teeny wooden table between two square storage boxes forming a booth. I covered the boxes with plush imitation sheepskin covers for a warming bum cuddle. Behind the driver's seat, stood a very compact showering area with plastic lining. It housed the portable toilet. The floor was dark wood-effect lino, faux parquet. Curtains masking the rear doors were white and grey, with black and silver trimming. Tacky fairy lights strewn around the head of the bed give off a mellow ambience. The sleeping area had a permanent structure with a small look-out window, the light almost always blotted out by an abundance of odd-shaped cushions.

Underneath the bed there was an enclosed but potentially empty void that Vanlifers refer to as the 'garage'. I could assess mine through a tiny cupboard door on the floor next to the fridge, or via the two external rear doors. It was already a veritable tip of deck chairs, straw mats, old curtains, a hose, a barbecue, a trolley for waste disposal, a large water tank, three broken iPads, as well as a liquid propane gas canister enclosed in a carpeted locker. Also stored there were the additional batteries and a myriad of electronic gubbins for converting the solar power to electricity through a modicum of magic known as amps, volts and watts, and other matters pertaining to physics that I have never knowingly made head nor tail of.

Having completed the V5 documentation, I cruised The Shitron home. Departing from a typically over-stuffed, car-strewn, 1970s housing estate to chug along numerous A-roads, it was not long before I lurched into squirrelly country lanes luring me back to the Cotswolds. The maiden voyage gave me the sensation of being a bus driver of the double-decker variety. That was all it took for me to morph from a reasonably-careful-middle-aged lady driver of the white Nissan Juke stereotype into a middle-of-the-road, wildly gesturing, white-van owner of the objectionable variety.

It was only after I had safely returned to my country abode that it occurred to me how cannily similar my soon-to-be-living space was to my soon-to-be-abandoned bathroom space. The only upside I could readily conceive was that my menopausal brain would never again arrive in a room and wonder why the hell it had done so.

****

Packing up a one-bedroom cottage should have been a fairly straightforward process for any experienced world traveller. And it was a fairly straightforward process, except for my first, and hideously dire, bout of Covid. It arrived the day after I snagged a nerve in my lower back. Both afflictions had me straightened out longitudinally for the most part, and they, of course, coincided with the first heatwave of the year. It was hard to determine whether I was suffering from a virus-induced fever, a menopausal flush, or if I was simply slow-cooking in the extreme summer climate.

Lying there, I mentally committed to doing a thorough spring-clean but also a ruthless one, indeed some might say, reckless. I was going to out-*Marie Kondo* Marie Kondo herself. I was going to feel the love, and abandon anything that failed to meet my exacting expectations. First up for banishment: the marital sofa. The place my husband had last sat and grumpily explained how stressed he was at work. "No!" he had snapped: he did not, "want to talk about it".

He was gone the next day, failing to mention that he was not coming back. Consequently, I spent many an hour idling on that corduroy corner sofa, drunk, alone and terrified. Our life together unravelled to the point that I doubted its very existence. The once eternal optimist changed course, then ultimately abandoned ship. I think of those days now as the dark ages. Then I learned to walk. And I walked until I could walk no further. One step, then another, then a bazillion more.

I had long since disposed of the marital bed; my first act in reclaiming a home for just myself and the cats. The cats used the replacement as a scratching post, only permitting me to use some of it, some of the time. I bought new duvet sets, but kept old towels. So much of it was still new back then, new for the home we had been building. I had kept the crockery – his choice – cutlery, likewise. There were two oversized 'his' and 'hers' tea-cups for hangover days, unused once my sobriety kicked in a year later.

When I moved into this cottage, I celebrated by purchasing a stylish, artisanal desk, elegant lamps and lampshades, a dedicated space to write my first book. I had picked other bits and pieces in the intervening years too – a Welsh dresser, coffee tables cut from reclaimed railway sleepers, an old church pew for a shoe rack. Antiques to me, although others might say, dead people's furniture. The remnants of someone else's past had become a hotchpotch of several lifetimes all mashed together under my roof. Now I was to dismantle it all again. Some bits would not survive another journey. The time had arrived to oust the rest of my marital life: it was like being a custodian of his old belongings.

Packing up ruthlessly is nothing but endless decision-making: "Have I touched this in the last year?" "No? Well, to hell with you!" I would exclaim, usually aloud. 'Hell', of course, was the local charity shop or the nearby 'recycling centre' which seems to be a lousy euphemism for landfill. On and on I culled belongings, moving from drawers to cupboards then back to drawers again where I had reserved pieces of my indecisiveness. Do I really need a hand-mixer in my new life? I certainly did not need three, which is what I actually had. What about soup? Making soup has long since been a therapy for me, possibly because it is the way I wield a knife into cylindrical vegetables.

I moved on to extracting the least scratched cutlery and put aside my favourite teaspoons. Baffled as to why I had so many, and originating from differing sets. Pegs, clips, sandwich bags? Corn on the cob forks? How many sharp knives? Would they clang or rattle, and roll around and generally be a nuisance as I trundled along? All my old baking trays, telling a culinary story of their own, caked with charcoaled remnants, scratches, scars and dents were clattered into the recycling. And seriously, just how many spatulas does one actually need in any-sized house? I seemed to have enough to stock a professional kitchen. Whimsically, I selected the least stained one, and two wooden spoons, clueless as to why I required two.

Would I keep my emergency cheese slicer? I had purchased it upon my return from America in 2020, just as England was stymied by yet another fiercely-restrictive lockdown. The local Tesco has a mezzanine floor stocking the homeware goods. A shop assistant-cum-Covid-prevention-worker blocked anyone using the escalators unless they had a very good reason. "I need an emergency cheese slicer," I muttered, prompting the guard to stand aside to permit me access to the hallowed kitchenware section. At the polar end of the escalator, a second sentinel commanded shoppers to go directly to the necessary aisle. I repeated my need for an emergency cheese slicer. He deftly pointed to a spot six aisles down, only to interrupt his otherwise clear-cut directions to admonish an elderly couple daring to admire a pretty dress as they were vacating the vicinity.

There is something about discarding household implements, just like packing up ornaments and souvenirs, that makes one want to say, "I remember when…" To reminisce about the mundanity of a shared life, to conjure up a place, a sensation, an interaction. Or perhaps that is just me. Perhaps I am the only one who finds resonance in azoic possessions. What lingers long after the anger, hurt, sadness and regret that abounds from a failed marriage ebbs away is the loss of being able to say, "Do you remember when…?" That there is no one to titter absentmindedly to is the uppermost downside of singledom, I believe. In the absence of a fellow human, I chunter to the cat, even though, as a conversationalist, he is truly abysmal.

****

Nelson had been first spotted as a weeny, mottled grey bundle of fluff hanging upside down, eighteen claws hooking the bars of the roof of the cage he was trapped in. His tiny prison was set on the floor of one of the many shops on Chungmu-ro Pet Street in the Jung-gu neighbourhood of Seoul. I'd taken a four-hour train to the capital to sit an exam and I was intent on returning with a second cat.

His upside down wailing revealed a florid pink mouth and way too many fangs for comfort. With tufty ears, he was more bat than cat. "Him! I want him!" My husband squatted down. The kitten snatched at his finger and gave it a Velcro-ey lick. "He British Shorthair!" the shopkeeper announced. We both nodded, as if we knew what that meant. Rings of darker fur wound around his ratty tail, and lighter frown lines of pissed-offness creased above his intense grey eyes.

As Nelson adulted, his face became far too slimline and his muzzle lengthened to pass as anything resembling a British Shorthair. He acquired jowls rather than chubby cheeks. He'd fix me with an unrelenting grey stare attempting to transmit something, but what that might be was anyone's guess. Then came the night I went to bed, as usual, steadily observed by the wide-eyed granite wonder squatting on the bedside cabinet, only to wake up the following morning to find two luminous orange marbles boring down on me.

Nelson is a lover rather than a fighter, and since his castration, he is equally as bad at both. These days, when he's not suffering from arthritis, he's nearly bankrupting me with his hypochondria. At six months old, he fell silent and was rarely able to rouse himself. After many, many trips to the local vet, he stopped using one of his legs altogether, and it withered quickly into a dangling appendage. "Avascular Necrosis," the vet tapped at the words in one of his veterinary medical books, written in English. Dr Kim could not express himself verbally in my mother tongue, and to my shame, my Korean was just about good enough to say, "Hello, goodbye and thanks for all the fish," albeit without my making any reference to marine life.

Over repeated visits, Dr Kim and I communicated through diagrams and early editions of Google Translate. At that time, the app was about as efficient as making smoke signals using a bubble machine. I went back for a final visit to discuss euthanasia. Relying on a crude sign language, it was the best that my imagination could muster for my hands to indicate decapitation: a swift chop across the neck. Alarmed, Dr Kim pointed at his calendar to show that I should wait another month. The muscle rebuilt slowly – very slowly – until one day all that remained of Nelson's ordeal was a subluxing patella. There are probably more everyday names for these afflictions, but my regular communications with Dr Kim only improved my Latin, previously non-existent, and regretfully, not my Korean.

I do know that somewhere along the way, Dr Kim fell in love with this happy-go-lucky bundle of sharp claws and teeth, because the day came for us to depart South Korea and I took him for his pre-flight check-up. Dr Kim simply uttered: "Problem airport. Give me!" he commanded as he cuddled a farewell to Nelson, who remarkably bore him no grudges despite all those penetrations with the thermometer, his loss of testicles and invasive knee surgery.

The only adult who has ever been averse to him was the now departed husband. Relations had soured abruptly overnight while I was away on yet another trip. Said husband had awoken mid-slumber to find the admirable Nelson curling one out on his head. Matters were not helped by Nelson's eminently smug face. For quite a long time post-marriage, I cherished the memory.

One long-term legacy of Nelson's illness was that he stopped meowing and remained quietened for many years. Aside from intermittent 'akking' at flying life, dozing remained his preferred hobby. Sometimes he'd muster up the most adorable 'silent miaow' of the truly indolent. Then came the day that my other cat, Tess, passed. Realising that he'd have to sing for his own supper, he resumed the choir of his people, taking on a soprano role. Imagine hosting a party for twelve toddlers, but only having ice-creams for eleven – these days he sounds like the twelfth toddler.

Just as I am, Nelson is cresting the hill of maturity and has begun the slide into decline. His eyes are dimming to a burnt orange, and his previously perky ears are slowly slipping down the side of his head. His penetrating gaze remains steadfast and, in the night, I often wake to find his little body vibrating away next to mine.

Every home needs a second heartbeat, and his is mine.

****

To Shitterton and Beyond

I don't remember my first bathroom. Nor my second. Just my third. The bathroom suite would be called 'avocado' in today's parlance. It was a room made dingier by a lack of natural lighting. I think there was a lift shaft behind a solitary frosted window, but the details are woolly. I do remember it had a bidet, and a bath, also in fetching avocado.

At that time, I had not previously encountered an avocado, and if I had, I would have made the case that the colour of the suite was more akin to slurry. The tiles, with their olive and dark brown symmetrical design, only added a sense of busyness to the already dank room. There was a stark white wicker basket in which I once concealed myself in a game of hide-and-seek, jumping out like a jack-in-the-box when one of my non-kin uncles paid a visit to the lavatory. I could have said that he'd pissed himself, but he was already half-way done.

I have hazy memories of my bedroom, the first door on the left. Come bedtime, I would stargaze at the pellucid desert sky. On other nights, I kept the curtains closed. I could be anywhere, the only tell was the bed being clad in just a simple white sheet, top and bottom. The mosquitoes' whining was relentless and their invasions on my naked arms were bothersome. The only way to cure the itching was to ram my tiny nails into them, scratching and digging until they bled. I'd use the sheets to dab at the wounds.

I remember the night that the souk burned down. I watched from my bedroom window as the blaze danced furiously, flames grasping up at the pitch sky. I don't remember any noise, because it was far away on the horizon. During the daytime, the souk was a short drive away, but we took the more time-consuming buses, hovering under the shadow of a street light for shade waiting for ours to arrive. Nothing was predictable. My mother, already a short-tempered woman, wilted. We often visited that souk, catching the bus, of course. Of course? Of course: because women were banned from driving.

The national green and white buses would cough out their pollutants next to the rear doors marked for the females. I'd clamber up the huge, sand-strewn steps, jostling to find a spot amongst women doused from head to toe in black cloaks: the Abayas. There was barely a naked eye amongst them. It was always 'standing room only' because there was insufficient space for seats. Our compartment was probably no bigger than the average British bathroom. As Westerners, we didn't wear the overcoats, rather, we opted for kaftans and loose-fitting long-sleeved dresses, a simple scarf perhaps covering the top of the head.

Sometimes the bus driver failed to open the rear doors, at others, the bus pulled away without giving enough time for us all to embark. There'd be a fit of screams and hollering, mostly to no avail. On other occasions, the driver would omit to close the rear doors, making the journey unnecessarily perilous, but at the same time providing some welcome cooling draughts. Riyadh was always a city on the broil, but it was unbearably savage when compressed into a small vestibule adjunct to the rear engine. I can still cast my mind back to a pregnant woman falling backwards down the steep steps as the bus lunged forwards, my mother reaching to grab her to haul her back in. The stranger slapped away at her hand, and grasped at the rail. Words were exchanged, but none were understood.

On one trip I peeked through the window separating the men's quarters from ours. The pillar-box red velveteen curtains had edged apart in the centre. Unable to resist sneaking a look into how the male half lived, I was astonished by the men's quarters. They weren't just one half of the bus, but an entire three-quarters. Luxurious, wide, and vivid red high-backed seats sat two-by-two on the right-hand side, offering ample leg-space, just like an old-fashioned first-class coach in 1950s planes. Mostly, the armchairs – for that's what they really were – remained empty. I counted only the backs of three heads. They looked cool, as if their space was air-conditioned. Behind the glass, we females asphyxiated.

****

"One year, no fear!" I informed Nelson. It was to be my mantra. "There are only two ways of overcoming fear: drip, drip, drip or plunge in without hesitation". I kissed his little furrowed brow. I know that there is no half-way between the two. Just the two options: take the cat on tiny little drives, extending them, returning home, and before doing the do again and again and again. Stretching the time, the speed, the distance, the fierceness of competing traffic. Cats learn to fear cars by association, after all there is usually a vet trip involved. Or just plough on through.

The cat, not being as rational as I am prone to being, has no option but to defer to my superior logic. It was not as if Nelson had not been in a car and not gone to the vets. He is a well-travelled cat, and one used to ever-changing homes.

The conundrum on how best to condition Nelson to the nomadic life resolved itself when I was invited to spend a weekend in a town known formerly, and most amusingly, as *Godalminge*. Yes, I had to read it twice too and the variant pronunciation quickly fossilised, much to my host's horror. It was never going to be as simple as wrestling Nelson into a carrier and hitting the M4. This task would require some leash training. A few weeks prior, I had captured the unsuspecting feline and jacketed him in a harness. Until this moment, Nelson had never even worn a collar, although several incidents had caused him to wear the cone of shame. Now it was time to try out an entire padded coat, one covering most of his rib cage, a third of his back, and all of his fine chest. It looked reassuringly safe to my eyes.

Nelson, on the other hand, concluded that he had somehow got himself into a bind and stalked me from room to room, balancing himself against any solid objects. Anywhere I went, there following me was an incessant and slightly embarrassed, "Mom! Mom! Mom!" as he shadowed me pottering about the place. If I was not ambling around, he would poke me with a paw as if to draw attention to his predicament. He would almost roll his eyes that I could not 'see' the problem as he determined it. In the end, he would feign a faint, staring vacantly as if relinquishing his will to live.

I bought a simpler harness: just two simple interconnected straps, one a choker-type and a second, to prevent choking, wrapped behind his front legs. Peace and harmony were soon restored.

On his first ever crate-free journey, Nelson behaved admirably, tethered as he was from his harness to the front seatbelt in a small, open box. I kept the cat carrier on the back seat, just in case. In hindsight, it was probably a formidable threat from his perspective. He loved the ride home too. The only possible conclusion is that Nelson is an archetypal cat – especially weird, and pertinently unpredictable.

Trial over, it gave me the green light to just crack on and plan a journey around the UK. A single, motorised trip that would drag us from *Shitterton* to *Weedon*, through every county, or administrative centre in current existence, as well as anywhere else we probably never wanted to go. Along the way, together, we would learn quite a bit about overcoming fear, phobia and anxiety. Mind you, we would learn a great deal more of British history, geography and etymology.

****

It seemed apt to commence the journey at *Shitterton.* For the unknowing, this is a bona fide thousand-year-old hamlet adjacent to the village of Bere Regis, and one which is world-famous for its very unfortunate name. Until the week before departure I had no idea where exactly it was. Somewhere in the fog of my brain, I had placed it in Somerset, deep in the thigh of the leg that juts out at the base of southwest England. It turns out that *Shitterton* is slap-bang in the middle of Dorset, which is perpendicularly south, with a twitch of west, of Warwickshire, where we were ordinarily residing.

I readily confess that I am geographically-challenged, despite my worldwide travels. I have a tendency to get lost in my own living room and this trip truly reinforced to me just how disorientating English geography can be. For starters, the number of counties seems to vary depending on which political party is in power and what information one is looking for. An English map, I discovered two days after I left Cumbria, can also be re-drawn at a moment's notice.

For the benefit of other pseudo-foreigners, and for the authentic ones, I can only liken England's sudden cartographic adjustments to the Administration of the United States randomly declaring that Florida will subsume most of Georgia, then giving the remainder away to Alabama. One day there are fifty states, the next Americans are glorifying about forty-nine. Usually, the purported theory for this is the ruling-elite wishing to wash out one state's tendency to vote for the opposition.

Here in the UK we do not have senators but Members of Parliament, some of whom are appointed 'Right Honourable'. This epithet simply means that they are a senior rank to the elected politicians, who are often called backbenchers. It would be a misstep to presume the Right Honourable lady, or gentleman, is any more trustworthy than the overweening, self-aggrandising rest of the motley crew. In times past, the title was indicative that the politician was of a lesser rank and not born within the aristocracy. Our entitled folk once occupied both the House of Lords and Parliament, although not so much in present times.

If this is not hierarchical carnage enough for any democracy to fathom, more recent times have seen this country falling into the habit of changing Prime Ministers more frequently than we have elections. In the course of this year-long expedition, the Tory Government ejected three leaders even though the electorate had no hand in voting in any of them. If anyone else is similarly baffled by the antics of our national managing directors, please form an orderly queue behind me: I am the sane one chatting to a South Korean British Shorthair.

How England is carved up mattered, for I intended to seek out the most awful-sounding places in each county in order to pace my year around the country. I had envisaged writing each county as a chapter. It seemed, therefore, eminently rational to divide the number of weeks by the number of counties in existence, and take it from there. Alas, curiosity got me asking Google how many counties that would be, and the answer is, "It depends on what one means by county." Apparently, in England, a county can be taken to refer to an administrative region, or it may refer to a zone from Olde Worlde England, which may or may not align with a ceremonial county. It may exist this year politically, by parish, or in accordance with the Post Office or the Police's assignments. Only in England, the originator of imperial mathematics, could simple calculations become so terribly complicated, so terribly quickly.

Upon arriving in Dorset, I quickly discovered an absence of street signs for *Shitterton*. It transpires that they have all been pilfered over the years. Traditionally, such misappropriation is blamed on university students, rather than the local 'oiks'. Somewhat creatively, this unrelenting crime spree across parochial Dorset was eradicated once and for all when some bright spark decided that '*Shitterton*' might be better engraved into a ton and a half of Purbeck limestone. The appropriated lump of stratum was promptly dumped roadside in 2010, approximately halfway down the main drag that dissects the village of Bere Regis. Incidentally, 'Bere Regis' is a more pretentious title for King John's Wood. It is notable for being a minor village that is, funnily enough, tremendously well sign-posted across Dorset.

In 2012, Bere Regis, not wishing to be usurped by its smaller bedfellow, or rather 'to keep up with the stoneses', purchased its own near-identical lump of sedimentary rock and plonked it on the western boundary in commemoration of Her Majesty's Diamond Jubilee. Fast forward to 2022, while Bere Regis and the rest of the country celebrated the Queen's Platinum Jubilee, *Shitterton* could simply rejoice in not having had its bit of bedrock nabbed for over a decade.

One could say it is a tale of two hamlets, but alas, Bere Regis has a church, so, as far as England is concerned, that is what distinguishes it as a village. A very, very small village nonetheless. Still, it tries its best to outdo the significantly more famous hamlet of

Shitterton and fails woefully, especially on looks. Once upon a time, Bere Regis would also have been a huddle of picturesque wattle-and-daub beamed beauties, but they were carelessly eradicated by fires in 1613, 1717, and again in 1788. At the fourth attempt of retaining its existence as a settlement, all lodgings were sensibly brick-built. Despite its sparse population, Bere Regis offers residents a choice between a church and a chapel, the latter located on Butts Lane.

But before one proclaims Bere Regis for having superior moral turpitude, the village is tempered by two pubs and an off-licence-cum-convenience store. With so much ale available, it is little wonder that Wikipedia suggests the name *Shitterton* is quaintly derived from the Olde English to mean 'the brook that is used as a privy'. Even more amusingly, this brook, which bifurcates Bere Regis from *Shitterton*, is a tributary of the River Piddle. But most astoundingly, it was this little snaking latrine that prevented the immolation of *Shitterton* on three occasions and kept *Shitterton* the delight of black and white, but highly flammable, boxy thatched cottages that it is today.

Both settlements are recorded in the Domesday Book of 1086, a book which is thought to be England's first census of all its towns, hamlets and hovels. Back then, *Shitterton* was dubbed 'Scatera', with the 'scat' having the exact same meaning as it does today: poop. Scatera is also thought to mean 'farmstead on the stream of the sewer'. Somehow Scatera reconfigured, as the English are wont to with their language, into *Schitte*. Over the centuries, a few letters were silently obliterated, or possibly stolen, leaving us with a shit to give.

It is safe to say, and probably necessary to insist, that *Shitterton* is Britain's most misnomered hamlet. It is little more than a tiny kink of a road, bisecting a few furlongs of higgledy-piggledy blonde-maned, oak-framed cottages. All are painted an immaculate white and suffocate in well-tended but burgeoning summer blooms, making this the dream postcard composition. Except it is so confined, I found it terribly difficult to get a decent angle for a photograph.

Down in Dorset

First nights are always tricky. The smell of an unfamiliar bed, the shape and shadows of a room, and the sounds which reverberate softly around unfamiliar walls. A fridge kicking in perhaps, radiators tinkling as they cool. Things clicking or ticking. In a cottage, one might hear the whispers of breezes or rainfall. Perhaps, in the far distance, foxes barking, owls swooshing before abrupt screeches pierce the dark. These are familiar outdoor country babbles, but in The Shitron, they are so much more striking. In a house, I might ponder if they were ghosts or intruders, yet I would often remain immobilised by a combination of exhaustion and lethargy. Within weeks, any idiosyncrasies of my new abode were thus transmuted into my every day before eventually going unheard.

I had parked in what I had hoped might become a quiet lane just as the sun journeyed into the past. As night took control, my mind attuned to danger. There were five doors into my home and I could see all of them, bar the driver's door, from my pillows. I was relying on blind faith that the side and rear doors were locked because they would still open from the inside. I pressed the fob to 'lock' and external orange indicator lights flashed like beacons. I pressed the key fob again to be sure, and then wondered if I had now unlocked them. There was another surround sound of bolts slamming. I pressed it a third time. The door slid open. I closed it and clunked the locks again.

I had opted for a small layby surrounded by the Downs, but it was a poor choice. The van lurched as each passing car whizzed by. Nelson launched himself bedward for a cuddle, having wandered around the place unperturbed, with a look of "This it?" He glanced upwards then settled down beside me. He had already eaten several times, sauntered across the counters and sat like a loaf of bread on one of the seats by the table watching me as I went about my business.

A car pulled into the layby just as I contemplated extinguishing the lights. I could not see it but I could sense it. Nelson snorted out his tiredness and I felt his body release into slumber. The light switch was reachable from the bed, but I remained wary of plunging us into the pitch so hesitated until the car pulled off. With a sigh, I jabbed the 'off' button to cut the power to the five spotlights embedded into the pine ceiling and awaited the momentary blindness.

The room glowed cobalt. Just like a darkened cockpit, the buttons from the control panel mounted on the far wall directly opposite my eyeline tinged everything a bright blue. Beneath my bed, an electrical contraption blinked and orange and green blobs bounced off the rear doors. My WiFi with its two green eyes twitched and the fire alarm fluttered an angry red dash. It seemed as if I had been plunged into a veritable disco of traffic lights and I was now living in some childhood electronic game.

****

The town was festooned with colourful, brightly-lit fountains taking centre stage in the roundabouts and palm trees shuddered as expensive cars raced by, tyres squealing in the night's heat. I remember weekend trips to visit the desert, which was little more than miles of rocky arid outcrops baking in a midday sun, wisps of clouds barely marring the celeste sky. Tourism, aside from the Muslims' Hajj pilgrimages to the holy city of Mekkah, was outright forbidden. There were no mementos to purchase, no postcards of stunning red sands, of dunes and troughs sculptured by desert winds contrasting the shadows of the camel trains. Sometimes, cruel winds whipped up a sandstorm grazing my eyes and ruining the day. There was an undeniable luxuriance to these lands, with scorching sandpits full of golden ripples, a shimmering horizon and oil-funded wealth.

Once, we happened upon a large Saudi family picnicking between the dunes not too far from the road. Exquisite Arabian rugs placed directly on the ground, with women sat cross-legged around their edges. No chairs. No tables. They beckoned us over, although my father and brother were promptly whisked off to join the men on another side of a mound. As they disappeared, several women emerged with half-eaten plates of salads, leavened breads and sauces, placing them in the centre of the carpet. Right hands delved into the platters and scooped up the already-mauled offerings. There were rose-scented sweets beckoning too, out of bounds as they hadn't yet been offered to the menfolk. I adored the rich, sugary, lemon tea which was poured into tiny metal cups directly from the samovar. I asked for more, and then a third, which gleaned the grandmother's approval and had all the women laughing heartily. I'd like to think there was a communal understanding between the mothers that I'd be wailing, "I need the toilet!" within five minutes of setting off for the drive home.

Their veils thrown over their heads meant that one could read their moods, see their smiles and watch their eyes dance around; they hauled down the fabric the moment a holler was heard. Some of the younger women set off as commanded. Not too far away, there was a gaggle of 4x4s, and men in white thaubs appeared to collect them. We could hear them revving up and down dunes, smelling the faint whiffs of clutch oil burning. Later on, my father returned red-faced, thriving in the adrenaline rush generated by thrashing cars to his heart's content, revelling in his newly acquired skills of off-roading in deep sand. We females had sat through the racket demurely, not even spectators to their accomplishments.

One would like to think of them as Bedouin, but more likely they were just another family, albeit one of many wives and generations, out enjoying the world at large for a day – just a simple day of frivolity. Segregated frivolity.

The deserts that I most remember were stony and grey, rubble almost. Those were the best for foraging; we could scamper up and down, scraping knees and elbows in fervent exploration, all the while minding out for scorpions and flesh-eating camel spiders. Occasionally, we'd find the spiralled shells of the ammonites and perhaps a few teeth of some underwater predator. A pastime that was nothing but a dry fishing expedition. It was impossible to imagine that once these parched lands languished under oceans. We sometimes kept the relics from a bygone age, but mostly we threw them back for others to seize another day.

The remote deserts allowed my mother to take the wheel for short defiant bursts, countering her fear of losing the skill of driving. Cruising along undeviating highways just for the hell of it, her rebellion ran wild for a mere ten minutes: probably no more could be dared, lest another car passed.

Most days we'd go to the compound pool after we'd finished at the American School. We lived in an expatriate community, a workers' ghetto segregating us from the ordinary residents. I learned to swim there, fighting against a slathering in greasy sun cream. We'd eat crunchy potato sticks from a can and Pringles. Occasionally we'd go on playdates. I loved them because I loved electronic games. Space Invaders and some ping-pong simplicity that needed a full-sized computer could absorb me for hours. Then there was the ever-speeding up Game and Watches, challenging nimble fingers and the pursuit of scoring 999 so it began the count again. I didn't have such toys of my own in those days, but I hankered to borrow those of others. There was one toy that involved sedate driving. There were obstacles and other vehicles to overtake, I found it soothing and mindful. When my mother came to collect me, I showed her the game and asked if I could have it, perhaps for my birthday or Christmas. It was then I learned that it was a boy's toy.

****

So far, my journeying around Shitterton was proving to be gloriously twee, reminiscent of a bygone era of lovely ladies in frilly white dresses, soaking up the late afternoon rays, their legs tucked to one side as they rested on blankets laid on immaculately trimmed lawns, in summers that were just so perfectly set. One could almost hear the pouring of freshly brewed tea into dainty porcelain cups, the nibbling of cook's shortbread as they tittered to one another behind lace-gloved hands. In the backdrop, the occasional handsome man would pass by, rugged and swarthy from many an hour of wheat threshing. There would be more tittering. Such cinematic Englishness! Then the ladies of the day would return to gossiping about who had taken a charm to whom, who was falling out of favour, and of course, the high fashion of London Town. In reality, it would be more likely one of the women would exclaim, "The sodding privy is full to the rafters again and my bowels are fit for popping!"

Nowadays, the cottages are modified to include indoor plumbing. No more dashing to a creaking wooden latrine at the bottom of a muddy garden to wipe one's nether regions with leaves, moss or a pretentious shitty stick. Toilet paper, I have since learned, was only invented in 1857, and even then, it was dashed with splinters. These days, when it is time to put the kids to bed, it is one swift flush and off they go to la la land. The dilemma for the modern Shittertonian is whether to have contemporary bathroom furniture or boho enamel.

Shittertonians would not need to revisit last night's dinner in quite the same way as the van-dwelling itinerant, whose options are ostensibly confined to 'compost or potti' or some make-do vestibule. The Porta Potties use blue and lurid pink liquid chemicals, mixing with the contents to form a sort of putrid green sludge, which then needs emptying somewhere responsibly, usually incurring the cost of a campsite. Traces of irresponsibility occasionally bleach the ground and destroy all that lives beneath it.

Option two is the composting toilet. A top of the range composting toilet costs the same as an old car that has just about retained its MOT so I guess, it is not for nothing that old bangers are also referred to as shit-heaps. The second tier of composting loos are considerably cheaper, but still not cheap. Finally, there are a plethora of wooden boxes available, housing two vessels divided by a separator. One may opt to protect the 'solids' compartment with a compostable caddy liner available in all good supermarkets.

Irrespective of price, composting loos all seem to amount to the same thing: you sit on the seat and release whatever is clamouring to get out. If all goes well, the pee exits into the front hole, and the other drops into the wider mouth behind. It is best all-round if this happens before the blood circulating to one's feet cuts off entirely. Then, grabbing one's composting material - be it wood shavings, woodchip cat litter, coconut hair or shredded paper, one decorates the gently steaming reconstituted foodstuff. Note well: glitter is not a compostable substance.

Composting, I have since learned, takes around a year and a half. It is quite likely, therefore, that it will not be long before one utters something akin to, "By Jove, that privy is full to the rafters and my bowels are fit for popping!" in whatever dialect of the English language one ordinarily conveys their thoughts. Thus, like all good dog owners, one is required to bag it up and pop it into a communal rubbish bin, or bury it with a shovel in the hope that no one asks too many questions. The wee, on the other hand, assuming no chemicals have been used, can be chucked out pretty much anywhere. Coming soon to a hedge near you…

One notable difference between caravans and converted vans is the lack of actual compartments within the cabin. Caravans and motorhomes usually have a small door behind which one can stuff one's body inside and have a modicum of decency, albeit very squashed decency. Vanlifers are obliged to retrieve their preferred unit from underneath a fixed bench, or in my case from the 'shower area' and plonk it down in the minimal floor space available. Never before, at least not in living memory, have I introduced my insides to the outside while simultaneously sitting inside my kitchen, office and bedroom. Welcome to Vanlife.

Nelson's litter tray lies in the passenger footwell, just in case you wondered.

****

As I trundled across the rolling Dorset downs, it was not long before we became a mobile chicane for sportier traffic. Like a gaggle of ducklings, cars of all shapes and sizes skittered out then back, assessing whether there was space to overtake as we collectively wended our way through the desiccated lands, parching in the summers' heatwave. I pondered why English farmers have such an aversion to square fields, or just right angles in general. Too much mead in times yonder was the best I could conclude. It must have made maths a hellish subject, long before trigonometry became the bane of schoolchildren's lives.

From the confines of my windscreen, the landscape struck me as a fluffed-up duvet of celadon, gold and beige swatches. Rather than a neat and orderly patchwork quilt, it looked as if a humongous cat had played kiss chase across it, leaving pillowy lumps and concavities, not unlike my own duvet. It is little wonder that one of the Downs is called *Smacam*. I spent much of my time fruitlessly thumping down the bulges left behind by the furry one in order to maintain the illusion of a tidy tiny home; it was a war that I lost most days.

Perhaps all these mounds and hollows are the reason Dorset is a county dripping in offensive terms. One could almost conclude it is a veritable latrine: it has the highest bottoms to hectare ratio of all the counties in the UK. There is *Knights In The Bottom, Fishpond Bottom, Burnt Bottom, Little Puddle Bottom, Bramble Bottom, Charity Bottom, Rake Bottom, Littlecombe Bottom, Quarry Bottom, Boar's Bottom, Long Bottom, Chickengrove Bottom, Great Bottom, Broad Bottom, Wild Church Bottom, Slap Bottom* and my all-time favourite: *Picket Bottom*. Alas, not one of these place names made it to long-term settlement status and exist solely on the old cartes of yonder year.

Thankfully, there was still plenty of piddle to investigate. In fact, there was enough piddle to make a small child chortle so heartily they would be chanting, "We're not there yet, are we?" The *River Piddle* cuts across *Piddletrenthide* and *Piddlehinton* and trickles its way along to Poole, yet oddly by-passing *Tincleton*. Funnily enough, shortly after *Piddlehinton*, the piddles coalesce into puddles. The rumour circulating the internet has it that their names would most certainly not have tickled the virtuous ears of Queen Victoria. As a consequence, the Piddles of Briants and Turners were thereby puddled, as were the piddles of Puddletown, Affpuddle and Tolpuddle as she, and her delicate sensibilities, swept through the region for a royally-censored visit.

Yet, slap bang in the middle of such depravity, no one thought to dress the chalk outline of a giant with his oversized gentleman's genitalia standing out, loud and proud on the hillside of Cerne Abbas. For the unprepared, the colossus also wields a large club aloft an undersized head, as well as lopsided nipples and an under-serving of ribs. It is a steep climb up to the area of upstanding, unnatural beauty and just as one fears expiring from altitude sickness, wheezing like a former smoker does, one is greeted by a sign that says, "the best view is from the lay-by of the A352." Down I trudged.

I sauntered into the town to use the free local amenities, thankfully still in existence in the village of Cerne Abbey. A sign boasted that the toilets were cleaned three times a day. They did not stipulate exactly which day though, and that particular day was not my lucky day. Shortly after, Nelson and I, along with The Shitron, set off towards the lay-by to better appreciate the porn field.

According to Wikipedia, the origins of this gargantuan piece of graffiti are hotly debated by those who are fascinated about the history of such matters. I was simply surprised that no one thought to consider blaming the attendees of the nearest university. Whilst its purpose remains a mystery, the common consensus is that it is, "one of Britain's best known hill features". I beg to differ: it is Britain's best known hill feature largely because all the others lack any genitalia whatsoever. Surprisingly, it did not make for the main talking point amongst that day's visitors. "You can't really make out his ribs," one woman observed aloud as a gaggle of us collectively, and very silently, studied the life art intently from a park bench.

Shortly after, I hurtled off towards *Scratchy Bottom* and *Dungy Head*, both located on the crumbling Jurassic coastline. The route took me deeper into the glorious Downs, made moodier by a torrent of rainfall; a rare moment of respite from an otherwise stifling summer. We soon turned into the tourism vortex that is Durdle Door. There I could disembark and traipse across the dry, chalky farmland to the valley known as *Scratchy Bottom*, famed for being the location where 'Far From The Madding Crowd' was shot. It was nothing short of ironic that the place was thronging in the height of the school holidays, despite the dank weather. If I wanted to join in with the gaggles of holiday-makers on the itchy pilgrimage, I must first part with £15 to spark the van, and overnight staying was not permissible. For that price, I would expect The Shitron to be offered a wash, dry and wax at the very least so I took a swift turn out of the car park.

Dejected, I headed for *Dungy Head* but the thick mist that was still rolling in wiped away anything of interest so instead I continued towards *Shatters Hill*. To get there, one drives through several Ministry of Defence firing ranges, regularly passing warning signs exclaiming 'Sudden Gun Fire' so perhaps it was not difficult to reason how it came to be so named. That said, I was either profoundly deaf or our military was having a day off. The most alarming warning sign of all screamed out, 'Cat Firing Point' placing Nelson himself in mortal danger. If there is one thing one does not screw around with, it is cats.

If nothing else, *Shatters Hill* had me cull my itinerary. Too much time, fuel and faffing about parking would be spent seeking out inappropriately-named roads and hills. Otherwise, it would not be so much as 'one year, no fear' as 'one year, still down here'. From now onwards my explorations would be confined to hamlets, villages and towns, and all would require signage to make it eligible for inclusion in my very pointless book. My decisiveness thus ruled out a tour of the delectable-sounding *Knackers Hole, Crumpets Drive* and *Shaggs.*

With that revision, I concluded my day by finding a wonderfully secluded spot on the outskirts of *Happy Bottom*: a local nature reserve which, unusually, had its own sign. It prompted me into thinking that it was high time to make use of the van's ablution facilities. All that was required was a large pan, an electric shower head plugged into the wall panel, a flannel and a jug. Nelson took refuge, once again, under the middle passenger seat. Once I had finished spray-washing myself, and wrangling with my long hair, I casually observed that I had incidentally, and very thoroughly, disinfected the floor of the van with second-hand soapy water. It really was quite the palaver cleaning it all up, and soon induced a sweat.

The following day I dallied around the edges of Dorset and Somerset. The miles of shaved wheatfields but yet still sturdy corn crops made for breath-taking, albeit nasal-bursting, scenery. It was time to take in the hay, leaving the horizon full of bales and bricks, and the air full of dust and other sternutatory materials. The waft of hay cut through yet another mugging heatwave, and in between cruising, Nelson and I had taken to fighting over the sweet spots under the van's ceiling fans. It is the cat who suffers from hay fever, and when he sneezes, I get splattered. For that reason alone, he wins most of the scrimmages for the prime draughty spot on the bed.

The van has two fans; one is a sophisticated contraption directly above the bed that comes with a sizable remote control. When switched on, it automatically raises its large lid. One can set it to suck air in or expel it, as well as select its ferocity: it has ten levels from barely discernible breeze to almost detectable wind. This fan is fairly quiet, unlike the second one, just above the stove top, which is capable of silencing a hurricane. I only put it on when leaving Nelson alone in the van as he was seemingly ambivalent to the racket above his head. Nevertheless, I usually returned to find him basking in a sunbeam shooting through the windscreen, ostensibly microwaving himself on the driver's seat.

Having slashed my itinerary, I randomly found myself on the outskirts of *Sydling St. Nicholas*. I thought the village's name curious, mostly because it conjured up notions of committing frotteurism on Santa Claus. One ought to be keenly aware that molesting Nick the Christmas Wonderworker will not only result in an absence of presents on Christmas Day, but also see one consigned to the sex offenders' register for the foreseeable. I soon realised the intriguingly named village had not been picked up by the cartographers of Strumpshaw, Tincleton & Gigglewick's Marvellous Map of Great British Place Names, which had been my source of information hitherto.

Sydling St. Nicholas is an olde-worlde name for an olde-worlde village: full of squat, thatched terraces, rumbling along the Sydling Waters, a mere trickle of water that feeds into the river Frome. I did not lurk for long, largely because parking was impossible, but also because I risked being charged with loitering with the intent of ruining someone's day. Several curtains twitched and one door was held ajar, permitting just one eye to peer out. It struck me as the kind of village that is very attractive for highly suspicious people with a penchant for lace-obscured windows.

Instead, I headed off to a string of hamlets that collectively sounded like a series of disappointing love affairs, commencing with *Evershot.* Contradictorily, *Evershot* is the source of the River Frome and runs parallel to the *River Piddle* to meet its maker at Poole. It was dribbling away like a Great Dane at dinner time. The former bustling market town has been reduced to being the backdrop for period dramas and, as such, usually appeals to fans of Thomas Hardy.

Evershot's most redeeming feature is the 'Three Dumb Sisters'. Three megaliths, the tallest at just five feet, are set in a line. Legend holds that these stones are the lapidified remains of a trio of girls who dared to dance on the Sabbath. Presently, they suffer the ignominy of being converted into a bench which were just as uncomfortable as the van's fleece-covered wooden boxes.

One quick tour of the village later, I made my way upwards to *Penselwood*, just across the border in Somerset. The Shitron lunged over hill after, and having peaked of driving, I decided that the freedom of the road allows the freedom to tear up confining itineraries. I settled in to absorb the stupendous views of the place where England's finest are said to have made a stand against the Great Cnut in 1016. Somewhat predictably, they lost.

England's media was still basking in the glory of our Lionesses winning Football's European Cup. Women's football had at long last been televised after years of being a barely passing reference in late-night editions of 'Match of The Day'. It was once deemed unsuitable for women by the almost all-male powers that be, and in 1921 women's participation in the game, like dancing on the sabbath, was formally banned, despite it previously having been enjoyed by all and sundry. The decision was only reversed in 1970, although who would have known? One does not need a law to forbid women's participation, when it can simply be banished or scorned by popular media altogether. Finally, just before the pandemic, the nation's television executives revealed to the general public what they had been missing out on for nearly one hundred years: a football team capable of trophy-hunting. The Lionesses had been on a formidable charge at the 2019 World Cup and suddenly someone, somewhere in the BBC woke up that maybe the Great Unwashed needed something to cheer for. The women exited at the semi-finals, not unlike the men had in 2018. It had been the men's best performance by far for years, but just three years later, I cheered as the women conquered all in the Euros.

I had been hankering for some live sport to support for some time. Divorce had stripped out my passion for Formula One and Rugby for their association with marriage and the memories they stirred up. With the advent of women's football being shown during prime time and live, I could appreciate the pastime I had previously and vociferously denigrated. Their struggles, the lack of investment and the begging to be taken seriously and given equal access to amenities. I could relate to all of that. I need role models, inspiration and relativity to show me courage, fortitude and the importance of perseverance. And I need them to resemble me, albeit, in this instance I do have to overlook their lack of cake-eating excess.

For women, there remains an ongoing fight against the invisibility cloak that has all too often been thrown over us: especially middle-aged women. I suddenly realised that is what I want to write about – the Englishwoman's England. Our stories, our culture and our history; or at least, my experiences of it. So I will, but only later in this book, because first I must get to grips with the basics of vanlife.

The most frequent question I encountered in these initial months was, "Aren't you scared?" Once I realised only I knew where all the heavy objects are as well as the knives, my fears dissipated. If someone was to break in, I would have a head start on the carnage so soon enough sleep came easily. All the same, I did consider whether I should get a sticker that says, 'Only two tools are kept in this vehicle overnight and both of them are useless!'

The tranquillity of *Penselwood* kept me for three days before I popped down to *Droop*. There was bugger all to be said about *Droop*. Signposts aplenty bidded us a polite, 'Thank You For Driving Carefully' but of *Droop,* not a word nor a letter was forged. The houses, substantial though they were, were obscured by thick hedging, making life difficult to discern and interest difficult to maintain. Full of dismay, I headed off to the outstanding village of *Tincleton*. On parking up, I asked Google, the font of all my knowledge, for interesting facts about *Tincleton.* The tinny voice came back with the announcement that, "There are no interesting facts about Tincleton." I trundled on.

The daily flirtations around Dorset ended with my hunting for suitable one-night stands for The Shitron. Ideally, a bare patch of gravel high up a Dorset down, offering a stunning panorama of rolling English hills and incidentally supplying me with an ever-changing, but breath-taking view from the loo. Too often, though, I was making do with whatever came my way, and sometimes that felt far too close to the madding crowd. My first fortnight saw me sneaking into villages and suburbs come dusk to tuck myself away unobtrusively behind another work van. I quickly realised that I did not sleep so well in the settled zones of England.

After a few weeks on the prowl, I was becoming attuned to isolated, informal and rough car parking spots worn in by dog walkers' vehicles. On other occasions I would make do with a layby, although experience quickly taught me that it was optimal to choose ones set away from the main road that they serve. Without a row of trees or bushes, vehicles swinging by suck the air away from those who are parked up. This is at its worst first thing when the great-employed hurtle into another paid-for day. In their wake, the bed-ridden occupants still stationary in the layby lurch about as if the tarmac was nothing but a superhighway of water. If the van's a-rocking, don't come a-knocking: the occupants are likely being sea-sick.

It is far better, then, to choose the dedicated cul-de-sacs for truckers. These still require one to tune out the hubbub of traffic, as well as position the van so that the camber of the road does not result in having one's head below one's feet when in bed. On my final night in Dorset, I found one which offered a stupendous view of the sun descending beyond the Downs. Locals brought with them camp chairs, small tables and picnics to look on peaceably as the yellow orb dipped down before quietly disappearing into the night to trigger a yesterday.

I bedded in, thinking to commend the location on Park4Night, an app like Tinder, albeit this one matches chaste bedfellows in vans with good resting places. That was how I discovered that come half past ten, that this popular site morphed into a dogging spot. Seemingly, this is yet another predominantly male sport, and needless to say on this particular night, there was to be more than one full moon. Too tired to move, I simply changed channels by stuffing all my windows with sun reflectors and hoped, and thankfully got, a full night's uninterrupted sleep.

A Rummage in the Undercarriage of Hampshire

I remember when the bath was decommissioned; I say decommissioned, I probably mean requisitioned. We had a second room for ablutions: a tiny closet really, beside the front door. It contained a deep, white shower cubicle and a grotty white toilet. The drains stank. Ordinarily it was a store room cupboard for cleaning paraphernalia: mops, brooms, brushes, buckets and stale stench. Then came the day that I was old enough to shower. It was not so much a rite of passage, but a moment of necessity. The bathroom had been sequestered.

The supermarkets knew all about foreign psychology, but even if they didn't call it that back then. I doubt they called the aisle 'World Foods' either. Nonetheless, the sugar, the baker's yeast and fruit juices always sat side-by-side, enticing to many Westerners' trolleys.

Fresh grapes were purchased from the fruit stands, all containing bitty seeds. Despite the abundance of varieties, seedless grapes had not yet become a modern-day convenience. The arithmetic would require a calculator, paper and a pen. If each bunch of grapes has close to one hundred berries, but a punnet only fifty, how many clusters are needed to fill a standard bathtub? And if each bottle requires around five hundred grapes, then how many fruit stalls would one need to visit? From there, the bath and a pair of washed feet could then be reconfigured into a wine press.

Later, I was to learn the riskiness of such ventures. My father only knew two other names, the men to whom he'd sell on his wares. If he was caught, he'd protect his network under the threat of lashes and other presumed acts of police brutality. Chemists, like prisoners, can be very enterprising. Foreigners bring with them foreign behaviours. And where there is foreign, fear can follow.

****

I thought it useful for me to learn a little about the historic significance of Hampshire before I set off, particularly given its strategic seaports of Southampton and Portsmouth, so I sought out my favourite historian: Wikipedia.

One commonly overlooked port is that of *Buckler's Hard*. Intended to be a thriving landing place for the shipments of sugar, all that remains are the delightfully twee rows and rows of rusty red terraces, glowing in the summer heat. It is a sight which brings about a large, satisfying sigh. England's candy revolution, however, was scuppered by the French capturing and colonising the West Indies. Humbugs! Or not, as the case proved.

Hampshire's potted history reflects much of England's past as it is recited in school history books. Hampshire was the first region to fall to the might of the invading Italians as they set about expanding their Roman Empire. It was they who displaced and enslaved the native Britons in the first century. Apparently, there was a period before the first century, but that seems inconsequential to the people who designate historical time frames.

After the Romans exited stage left some time in the fifth century, Britain was plunged into the Dark Ages. Since I left formal education, this period seems to have been redefined as the Early Middle Ages. During this period, the Germanic Jutes took to occupying parts of the county, although they quickly capitulated to the Angles and the Saxons coming in from the east, the east largely being a euphemism for modern Germany. England was, given the sudden abandonment of the Romans, without an effective defensive army; a tradition that is seemingly re-enacted every few years in men's football tournaments.

There was also the small matter of the rising tide of climate change which forced the Danes, Dutch and Belgians, flooded out of their coastal homes, to venture and settle into these fine shores. Drawn, I suspect, by the attractive temperate climes of the times which permitted England to be a land abundant with grape growers. So, for five centuries, Britain remained middle-aged and just dandy – right up until William came along to spoil the party.

William the Conqueror, he of the Norman invasion, was a decisive man. Declaring that Hampshire's New Forest would exist solely for the hunting of venison, he evicted all the peasants residing within. There was no discussion or eviction paperwork: he simply fire-razed their homes by way of persuasion. Concerned that the now well-intermarried natives were not being entirely honest when it came to paying their dues, he commissioned the Domesday Book. Its purpose was to list 'his' holdings and demand the taxes owed to him from his recently-acquired assets. Until this point of English history, only one thing was certain: death. Now, thanks to the Normans, we have taxes too. Hampshire has not supplied us with a happy history.

The aforementioned might go some way to contextualising the string of villages entitled: *The Wallops, Faccombe* and *Gore End.* The Wallops are a trio of distinct communities, nowadays bisected by the A343. Previously *Over Wallop* was segregated from *Nether* and *Middle* by the oft-flooding *Wallop Brook.* The Walloping residents were disinclined to mingle, and any accidental encounters typically resulted in fisticuffs: that is if local lore is relied upon as a witness.

Nether Wallop's former name was *Wallop Inferior.* It is now a quintessentially countrified English village whose houses form the backdrop to many a Miss Marple whodunnit. Agatha Christie's most acclaimed female detective was not a well-travelled woman, shrewdly solving crimes from the comfort of her own home, barely moving her posterior. I consider it the perfect job. In fact, Miss Marple's very existence is said to be the consequence of the director shrinking an old maid into a young girl when 'The Murder of Roger Ackroyd' was re-cast from novel to stage play. In defiance, Agatha Christie was determined to sabotage the age-old tradition of making old maids voiceless and seemingly without utility. Thus Miss Marple was conceived and went on to become an iconic English character.

Faccombe's history, on the other hand, more factually recalls the repeated invasions and immigrations of foreign entities and male leadership. The village has the several derivations recorded in local annals: *Faccumbe, Fakcumbe, Facumb, Faucumb, Fackombe, Faccum* and *Fachum.* These days it is best known for *Faccombe Hall* – a site with a long, acrimonious and litigious history of male succession and inter-family friction; similar to most of England's grand estates.

The usual recital of English history usually culminates with *Gore End.* For future reference: the place itself does not merit a visit unless one has a fascination with modern, bulky, two-storey, oblong houses with identikit window frames and common red brickwork; but it might be of use if one is in need of a plumber's merchants called 'Fix the Bog' – I was not.

Perhaps, though, Hampshire is better known for being the departure point of the Titanic and the home of the Mary Rose. I think it ought to be infamous for the hamlets of *Panters, Woodcock, Goldenballs* and *Gobley Hole*, but like the famous sea-goers, these former settlements have long since sunk into history. Instead, we are left with *Dummer.* It seems there is much to occupy one in the village of *Dummer.* There is *Dummer* Village Hall, *Dummer* Cricket Club,

Dummer Farm, as well as a pair of guinea fowl with an inclination to play chicken against The Shitron. They won.

Although it is invisible when one travels down Up Street to turn left into *Dummer Down* Street, the bird's eye view of *Dummer*'s boundary on Google Maps looks akin to a chalk outline of a homicide crime scene. Coincidentally, *Dummer* is not too far from the village of Alton, which was the birthplace of the phrase 'Sweet Fanny Adams'. The town's legacy tells the especially tragic story of the senseless slaughter and dismemberment of an eight-year-old girl back in the 1860s by the village postmaster. Unusually, and most notably, this victim's name lives on, long after that of the murderer has been consigned to oblivion.

Before anyone deduces that Hampshire is all doom and gloom, that it is not the case. It offers tourists the most delectable of holiday destinations: *Sandy Balls*. The site really is, and was, and has always been called that. These days, it is a haven for the static mobile home holiday-maker with a penchant for living amidst many neighbours and thin walls. What is most peculiar is that it is called 'sandy' when, in reality, it is a suffocating forest, albeit one that provided some glorious respite from yet another ever-blasting heatwave. I could park under the thick canopies and cool a little during the height of the midday sun, the time when only mad dogs and Englishmen are said to venture out. The cat and I wisely declined to do so.

Confined by the woodland, no more of these quadrangular boxes could be stuffed into *Sandy Balls* without building skyward. At the time, many Britons were, by and large, continuing to staycation, so *Sandy Balls* was as busy as a container shipyard. With the ongoing concerns surrounding global warming, global travel and global issues inducing a national fear of travelling, perhaps we should worry for the coastal dwelling Danes, Dutch and Belgians, especially with England's participation in another empire having similarly recently ceased. At the very least, these types of houses might be commended for their buoyancy should sea levels rise even further. An Englishman's home may once have been his castle but such abodes may soon become his main floatation device.

Photo snapped, I was happy to depart and head back further inland, diving into the New Forest in my quest to find *Butts Ash*. Never before has anything been more misnomered than the New Forest – it was so absent of trees; I might as well have been in a denuded Brazilian rainforest. Clusters of copse dotted here and there gave the impression that the Forestry Service is, shall we say, a tad lackadaisical and in need of a fresh razor. My tour of this area of outstanding, but not altogether natural, beauty left me with the impression that wood was available in the event of an emergency, but overall thick bush was more the fashion of the day.

The wildlife, on the other hand, was exceptional. I briefly stopped at *The Fighting Cocks*, a well-known public house that is well frequented by asses. Some clearly looked to be in a state of advanced pregnancy, and not just the jennets. There were more donkeys than people that momentarily I feared I had taken a wrong turn and had somehow ended up in Bethlehem.

Hampshire seems to remain as vulnerable as ever to annexation by foreign tongues. The invention of the Internet has introduced new weapons with which to fight the war on words. One such method is called the word filter, and some of them are spectacularly ineffective. They are designed, apparently by necessity, to filter out offensive language. Words such as 'ass', which is the American English for 'arse', are particularly in peril. Unfortunately, some of these word filters remove the 'ass' altogether, some replace the offending word with an eye-contorting gap, and others opt for asterisks. At least with asterisks, one can make a fairly decent stab at what Sweet F*** A** may well be. But none of this is helpful, however, when one is trying to locate *Butts Ash* on Google Maps.

Butts Ash is not, nor ever has been 'Butt Sash' nor 'Buttsash'. It is most definitely *Butts Ash.* Two words separated by a space. Most amusingly, its postcode is SO45 3PP. Yes, PP. It is just its name cannot be found on Google Maps lest it offends. In spite of these Google-initiated hindrances, I managed to photograph the sign welcoming one to *Butts Ash.* The village's name was prominently displayed, and adorned by blooming, and very bushy, hanging baskets, on both sides of the roads, and at both entry points. The town councillors clearly spared no-one's blushes by making the sign quite substantial and there was even sufficient space to boast that it is twinned with Mauves-sur-Loire in France. A quick gander on Wikipedia had me noting that our French cousins believe they are twinned with Hythe, some six miles north of *Butts Ash.*

Granted, *Butts Ash* is not a place that one would get excited about visiting. It is nothing more than one of those ubiquitous 1950s or 60s red-brick housing estates that is purposefully regimental despite lacking an army. They are made slightly more upmarket with the addition of weatherboarding to soften the monotony, and all have typical postage-stamp gardens. The fronts are lawned or crazy-paved, giving sufficient room for visiting cars to park off-street. Aside from that, it boasts a red-façaded post office and a red dog poo bin.

Our days had quickly settled into flexible routines. My time was spent writing, researching and driving. In the long late summer evenings, I might explore the rolling countryside a little on foot. A short walk, not even of the brisk variety. I came to the conclusion that I was not a fan of walking during the pandemic, so life had rapidly become quite idle. Some days, I might decide to do the housework. Just twenty-minutes of faff if I really did an intensive job of it. At other times I might head into a supermarket or treat myself to a cafe outing just to have a change of scenery from Britain in bloom, farmers in fields and cottages in quaintness.

So far, friends and good weather had availed me of washing machines and hot showers, as well as coffee and companionship. Days were no longer defined as 'weekends' or 'work'. There was a peculiar absence of stress to this expedition of England. Elsewhere, Nelson's existence seemed to dissipate into snoozing, sleeping and napping so I decreed the time and place had arrived for venturing out on the leash.

We had just made the leap of faith from van to solid ground when a cyclist slogged by. In the flash of an instant, Nelson slipped his harness and bolted. Waves of terror and grief kicked in. It is not a heart-stopping moment when one's heart is hammering away. Self-loathing swiftly. Calling fruitlessly for him left and right, I increased my circumnavigation at each rotation. Minutes stretched into half-hours. I returned to the van, then out again, to circle around again. Dusk was threatening when a knotted-up bundle of hawthorn caught my top. My sight keen, I looked down, and there, deep inside, were two orange eyes and a mess of a cat. I scrambled in, and dragged him out, pressing him hard to my chest. Angry, yet relieved. All that truly mattered was that we were reconciled and life could mellow back into malleable moments.

We quietly found our own individual contentment in our ways of being. Sometimes we might sit together, my legs hanging out the van, his firmly next to mine, with the side door open to just take in the hills, the woods or the birds flying high. Nelson showed no interest in leaving after that first experience and I deigned not to push him. Better that he should be chief of his own fear. Excitement for Nelson came in with doses of catnip, and a regular wafting of wand toys. I suspect that I was probably keeping a small town's economy afloat somewhere just trying to keep things fresh.

Pootling along, Nelson would usually snooze under the middle passenger seat on some towels. On a whim, I treated him to a plump-cushioned cat bed, placing it under the gear stick. In my imagination I could lean down and stroke him more readily when stationary at lights, or when I pulled over to write notes. Much to my astonishment, he defied the disobliging laws of felines by actually using it.

Our little tour of the county of Hampshire concluded at a squiffy sign into which '*Stoner End*' had been chiselled. Britain, or rather its inhabitants, was to commence ten days of national mourning. I, for one, lamented the death of the monarch as the loss of a female icon. After snapping the obligatory photograph of its wonkiness, we settled into a small copse nearby, intent on whiling away a few days for a respite from driving and a life on the go. It had appealed for its cooling temperatures under canopy, yet offering a real test of The Shitron's battery life. I could just run the engine a little to top up if necessary, but I wished to enjoy a few peaceful days absorbing the magnificent panorama of the forthcoming Sussexes, as well as wait out the day of mourning when all non-essential businesses would be closed. What I had not planned on was running out of propane just as the funeral bells began their toll to accompany Her Majesty's cortege.

****

"So are we going to live here now?" I think I remember asking that, or at least I recall contemplating the notion. We'd been on holiday, a visitation to the mother country, but now I can barely remember a jot about it: where we'd gone, what we'd done, or even who we'd seen. Grandparents probably, for one set were still alive, Londoners now living in the north, and thriving. A maternal aunt and uncle most definitely, on the east coast. Perhaps we visited all four corners of England, after all there was a relative's holiday cottage in Cornwall too, but I don't think we turned southeast. I remember strobes of motorway lights, white, yellow, sometimes orange, some not working at all. The smell of cigarettes wafting from the front seats.

I remember my aunty's wrought weeping as we said our goodbyes, screeching at us to, "Just go!" so that she could suffer her distress at our departure more privately. I remember it was a terrible fuss, and yet we'd already been gone for so long. Perhaps it just seemed that way to me. I couldn't fathom all the hubbub.

We were supposed to be flying back but we didn't. We lived here now. This particular house had five bedrooms, two sitting rooms and carpeted stairs that changed direction four times before reaching the upstairs bathroom. It had peach-painted anaglypta wallpaper and cream carpets. A shower cubicle in one corner. A peach bath in the opposite corner, a white toilet in the third. The fourth was empty.

We weren't supposed to be here. We were supposed to be over there – only my father had been fired. No longer were we on holiday, now we were in strife. We let ourselves into a house that didn't belong to us, but it wasn't unfamiliar either. I'd been here before as a visitor on play dates although reminiscences are vague. It was empty of them; empty of their furniture, empty of day-to-day life except for our holiday suitcases. The sum total of our belongings. No mosquitoes. No toys. No friends. No school.

The Battle of the Sexes

It was at *Titty Hill* that I commenced my adventure around Sussex, a county divided into two for ceremonial purposes. Thus, some would differentiate them into East Sussex and West Sussex. The latter should not be confused with Wessex which does not exist whatsoever in contemporary England. *Titty Hill*, I discovered, was nothing more than cleavage: a road between two mounds and probably good for a quick walk, but little else.

Driving solo provided plenty of opportunities for Nelson and I to glean knowledge from those more erudite than I. That morning, I had been inspired by a CNN article claiming that swearing is a sign of intelligence. "Long may my middle years have me foul-mouthed," I declared to the utterly indifferent cat as we learnt a little of the history of swear words.

It seems that I have determined the wider world should know that behind this invisible exterior, a bright woman shines and swears. A most spectacular proliferation of obscenities emerged as I hunted for LPG gas in order to refill my container. In desperation, I turned to Facebook, where I learned that the G in LPG denotes 'gas' so I was ostensibly asking tellers and attendants if they supplied Liquified Petroleum Gas gas. Thankfully, advice was readily forthcoming, despite my incidentally triggering a right royal row on which was better: Calor or LPG?

Multiple visits to various service stations and caravanning sites soon taught me that Calor Gas is a significantly more expensive but much more readily obtainable fuel for cooking. SafeFill containers, which is what I had, require one to own a monkey wrench: a tool I discovered I did not have. I also learned one should not travel too far from a supplier who is willing to let one self-fill, but such places, it transpires, are few and far between. All good reasons, I believe, to swear under one's breath, in one's head, and once safely within the cab of the van, aloud to the cat.

An entire day was lost visiting possible outlets in Sussex, and finally culminated in my charging back to Fleet, Hampshire. There, probably to the chagrin of feminists worldwide, I appalled myself by shamelessly engaging 'Damsel in Distress' mode to borrow a suitable wrench from a kind trucker. Another kind trucker unplugged the container, and a third kindly watched on, loudly expressing mostly incomprehensible instructions in part-Chinese, part English. I decided I ought to do the actual filling up, after all, I would need to know how to in future. The now-weighty canister near flew across the forecourt as I detached it, giving me yet another opportunity to demonstrate my intelligence to all and sundry.

Relieved, I could make a decaffeinated coffee to salve my jangling nerves, already heightened from being forced to succumb to garage-station coffees. I typically avoid the stronger stuff since caffeine is thought to terribly exacerbate one's anxiety. So does obtaining LPG gas it transpires. Naturally, none of my knights in white shining armour offered to pay, but my Facebook contemporaries are quite right: LPG is indeed astonishingly cheaper than Calor gas, but only if one extrapolates out the cost of fuel trying to locate some.

Falling short of my day's ambitions, I decided to call time near to *Cocking*. *Cocking* sits deep inside South Downs National Park. Although the settlement itself would not land a slot inside a Christmas Calendar of Pretty English Villages, some of the houses loudly advertise their existence with their mustard-yellow framed windows. Supposedly, the yellow is to indicate which abodes belong to the liberalist, and very aristocratic, Cowdray family. The colour sets the residences apart from the privately-owned imposing five-bedroom red-bricks that proliferate throughout *Cocking*. It is one way to discern who owns and who rents, which is practically a British obsession.

With the day's stress now behind me, I was looking forward to spending further time researching and quaffing decaf coffee. Except the gas would not fire up – no hiss, no burble, no toxic smell. "Cocks!"

was my profanity of choice as I clambered into the garage and set about dismantling the gas locker once again. There I observed the hissing sound, with some dribbling too, and the frozen dry ice-caked head of the container. Off I went to find a garage proper, preferably one with a monkey wrench to tighten the neck. In the interim, Nelson was promoted to chief canary.

My stay near *Cocking* permitted me to further investigate the language of swearing. Two researchers, Virginia Braun and Celia Kitzinger, reckoned that there are five hundred words for 'penis' but nearly twelve hundred for 'vagina'. In the following days, as I drove between the revolting villages and hamlets of *Lickfold, Hooe, Balls Cross, Netherfield, Pett, Wartling* and *Cock Marling*, I amused myself by reciting to Nelson all the words for genitalia I could think of. It turns out that I am quite linguistically inept, albeit intelligently so.

'Cock' is one the few words of the male anatomy used to insult a fellow, the others, of course, are 'dick' and 'prick'. Female obscenities include 'tit', but the unspeakable one is universally condemned as much more severe unless one is Irish. Swear words almost fall into three broad categories: sex, excrement or specific bits of human anatomy. A fourth group exists for those deemed to offend religious virtuosity. It is the latter that are almost always quite feminine in their derivation, such as, 'bitch', 'whore' and 'slut'. There is no real male equivalent for these. This arguably reinforces a misogynistic society that requires us to be ladylike, while simultaneously hindering our ability to demonstrate our intelligence.

Through other clicks on my phone, I was fascinated to read an article by a Mr Guile that tween-aged girls outswear boys by as much as one and a half times. Then the teenage years grumpily announce themselves and it swings three-to-one the other way. Society, culture, family and schools condition vulgarities out of us, and if women do not play the game, they are deemed to be less professional, less intelligent and less sophisticated. I could not resist decrying my sense of unfairness to Nelson, who wisely kept schtum.

A day of driving or so later, I was thrilled to pull into a picturesque parking spot just outside the heart-breakingly divine village that is *Fulking*. Sounding somewhat like a portmanteau of fucking and sulking, there was the requisite *Fulking* village hall, a *Fulking* pub, a *Fulking* Village Store, a *Fulking* parish church and if that was not entertainment enough there are some fabulous *Fulking* walks where one can discover the *Fulking* Lime Kiln and the *Fulking* Pump House. Most peculiarly, though, the locals' sports society is called the Preston Nomads Cricket Club – they are certainly a long way lost, given that the nearest Preston is in Hertfordshire, and the largest is in Lancashire. Nonetheless, their proclivity for losing can be witnessed from the glorious *Fulking* Hill.

It was while at the Fulking public house that I learned that swearing quells pain. Professors from Keele University concluded that swearing after the thwacking of a hammer on one's thumb enables the sufferer to overcome the pain sensation much quicker. Imagine that: just as a girl's period pain rips through her insides, society drums out of her any urge to swear. Still, by regularly bashing my head on my cupboard units, I can at least medically alleviate my injuries by swearing loudly on each occasion.

The Battle of the Lexis

We lived here now. Not there. We were back in the house I was born in, although it was as if I had never seen it before. It was cramped. It had been rented out and we had had to wait for the tenants to be evicted. It was shoddy, a true mess of a neglected house. The walls were littered with markings from crayons and felt tips; the carpet heavily stained, somewhat threadbare; the furniture scratched, torn and smelly. I had a vague notion of the family dog but he was put down just after we left. I sensed him occasionally, oddly missing him.

The bathroom had tatty black and white laminated flooring. It was the only room free of childish scribbles. It had a cold enamel white bath with lime-scaled taps and a wire bath shelf slung across. An odd blue stain headed towards the sinkhole. There were no radiators, just a gas fire in the living room with two settings – four panels or two. Its heat scorched the legs of the sole occupant who could sit next to it: mother's chair. We rarely sat there. My parents had a portable electric three-bar heater in their room, but never was it shared. Perhaps that was why I liked the bath, a place to be warm. Then a neighbour's son fired off an air rifle, smashing the frosted window, damaging the only undamaged room.

We were still in the throes of nothingness, and money was tight. The garden was overgrown; the perfect jungle for a plant-starved child. I loved foraging in the blackcurrant bushes and raiding the apple tree, which supplied bitter cooking apples. Apple crumble was the most delicious thing on the menu, despite being served with the powdery, lumpy Bird's custard. My father cut the tree down shortly after the harvest finished – I know not why. Everyone was always silently seething – I knew not why. Stress polluted the air. Now I understand why.

It was decided that I should be homeschooled, and only my brother should go to the 'local comp' as they called it. I know not why. Then our father left for another country and I went to school proper. Bafflingly, I shared the same class with my elder brother. I know not why. At school everyone knew everyone, and always had done. My mother claimed that my brother was too advanced for his school year, a result of the American school being better than a comprehensive, or something to that effect. I found it all odd because she told me I was behind at my last school. We'd walk to school everyday, sometimes in the rain, sometimes with a neighbour and we were forever cold. I missed the desert buses, the chattering to the other children, the daily journey between school and home when we'd share our snacks with our seat-mates. I missed the heat. I didn't belong here. I did know that, although I didn't understand why.

****

When the Anglo-Saxons gallivanted into what was not then called the Kingdom of England, in the fifth century, they brought with them the rudiments of modern-day English. Somehow, although no one really knows how, the majority of natives adopted the language of the incomers. Despite this auspicious start, in contemporary times, English people have a global reputation for being dire at learning languages. The exception to this is, of course, when it comes to reciting swear words or ordering beer. Whatever methods the invaders did to help us master their tongue, we should probably adopt today though I suspect that it might result in a long prison sentence!

The other reason, which I realise may be offensive, is that Old English, fashioned by our Germanic cousins, was probably a lot simpler than the original Celtic language. When I studied Welsh, a fabulously melodic but very phonetic prose, I was told that the word 'tomato' can be pronounced, and thus spelled, 'tomato, domato, dhomato, nomato, nhomato or thomato'. There are probably even more mutations than that – and that is just a simple word. Imagine a whole string of tomatoes: "I went to the shop and I bought some ripe tomatoes, some squishy domatoes, a few green nhomatoes," I would never go to the jeffing greengrocer's again! I feel a strange sense of relief that, by virtue of being born across the border in the Lost Lands, Welsh is for me an additional language.

It is a tad unfortunate that the Anglo-Saxons as a collective were not known for their wild imagination. Towns, or tons, which can also be 'dons' or 'tuns' or 'duns' were often named by their relation to another 'ton'. Hence, England has a plethora of Nortons: North Towns; Suttons: South Towns, and Middletons, a few Eatons, a famous Eton and quite a few Weedons.

If it was a particularly long town, it might, just might, over time end up being elided into 'London'. If there was a bridge, it would be affixed with a 'Brig', a road made for 'Rad' and if it was a farm, it would be a 'stock'. Woodstock, for example, could well be a farm specialising in the cultivation of trees; something Britain used to be blanketed in. Or perhaps 'Stockwood' was just a forest minding its own business until some shady developers annexed it.

Sometimes, though, farms were called 'hams', or 'steads'. Or 'farmfarms' in the case of Hamstead: "Aye, it's not just a farm, it's a farm farm!" as if all the other farms were actually just fields being tilled for tax-dodging purposes. And as for Hamstead Heath – the mind boggles: it could be translated to mean 'a cultivated farm of uncultivated fields'. Sometimes an entire area was full of hams, which could also mean meadow rather than farm, as likely was the case for 'Hampshire'. Once London became overpopulated and people were compelled to move somewhere cheaper, nothing proved cheaper than Ye Olde Field.

The intervening Romans insisted on latinising our towns, making things terribly multi-syllabled and fortified. Following their exit stage right, Uncle Norman bumbled in, causing even more havoc. That carnage only ceased when the Scandinavians, speaking Old Norse, froze him out of the picture. On the east side, they left their mark by re-suffixing our 'tons' into 'bys' and 'thorpes'. Mixed with a Geordie accent, it is easy to hear how the Scandis became the Scuns, resulting in Scunthorpe becoming a particularly attractive holiday destination for our Viking cousins.

Anyway, having arrived in the Kingdom of the West Side of Sex, presumably a derivative of 'Saxon' I then headed down to the Kingdom of the South Side of Sex. All this learning had left me to ponder who exactly should be blamed for *The Dicklands* and *The Dickers*.

Novelly, it had a separate toilet: the bathroom was an entirely unitary room, making it a true bathroom, although it also contained the standalone hand basin. Above the water closet were three grubby horizontal window panes permanently open. The window was blocked with dusty flyscreen, keeping away the worst of the critters, but still piped in the rich and melodic birdsong. An occasional annoyingly repetitive and shrill screech would break up the melodies.

Both rooms had lurid green walls but here was nothing much else to make them remarkable, not even the occasional bird spider that found its way in. Being the size of an adult hand, they were certainly something one did not wish to encounter next to the plug hole. Outside, watching, waiting through their many eyes, they would drape large cobwebs, weaving curtains between the trees and bushes that crowded around the home.

The walls were made of wood. All the walls, in every room, were made of wood. The external ones were slatted, but inside they were beige painted panels. In my bedroom, the painters had changed colour half way down one – from brown to cream. Haphazardly, as if they'd made a mistake, realised it, but decided against fixing it. The roof above was nothing but thin tin sheets. The daily afternoon deluges thrashed down relentlessly, forcing the inhabitants to shout to make themselves heard. One time, lightning struck the roof, throwing out the electricity for days, but power outages were a regular inconvenience in any case. Another time, a tree fell, whipping its branches across half the house. Periodically, earth tremors shuddered, the structure rumbling, crushing, grinding until the underground settled again. It was a rackety home even when the family was absent.

Underneath the house, we had three cars; two barely working, one a wreck for parts. Adventure, Joint Venture and Misadventure. My father would tinker with them when he deigned to venture back to his house, which was rare. Next to the cars were two large cylindrical water butts there to collect the daily convectional rainfall for pumping up to a heating tank. Water was always plentiful, even if sunshine was in limited supply. If there was no solar that day, there would be no hot water. Lukewarm baths make for a miserable pastime, cold baths are worse still. Sweaty tropics make for sweaty bodies, and sweaty bodies also make for tropical ulcers.

I did not mind the toilet during the day. At night a quick flick of the light switch unleashed mayhem as cockroaches, some the size of my big toe, scuttled frantically in every direction. Within seconds a path was cleared to the loo. Where did they live during the day? I wondered. Where did they go then? After demonstrating his capabilities for chasing them off, the cat, much detested by my mother, was allowed to move inside the house. Blackie, the Chief Roacher, loved nothing more than someone padding to the loo in the middle of night, with Rita the mongrel dog joining him to investigate human doings during the wee hours. They were my best friends, my confidants, my warming snuggles. I was given my very own horse: Hey Girl! Life was settled. Life was good. Life was an adventure again.

****

A coffee cup attached to a man exited the beige campervan. I waited until he had perched himself on the low sturdy coastal wall before self-consciously reversing The Shitron into the gap between his motorhome and a second one. Behind him, a pebbled beach spread out and a becalmed sea lapped gently. This was a true sanctuary. In the distance the white cliffs of Dover evoked patriotic sentimentalism so I began warbling Vera Lynn's wartime anthem to an unappreciative cat, who clambered up to sit on my lap. Together, we watched terns bobbing up and down near the shoreline, while others glided effortlessly on invisible thermal currents. Walkers came and went, dogs trotting alongside them on leads. People smiled, full of summer conviviality. Nelson's paws gripped the steering wheel as we both soaked up the marvel of this most tranquil vista.

Vanlifers with an affinity for social media like to pose their vehicles in such places, as if they are truly remote. Particularly if they are flogging their van, selling the wanderlust dream – although sometimes the Photoshopping is quite exceptional. Two nights prior, I had headed to a popular Kent beach only to discover the shore was held back by a man-made bluff so tall that it hid the horizon and the twinkling sea. Overlooking the marshes still made for a reposeful night for a good dozen of us, despite several motorhomes blotting the breathtaking sunset copybook. Truth be told, such epic sea-side panoramas are typically restricted to day-time enjoyment only. Councils pin in 'no overnight' signs even in the most discrete areas, and by day, they charge the everyday citizens for parking. This, of everything, is what baffles me most: cherishing one's country's natural amenities almost always comes with a fee. This particular spot was almost unique in that not only was it stunning, but it was also gratis and without restrictions.

I took a cup of tea to the low-slung stonewall, leaving Nelson to his birdwatching. Martin, thin, wiry and naked bar a pair of shorts, asked if I was up for a conversation. I liked the request, rather than the presumption and nodded my amenity. I slurped on my drink as he chit-chatted about our way of life. He had been at it for fifteen years, always solo, and mostly in Europe. "Europe is the haven," he said. "They love motorhomes there. Here, they hate us. Now with Brexit, I can only do ninety days at a time, so I mostly live here. Besides, I have colon cancer and have just had a colostomy bag fitted," he patted his khaki shorts, "so I can't really go far from the hospital."

He spent his days keeping an eye out for taps, doing a gentle top up, just taking a few litres here and there. Heading my list of chores was refilling the water tank. Until now I had been relying on friends' generosity, but by flinging myself further afield this option had fallen off the table. Although there were a few people this way I had known once upon a marriage, I thought it a bit cheeky to start ringing around with, "Hello, how are you?...Yes, I know it's been a tremendously long time, but would you like coffee? Oh, and can I have a shower at yours, and while I'm at it, would you mind awfully if I pumped some tap water into the van?"

Martin proved to be the very oracle on Vanlife I sorely needed. "Cemeteries," was not the solution I had anticipated though.

"So, do I just drive in there, park up, and presumptuously plug in my hose? Just like that?" I asked incredulously. "No, the trick is to park and, out of respect, wait for any mourners to go. No one mourns for more than ten minutes at a time, then you can whisk out a container, and fill it up. Never drive past a church without inspecting its cemetery. Perhaps leave a few coins if the door is open," he instructed. All I had ever done at English churches was park up, snap a few pictures, and move off, usually perplexed as to why such tiny villages are dominated by such spacious, ornamental houses of worship. The congregations must have been paltry given the size of most hamlets, even prior to the passing of the Tolerance Act of 1688 which had eliminated mandatory attendance.

"In Europe, France especially, there are taps everywhere. Parking is hardly ever forbidden, and they'd certainly not put in height restrictive barriers. Germany too. Fabulous place. Farms and such like let you pull and top up your water, permit you to get rid of your grey water, your rubbish, and even your porta potti if you have one. They barely ask for a Euro. Here it's a battle trying to find rubbish bins, water, and sanitation places. It's fine inland because you can use the canal facilities, but at the coast, they make life so hard. Councils blame us for the litter, and for tipping toilet chemicals pathside. It's like they want to eliminate us, and parking is becoming such a chore." Martin shrugged, "It gets harder and harder every year," he trailed off.

"You know why New Age Travellers only buy blue or green vans, don't you?" Martin changed direction. I didn't, actually. "So they can more readily hide in woodlands and be left alone," Martin informed me. "I don't hang around with those types though, too much of the old puff," he mimicked smoking a joint. "They're not any trouble, but just not my cup of tea."

"I see you have a dog or two," I waved toward his van. "Oh, no!" he laughed. "I always put out two large dog bowls, one filled with water, and leave a large dog lead splayed on the ground. It makes people think there's something vicious inside. I don't even own a stuffed toy dog," Martin chortled. "It makes me feel safe, although I've never once had a moment's bother in fifteen years. You hear horror stories, you know, but they are not mine." Martin smiled reassuringly.

Later in the afternoon, a new neighbour introduced himself. "I'm homeless, I've been thrown out of the house so I'm car camping. I hope you don't mind me parked up next to you?" He cocked his head. He did not offer his name, but he was thirty-something, clean-shaven with a beaming smile and very affable. "I'm working right now. I work from home so I can't chat for long. I'm a helpline for people using IT," he shrugged. "I hope I don't disturb you but I've got to keep the windows open to run the engine for the power." The day was baking away and home, for him, was a black Fiesta.

"So, how do you sleep?" I enquired. "Oh, I just push the passenger seat back as far as it'll go. I have long legs, see?" He waggled one of them at me. "It's not great, though." I'd love your set up. I think camping is ace. I'm a Londoner, so I really like getting away from it all. I really want to do more but round here it's not so easy unless you pay, and sometimes you get aggro, y'know? Besides, I'm still needed here to take my children to school. They are only little and there are no buses." All too soon his break time was used up.

A second car arrived. Another friendly face, full of laughter and ready smiles. "My wife and I, twenty years married. Can't do it anymore. I'm converting the van," he tilted his head, "I can't even afford to rent. Self-employed, you see." It was a small Berlingo:

everything must be done from a crouched position. Later, the smell of a spliff seeped through my flyscreen keeping the evening gnats out of the van as the shoreline turned dark. Staying in Kent had been a rare social experience. Up until now, Vanlife had been a very solitary existence, a few brief hellos here and there.

The following day, I dashed off to Tesco. Supermarkets, but pertinently Morrison's, had been Martin's other suggestion. Two men sat kerbside waiting to start work at the Waves Car Port. "We don't open until twelve," one man muttered. "But can I just use your taps while you're not?" Inwardly I cringed at my imposition. Turns out they are turned off to prevent the brazen helping themselves. Nonetheless, the men kindly did all the work for me – filling up the entire seventy-litre tank. 'Every little helps' and all that.

Guilt compelled me to go shopping. I adopted Martin's recommendation of buying El Cheapo own-brand two-litre sized bottled water; the containers could be recycled again and again from bathrooms. Although not potable, it would be useful for washing up with. If necessary, I could always purify it through a filtration kit I carried. I lobbed a pack of four into my trolley. Much later, I discovered the underlying taste of carbonic acid, from the sparkling water I had accidentally purchased, utterly decimated the tea-drinking experience, but it did not half make the washing up bubbly.

A few days later, with the tank filled to capacity, I could again relax and look forward to spending a few more days free of driving. I wished to bask in the balmy late August weather, but not wanting to overstay my welcome, I had taken myself off to another beach-side location. This one, with a pretty walled garden and a dedicated 'pop-up' cafe, offered no direct view of the sea, but there were lovely promenade walks in the evenings.

I introduced myself as a neighbour to the woman running the cafe. "You staying here long?" she asked me as she flipped my grilled cheese sandwich. "Probably three nights," I answered. "Would that be a problem?" She shook her head, "No, they love you motorhoming types here. This road used to be used for drag-racing until your lot took over. Residents like the security you bring, houses on this road don't get burgled anymore." She handed over my greasy breakfast and hot coffee, and I perched on a tiny garden chair. "I just think you should always contribute in a way that benefits the local economy," she smiled at me. "Like you just did. If everyone did that, everyone would be happy."

That night, heavy storms broke the insufferable heatwave. I set my speakers to max to overcome the rain clattering on the van's roof in an attempt to enjoy the evening's television. As the sleeping hour crept in, I turned to the cuddling Nelson, "I can't imagine we'll sleep a wink through this," I stroked his furrowed brow. Lightning cracked in the far distance, and thick winds thrashed the greenery, which in turn, thrashed the van. By morning, the storms had blown themselves away, taking with them the muggy humidity and leaving behind a spritely cleanliness. Turns out, neither of us had any difficulty sleeping despite the raging weather system or the metal roof.

Elsewhere, torrents of rainwater had overloaded hidden drainage systems serving the towns. A network usually unsighted, unheard and unthought of, the storm had inadvertently forced an unceremonial dumping of untreated sewage into the land's rivers. Flushed out to sea, the coastline soon became an repulsive rim of brown sludge. I abandoned any ambition to partake in a little wild swimming. I learned that Britain's water companies can lawfully blight our natural wonders each and every summer, and there is little that can be done about it, beyond fines. These, of course, are just passed on by way of increased water bills for Joe Public to pay somewhere down the line. Such is the circle of life.

****

I sat down in the third row. Class had already begun and the children, a community of yellow shirts and brown shorts, were from here, there and anywhere. They were engrossed in the morning's task: diligently attending to the bookwork on cursive handwriting.

I didn't know what cursive meant but I could decipher the word. I stole a look across to my neighbour to try better to comprehend what to do. Her arm obscured my noseying as she concentrated intently. I could just about snatch a glance that she was drawing a cluster of letters over and over, all neatly running together. I gathered up my pencil, not even sure what page to begin on, and quietly scratched at the dots and the lines.

"Oh, you don't know cursive?" the teacher came across. I shrunk back. She left the room momentarily before returning with an earlier year's notebook. We should study the letter, observe the flow, then mimic it, following the arrows. She cracked open the book half way in. I was back to learning how to produce a single symbol. How I printed my alphabet was not at all acceptable to the Australian school

system so now my book was red while everyone else's was blue. I loathed cursive immediately, and Mondays became a painfully tedious start to the week.

The smell from nearby firepits, called mumus, wafted across from the nearby market. It was the only place to go for fresh groceries. After school, I nagged to go there for a snack. The local women, 'meris' they called them, mostly sat behind trestle tables, but sometimes on reed-woven mats, trading their home grown produce for coins of Kina and Toea. I tasted yams, hot roasted kaukau and corn on the cobs as all around us, brightly coloured bloused women barged their way from one stall to the next, many cradling their babies in their bilums. Others carried firewood or their days' supplies, sometimes even live chickens. No woman left home without her bilum. The stringed bags were highly-decorative, with individualised geometric designs. Like them, we would wander from seller to seller "Ha Mas? Ha Mas long dispela?" trying to barter the best deal. "Ples bilong yu?" some would enquire, "Yu kam long wanem hap?"

"England," I'd say. "Ples bilong Kwin" The place of the Queen. She had visited here once, and many had shook her white-gloved hand. Almost everyone had seen her and found it especially odd that I hadn't met her.

Back in the classroom, I interrupted the quiet. "Can I go to the loo?" I raised my hand. "Dunny," the teacher corrected. We go to the dunny at break times. Irrespective of what it was called, there was never any dunny roll supplied. Later, I learned that most of the children called it the 'Liklik Haus' or even the 'Sit Haus' because this wasn't Australia either.

****

Circling around the county's chief city, the Bury of Cant, or to use the more modern vernacular, Fort of Kent, it occurred to me that I had never gone to so many places and completely passed them by until I arrived in the county of Kent. I had hung about Kent for years: I even took my driving test there and passed, much to the astonishment of at least three people – me, and the two drivers who had honked their horns furiously at me that morning.

Until now, I was ignorant on how utterly insouciant Kent's Administration could be. Once upon a time, Kent extended into parts of Surrey, Sussex and Greater London – not so any more. As recently as 1988, Kent has had lumps chopped out of it. One can understand why the county was content to give away *Pratts Bottom* to the newly-established borough of Bromley, but to also forfeit Bexley, Greenwich and Lewisham without a smidgen of outcry is a tad remiss.

Such annexations have Nigel Farage, he of the far, far right, born in Kent but he is no longer a man of Kent at all, but of Bromley. Oddly, Julius Caesar considered the 'Kentish people' to be the most civilised and yet somehow he distinguished them from the 'People of Kent' whom he utterly maligned. I think Julius was being, at best, diplomatic but more likely disingenuous. I would argue he meant: pliable. It seems the Kents are a devotedly people-pleasing clan, albeit perhaps bordering on neglectful. As London expanded, it took to expropriating entire chunks of the county and yet there was not so much of a sniffle of civil disobedience, nor indeed, even covert resistance from the Kent folks.

In more recent times, Kent has permitted the breakaway group now fashioned as Medway. Although Kent County Council claims it is still a part of Kent, Medway County Council announced itself as a unitary authority in 1998. This might explain why the council of Kent-but-not-all-Kent, has the dubious honour of having the only metropole in the world that forgot to re-register itself as a city. Rochester, a noble city for eight hundred years, was demoted to a simple town despite formerly being Kent's second in command. It took the council four years to notice.

Given such lackadaisical behaviour, perhaps someone should write to inform Kent's overseers that the towns of *Twit* (Twitton) and seventy miles to the west, the homestead of *Twit* (Twitham) seem to have been rebranded into Otley, or just plain ignored after Sandwich. I found such non-discoveries especially disappointing – where did all the village idiots go, I pondered?

It seems that Kent County Council was prone to omitting to signpost its villages, making perfectly amenable hamlets seemingly unworthy of a formal place name. Added to which, there is also the 'missing in action phenomena'. My phone completely forgot to store a picture of *Pett Bottom* and I completely forgot to take a photograph of *Lyminge*. 'Ly' in Old English means 'having the body of' or 'being like something'. And 'minge' is the Romani Gypsy word for 'minge', or vulva if one prefers to be anatomical about it all.

Being so starkly descriptive is atypical of Kent. It comes across as a terribly prissy place and local councillors are quick to remind everyone that Henry VIII proclaimed it the Garden of England. Well, he would know. But the administrators of Kent seem very keen to dissolve certain hamlets or districts of interest. Hernhill, for example, is widely considered to be an exquisite, and much extolled village, grossly inflating its house prices. It nestles amidst many equally charming hamlets, one of which was called *Slutshole*. Not so anymore. Likewise, *Clap Hill* is more commonly known as Aldington.

Further on, the very long hamlets of *Bush* have divided themselves into *Upper Bush* and *Lower Bush*, but one would be hard pressed to know because they do not like to show themselves to passing motorists no matter how frequently one kerb crawls around the surrounding lanes. Similarly, I could only assume the former hamlets of *Butthole* and *Milebush* have been vanquished for their censorial qualities. *Stiff Street*, which was a hamlet snuggling into the fast-moving M2, has also seemingly been eradicated.

It was almost a relief to get to *Shorne* and *Thong* because at least there was something to write home over, or rather, make a Facebook post about. It was also impossible to miss *Lordswood,* although *Shorne Wood* was much more appealing, being less built up, and in reality, a rather glorious forest. That is about as filthy as Kent gets, nothing more offensive than a bloody good euphemism. I can only presume that this is to prevent the residents getting up and sodding off to Bromley.

Aside from gazing out at rocky beaches, the highlight of my trip was happening upon *Noah's Ark*. Not that there's anything worth tittering about there but I had always assumed it was in Iraq. Mind you, given the above, it is perfectly feasible that the Kents either made Noah's Ark up, misplaced it or gave it away, most likely the latter. Assuming the story is rooted in fact, it is clear that Noah expected the animals to fornicate without much assistance regardless of whether or not there was any mutual attraction. Quite why he made an exception when it came to badgers is anyone's guess, but *Badger's Mount* does not half sound like an instruction.

Slanderous Surrey

"She lives in a treehouse!" one of the girls exclaimed to the gentleman.

A huddle of ten-year-old girls, dressed up in our finest for a rare excursion, had been bussed to the opera: the plot of which I didn't so much lose, as not acquire whatsoever from the instant the curtain raised. The interval toilet trip provided much-needed respite from the confines of a thinly-cushioned seat, and our even more ludicrous uniform. In the stiflingly hot opera house, we sweltered.

It was a Saturday, but we'd been ordered into our Sunday poet blouses with their pointless ruffles just waiting to catch gravy drips. The blouse was mostly covered by a grey knee-length tunic. In turn, our tunics were clad in pillar-box red blazers, then drowned in full-length heavyset, grey woollen cloaks, complete with sagging hoods that must never be used. Nonetheless, they provided a useful hiding place for tissues, forbidden sweets and secret notes. On rare occasions one might discover other people's litter. The cloak could take a stranglehold of the neck if one sat down too quickly and was an obstacle to push to one side when using the loo, lest it become accidental toilet paper.

Outside, our cloaks offered little protection from the fierce Autumn winds, which would blow straight up one's legs given half a chance. Our attire was topped off with brilliant red tricorns, under which hair must always be pony-tailed, bunned or plaited. Bands and clips had to be brown or black. Never silver, or God forbid, coloured. Shoes brown. Knee-length grey socks, bare thighs. Two pairs of knickers, the thick outer set compulsorily blue, were inspected regularly. We stood out from the other concert-goers by the sheer idiocy of our striking outfits. I had just returned from the lavatories and the kindly man was enthralled by this gaggle of oddities. "Where do you all live? Anywhere exotic?" he'd quipped. It being self-evident we were from a boarding school. A classmate pointed at me and exclaimed, "She lives in a treehouse!"

I lived in a stately home now. A fee-paying school for the children of perennially abdicating parents. "I'm from Papua New Guinea," I told the man.

"No, you live there, you're not from there," the housemistress bellowed across me. "And she doesn't live in a treehouse. She lives in a house on stilts," she corrected my companion, "because of the earthquakes." I nodded. Homesickness raged through every cell of me. I didn't cry anymore. I'd stopped that nonsense several moons prior. This was many of the girl's first dreary Autumn term and I had to be brave for those still drowning in it.

****

In the event of another national toilet roll shortage...

...use this page!

I have a favour to ask...

I would love it if you joined me in a little Internet game of 'Hide & Seek!' If you could find a little space on a forum, a Facebook group, your own page, Instagram, Tiktok, YouTube or something similarly social-mediary!

1) Place this book on your toilet lid,
2) Take a photograph
3) Add any thoughts you might have,
4) Finish with the the caption:

#ViewofMyLoo
@PersonIrresponsible
Here's a place you haven't been!

I will try to find you even if it's just to say 'Thanks!'

A dork is a socially inept, contemptible individual, so presumably if one is behaving in a socially unacceptable, contemptible manner one is *Dorking*. Ordinarily *Dorking* is a charming market town, one of the many pockets of dormitory towns fiercely competing against the municipal green belt to feed an avaricious London. Its town mascot is a cock, which struts above the bespoke gridiron road sign. Painted black, it is camouflaged by the shade of the broadleaf woodland that smothers much of Surrey Hills. Its most famous coppice is *Glory Wood,* a designated sanctuary for oak, sweet chestnut and beech, short glades and even smaller ponds. Winding paths make it a dog walkers' haven. The clock had struck Autumn yet abscission had not begun except for the glut of apples which rained down. Everyone, it seemed, was trying to offload a bumper harvest.

Surrey means 'the southern region'. It is quite literally the leafy undercarriage of London. At its uppermost point sits the massive commuter conurbation that is *Staines*. These days it is called Staines-upon-Thames: a direct result of, some-might-say, the socially contemptible Alistair Leslie Graham. He brought world-wide attention to Staines, sorry Staines-upon-Thames, which was, until its unveiling, largely invisible under the smog generated by London's busiest airport: Heathrow.

Alistair Leslie Graham is a fictional stereotype whose dubious humour revealed Staines-upon-Thames to the world. His character was retired in 2007. Such was his legacy, it was repackaged by local councillors into Staines-upon-Thames in 2011. Provincially it is still referred to as Staines, just as Alister Leslie Graham is still world-renowned as Ali G.

If calling it *Staines* is deemed offensive, one might wish to swerve the entire county of Surrey altogether. It is a county teeming with British vulgarities just waiting to be invented. Starting with *Effingham*, the potential birthplace of effing and jeffing, the polite alternative for expressing annoyance. Effingham was a place strangled by roadworks, providing opportunity galore for a bit of cussing and beeping. There is nothing like a traffic jam for a memory to come for a haunting. The town of *Hurtmore* conjures up reminiscences of boarding schools that are better off quashed.

Nonetheless, Surrey offers an abundance of low-grade childish smut, like that of *Tongham*. Its primary purpose has always been to house London's labour force, and if the hustle and bustle of train travelling does not appeal, *Tongham's* major employer is Hog's Back. Surprisingly, this is a brewery, I had presumed it was a manufacturer of bacon butties for the blurry-eyed commuters. From there, I ventured on to *Willey Green* followed by the more worrisome *Trumps Green*. Both had evanesced, having been subsumed by larger estates.

Further on, the hunt was on for *Donkey Town*, which, surprisingly, is actually a village. Donkey Town's existence is a modern parable: a collaboration between the Earl of Onslow, owner of West End, and the churchwardens tasked with caring with the labouring poor of the parish of Chobham in the Georgian era of the 18th century. *Donkey Town*'s earliest settlers were demobilised servicemen who became surplus to requirements upon the end of the Napoleonic Wars. The bequeathed land gave them the chance to build their own homes from whatever materials could be salvaged. Surrey Live, the county's paper, suggests the locals of West End referred to these incoming inhabitants as 'donkeys'. But a kinder theory is that perhaps a drove had simply wandered there, braying their way into the annals of history and a sign post.

As we hurtled into the village, a dainty little sign declared, "Welcome to Donkey Town West End". It whizzed past me so fast I opted to seek out the East End – none existed, just a dead end. We trundled back towards the original sign, and I parked up at the first available space before setting off purposefully into the distance to photograph the road sign. I marched quite some way. And some way more. All the way to the main road, in fact, still unable to locate the sign I had clapped with both my eyes. Thankfully, I found it on the way back bang opposite The Shitron.

Following that, this particular donkey moseyed on to the towns of *Leatherhead* and *Hindhead*. I have no idea why these are not contemporary insults because they really ought to be. Perhaps I should nominate a name change to Knuckle Head and Butt Head respectively.

By far the most amusing day trip was exploring the sedate suburb that is *Nork*. *Nork* is thought to descend from the word for 'stepmother', a woman who is stereotypically depicted as a mean old nork! Thankfully, the townsfolk of *Nork* like to celebrate their norks with signage galore. I could have spent a full day just taking photographs of all of its norks. It was quite unlike the village of *Titsey* which is, in fact, an imposing manor house of the stately home variety in Oxted, and very much hidden behind an imposing wall.

That said, my favourite villages were those of *Fetcham* and *Bookham,* invoking scenes of law and disorder. With the two signs sharing one roundabout, it seemed like they existed to direct the local bobby as to where to go and what to do. Having snapped the mugshot,

I found an isolated road on which to park up, not too far from the invisible perimeter of Hampshire. It was there that I had my first ominous 'rap on the window' moment that signalled the breaking of one's Vanlife virginity. I was to be moved on by the Forestry Service. I say 'moved on', I was, in fact, merely asked to park on the other side of the road behind what I suspected was an abandoned car.

The following day, the little Volkswagen remained. Using all my finely-honed observation skills, I noted a fine layer of dust covering the car. There was no indication of a door handle having been used in some time: spiders had laced themselves to it. A window was left ajar, as if to prevent too much car sweat, but the vehicle was absent of a note or 'police aware' stickers. Being far enough from inhabitation, it seemed an odd place to strand a vehicle. I pondered whether to call the local constabulary and raise my concerns.

Google location quickly generated the location of my closest police station although upon closer inspection, I was taken aback to read a notice that they had ceased their occupancy on *Crookham Road* in the latest implementation of cost-saving measures. Confoundingly, I felt robbed of what must have been a very predictable joke.

The Royal Berks

I don't know if it happened before I went to boarding school or after, I think perhaps, before. Memory is like that: it fades, rearranges, reconfigures and lies. I do know that it happened though, although a right royal row would be had if I ever told my version of events. Still, I shall. We'd been out to visit mother's friend on a tea plantation. We lived a good half hour from the main town, and they lived a good hour in the opposite direction. It was night time in a world that boasted not a single street light.

Some roads were tarmacked, but mostly they were not. Mostly, they were compacted red clay, especially slippery after rainfall, and made lethal with deep chassis-battering potholes patiently waiting to devour entire cars. There were no barriers to prevent skidding off down deep valleys, the threat of death or serious injury was all-pervading for those with precarious driving practices or those not fully concentrating on the task at hand. We lost a family acquaintance that way, but I believe that hadn't happened yet.

We were in our only reliably-working car: a twenty or thirty-something-year-old Land Rover. One that occasionally required starting with several spine-snapping turns of a crank to kick into life. Even when the going was good, it was a vehicle that screamed out for hours of mechanical intervention. It had two front black tattered passenger seats and a windscreen made up of two windows. The cab's centrepiece, between the two occupants at the front, was a dashboard of just two dials. The broken one would have indicated the speed. It never acquired much speed in any case, terminal velocity was probably no greater than thirty miles an hour. There was nothing for comfort and nothing for protection. It was a mangle of chipped blue painted metal, dents, cracks and exhaustion.

Behind my parents, in the boxy rear, we children availed ourselves of one of the two rectangular metal wheel arches. No seatbelts, no cushions. Sometimes, it was less jarring on the floor but usually there were saddles, bags, dogs and shopping bilums occupying that space. We gripped tightly to whatever we could – things had a tendency to bounce up and bruise.

*My mother usually drove but only in the absence of my father being present. On one particular night, he was present. Typically cantankerous, but present. We were cresting a hill, but he had forgotten to refuel, coasting his way back, eking out the small supply and hoping that gravity would push us all the way back home. The car shuddered as he accelerated, and juddered when tilted. There was nowhere to obtain fuel, no formal service stations, no help to call for, no phones to use in any case. This was as remote a town as any on earth, only serviced by small prop planes twice a week. Out in the darkness lived the '*raskols*' as all and sundry called them. Raskols were hordes of opportunistic young men, tooled up with sharp knives, axes and other fashionable weapons of the fatal kind. Some had advanced into carrying unpredictable homemade guns; rumours abound that a few sent the shot backwards, an event that would have brought religion to even the most atheist of victims. Raskols came with a gang warfare mentality, haunting the most vulnerable.*

The fear always lingered because talking about them was common parlance. Family friends had once been carjacked, so we knew they were real. On this night, just like every other night, one could never assume one was secure. By comparison we were wealthy, with our car ownership, one bedroom per child, food to eat, horses, foreign holidays, and household help. We were startlingly white and strikingly foreign. One should never risk running out of fuel while in such a place.

But it was the entire wheel flying off ahead of us, bouncing up, then down, careering away, hurling itself into a valley that terrified me. That, and the Land Rover tipping over. That is what had me screaming, piercing the air in a way that had the adults lose their temper. I still feel justified about shrieking on that occasion, even if it wasn't the end of the world.

****

Sounding like a retirement destination for your local village idiot, Royal *Berkshire* is a long slither of a county resembling a hamburger clamped between the two buns that constitute the shires of Oxford and Hamp. If one is unfamiliar with how ludicrous English place names can be pronounced, I ought to point out that it is "Barkshire" as in 'barking mad', rather than "Berkshire", as in 'acting like a complete prat'.

Berkshire is said to mean 'birchy and hilly', and I can attest that, at times, it is indeed very birchy and tremendously hilly. For the most part, however, Berkshire's golden fields give the vista a true *Honey Bottom*, which incidentally is a piffling hamlet of just one house. Other wonderful sites of interest include: *Hell's Corner,* which turned out to be nothing more glamorous than a farm, and a farmstead of crooks: *Crookham*. There is something terribly disconcerting when 'Alexa' tinnily pronounces, through the medium of SatNav, "You have arrived!" only to find there is nothing to see but a long and empty road.

Berkshire is predominantly arable but by our arrival it was an especially stubbly place now that the wheat was being harvested. This annual event of the farming industry had left behind a gloriously flaxen hue to undercut the horizon. That said, I would argue that the county is better known for the stupendously glorious houses of the extortionate kind and for being a shire that takes its royal title very seriously. Royal Berkshire is also home to that most renowned of Stately Homes – Broadmoor Criminal Lunatic Asylum, whose very first patient was a feeble-minded female, of course!

Berkshire is a county that revels in its full title: The Royal County of Berkshire, although this may change now that a new King has been installed. At the time of writing, it remains the only county in England to use the honorific Royal prefix. This is attributed to the presence of Windsor Castle, which was the late Queen's principal home, and not, as many assume, Buckingham Palace in London.

If the King were so inclined, he could deign to erect a purpose-built castle in *World's End*. I quite like the idea of having a town called Royal World's End, not just because of its tongue-twisting matter of factness, but how it would make this catastrophic-sounding hamlet an even more superlative one. It would be situated between the melancholic-sounding *Downend*, and the incongruently-named *Marquis Motorhomes*.

Another location potentially suitable for nomination is *Crazies Hill*, a name which belies just how beautiful the hamlet is. Its residents are inclined to guard themselves behind tall, bristly hedges and strong wooden gates. Any monarch would fit right in. Hedges are a fine impediment to ascertaining the residents' certifiability or their delinquency. 'Crazies', according to the Journal of Antiquities, is said to mean "The fresh, clean water of the waterless place". I think that makes the royal point quite precisely.

Still, someone, somewhere, once upon a time, decreed *Crazies Hill* to be the upper echelons of homes that are dotted along the single-track road as opposed to the lower echelons on the very same lane. Those unfortunates inhabit *Cockpole Green*. Rest assured *Cockpole Green* was most certainly green despite the summer having now fallen away, but there was a notable absence of cockpoles. I have since learned that a cockpole is a gathering place for cocks. Much fighting used to occur there, possibly long after it was outlawed. Still, some fantastical trees remained upright and thriving for Nelson and I to admire while partaking in our respective lunches alongside the very green, green.

I presume the residents of Berkshire are tremendously British about any matter that does not meet their distinguished approval: only deigning to demonstrate their feelings with a contemptuous tut. While we all may love a good whinge, it appears that Berkshire residents have a gathering place to emit their collective sigh of disappointment: follow the road called *Rotten Row Hill* and Alexa will soon notify you that you have arrived in *Tutts Clump*. Even the Methodist Church has an appropriately mortified façade.

It was quite the relief, then, to depart the area and head towards the less salubrious-sounding *Binfield*. While on my way, I spotted a layby dotted with a trio of black litter receptacles of the very type made suitable for visitors' use. Not the kind best described as a private wheelie bin, but large, cylindrical metal bins of the unambiguous 'for public amenity' variety. I had been in need of a bin for quite some time.

Having a cat aboard, and there being a national shortage of compostable woodchip litter, a consequence of Russia's invasion of

Ukraine, I was forced to rely on the less environmentally-friendly clay pellets that are available in all adequate supermarkets and pet stores. This practice upped my bin usage considerably despite my tutting loudly about the lack of selection of cat litter at every store I visited. I once even joined in with another woman's tuts in a Sainsbury's, but it availed not a jot of difference: there continued to be a dearth of woodchip litter. It left me carrying more rubbish on my passenger seat than was desirable.

Pulling into a layby with the trio of bins, not far from the roadway hubbub of the large roundabout it serviced, I commenced the hideously repugnant task of decontaminating Nelson's litter tray. The stench of stale cat pee settles to the bottom of his deep-sided tray, and explodes out as one gets around to disposing of all the contents. Task complete, mildly green in complexion, I spun around to find myself nearly colliding with a similarly coloured electric car. It appeared to have been deliberately parked in my way by an absolute bin lid of a grey-haired bloke. Despite being safely protected by his driver's window, he felt it necessary to glare at me in a manner most intimidating. I interrupted the passing of time by cocking my head, and raising my blonde but barely discernible eyebrows in a pathetic attempt to communicate, "What?" After a substantial period of time of my looking at him quizzically, and him staring back angrily in an vain attempt to have me read his mind, he felt it sensible to wind down his window a crack and actually utter some comprehensible words.

"Where are you putting your rubbish?" He did not so much enquire as demand in a bellowing cut-glass accent.

"In the bin," I announced. "It is the responsible thing to do," I added a little too glibly in my similarly elocuted accent.

"The responsible thing to do?" His spittle splattering on his windscreen as he echoed my words but totally re-stated my intonation several octaves higher. "The responsible thing to do," he barked, "IS TO TAKE IT HOME!" His apoplectic rage was now fully unleashed.

"I am home," I replied, astonished at my level of calmness.

With that, I left him to lose more of his shit in the direction of his windscreen. Squeezing through the gap between our two vehicles, I strode off towards the bin.

I do not think it wise to ever pick a fight with a woman who has a bag full of used cat litter. It is practically a nuclear weapon. Forgot 'restraint of pen and tongue', this was restraint of turd and ammoniac contamination.

It was, incidentally, collection day so I could have got away with appropriating one of the towns folks' bins. But I am a responsible litterer: I use the bins provided for public consumption. Always. My actions were not exactly the end of the world.

Going round in Circles in a Wilting Woo County

Michaelmas was the worst term: the longest, the coldest and the cruellest. Nonetheless, round and round the termly cycles went. Some could count the days until exeat: a weekend treat either side of half-term that permitted them a visit out of the school's confines. Cars crunching along the gravel driveway would slink in to take them away. A moment's respite. The Saturday morning minutes stretched out as the fortunate girls' necks craned towards ticking clocks. Their agitation was visible – for even on a special day, one dared not sit on their pristinely made-up bed, each covered with an identical counterpane. The rest of us were left to just watch them watch. The grand entrance doors, forbidden to us except on Sundays, would squeak open and clatter closed. We would guess whose parents they were by the shrieks of delight ringing round the corridors; the absolute rule of 'not running indoors' was wilfully contravened.

Other girls counted in weeks until half-term. Their travel arrangements were too tiresome, too complex or too inconvenient for a weekend. Some were plonked at railway stations, tickets in hand, left to navigate British Rail alone. Their smuggled-in prohibited personal clothing crushed into suitcases, just waiting to be put on in the station's WCs. Trains were occasionally missed if the girl took too long stepping out of her uniform. One time the matrons did an impromptu inspection, catching all the miscreants who were not beacons of their private school education as the rules stipulated they must. "We are a target for bullies," was a defence that fell on deaf ears.

Finally, it was the far-flung expatriate waifs who counted in months. There was always a steady flow of silent tears shed in the planes' toilets when heading west, but unbridled euphoria heading east. Come the end of term, a taxi would drop me off at the local airport to catch a short flight to Heathrow Terminal Four. I'd check in, wander around the duty free, buy some coke and gorge on otherwise unobtainable crisps and sweets. No adults. No corralling. No yelling. The irony of the peace of the hubbub. The smell of the foreign. The glare of yellow signage. The chest-swelling appreciation for the freedom of the transit halls.

Going east, I'd leave school in the morning having scoffed British Weetabix, and two days later, I'd be feasting on Australian Weet-bix, decidedly more cardboard-tasting. I would be reunited with Blackie, Rita and Hey Girl, along with Anna, the cheerful house girl. She did everything except make lunch. That was my job and not my brother's. He was still getting ribbed for making angel cake several years prior and I needed to learn that life wasn't fair. My mother usually popped home for lunch, but not always. Our father, never. My brother and I rarely flew together, our term times never really synched. Besides, he'd taken up smoking so he elected to sit at the back of the plane to make use of the ashtrays.

The journey home took two days, yet the return was so rapid, just a day and a bit, using four planes. Our personalities were recast before the plane's wheels smashed down on the Singaporean runway, no matter which way we were heading. Oftentimes one would hang out with a fellow boarder from another school. It wasn't hard to spot other underaged solo travellers despite the absence of a school uniform, we'd reek of worldliness combined with anarchy. Fast friends within minutes. We would become the pillocks walking backwards along the travelators, gallivanting around to break up the monotony of long-haul journeys and the interminable waiting in airport lounges for flights to be called. We'd babble about our plans for the holidays until our planes had us dispersed in different directions. We were less convivial on the return journeys, quietly contemplating, silently dreading. We swapped stories of mardy matrons, the tedium of waiting for prep to end, what time was lights out, the endless restrictions on our lives, and, of course, the salacious gossip of someone being expelled. Sometimes we'd see each other a few terms later, but usually they were instant companions we had never met before and not see again.

Occasionally, the check-in personnel would offer the option of going with the other Young Travellers, but we were sniffy about that. We thought it only suitable for primary-aged children. I always said no after they lost my passport one time. It had been left at Singapore and it was all a bit of a faff getting into Port Moresby. I once heard they had sent the wrong passport with the wrong child. No one ever insisted we travel as unaccompanied minors, which they called 'U.M.'

I so loved the stories of adults cocking up. I was proud I'd never missed a flight. Except for that one time I had had food poisoning, vomiting the length and breadth of Jackson International Airport. I had woken up at a stranger's house that morning feeling queasy. When heading west, we'd always stay at a stranger's house in

Port Moresby, having flown in the night before. It was never the same stranger. The man of this house, whose name I don't recollect, called my mother saying I was too ill to fly. She insisted I return to school.

The airline purser had threatened to hospitalise me at Manilla, but I lied and said I was okay because I had heard there was a civil war there. A few hours later, I was medevaced, unconscious, to the American Military Hospital after landing at Changi. I vaguely remember coming to and seeing the blue lights bounce off a wall. No one bothered to inform anyone else. For four days, only the medics attending me knew where I was. One even brought me a care bear for company. When I came to, I remember asking if I could use the toilet. The male nurse snorted. He chided that I was big enough to go on my own. It was an en-suite. I hadn't meant I needed his help; I meant I wanted the freedom to go. I knew the rules changed from west to east, I just didn't know what the rules were in the middle bit.

I flew back to school on the fifth day, surprising everyone with my late arrival. Back to a world of bells and regulations. Of decorum and obedience. Back to asking for permission from everything from going to the toilet, to having an extra piece of bread to satiate ever-gnawing hunger, or obtaining stamps to send letters to friends made on planes.

****

The circle of the seasons rotated further into autumn, greying out the skies. Wilting rusty leaves shedding from trees caused, one presumed, all manner of train delays. They prettied up otherwise litter-strewn kerbs, and brought a magical fuzzy beauty to this sometimes dismally grey country. The sun, usually weakening by now, glowed powerfully on; making most days gloriously long and warm.

The Shitron had rumbled into the county of Wiltshire: its wheels going round and round just like on the proverbial bus, albeit he was now minus just one, quite useful, off-side wing mirror. Apparently, my Citroën had taken a liking to an oncoming van of similar proportions and their mirrors had kissed at fifty-five miles an hour. It had been a fleeting love affair, but one that jettisoned a bit of weight after the break up. It took a while to get it sorted, leaving me plenty of time to delve into the history of Wiltshire.

Wiltshire is not only famous for the neolithic circular arrangements otherwise known as Stonehenge, but the county is also a stable for eight white horses. Visiting each one makes for a ninety-mile circular trek. There used to be thirteen but neglect had them devoured by the surrounding turf. They are nothing but chalky hill figures etched into shallow bedrock, high up on Wiltshire's hills, and to most people's surprise, they are less than three hundred years old. Those that remain come with wonderfully peaceful parking spots with far-reaching views where I could settle for days and write what I hoped would provide some income: a talk on women and bravery in order to stem my dwindling funds. It is one of the few downsides to single life: earning enough to keep everything moving.

Nomansland, I determined, would either be Britain's only matriarchal hamlet or an uninhabited area between two occupying armies. What it was, I discovered, was an underwhelming morning: the houses were plain and ordinary, and there was a disappointing absence of war. In fact, the only signs of life were six horses merrily munching away on either side of the road, the smallest – a Shetland and the largest akin to a former thoroughbred. Perhaps having escaped a dog food abattoir, presumably sited at the nearby village of *All Cannings*.

I departed *Nomansland* on the assumption that the absence of anything identifiably human was more to do with the deluge of rain tipping from the autumnal October sky than an abduction of mankind by aliens. Wiltshire stakes a claim for being England's most mysterious county, holding the national record for the number of UFO sightings. Further digging on the subject revealed that Ms Natalie Myres had found it necessary to submit to Wiltshire's constabulary a 'Freedom of Information Request' in December 2020. I presume she also paid the attendant £25 administration fee compelling the police to disclose that year's frequency of visits by unidentified aerial phenomena. The police declined, stating it would cost £450 to do so. It struck me that the charge was not only a very defined sum but they had also omitted to deny the existence of aliens. The answer 'none' would surely have been a significantly in-budget answer.

Wiltshire is not quite, but almost, the birthplace of the universal happenings known as 'crop circles'. Wikipedia oozes cynicism when it observes that these flattened spheres of wheat stalks are "not distributed randomly across the landscape but appear near roads, areas of medium to dense population and cultural heritage monuments such as Stonehenge or Avebury." If I am not mistaken, there are hardly any substantial areas of nothingness in England, given it is the second-most populated country in Europe.

Granted, there were occasional patches of nothingness, like the village of *Snap*. *Snap* is a former settlement most notable for being abandoned. This is especially peculiar because it happened quite recently: 1914. It was the arrival of The Great War which coerced the last resident into removing herself to a local people's home. Upon her evacuation, the military moved in and used the village for target practice, readying soldiers to fight in the great battles of those times. Consequently, the army obliterated most of the houses; I guess they were not very adept at the targeting part of the practice. After the war ended, wily pilferers requisitioned all the brickwork and rubble including that of the still-intact school and the chapel to establish buildings elsewhere. Naturally, no one saw nothing, guv. If one looks carefully, there is still signage for *Snap* but having scoured the countryside, it became apparent that all that remains are fields of harvested wheat. Not even a rocky outcrop nor a hazy crop circle was to be located. So, was *Snap* vanquished or did it simply vanish?

Concluding nothing, I resumed my wilting quest. Inspired by Wikipedia's scepticism of the supernatural I sought out nearby *Crooked Soley*, a hamlet on the east of Wiltshire, adjacent to a similarly-sized hamlet called *Straight Soley*. At first, I thought they sounded like a place where one should confess one's degree of honesty in their tax returns.

Situated just south of the M4, which tears across the county, even the signs were ironic: with *Straight*'s post being crooked, and *Crooked*'s being straight. Never before have two settlements better described the dichotomous, if not sometimes fractious, relationship between peoples with contrary belief systems. One is either a scientist or a cereologist; a believer or a non-believer; a player of the cop or the robber. Indeed, if Doug Bower and Dave Chorley were the originators of Wiltshire's crop circles that proliferated in the 1980s, then why were they not charged with criminal damage? I assume that it is quite hard to harvest flattened wheat and corn, which subsequently deprives the farmer of income. Farmers are, after all, world-renowned for cost-centrism. I left the area with much to muse over.

Incidentally, *Crooked Soley* is the title of a book by Allen Brown and John Mitchell who claim "crop circles are the finest, most beautiful and original art forms of *modem* (sic) times." I can only deduce from their brief synopsis that the purpose of the crop circle is to enable the modulation and demodulation between beings of far flung planets and ourselves. Alas, it was all binary to me. The book, incidentally, scores 4.6 stars out of 5 on Amazon, not unlike my first book, albeit theirs comes from a combined average score of eleven reviewers. Perhaps readers are put off by the one three-star review by A.Gal who stated, "… Yes the mathematical theories are awesome but meh". I completely concur with the sentiment even if I was not impressed by the lack of punctuation.

Snap was not the only place missing in action. *Wilsford cum Lake* is a lengthy, winding village. Foliage and high-siding fencing obscured any possible sighting of the cum lake, let alone permit a peek at a substantial body of water. From Google Maps, it seems to be more of a bulging river but this could not be verified, given parking was impossible. Later, I discovered it is a place quite unsuitable for any form of sailing given the area is a triumvirate of three settlements: 'Wilsford' and 'Lake' although why Normanton has been dubbed 'Cum' is anyone's guess.

I followed up with a quick morning's detour to *Cuckoo's Knob*, adorned with much prettiness by way of gardens. Alas, the small modern brick boxes were of the 1970s bungalow variety. Perhaps, as many an ugly girl is told, it is what is on the inside that counts, but were I to demand a house inspection I suspected this would greatly startle the elderly population therein. I reluctantly decided against being the object of a police investigation, even if there are supposedly enough UFO abductions going on to keep the local constabulary occupied for quite some time.

Photos snapped, I returned to The Shitron, which whisked me along narrow twisty lanes to *Clench*. Having been waylaid for a few days getting The Shitron repaired, I was, more than ever, disinclined to hit objects best avoided. I thought it beneficial to hold my breath and lean over as we passed oncoming traffic, or stretch myself upwards between high-sided hedgerows to help protect The Shitron from further incidents. Getting to and from *Clench* required a great deal of breath-baiting, not least because one of the roads had been washed away in a tremendous rainstorm the previous night.

From there on the mysterious Wiltshire degraded into smut as I embarked on a series of concentric tours of the county. Just like a 1970s pervert, I started at *Patney* with the ambition of quickly getting to *Chicklade*. *Patney* still boasts that it was the awarded best-kept village in 1992. It certainly continues to age delightfully but given it has been on the go since Plantagenet times, I imagined that the ageing process of any village is especially languorous. Once upon a time, *Patney* boasted its very own 12th century church until a lack of attendance had it shutting its doors. It happened the same year the village received its crown of pageant beauty. If anything, *Patney* disproves the adage that, "It's what's on the inside that matters".

Frustratingly, I failed in my *Chicklade* conquest because the only signage sat astride the fast-moving A303, and having whizzed past in the blink of an eye, it was clear that getting a photograph would have risked life and limb. Given it is illegal to use a camera while operating a vehicle, and the cat remains all thumbs, I opted instead to tootle off to *Limpley Stoke*.

Limpley Stoke is a place that demands one is careful to check the spelling of, let alone risking unpaused enunciation. It seems to be a very easy faux pas. Shortly after, I was somewhat startled to find myself in hot water, or to be precise, Bath in Somerset. Not five minutes later, I was even more alarmed to have myself pulled over by a French woman police officer.

Although, that definitely is a tale of '*Lacock* and Taureau'. *Lacock* is described on one website as being 'lost in time'. Assuming that time is, in fact, perfectly pinpointable another website has it chronicled as a Saxon village. A few of the older structures, including one from the 12th century, originated in the High Middle Ages, but most of its buildings were constructed in the 18th century. Hence, it is more accurate to say *Lacock* is a village that is baffled by its timing. I was just impressed that any of it has withstood the ultimate tests of time: weather, fire, pollution and Harry Potter, given much of it was filmed there. *Lacock* is also notable for two other things. Firstly, that it is illegal to affix TV aerials or satellite dishes to the buildings, and secondly, its annual Scarecrow Festival. Well, if one cannot receive a decent television signal, what else is there to do but dress up effigies of visitants, martians and bogeymen for entertainment?

Other throwbacks dotted around Wiltshire are the ubiquitous red telephone boxes of yonder year. At first appearance, it is as if no one wishes to recognise that they have been gazumped by the realities of modern communication. Once upon a time, these cultural icons were frequently confused with public toilet facilities, or at least they smelled as if they had been. Nowadays, the whiff of latrine has often been replaced with a much more nostril-appeasing bibliosmia.

Every village seemed to retain at least one of the old poppy-red kiosks. Just outside of *Nomansland*, an actual, proper telephone idled, minding its own business, which in all probability is zilch. Others had been converted to house defibrillators, so if you are planning to have a heart-attack, Wiltshire would be an excellent place to spend the holidays. Most, though, have been converted into teeny-tiny libraries or tourist information booths. Considerable time can be lost scouring for a good book or pamphlet. I was especially delighted to find a brand new five-hundred-piece jigsaw puzzle depicting a scene of British woodland wildlife in *Patney*. After the cat got involved, it obtained its very own crop circle.

Not long after, we happened upon *Spirthill.* It was a surprising destination where we had a most astonishing encounter with actual British wildlife. I had parked up, ostensibly to photograph the Hill of Spirt. By doing so, I incidentally positioned the van so the sun reflected a stern glare from the darkened privacy glass on the side door. I returned to find a territorial blue tit dive bombing into itself, clattering against the window in rage at his perceived interloper. Bashing itself repeatedly. On the other side, a similarly territorial British Blue-ish shorthair, was indulging his instincts: pressing himself hard against the glass panel delightfully anticipating his lunch. Only his preferred master tactic of lying back, mouth agape, waiting for something to land directly into it was thwarted by the invisible force known as my 'kitchen window'.

Cue two furious, and very exasperated, animals. The ceasefire occurred when I bumbled off towards *Rotten Row*, where I pulled up at a wonderfully flat square of concrete on the outskirts of the revolting-sounding hamlet of *Horpit.* A place where lunch could be properly lunched. *Horpit* is a miniscule agricultural hamlet on the outskirts of the Town of *Swines*: commonly referred to as *Swindon*.

I had mistakenly thought *Swindon* was a city, but it is still a town. Downtrodden, and coming in at No. 31 on 'Britain's Worst Places to Live' list, a ranking compiled annually by www.ilivehere.co.uk. *Swindon* has the saddest of tag lines: "Broken Britain in a Microcosm". If that was not condemnation enough, it is also described as Britain's most average town; a destination so utterly dull that one might consider its most redeeming feature to be the sheer number of roundabouts that befuddle drivers new and old alike.

Roundabouts in Britain, I have learned, are formally known as 'Ring Junctions', a term I have never encountered in my life, let alone heard someone else refer to. I grew up in places where they were called road circles, or just plain circles.

I suspect that the popularity of roundabouts amongst *Swindon*'s urban planners is down to their utility as an escape prevention measure. Notionally, they induce such a level of dizziness in motorised Swindonians that they could feasibly deter a mass exodus. What other possible explanation is there to justify *Swindon*'s most remarkable ring junction: The Magic Roundabout? It even has its own traffic sign to direct road users and visitors. For the uninitiated, this vehicular circus is best described as seven circles of contra-travelling hell for a lost, long-wheel-based white van driver in rush hour with a 'hangry' cat still sulking about the lunch he failed to catch that day.

One plausible alternative explanation for this geometric abomination is that the designers of local infrastructure, back in 1972, spent their lunch hours in *Tiddleywink.* If anything captures the evanescent phenomena of Wiltshire it is *Tiddleywink.* It is not an especially grand place: Established circa 1881, the settlement is nothing more than two sets of slightly grubby terraces combining to make eight humble abodes. At some point in the past, one of the inhabitants of Tiddleywink Cottage served their own home-produced hooch to passing drivers of the cow-droving variety. Hence, travellers would meander down the lane for a quick snifter, or rather, using rhyming slang to obfuscate their illegality: a tiddleywink.

Then the hamlet of *Tiddleywink* slipped into obscurity. First, it was overlooked by the Bartholomew Gazetteer of Places in Britain, a publication I was clean ignorant of, and then eliminated completely by what was once the road-goers' bible: The Collins British Road Atlas. That was the formal name for the oversized A-Z book of maps that once dominated the windscreens and passenger seats of the intrepid British motorist. Nowadays, they have been rendered near-obsolete by the emergence of Google Maps and other directional apps.

Having been ignored by both epochal tomes, in 1998 *Tiddleywink* went on to lose the only remaining evidence of its existence: its unitary road sign. A driver, presumably this one of a car-droving variety, and perhaps having indulged in a few too many tiddlywinks, crashed into the eponymous sign and obliterated it.

"I haven't had a catalogue delivered for nine months because the postman just can't find us," a resident complained to a BBC reporter. The hamlet's sluggish dematerialising ceased five years later only after a new sign was erected. From then onwards, to the delight of the handful of occupants, Amazon deliveries could be received for the first time. Alas, there was no happy ending: the road sign was stolen ten years later. "People will nick anything these days," mourned the local councillor to another BBC journalist. I wonder how he knew it was people? It is as if he knows something the rest of us do not: after all, no one thought to bother the police regarding this act of larceny.

With some trepidation I headed off to *Brokenborough.* Borough in Old English means 'fortified place'. It was probably established to keep out the lucky few who had found their way out of

Swindon. It is a rather grand place, pricey most definitely, although not best known for its religious piety: its chapel was a rather pitiful affair. Ramshackled and well along its way to being devoured by the village's vociferous and ravenous nature, it left one fretting for the inhabitants' souls. My angst was soon soothed by a quick visit to *Hankerton* with its tremendous Grade II-listed church dating back to the 12th century. Even today it preaches good, honest values to the villages of *Crudwell* and *Bullock's Horn*, places which sound like they need it.

****

I spent my final nights in Wiltshire atop the Ridgeway, soaking up its rolling hills at the site of yet another white horse. This one is accompanied by an actual white horse and two skewbalds. Loving creatures, they snorted contentedly while tearing at the grassy meadow. Between mouthfuls one bellowed shrilly to a trio of horses fenced in on an adjacent hill. It would have been idyllic except for it was bisected by a popular road; cars came and went, bikes too and the occasional truck huffed its way uphill.

I had taken a break from sitting on my arse-numbing square wooden box tapping away to chat to the horses. We had been here two nights already and I felt I should be moving on. Cheekily, I opted for a third. The period of stasis had given me time to rehearse the presentation material. I had written a short talk. I loved how the seminar unfolded after a few stop-start attempts, almost writing itself. These few days were supposed to, somehow, compel me to commit the dates, the percentages, the numbers, the names and the references to memory. To remember the hidden clues embedded into each slide to remind me to say what, instruct what, illustrate what. To learn to segue from slide to slide, from image to image, from notion to notion. To remind myself to stop saying 'umm', to enunciate my 'b's from my 'm's. According to the voice coach app, I keep mispronouncing 'anxiety', inducing an ironic anxiety of its own.

My early attempts at presenting had me jabbering for an hour and twenty; in front of a real audience, I would run way over. I trimmed and trimmed some more. I panicked that it was now too simple, too stating the obvious. I recorded myself for the umpteenth time trying to remember when to swipe my screen. I trimmed again. I thought it a shame I could not present everything I had researched. Now I had to remember what I had deliberately omitted and to prevent myself going off on a tangent again.

Recording a satisfactory attempt, I took to walking and listening to my own voice. I could then hear every 'umm', like the bashing of a gong. The recording had picked up some background roars from outside the van, and I sprinted off to one side convinced I was being chased down by a tractor. Thankfully there was no one around to witness it. I walked some more along the dry ridgeway. I had already reserved a village hall, paid Facebook to promote my adverts and so now it just left time for the headmonkeys to crank up. Of course, no one is interested in fears, phobias and anxieties in womanhood. No one cares about how bravery differs between the sexes. No one but me finds this topic fascinating. No one else wonders how invisible societal forces can push and pull us around like sycamore pods in a whirlygig until we come to believe that being perennially afraid is normal.

I was on my final walk of the evening and nearly an hour into my recording. I could already see my van atop the hillock. My voice, my recorded one, reminded me that the only way to build self-esteem is to 'face everything and rise'. To ignore the Twitter Trolls, the Social Media Smiters and our own internal critics marking out the boundaries of stereotype, condemning us for daring to step out of our circles of containment. Because bravery is directly proportional to how much fear we have. The more neurotic we are, the braver we have to be. Courage is not the absence of fear, but the proof that fear exists.

Toward me strolled a diminutive woman. Dark haired. Dogless. A decade and a bit younger at least. Wrapped up in a dark puffer jacket. I was still half-listening to my implorations, while the other part of me was concentrating on the message conveyed by the head demon calling me a fraud, that no one would come in any case. I smiled notionally as the stranger came within a few feet of our passing place.

"I'm glad I'm not the only woman walking alone out here," she blurted out quite unexpectedly. I could not recall it being used as an ice-breaker before. Typically, those unfamiliar rely on a safer but mundane, "Grotty weather, isn't it!" or "Sorry about my dog," as some breed or other attempts to wipe its nose on me. Most often, it is a nod and a quick diverting of the eyes.

I pulled out my ear-piece. "I'm so glad you said that," I replied, half-laughing.

"What is it about women being out on their own? I had to get out of the house but why is it such a big deal being out on your own?" She stood stock-still quizzing me.

"You've just asked a question on my specialist subject and I'm just rehearsing for a public speaking event on women and fear. In 2020 I walked across the American wilderness alone."

Even I could not believe this conversation was happening at the very moment that my anxiety had crept back in via the secret door that I still had no idea how to seal shut.

"Is it societal?" She asked. "Yes, we're taught to be afraid from a young age. Boys are taught to be brave, girls are taught to be perfect. Girls are pushed into adjusting our behaviour for our own safety. Did you know that men are one and a half times more likely to be victims of crime? But we're the ones told we're vulnerable."

"Really? But on TV the victim that is stabbed is always female."

"And white. Preferably blonde." I added.

We laughed. I had finally found my moment of woo in Wiltshire.

The Yle of Wihtwara

Each September we'd be allocated new beds in different dormitories. As we graduated up through the forms, we'd eventually leave behind our bunk beds with their stretched and weary bedsprings, straining under heavily stained mattresses. We yearned for the third form: the time when we would no longer have to weigh up sacrificing one of our four mandated blanket to prop up the sagging berths against better respite from the bitterly cold dormitory air. In the third year, one could be trusted with a single bed. No bed mate above or below, one whose rolling over would have the other shuddering awake. It could be worse, though. It could always be worse.

The smallest gaggle of boarders were the juniors. This dormitory of bedwetters was closest to the matron's room. Never a night passed without someone getting the matron to sigh in frustration. It was only the slumber of the oblivious that would prevent her shouting. Her fury supplied the day-terrors, which were worse than any night terrors.

Across a short corridor, stayed the eldest of the juniors and next door was the first form. Then, further along the second year, nowadays called Year Eight. By then our numbers would have swelled so we would be split across two rooms. Upon reaching the third year, we would be eligible for a precious single bed. Classmates were spread across into three dormitories, located on the east side. The fourth and fifth forms were scattered amid pokier rooms on the top floor, the old servants' quarters, and down various nooks in the wings, further from the ever-stalking matrons. There were only one or two around at night, but they could be everywhere, all at once.

We queued for breakfast, lunch, dinner, school, church, sport, indeed for our very existence, and always in pairs, grouped together by our allotted dormitory. Come September, we might not sit next to or see our closest friends from our earlier years until school, and then only in break times. Friendships fractured, rows exchanged and jealousy grew. Pettiness prevailed. Allegiances broke down each new academic year only for new ones to build again in the following terms.

Beds were always assigned. Duvets, typical in most family homes, were strictly forbidden. A girl arrived with asthma. Her parents had insisted on a hypoallergenic duvet, even though all other parents previously had been told no. How we all suddenly wanted asthma, even those who actually had it. Given they had managed so far, they could not claim to be special cases. Shortly after, another girl arrived who was just seven, a whole year younger than her dorm-mates. She was allowed an extra cuddly toy and sensibly allocated a bottom bunk.

The beds were covered in matching bedspreads, and all layers had to be tucked in with hospital corners, including the unsighted sheets. Dorms should be immaculate at all times, with nothing ever allowed on the hallowed wooden floor, or crusty rugs. The bedspreads varied in colour and design according to the name of the dormitory. They were washed annually, and one must never be caught sitting, let alone lying, on them during daytime hours. No TV. No games. No playing cards. No electronic equipment of any kind except a scientific calculator, which must be stored in one's school desk or in one's briefcase. No comics. No dolls. One cuddly bear. The fifth formers, who lived in a faraway side-wing were permitted the luxury of a radio, but it must only be played on a Saturday. Despite this, once they forgot to switch off their illegal listening before heading to the schoolrooms and so the privilege was withdrawn for all succeeding years. "What music do you like?" became another unanswerable question.

We took to spinning. Literally. My roommates and I would twirl ourselves around and around until we felt queasy or staggered over, sometimes bashing a forehead against a bed frame. It was something to do in the mornings while we waited for the bell and kept us occupied for an entire term. It was demented, laughably demented!

At the end of the school year, we'd recover our trunks, which had hibernated in the cellar for the duration of the school year behind a locked door, in an area we called the crypt. We'd haul these beasts of burden upstairs, never via the central staircase, only ever by the tighter, twistier servants' stairs, and place them beside our beds. The night before the school year ended, we'd empty our two allocated drawers, folded in our school uniforms, after-school trews, airtexes and jumpers, our cloaks, summer boater hats, winter tricornes, shoes, gym kits, as well as briefcases crammed full of note books, pens and pencils. We'd then drag the sodding thing, which was as long as most were tall, back to the crypt.

After the summer holidays, we'd dribble in early-evening, put our possessions into our newly allocated drawers, and then pack our casual wear into the trunks. The canny stashed them somewhere else, usually in the unlocked portion of the mildewed cellar behind the ranks holding our Sunday shoes. Then we'd wait to see who our new roommates might be, hoping for one's closest friend, or dreading the one that wasn't.

The first bell of the term would ring. We'd start to queue, waiting to be instructed to haul our emptied trunks to the crypt. New girls would chatter away excitedly, already anticipating midnight feasts, lashings of lemonade and jolly hockey sticks. Newly-appointed prefects would march up and down, dishing out power-crazed threats while the matrons were busy shrieking about the stacking of trunks in the cellar.

Then we'd return to our four-hundred-year-old rooms to welcome these now silent arrivals, who were already realising things weren't quite as depicted by Enid Blyton. With no prep that night, the only night there wouldn't be the onerous task of homework or letter-writing, we'd tell these now horror-struck novices all about the ghosts that we'd witnessed traipsing up and down the Elizabethan corridors. The toothless vagrant who lived in the crypt; the country squire in the kitchen chasing after the cook's assistant. Of course, there was a soldier, blood dripping from a mangled arm. The moans, the yawns, the black splodges that shape-shifted through dorm walls. We'd remind one another to worry about the girls in the third form for on Friday the 13th, their beds span into coffins come midnight. Then the ghosts would come to feast on the weakest, sometimes watched by the petrified one who wasn't yet asleep.

Then another bell would ring, commanding the juniors to bed. The occupants would bellow, "Nobody look!" as they attempted to remove their trews and jumpers, and get into their nightgowns without revealing an inch of naked flesh. Fifteen minutes later, the eldest juniors were corralled into their bunks, with matron frequently returning back to the first dorm holler at the younger ones for not being sufficiently asleep. Dorms were put to bed in fifteen-minute cycles until the time came for us to settle into our new beds for our first night in the latest room that would now be our source of identity.

Only this time ours came with bed bugs. A few days of complaints saw us billeted into the school's sanitarium. With only two beds, most of us were forced to sleep on the carpeted floor for the week so the dorm could be fumigated. Far from the madding matrons, just above the kitchen, we snuck down a secret passageway to have our first and only midnight feast with lashings of milk, scrummy biscuits and pilfered jam.

****

Sitting like a sharp pebble under the butt of England, the Isle of Wight is for the most part a lump of white chalk roamed by cows. Some allege it is host to England's largest population of ghosts, ghouls and other paranormal *wights*.

Incidentally it is *Wight*: not be confused with its homophone 'white'. The word *Wight* is thought to be derived from 'Wicht', Dutch for 'little creature' and German for 'little child'. Perhaps for some, this amounts to one and the same thing. Somewhere along the line, though, the English language evolved in its contrary way, changing the 'c' to a 'g'. This single additional stroke quietly unleashed all sorts of pandemonium.

One might contend that the English deliberately set out to make our spelling system bafflingly incomprehensible to children and foreigners alike, in keeping with our Island's defiance. Others may claim the complexity is nothing but an enterprising conspiracy to industrialise the English language into family fighting games such as Scrabble, Wordle and Pictionary. Elsewhere, pedants far and wide can whip out their phone cameras to record the best of misspelt words for eternal mockery. I have always quite appreciated that hobby though.

I was once immersed in a system that declared that rules matter. They mattered even when one did not understand them. They mattered even if one did not agree with them. They just mattered because one was informed that they mattered. I was told that without rules, there would be disorder and chaos, and no one would be able to cope. It is also why Modern English spelling provides a sure-fire device for winning any argument on the world-wide web: spot a typo and the hapless eristic can be magically obliterated, a form of linguistic quick draw, a linguistic battle of the *Gunville* variety.

Coming off the ferry at *Whippingham*, it reminded me that one cannot always know how a place is called unless one is local to that region or has been corrected by someone who is. Despite my elocution teacher demanding I aspirate the 'h' in 'wh' words, yet drop the 'h' sound to say 'aitch, not haitch', I realised it had been many years since I had obliged her. Worse, I have become inclined to drop the 'h' in the 'ham' too. How fast the elocution teacher must spin in her grave!

Regardless of the similarity between 'wicht' and 'wight', some assert the word is a derivation from the Celtic language for 'working fort'. In spite of the island's unitary defence, the Romans brought with them the Latin Alphabet, which was fine for Rome, but Italian avoids words beginning with 'th' sounds: as in *the* Romans. Hence, we nabbed a few characters from our original runic script, which culminated in our alphabet having thirty-three letters to play with. This blend of alphabets was known as Futhark; not that I have any idea how one pronounces that, but please avoid any spoonerism.

The Normans, unsurprisingly, were all about minimal living. Subsequently, they declared that one letter should resemble many sounds, with that they deftly swiped away seventeen of our symbols. Thus, the early history of the Isle of Wight is more a tale of liberating superfluous letters: the Isle of Wight going as it did from Wihtwara to Wihtland to Wiht to Wit.

Then came the turning of the tide. Or tyde if one wants to be archaic about it. Once upon a *tim-e*, of course, we would have pronounced the 'e'. This continued until the day we simply stopped saying 'eeee' in a life-affirming way. Across the lands, all the 'eeees' fell as silent as muted ghosts, until finally the 'e' would only be recalled on parchment. Also, during this period the letter 'y' was agreed to have an 'oooo' sound, rhyming with the ghoulish 'boo!' That is how *Ryde* was rude, albeit nowadays it sounds like 'ride'.

Scholars of the eras find all this befuddling, but thankfully in times past your common or garden Englander could revel in their illiteracy. Eventually, the erudite classes came to a consensus that by adding an 'e', and changing the 'y' to 'i', we could all get pie-eyed, to rhyme with ride. Although nude was still rude. Thus began the beginning of the end of the age of simplicity. If things were not complex enough, the Islanders below, just as much as the Mainlanders above, were dragged through The Great Vowel Shift. This occurred between the fifteenth and eighteenth centuries, and leaves one to infer that we had been terribly constipated about matters up until this point.

Some claim that the shift occurred by the rapid migration of peoples from the north of England to the south, or labour movements induced by the Black Death, diluting previously distinct dialects. Others attest that Londoners switched out their vowel sounds to distinguish them from their rivals in Birmingham. More still blame the French, which seems to be a typically English thing to do whenever in doubt. Perhaps, though it was the middle classes who simply desired themselves to be more *Anglais* than Ing-lish without actually having to fork out for the ferry, which admittedly is exorbitant.

Cometh the hour, cometh the arrival of the Dutch. Into this melee, they threw in their printing presses. The advent of mechanised writing demanded additional ink left, right and centre as reading became a new and fascinating means of communication. The need for convention became paramount. What the English language really did not need, then, was for the printing men to add silent 'h's to words that had previously been deciphered perfectly well without. It was they who burdened our ghosts and ghouls with the deathly silent 'h'. And that is how *Wiht,* which had already simplified to Wit, morphed into *Whit*. So that is all very *Whitwell*, isn't it!

Where consistency was key, labour rates varied, as did literacy levels. Being not of the mother-tongue (whatever that now was), this new literary industry saw its Dutch workers paid per line. This was incentive enough to throw in a few silent letters: just a few soft and hard 'g's to help string things along. It certainly gives one much to cogitate as one counted gnats gnawing on fungi growing in the heights of the gentle *Godshill*. So, perhaps this is how Whit became Wight. But even so, quite how *Niton* and *Knighton* are homophonic hetero-tons on the same island is far beyond my wit.

They say that knowledge is power, but knowledge is also connected to acquire. This "Is it Latin or French?" conundrum precisely demonstrates why the philologists of Latin fell afoul of French linguists, both of whom battled against Germanic lexicographers in order to determine whose spelling was the one true ruler of symbols. On occasion, when a word could not be claimed as either Germanic, Latin, French or Celtic in origin, it was assumed to be Greek. This saw them add in the letters 'p' and 'b' as a nod to their heritage, and to compound matters, the added letters were to be unspoken, giving us debt, doubt and receipt.

'Island' with its soundless 's' was said to have derived from the Latin 'insular'. Elsewhere, someone pointed out that surely it was related to the French 'Isle'. Presumably, war broke out somewhere, as thereafter we adopted not only the French spelling, but also their pronunciation. Of course, the French like to ignore their letter 's'. It turns out that it was from the original English 'yle' but the original Celtic languages had become, mostly, the lexicon of the ghosts.

Added to this complexity were accents and speech impediments. *Great Thorness* would be a lispy way of describing my thighs having staggered down to some of the Isle of Wight's bountiful coves. The one at *Niton* was definitely worth the mud-riven hike, albeit an extraordinary amount of it was spent descending on my arse. Although, I spent much of my week-long sojourn on the micro-island: not so much hiking down to coves but rather researching English spelling - just in case anyone else ever wondered how the Isle of Wight grew up to become the ultimate chef of word salads.

The advent of a universally acceptable dictionary should have brought some finality to the occasion. Alas, it simply generated further mayhem. By now the linguistic wars had gone global. America reformed their English, whereas Canada opted not to. Hence, the Americans and the Canadians differ on the spelling of centres, cheques and modernise.

All considered, we had a jolly old time on the Isle of Wight, a place whose name has absolutely nothing to do with its chalky whiteness: that was just the fog, which smothered almost all the views as I toured across this tiny isle. Despite the claim it is the sunniest place in England, outshining many Spanish holiday destinations, it was most definitely the Isle of White for the duration. I still wish it were spelt 'Wite' as it would also permit my trusty old elocution coach to rest in peace. On the other hand, visitors can rest assured that should they encounter one of the Isle of Wight's legendary ghosts, chances are one would not comprehend a word all because of that bloody Great Vowel Shift all those years ago.

Fascinatingly, this Isle of Ghoulish Children is most famous for garlic, and yet the Isle of Wight's alliums fail to repel nearly two-million visitors a year, all of whom are obliged to pay the equivalent of 750 garlic bulbs per return ferry in peak season, a journey that lasts exactly one hour. It is sensible, then, to come to these isles in winter, where one can spend the equivalent of two hundred and fifteen bulbs, or, if one prefers, twenty-five hundred cloves. Unless one comes across in a van, then the prices suggest it is summer all year round. Still, it gave me the enormous privilege of being able to sail on the truck ferry. Aside from segregating truckers from the hoi polloi, this speciality voyage offered the additional perk of free tea and coffee during the crossing, making it probably the most expensive cafe in England. I had two just to cheapen the price per cup, as well as ensuring I availed myself of the ferry's very clean toilets for what I have come to dub 'a posh pee'.

This island-below-the-island boasts that its biggest summer show is 'The Garlic Festival', attracting nearly twenty-five thousand vampire-slaying aficionados to *Fighting Cocks Cross*. This claim might upset *Cowes*, which attracts nearly one hundred visitors a year to its week-long sailing regatta. In 2021, The organisers of *Cowes* Regatta changed one the Tuesday, from Ladies' Day to Women's Day: an act which The Daily Mail derided as 'woke'. "It would be terribly sad if ladies were no longer welcome," the tabloid quoted a member of the Royal Enclosure. Like the so-called educated elite of yonder year, he too fathomed the beauty of the English language in quite a fascinating way. For him, August 2nd, 2021 was the year that England silenced the female of the species. Again.

Incidentally, *Cowes* is named after two bovine-shaped sandbanks on either side of the Medina Estuary. Whatever happens, please never enlighten the members of the Royal Enclosure that in some places, like in modern English, cowes are more contemporarily known as cows, and most women object to being called that too.

Scandalised and Vandalised in Gloucestershire

I remember when the bell rang in the classrooms. A few of the obedient little cherubs we were occasionally inclined to be, dashed off to the lavatory. Charging down the tiled corridor, then the hardwood stairs, they would dive into the room on the right. The facilities had a tiny obscured single-paned window, a crack across it and a chunk missing from the bottom right-hand corner. Certainly no one thought to repair it during my confinement.

My memory says that particular lavatory was called 'Cloisters'. Although, that cannot be right because cloisters are an open-air hallway. Given they were extremely draughty, perhaps my doubt is the issue. The black and white tiles retained the cold all year round. Black cisterns affixed high on the wall, chains dangling with chipped flush pulls. Pipes rattled and clunked, reverberating around the building, unless of course, they had frozen in the deep midwinter.

Such periods saw the ageing Armitage bowls become particularly squalid. Ironic, for the purpose of the place was to form us into demure young ladies for the future.

Spared of hot water to wash hands, one would avoid the Cloisters unless the lesson called for mapping the outlines of countries. Then a scrummage of grey, woollen tunics and red-cardigans piled down the well-worn stairs, hands gripping the bannisters to avoid the shunt from above. All of us were desperate to be the first to obtain the prize of 'tracing paper'. The day school toilets were stocked with, I can only surmise for the convenience of art and geography studies, Izal's medicated toilet tissue. It was waxy, acrid and most impermeable to liquid matter. It mostly scoured, and was barely flushable.

It was the commodity that was never depleted, for the softer toilet paper was only available in the boarding house. Woe betide anyone caught smuggling the luxuriant, and much more effective, equivalent. Special dispensation was sought, but not necessarily granted, when afflicted by head colds, or summery hayfever. It was better, we were informed, to use the same embroidered handkerchief day after day up until wash day. Pockets were not private spaces, so smuggling came with some peril.

Just a smattering had charged off to the Cloisters when the bell signalled the end of the English lesson. The bells ushered out the "Miss" from the school room, which would be replaced with another "Miss" upon the ringing of the next bell. A raft of dictionaries, usually stacked haphazardly on the windowsill, remained scattered about the two-person Welsh desks. They were well-thumbed, tatty and largely neglected. With nothing to do until the arrival of the next teacher, the room became unusually hushed as a frisson of excitement took hold as we collectively discovered the dictionaries contained rude words.

Vulgar. *That word was italicised after* 'shit', 'fuck', 'sex', 'bugger'. *So many hitherto unspoken words of mortification. Suddenly the challenge was on to recall more forbiddens, and that meant uttering profanities in hoarse whispers, masked only by one's hands, between giggles and shushes, pierced by the squeals of someone discovering that a word had already been underlined by one's elders.*

Oh, to be stuck in a priggish boarding school when one happens upon the sheer joy of an adventure by dictionary!

****

My quest remained a simple one: to determine exactly what is the source of Britain's lavatorial demise. With ironic timing, my arrival in Gloucestershire coincided with England's elected and unelected leaders' indulging in yet another scatological rumpus. Our ruling elite were again proving themselves incapable of navigating their way out of a toilet with an open door. We were, for the third time this year, seeking a new Prime Minister.

It made sense to me to start at *Ready Token*. A place that most sounds like that particularly essential coin one must always carry in order to access public conveniences, which are only convenient if one has the correct denomination. No penny? No spendy. Even though these days, way more than a penny is demanded.

Ready Token is a ridiculously tiny hamlet of warm honey-coloured stone. It is most famous for being the meeting place of six country roads and nine parish boundaries. It is not the sort of place one wishes to encounter a large yellow sign that screams out, "Don't follow your SatNav!" Carnage unfolded, as drivers repeatedly failed to make their escape. It certainly gave ample time to conjure up a scene of local councillors bickering over who was going to shun responsibility all the while referencing fine print that needed to be magnified in order for matters to be ignored.

On the surface, Gloucestershire is the county least likely to stake the claim of being England's lavatorial destination, given that there is only *Cockadilly, Ball's Green* and *Lower Swell* to get one's immature inner-child sniggering. Oh, and *Boxbush* which sounds like it should be obscene but is not, although curiously the bushless *Box* is. In fact, it is safe to say that Gloucestershire is considerably primmer and more proper than the average English county. It is only periodical acts of vandalism that has the village of *Uckington* made salacious before the council returns it to its otherwise strait-laced existence.

One could argue that Gloucester has all the hallmarks of a proper gentlemanly demesne, and its stuffiness is best encapsulated in locations such as *Tutshill, Old Sodbury and Miserden*. The latter was once famous for having the worst bandwidth in Britain. Well, I would be quite miserly too, given I would get neither entertainment nor income without the internet. That aside, the village was quite the remarkable piece of Merrie England.

Belying Gloucestershire's superficial decorum, there are clues frittered all over the place, that all is not what it appears. It is certainly the most violent county I have visited thus far: *Slaughter, The Camp, Bulley, Sharpness, Knockdown* and *Boxwell.* Following a furtive snapping of their road signs, I high-tailed away as fast as The Shitron and the speed limit permitted.

Gloucestershire's prudery is only true if one ignores the beauty of the Englishperson's penchant for a good euphemism, a practice that is especially popular amongst the kind inclined to take offence to more precise terminology. For it is here, well below the surface, that Gloucestershire shines in all its degeneracy.

This tale of urban sewerage begins at *Kemble*. Back in 2006, an anonymous being going by the inspirational pseudonym of 'Villager', stated that the place was, "a very shite village where nothing ever happens and nobody ever goes." Immediately, it struck me that the residents might be in urgent need of substantial doses of laxative. More pertinently it was this assertion that piqued my curiosity and diverted my attention to the hitherto unexplored underworld better known as www.urbandictionary.com.

With one click, and one eye closed for safety, the other squinting, I was expecting to be plunged into depths of depravity hitherto unplumbed. Except I discovered that if I wanted to investigate *Kemble* further, I must first get myself disbarred from 'top-shelf' content by proving my eligibility to my phone provider. Apparently, Britain's adults cannot cope with unfettered access to The Urban Dictionary, the content of which has probably been conjured up by teenagers nationally. This submission I only make given that its founder was a mere fifteen years old when he built the site back in the innocent days of the world wide web. Since then, its contributors have conjured up all sorts of lewd and outlandish lexicography: perhaps they all hail from *Little Sodbury*, the borough of little sods.

Some twenty-four hours passed before I was able to dive headlong into this unfamiliar den of interweb iniquity. Gloucestershire ended up becoming quite the grand tour, and one that was quite pornographic at times. I shall leave you with your own minds to litter with filth, as a parent might say. For those of a sensitive disposition, please avert your eyes, but *Quedgeley, Bussage, Slad, Quenington, Brimpsfield* and *Poulton* are nothing short of face puckering. Whatever you do next, it is probably best if you resist researching your own homestead, as the answer may well devalue your property faster than the current administration's economic policies.

With those ticked off the list, it just left me to defy 'Villager's' postulation that *Kemble* is a place where "no one ever goes". For clarity, that is not a euphemism for my doing anything but visiting. So, somewhat apprehensively, I crept, stealth-like, in broad daylight, in an oversized, diesel-engined-roaring ubiquitous white van. While there, I learned that *Kemble* is the source of that most famous slow-moving cesspit of slurry: The River Thames.

Thames Water was fined £4m in 2016 for discharging thirty-hours' worth of gastrointestinal gloop. Four years later, it was revealed the 'water' treatment works dumped a further two-thousand million litres of excrementum eruptio - its worst on record. On the day I arrived in *Kemble*, Thames Water was once again liquidating its assets. Thankfully, but only for the residents of Gloucestershire, this all takes place downstream in Oxfordshire. Proving, possibly, that *Kemble* is indeed a place where "nobody ever goes!"

Thus, my little voyage of vulgarity necessarily came to its natural conclusion, and it was time for me to make my way out. Despite my intention of visiting only those places of disgust or offence, I could not resist a quick diversion to the gloriously charming olde worlde *Bibury*. Clusters of seventeenth century weavers' cottages sit across from a gentle river, roamed by puritanically white ducks. It is truly the best of middle England. Some believe *Bibury* to be the most beautiful village in the country. It has been described as "utterly picturesque" on Fox News, and a "most charming town" by the Huffington Post.

Although, that is not what is asserted in the Urban Dictionary.

The Game-Changing County of Bristol

It was always a Saturday evening when the matron in charge distributed our letters from home – right after the bell had rung to indicate the end of prep. Just like in the rest of England, the mail was delivered twice daily; deposited just inside the grand entrance of the boarding house while we were cooped up in the school rooms. The bundles would be swiftly retrieved then stacked in a white wire tray kept on a table in the bursar's office. One could witness the piles growing through the doors' glass panels as the weekdays crawled by.

A dorm mate might spot my letter and inform me of its existence. They were usually blue aerograms adorned with large stamps depicting the gloriously stunning Birds of Paradise that were symbolic of my home. Papua New Guinea's stamps were far more alluring than the squat squares used by the Royal Mail, which were most often solid backgrounds set against the Queen's white profile. The colour of a British stamp was the key to how heavy the contents were, or what class, 1st or 2nd, the letter-writer had delegated it. It is amazing what one can affix an interpretation to in the absence of humane reassurance.

Very rarely, one's own post could be pilfered from the masses waiting to be united with their owners. This discovery had to be kept secret, best read when hiding in a toilet, lest it unleash a race to the offices among girls deprived of a full life. On rare occasions, the administration would forget to lock the door as they left for their private lives in the afternoon. We would always try to twist the door knob if we were in the vicinity without authority. Less seldom was happening upon the office being temporarily unsupervised. Usually such opportunities occurred on the way to the library, or if permission was granted for a dash to the mid-corridor toilets reserved for visitors, or when being summoned to the school principal's rooms,

The latter event was usually for a reprimand for some misdemeanour that, in all likelihood, one had already been admonished for at the time. Following the principal's telling off, the usual lecture on how one is a disappointment to the universe, one's parents, one's house, and oneself, a 'Black Mark' would be issued. It was not a letter nor a spot but a spoken notification that one had displeased one's caretakers. The punishment would be served the following Friday when any already chastened recipients' names were recited in assembly. Following which, the delinquents would haul themselves up from the floor, stumble around one's still-cross-legged classmates, to present oneself at the foot of the stage. There we would stand, backs to our peers, head dropped for the remainder of the formal school gathering. Come the end of term, the number of black marks would be deducted from the number of house points, reminding the second-placed house which malefactors who had the most impact. For some reason, shame works best on girls and the stigma remains ingrained for a lifetime.

The distraction of that week over, we could then yearn for Saturday. We'd wait for bells to signal the end of dinner; for the end of prep and wait for the matron to turn up bringing with her a roll call of lucky letter recipients. One by one, we'd leave our benches, to be handed the bundles or singles of a window into the free world. Woe betide the child who forgot to loudly thank the matron for her gift, but more unfortunate was the child with no post, and there were always such unfortunates. I was a good letter writer, and quick to make friends with whom I could pen-pal so I never felt that particular brand of humiliation. My mother never failed to write, my father never failed to not write. The vagaries of international travel meant months might pass between letters being sent and my receiving them. Amusingly, the steady aerograms landed, not always in the right order, and often after a school holiday had already caught us up with one another's news.

I remember it had come as quite the surprise one Saturday evening when I was expecting to receive precisely nothing. I knew my name would not be called out for I had spent quite some time on the loo that morning. It was therefore a tremendous shock to receive a letter with a stamp from New Zealand. My parents, I discovered, had popped off to Rotarua and were having a marvellous time of it despite complaining that the place stunk of raw sewage.

****

The only thing I knew about Bristol, prior to my arrival, was that it was famous for devising the globally-recognised 'Bristol Stool Chart'. It is a ranking system which does not specialise in the categorising of foot rests. This ostensibly useful medical aid was produced by researchers at the Bristol Royal Infirmary, which incidentally is a hospital that treats all classes, from the infirm to those with a most robust constitution.

If one wishes to undertake one's own anatomical research of one's innards, one simply needs to study the deposits of the rear end. Apparently, it is largely advisable that we should do this once in a while. Like daily, if not regularly. One 'wins' if one ranks between three or four. Anything else is less than desirable. A score of one is indicative of what is best described as system inertia. At the opposing end of the scale, a score of seven indicates one's regulations shift with unedifying swift velocity. Speed kills. At least that is what Bristol's road signs caution.

Perhaps what is most astonishing, at least to me, was learning that Bristol is not only a city but also a county. Even more astonishingly, it always has been a county, except for those periods of time that it was not. This occurred twice. Despite only having 'town' status, which was bestowed in 1155, King Edward III conferred upon Bristol the esteemed ranking of county in 1373 and it remained the case until 1974. Then, via an Act of Parliament, Bristol was subsumed into a more-artificial-than-the-usual-man-made boundary called 'Avon' for the reason of, well, politics. 'Avon' is still sometimes listed as a county on a company's drop-down address menu. This oversight is largely attributed to the phenomenon best described as 'system inertia' whereby the technology has yet to recognise the new geopolitical landscape – even though the disintegration of Avon occurred in 1996 when Bristol resumed its countydom.

That Bristol is not in Avon comes as news to many; even to some Bristolians, according to the very-challenging-to-read-online Bristol Post. The Bristol Post is the county's premier source of news production, or it would be if one could navigate through a bombardment of bouncing, oversized advertisements. These expand across, if not outright demolish, the already screen-dominating imagery that accompanies each article. Intact sentences are particularly difficult to locate. Navigating the website, let alone successfully clicking upon anything that might be deemed 'noteworthy', is a game within itself. I can only liken it to an activity that is slightly more frustrating than playing *Frogger* upside down while simultaneously trying to worm the cat.

What I did learn is that Bristol was established as a county exactly one hundred and sixty-nine years before it was appointed as a city. For the unknowing, a city can only be a city when the reigning monarch decides it is so. Bristol much pleased Henry VIII in 1542. Prior to that it was a town, and we know it was a town because it had a market, which is what historically separated a town from a village in this Land of Eng. Even today, the demarcation between the two statuses has nothing to do with population-size. Bewildering, I know.

There are absolutely no perks to being a city over a town, although town councillors, mayors and other dignitaries of lofty purpose beg to differ. Nevertheless, at every royal commemoration or jubilee, a competition is opened to elect 'Britain's Next City'. It is akin to the X-factor but for local civil servants and Simon Cowell is King Charles III. At least, this was the case at the time of writing - any information here may already be obsolete as British governmental leadership changes hands at an unedifying swift velocity, although the sovereign has struggled with some system inertia.

Tradition would have it that a town must have a diocesan cathedral in order to qualify as a city-elect, and indeed until 1889 this was a fundamental requirement. The investiture of the cathedral-less Birmingham in 1889 still causes friction in many a modern pub quiz. Following that monumental act of apple cart upsetting, the obligations upon wannabe city candidates were finally fossilised in 1907 in a secret agreement between Edward VII and the Home Office. That unratified edict stipulated a town to have a population of 300,000; a record of good local government, and a local 'metropolitan character', whatever that might mean. Back to that elusive 'X' factor, which I presume to be largely contrived in the eye of the business beholder. Despite the protocol, the ruling monarch is not required to pay any heed to this, and so usually does not. Thank God for England's ruling classes, otherwise, things would be clear, efficient and comprehensible, and us lowly English civilians would probably expire from boredom.

In other matters useful for pub quizzes: every county, including Bristol, is headed up by a Lord-Lieutenant who has been appointed by the incumbent sovereign ruler. The Lord-Lieutenant acts, just like a current monarch, as a powerless, but yet obscurely powerful, unelected leader of the county. Their roles include organising royal visits to the region and nominating individuals for royal honours.

Bristol's Lord-Lieutenant is the American, Peaches Golding, who is lauded for being the first black woman to hold the position. 'Naturally', women could not do so prior to 1975, when the passing of an Act of Parliament better codified the Englishwoman's ability to mobilise herself socially, economically and politically.

Born in Spartanburg, South Carolina, Bristol's Lord-Lieutenant comes from a long line of game-changers: her father was arrested for refusing to move to the back of the bus as the then southern-states' Jim Crow laws obliged him to do. Seven years before the more famous Rosa Parks was arrested for the very same act, Ms Golding's father had realised federal law overrode the racist mandate when travelling across state lines. He sued and was awarded $2,000 compensation, with which he sensibly bought a car, thus avoiding the buses in future.

Bristol's other contributions to a more egalitarian society are similarly commendable: their university was the first to accept women on an equal footing to men back in 1876, albeit women were excluded from studying medicine. Elsewhere, the Bristolian company, Fry's, arguably made the greatest contribution ever to women's wellbeing: they enabled the mass-commercialisation of the chocolate bar. Prior to this, chocolate offerings largely scored at the high or low end of the Bristol Stool Chart. Somehow Fry's recipes mastered the 'winning formula' of producing it at grade three/four. I believe their contributions have been successfully alleviating menstrual tension since 1847 and I consider it an outrage that they have not received any kind of Royal Honour. It is my current hypothesis that chocolate is similarly helpful for soothing menopausal brain fog. Further research is being vigorously undertaken as I write largely because I keep forgetting to record the outcome.

Despite the university's bar on women doctors, Bristol was the birthplace of America's first recognised woman Doctor of Medicine: Dr Elizabeth Blackwell. She emigrated aged eleven to New York in 1847, but on a return visit to these fair isles, she met with Elizabeth Garrett Anderson and inspired her to become Britain's first fully-trained physician. Together, they were a compelling force, which has resulted in 47% of currently-registered doctors being women.

Finally, just to demolish a popular myth, Bristol is actually Britain's smallest county; and not Rutland nor the Isle of Wight (when the tide is in) because according to my calculations, Bristol is a county of forty-two square miles. Rutland is a gargantuan one-hundred and fifty square miles, and the Isle of Wight is one-hundred and forty-seven-ish square miles depending on the hour.

There is a lot for Bristol to be proud of, and for women especially. I am not sure that *Horfield* is the jewel in its crown though.

The Swamps of Somerset

My arrival at *Dunkerton* got me contemplating personal ablutions. Interestingly, www.soakology.com claims that the average Brit has five showers and three baths weekly so the nation's proclivity for cleansing is way more than the prescribed two or three times per week touted by dermatologists. Unsurprisingly, women require eight minutes to the men's seven in the race for cleanliness. Thankfully, it rains a lot in these lands, permitting the luxury, although I will confess: it is only the many foibles of service stations showers that forced me to be compliant with the expert's recommendations.

At Gordano Services, Somerset, one asks for a key from the attendant at WHSmith. In response, the server will wordlessly thrust a cup towards you. In it, you will chuck your van keys by way of deposit. Then, with strides of purpose, you should saunter into the men's toilets to use one of the three available cubicles.

Motorway services have a legal requirement to provide shower facilities, even if it is just one solitary unisex cubicle. Seemingly at Gordano, it is only men who shower. Elsewhere, non-motorway service stations are 'strongly encouraged' to provide working showers for those who spend their lives on the road. Alas, that encouragement is rarely heeded. Experience has taught me to plan my routes judiciously, making sure that at least twice a week I cross paths with a motorway or a very good friend. On arrival, I always send up a prayer to the God of Divinity that it might be clean, hot and free of the smell of shrimp. Why shrimp, I have no idea, but more than two of the four stalls stink of such matter at Oxford Services.

There is no legal obligation for showers to distribute hot water nor even to install showers that actually spray water in the direction of the naked person. Some are nothing but a mere trickle struggling to burble down the wall, whereas others have fixed heads that jet wash the opposing door, bypassing the human being altogether. I cannot think of a suitable word to describe the disappointment of actually locating the shower room only to find a tatty piece of ageing paper declaring, "Shower temporarily out of service, we apologise for the inconvenience." Being temporary for years probably makes it permanent.

Moto, Britain's largest operators of motorway services, boasted, "We're proud to be investing £12.5 million into our showering facilities, upgrading every single Moto shower before the end of 2022." It was December 2022 at the time of writing, so I can attest that Britain's biggest chain of motorway services is in need of the website update. Hopefully, the work will be completed by December 2024.

Then there is the unfathomable inclination of engineers who opt to fit specialist showers with infra-red sensors, presumably more expensive that the average household shower. These high-tech alternatives supposedly detect that a person wants water to cascade over them. Puzzzingly, I have proved myself invisible several times at Warwick Southbound services: that one distributes lukewarm water for a full five seconds before the wishing-to-be-washed seemingly dissolves.

Most service station showers are free in the southern regions. This radically changes the further north one gets, where the facilities are restricted by a timer. Some permit two minutes to undress before spurting out water for precisely seven minutes, others require you to prepare for a rapid undressing as the clock commences its countdown the moment you enter the stall. Despite the timers, the showers nonsensically demand that the user push a button every ten to fifteen seconds in order to source water. In private facilities, like specialist truck stops, one might be obliged to pay four or five pounds for the use of the shower, on top of the day charge, but sometimes women go free. I presume this is because there are so few women HGV drivers, attendants are barely required to attend so, for once, and very illegally, we benefit.

In Winter, rarely do I queue, which is a major plus when there is a two-hour maximum stay at such facilities. One could argue that I am receiving a gratis service, unless, of course, I treat myself to a coffee or I am overtaken by the urge for some obligatory cake. HGV drivers' tachographs compel them to park up and rest for designated periods of time. May I dare suggest that those who work day in, day out in tin cans to ensure our supermarkets are stocked with luxuries such as woodchip cat litter are afforded a little more decency.

Thankfully, the cubicles at Gordano are situated quite near the entrance, so aside from being somewhat self-conscious as I marched into the men's, I did not have to avert my eyes as men do whatever it is men do in men's toilets for too long. Quite often, public showers are deep within the labyrinths of the toilet block, ensuring that one has to walk through a fugue of poo particles and then back again, negating much of the benefit of the shower.

This particular shower room was clean, simple, perfunctory and set to fridge temperature. Usefully, there was a single stained chair, as well as spotless floors and walls free of mould, graffiti, crusty snot blobs and stray pubic hairs. In fact, this appears to be true for most services, except few have a convenient chair or stool. To my delight, this one had a regular see-through plastic cubicle: many service stations opt for walk-in types ensuring my shoes, towels and fresh clothes also get a thorough dowsing despite being hung up. On the inside wall a small, luminous yellow sticker screamed out, "Caution: Hot Water!" Experience has taught me to be sceptical, but in fact, this one was wonderfully scalding and it had a reasonable flow. Alas, it only lasted for twelve seconds before I had to push the button again.

Most showers are of the push-button variety, ensuring one only gets what one is given. With some, one can maintain the hold while one-handedly wrangling with shampoo, conditioner, soap, body and hair. There is rarely any temperature control. It is a true gem of a service station that trusts a person to run the water and remember to turn the handle back on one's own accord just like the home-dwelling members of the population manage. One really does not wish to spend a moment longer in public toilets than is strictly necessary but this bleedingly obvious fact has yet to occur to service station designers, whose specialist showers compel one to remain in the vicinity for much longer than the average Brit's shower time.

****

The Michaelmas term was about to rotate away from, "Aren't you afraid?" as we headed towards the Christmas break. All too soon, we would return for the next leg: the one in which everyone asked, "Aren't you cold?"

I was now so far advanced into the menopausal years that I was, for the most part, feeling as if I was languishing in a water bath steeping at forty-one degrees almost all of the time, and Nelson has fur, so he was just dandy. I, for one, was delighted by my body's inability to discern the current temperature. Timing is, after all, the main ingredient of luck. For all other times, we made use of an incessantly clicking diesel-run air blower. We could only use it for an hour at most before I started to believe I had decamped into someone's sauna.

Bath, named after the springs which sprung the bathing epicentre of the British Roman empire, is Somerset's principal city. *Wells*, England's smallest city, is built on an agitating aquifer and *Simonsbath* is so called because a parent finally persuaded their manky teenager to tidy their room and clean behind his ears. Possibly. Dashing between villages on their outskirts all provided a glorious, muddy swamp in which to career around in a van, making a splash and dowsing the hedgerows.

I had been exceptionally fortuitous in selecting 2022 as my starting year of Vanlife as it was working its way up to becoming the UK's warmest winter on record. In fact, it was only when I passed through *Coat* that I was reminded that this stroke of fortune goes against my personal grain: I once accidentally relocated myself to Siberia and that particular winter saw Russia endure its coldest documented year.

I arrived in England's most freshet-inclined county just as there was a dramatic change in climatic conditions. England shuddered into her first cold snap of winter. About me, outdoor types and dog walkers shivered their way through the minus figures. A dumping of snow repainted the landscape into a magical winter wonderland and the roads around *Watchet* became suitable for a jolly game of curling. I laughed maniacally at every single second of it.

The joy of smashing through swollen fords, burst lakes and oversized puddles had me a little too exuberant at times. Very much appreciated was the random woman flagging me down to warn me that should I continue, we would probably float off just past the church. Reversing in flood water is slightly less entertaining and I thought

Nelson likely averse wild swimming. "One year, no fear" was starting to become a liability as my confidence soared.

The first evidence of the coldwave seizing our climate occurred when my washing up water failed to drain. There before my very eyes, the remnants of the cat's bowl, along with other foodstuffs, floated in a manner most unbecoming and refused to evacuate, no matter what I tried. Like most cats, Nelson has the tendency to lick the jelly off the cardboard pieces, chasing them out of the bowl, over the rim and across the floor, leaving a trail of smeared detritus. Having spread his dinner, England's second-most obnoxious-smelling substance around the place, Nelson will go on to complain shrilly that he is hungry even before I have finished cleaning up the previous meal. Inspired by Somerset, I have taken to calling Nelson's leftovers: *Catsgore*, after the revoltingly awful-sounding, but rather lovely, tiny hamlet in the south of Somerset.

Shortly after, I noticed that Nelson's drinking water had solidified. Situated by the side door, it was nothing but a frozen lump with a few dusty specks in. I am clueless as to why I provide Nelson with a bowl of water: no one has ever witnessed him sampling any.

Bumbling around the hilly Somerset with a sink full of dirty washing up liquid was a begging bowl of trouble. The night before a rogue cushion had inadvertently knocked over a very homely hot chocolate, gloriously pebble-dashing all the wooden walls and surfaces. While the smell was currently delectable, it would only be a short while before heat, time and bacteria would combine to cause an assault of chemical warfare. Now with the sink in such a state, our home was under further threat of putrefaction.

Cross is not a bad place by itself, but it certainly represented what I felt when nothing I tried would coerce the water to slink away into the grey tank. In the end, I resorted to flinging it out of the door, one cup at a time, making a right royal mess. Alas, I lacked the forethought that I would be stepping out onto that first thing in the morning, the pain lasted for days. Nature's karma.

Thankfully, in another moment of felicity, I had had my acid battery bank replaced with a single one hundred amp-hour lithium battery. It meant that, firstly, the van had a stonking new, longer-lasting battery life, and, secondly, I could now fire up the diesel heater without actually vacating the bed first thing in the morning. Until this point, awakenings had been spent dragging myself out from under the duvet, hauling open the side door, tip-toeing around to the driver's cab, turning on the ignition, darting back to the rear of the van, firing up the heater, scuttling back to the cab, turning off the ignition, sprinting back before slamming the side door and diving back under the duvet. A series of manoeuvres accompanied by a continuous thought of swearing on the sake of the hamlet of *Four Forks*.

The new battery permitted me to switch on the heating from the comfort of my bed until four days later, my entire electric circuit cut out for reasons of a no longer working charging unit. As a matter of frustrating coincidence, I had been idling near the suburb of *Failand* although I was somewhat appreciative that my power outage was concurrent with the Great Big Freeze thawing and temperatures swinging up to ten degrees.

Once the holy trinity of volts, amps and batteries were back in harmony, thanks to my newest Facebook friend, Andy The Diesel Heater Guy, The Shitron, Nelson and I resumed our grand tour of what was now the waterlogged lands of Somerset. The Shitron in particular benefitted from a thorough dowsing. It had long been the case of 'single white van seeking single yellow sponge for some dirty fun!'. I had hopes for a thorough cleansing at the antiquated *Washford Station* but was disappointed to discover it was nothing but one of England's marvellously twee heritage railway stations built in 1847.

Having exhausted myself exploring *Williton, Hinton Blewitt, Lynch and Puriton,* I parked up for a few days' respite in the stunning hills of the *Mendips*. There I discovered it was less than a hundred years ago that a bathroom was considered a luxury. In fact, the 1967 House Conditions Survey found just three-quarters of homes reported having an indoor WC, bath or shower. Back in the 1800s, only the wealthy bathed a few times a month, and the poor, probably just once a year. By the 1900s, Saturday night family bath time had become a thing for those in possession of a tin tub. Bathing was undertaken in a strict rotation starting with the father, then mother and children thereafter. It seems that only when the ship is sinking are women and children sent first. One can only assume that by the time the youngest child was ready for a thorough dunking, the bathwater looked not unlike the stuff that had been sloshing around my kitchen sink.

Interestingly, and confoundingly, at least to me, surveys reveal men wash more frequently than women in modern times. Moreover, Men actually wash more body parts than women, including thoroughly scrubbing ears and legs, rather than letting the shampoo cascade down one's body parts and hoping for the best. I assume the data for this research was self-reported rather than actively inspected by the journo working for www.bigbathroomshop.co.uk. Women are more likely to spend their time mentally rehearsing their to-do lists and pondering on the meaning of life, including, presumably, matters such as how exactly did *Hinton Blewitt*? Or perhaps they are distracted by more deep and meaningful matters, such as whether indeed, "Cleanliness is next to Godliness". Alas, cleanliness in that instance referred to one's morals, and not one's moping about in the bath. If the latter had been the case, I would have spent a proportion of my life being quite saintly, in fact, possibly holier than thou.

Until the nineteenth century, the medical profession advised against bathing, believing that it would increase infections. There was also, and still remains in many countries, a puritanical belief that women are unclean for one week a month. I probably was not the first girl to be deterred from washing her hair around her period, which is profoundly short of nuts with the benefit of hindsight. On occasion, my lack of inclination for meek obedience has been nothing short of a Godsend.

In the absence of women's magazines, the English had relied on the Romans to instruct us on all matters of bathing. Sadly, it was an activity that promptly went out of fashion upon the collapse of the empire, and did not return to favour until the twentieth century. No wonder that a large number of Somerset's towns sound like ominous Victorian skin diseases: *Huish Episcopi, Compton Pauncefoot* and *Mudford Sock.*

Naturally, after a bath or shower, one must dedicate time to rearranging whatever it is that needs to be rearranged, and Somerset also provides great instruction on what to do next: *Combe Down.* Although, I am at a loss to explain how a *Butcombe* is of any benefit.

LENT TERM

The search for identity and frequently answering the question:

"Aren't you cold?"

Denouncing in Devon

I pushed open the door with the image of a green woman set against a white backdrop. It had been perplexingly far down a dimly-lit corridor: not where you'd expect to find public toilets. They weren't at all convenient despite this being a large, bustling mall in the centre of a city. As the door swung open, three black women spun abruptly around. "Yours is over there, down the other corridor," the tallest hissed at me as the two other women glared. I let the door close softly before backing away, remaining mute for I knew not what to say. I may have let slip a very British, "Sorry!" for I knew I'd perpetrated some terrible faux-pas, if not an outright crime.

I followed the woman's instructions, and only then did I see the white image of a woman, set against a green background. These were my designated toilets. Signs tell a story even when they have no words.

****

And *places* convey a story all on their own.

'Hag' used to be such a positive word, derived from those thought holy and it was applied to wise women who healed, nursed and delivered newborns. Until one day, as if by magic, it came to mean reclusive, garrulous and spiteful. Today there are many more words for ugly women than for ugly men. An old codger is the only I can recall. I was provoked into judgement by my arrival at *Brithem Bottom*. *Brithem* is an archaic Gaelic word for judge or jurist, I learn. Rear of the Year springs to mind.

My now regular talks had incorporated a small section on how society condemns women much more harshly than it does its men even when it is subtle by comparison to other countries that I have lived in. If ageism is said to be the ultimate prejudice, after racism and sexism, it sort of suggests it is not the ultimate one after all. But there is one mythology that encapsulates all three and it is one provoked by Devon's place names. It was impossible not to fall into stereotypes given so many settlements conjure up images of witchcraft, villages like *Waggs Plot*.

'Wags' is a modern locution, and certainly in my lifetime, the wives and girlfriends have shouldered blame for the poor performance of their menfolk on the football pitch. Offering too much sex, not enough sex, or being just sexual to begin with. They are nothing short of a modern-day witch perhaps: beautiful, influential yet somehow machiavellian regardless.

In times past, being old, forthright and outspoken were deemed to be so threatening that they became the very foibles used to demonise the witch. Once these stereotypes were fixed as a collective mindset, it was an easy leap to denounce the lovers of magic as *Badworthy:* malevolent, vexed and bedevilled. But character is not enough, there must be a physical manifestation to aid the identification so the witch is almost always swathed in tattered, dank clothing, with clawed hands. Their faces warty and withered, it is unsurprising that witches are depicted partly shrouded by a black *Whimple.* Their companion is a scrawny cat: one with a penchant for hissing, spitting and offkey wailing. Unfortunately, Devon did not supply one of those, and Nelson is fifty shades of grey, so for the purposes of this allegory we will have to make do with *Black Dog.*

Villages, like *Sourton,* were not the tranquil havens of the well-heeled, as they might be thought of as today. They were instead a hotpot of labourers, spouses, children, influenced by men of the faith. Yet, amidst every village lurked a witch. It is readily forgettable that much of the population was confined to village life in the 17th century: the pinnacle period of witch-hunting, although such magical practices had a wide range of names: necromancing, conjuring, sorcering and enchanting. All were sought after solutions for physical ills in the absence of pragmatic medicine.

However, there is always poverty: a fight lost for limited resources. Limited by fiscal conspiracies: by favour, by fever and by misfortune. The poor are universally feared: a stark mirror of what might happen if fate deals out a bad hand. The impoverished represent an unthinkable alternate universe to one's current comforts. Rarely welcome in anyone's backyard. When the great plague blew through a parish, it took the weak, the infirm and the perfectly adequately fine, thank you very much, too. That is plagues for you. One day all seems well, then the next your beloved's health is nothing short of *Offwell.*

To the town's healers one must turn. For respite can only be found in the cauldrons of the medically-minded, the herbalists and the magicians and it has spawned a thousand stories of witch-quackery:

"Take yeself deep into *Cockwood* and gather me a *Crapstone* and while you're there, acquire the scrotum of a tufty grey squirrel as we'll need some *Nutwalls.* Just follow the signs, they will lead you…" a scratchy voice might list what is the beginnings of a recipe of a bygone age.

"...Then gather up one rat's tail...,"

"But where would one find a rat?" the desperate may quiz as they quiver.

"At *Rattery.* Bring also forth the red tail of a rooster...from *Cockington* and the toenail of a nun."

"And where would I find a nun's toenail?" The anguished may panic, for they know of no such place.

"Virginstow, obviously.*"*

Thereupon, the despairing would be led on a merry dance. A true tour of the countryside, with its harsh realities and dangerous foes until they have satisfied the witch's recipe. Only then could the cauldron bubble its toil and trouble. Should this magic potion fail in its optimism, dire times would follow. Swear words would proliferate, although the more politely-minded might emit a milder *"Shute!"*

But blame needs to land somewhere. And in very darkened times, blame often came to the door of the aged and the childless. Those who did not have the requisite *Mamhead* – witches rarely had children to advocate for them, it is what made them so vulnerable. Compelled to begging for alms, knocking from door to door, bowing as if stooped from hardship, their tatty clothes would see them besmirched as a *Bentwichen.* Fear of spells cast, might compel an act of giving, but any misfortune that fell upon a naysayer might be assumed to be retribution for the refusal. What to do? What to do?

Exeter was the first and last place that people were hanged for the dark arts of sorcery, dragged there from far and wide to face trial. Such events were usually no more sophisticated than a quick glance up and down in order to pronounce the condemnation. For the crime of witchcraft, hanging was the preferred punishment. Took up by the neck until the body stopped *Twitchen.*

In England, we did not bother with burning witches at the stake – that was more of a continental pastime. But of course, their guilt had already been established long before the trial with a simple question: Can it swim? For if it *Dunkeswell,* then it is not thought to possess the spirit of the devil. Except, in Devon, where they did not seem to follow this practice either. Instead, following a lengthy interrogation, witches were dragged away to be displayed before a baying mob. A public shaming like no other, a true *Horrabridge.*

The witch would be stripped down to the nether regions. It was the investigators' quest to find skin tags, piles or other lumps and bumps of the warty kind. Diligently, they scoured the body's nooks and crannies for the devil's teats from which imps and familiars could feed. Failing that, the erudite masters of witch hunts could interpret birthmarks or scars as signs from the devil. Once found, they were taken to trial before being sentenced to hang at *Heavitree*.

Even if your name was Richard Wilkyns and you are the first person to be hanged in the county for being a witch.

The Contradiction that is Cornwall

I'd been moved to the first years' dorm. Apparently, I was immature and so I belonged there. That was my shaming. That was how they would get me to grow up, now the blackmarks were having a diminishing effect. I didn't have the courage to argue, or perhaps I did and that was how I ended up being banished to the first years' dorm.

In the preceding three months, my parents had fled Papua New Guinea, and turned up at my school for the first time since they had been given the introductory tour of the buildings prior to signing me over the following Spring. I've no doubt they appreciated for a second time the Elizabethan façade, the long wooden corridors typical of a Tudor building, the turrets and its heritage. Impressive stuff for the eyes of the adult. No doubt they believed the brochure's promises of utopia too. So, the problem must be me.

My parents had let me in on the future, and by doing so, they had given me just over two weeks to say my goodbyes to friends and cuddle my ever-growing menagerie: Hey Girl, Bundaberg, Jessie, Blackie, Krallen and Rita. The ever-cheerful Anna had given birth and that was her dispensed with. She'd been replaced by Vivian, a stunted woman with a small affliction of kleptomania. She was not a cheerful soul, and regularly arrived at her place of work, our home, having been beaten all over by her husband. He'd taken a second wife; the jealousy was said to be crippling her. He took all her income too: that was the way of their world, and she looked like she carried the full burden of it.

I knew we were absconding but we had to tell everyone we were just going on holiday. I once overheard my mother talking about "When we come back..." It had ignited a false hope and my sudden exclamation, "So we're only going on holiday after all?" was followed by a swift kick under the table, and a bollocking later for putting the family in peril.

My father's management of his staff invoked strikes and riots. Time was moving on; old fashioned white autocratic management wasn't cutting it locally. When my parents arrived one half-term to collect me, their presence was the confirmation that it wasn't home anymore.

"Good news!" they announced. "We're moving to Southern Africa!" And off they went. The blue aerogrammes with the pretty birds ceased. The postcards that followed were adorned pictures of lions, elephants and cheetahs.

"Good news!" My guardians announced the following half term. "We're emigrating to Australia!" They had children so I was always in good company. They were a family that played endlessly, ate dinner together and chatted – just like in the television adverts. In my heart, I pleaded for them to take me with them, but I never asked.

As I traipsed my belongings back down to the first years' dorm, I was left to wonder: whose bathroom would I be using now?

****

The hand of England grasping out into the Atlantic Ocean is better known as Cornwall, a county synonymous with long golden coastlines, remote coves and crimes of the high seas. Cornwall's name, possibly, means horned foreigners. Quite why they should be foreign is anyone's guess, given most were Celts and as such the original inhabitants of England's soggy, but kelly lands.

Driven to the extremities by subsequent invading armies, the abundance of sea makes it rare for the natives to be depicted as occupational 'landlubbers': a word I find unsightly, possibly even unnecessarily derogatory. I think *Greenbottom* would be more apt.

Cornwall sits on the cusp of the European continent, strategically placed to lever its avaricious arm towards the sea-faring Spanish ships returning from exploits in the West Indies, lands the Europeans had begun to colonise in the sixteenth century. From then on, legends proliferated of sea dogs, buccaneers and privateers, heroes or villains who pilfered and pillaged homeward-bound Spaniards steeped with spoils from their travails in the South Americas.

Popular apologues set in the aeons of piracy would assert that women sea bitches were the ruination of male morality, instigators of mutiny and harbingers of oceanic catastrophe. And yet, melded to the ship's masthead was a buxom and half-naked naked woman to augur good luck and fair sailing.

The Cornish piratical stereotype has sunk deep into the English psyche and lingers long after the epoch has dissolved. Women from such times were almost always *Greenbottoms*, for the high seas were considered no place for those denoted as the 'fairer sex'. Our blandness in history means women's stories simply *Washaway*. Yet, the 1500s heralded in a string of female leaders of sea-faring industry.

The rights of succession preferred an infant son over an adult daughter as much as it required conjugal offspring over misbegotten conception. So it was thus that the Protestant King, Edward VI, Jane Seymour's first and only born child, and Henry's first legitimate son from three marriages, who acceded the throne in 1547. Edward VI was aged just nine, seventeen years younger than his half-sister Mary, the Catholic half-Spanish daughter of the divorced Catherine of Aragon, and four years younger than his half-sister, Elizabeth, from yet another mother. Elizabeth was the Protestant daughter of the beheaded second wife: the accused adulteress Anne Boleyn. The thirteen-year-old's constitutional legitimacy was already deemed controversial in religious and court circles, not only for the sins of the alleged debauchery of the mother, but also for the bigamous remarriage of her father.

Unsurprisingly, thanks to his unreliable and erratic father, the fifteen-year-old Edward VI's death created a complicated lineage headache for all and sundry. It was worsened by a dearth of potential male heirs to accede to his throne. Regardless, it does leave me to ponder upon what he saw in the similarly-aged Lady Jane Grey, Protestant niece of Henry VIII? *Ding Dong!*

Lady Jane Grey lasted a mere nine days, which proved inadequate time for the courtiers to organise a coronation. It left the door ajar for Mary I to sweep in and grab the diadem. Those opposed to their new queen were compelled to acquiesce with the striking off of their heads. Off too was lopped the noggin of Lady Jane Grey. *Splatt!*

With that, the hastily-crowned Mary managed to belt and brace herself onto the throne. Now ladened with fine assets, she surged up the marriageable rankings. This was pertinent as she was intent on obtaining a husband, ostensibly for the purposes of procreation and lineage protection. On the downside, she was at the advanced maternal age of thirty-seven, and had already had quite a history of paramour behind her. She had been first rejected for marriage aged two by the Dauphin of France, then briefly promised aged six to Charles V of Spain. Even by lowering her standards from heads of state to the kith and kin of heads of state, her forays into the dating world came to no avail, and eventually the well ran dry. *Knave-Go-By* best sums up her success with eligible men. Who knows how she felt when twenty-six-year-old Felipe II of Spain, and son of her former fiancé Charles V, was press ganged into saying, "I do." It was agreed that

Felipe would become the sole ruling monarch upon the birth of a live child - so that was perhaps motivation enough for him to lie back and think of England.

In the interim Felipe II would be England's co-ruler. This was partly because, by virtue of being female, Mary was banned from Parliament. She also avowed that a wife is best when obedient to her husband. Henceforth, the religious direction of England changed winds as she had been born and raised Catholic in defiance of Henry VIII.

No doubt England's barons of the scaffolding world rubbed their hands in glee each time our Monarchs decreed their subjects reassess their own religious ideologies: Englanders reconverted or else faced mounting *Slaughter Bridge.*

School history taught me that five years of bloodshed was splayed across the greenbelt, but with more women being permitted into academia, more recent scholars purport that Queen Mary's reign resulted in the death of just two hundred and eighty Protestants and the birth of a tomato juice cocktail. By way of comparison, her immediate ancestors are said to have condemned to death in excess of five thousand (Edward VI) and fifty-seven thousand (Henry VIII) in the pursuit of religious supremacy. Yet, she goes down in the annals of history for being 'Bloody Mary'.

Within a half-decade of taking the throne, Mary perished from ovarian cancer or cysts or some other belly-swelling phenomena that was not a pregnancy. Phillip II, who was mostly absent anyway, returned to Spain. True love did not conquer all.

So it came to pass that, in 1558, the feisty, but protestant, Queen Elizabeth could swan in and bag the hot seat for herself. Without much further ado, she arranged for the hanging and burning of another thousand men of the cloth, upending England again.

With that policy well underway, she began stoking the fires of piracy. Elizabeth Regina had little patience for her all-male parliament, seeing them as simply as controllers of her purse strings. In her mind's eye, the politicians' sole purpose was to furnish her with financial sway. On the other hand, her lords deigned to withhold their treasuries as a means of attaining more power. *Cocks!* may well have how she derided them but history rarely records women's thoughts.

Sixteenth century England also held that a woman had no independent legal existence once she entered upon marriage. Until women submitted themselves to the religious ceremony, they could inherit, command and self-determine. Consequently, women were educated to believe they were delicate and simple-minded: in need of a man to do her thinking. Elizabeth herself remarked that she was indeed a feeble woman, imploring her court to *Pityme*. The tactic worked a treat in charming the menfolk – except for her tight-fisted politicians, so she took to proroguing her parliament. This was the Elizabethan equivalent edict of 'Go and sit on the naughty step, and think about what you have done.' One might be inclined to call it such banishment *Cox Park*. Besides, the men of parliament were mostly obsessing over whom she should wed to best secure her Tudor line. She shut up the non-stop, 'You don't want to be left on the shelf' chatter by decreeing herself *No Man's Land*.

Her attention then turned to the shenanigans of her former brother-in-law. The Spaniards had detected lands in the west, then annexed and pillaged them. Thereafter, the seas were rich with merchandise and profits, slavery and stolen goods.

Queen Elizabeth sought to sunder the privateers from the pirates. The former were officials purloiners of loot from stranded or wayward ships, tasked by royal commission to generate taxes for Her Majesty. It enabled her to deftly bypass the parliamentarians' tight hands. The pirates, on the other hand, were mere tax-dodgers depriving the state of fiscal funds. Needless to say, both groups were in the business of ransacking ships with an intent to cause grievous bodily harm, leaving any crew to choose between *Hellandbridge*. For a time, Cornwall lay dormant with its grasping hand outstretched. And then, to prominence came the Killigrews.

The five wives of John Killigrew, albeit there may only have been four, but possibly six, are the device that contemporary historians use to tell the convoluted tale of Cornish buccaneering but be so very gender inclusive at the same time. All five women married a man called John, and with the exception of the last John, at least four of the parents deigned to call their sons and heirs, John. John, all of them, were ennobled folk, and thus all the successive wives were entitled 'Lady Killigrew'. These naming protocols make it all terribly confusing so this is the perfect opportunity to grab a coffee and *Park Bottom* while I endeavour to explain the sorry saga of two more Janes, another Mary and a different Elizabeth.

John Killigrew, who married Lady Jane Petit, died just a few years before Queen Mary I was born. Some claim he died without heirs but others say he had a daughter called Elizabeth. Regardless, somewhere in Cornwall an Elizabeth married a John, this one of Godolphin. Following this, somehow the Killigrew estate, incidentally called 'Arwennock' or 'Arwenack', was passed on to John of

Godolphin's brother, thankfully called Thomas. He, much to my relief, called his son 'Alexander'. Alas, Alexander died childless, so the estate then passed on to his second cousin, called, frustratingly, John. He married Elizabeth Mary Trewinnard, some would say in 1520, when she was two, but more likely in 1532 when she was eighteen. They named her firstborn male 'John'. Believe me: many pieces of paper got screwed up trying to make sense of all this. Thanks especially to the work done by www.cornishbirdblog.com who similarly researched this dastardly family.

When not being active members of nobility, the male Killigrews were occupied as commanders of ships, politicians, justices of the peace, magistrates and equerries to royalty – holding several esteemed positions concurrently. All of them were addressed as 'Lord', so by the laws of 'feme covert' all the wives became Lady Killigrew, henceforth to be the property of their husbands, freed of legal entity and responsibility.

Elizabeth's John Killigrew owned the land on which Henry VIII built the fortification 'Pendennis Castle'. It provided safe anchorage for passing ships beaten back by storms of a *Blowinghouse* nature. The future stately home had Lord John Killigrew, possibly the Third, also be monikered Captain John Killigrew of Pendennis, the First. His task was to collect shipping tariffs for his royal masters.

Under John Killigrew's stewardship, Falmouth became a commercial landing zone. However, its strategic location on the cusp of Europe ensured it was also a watery venus flytrap for John Killigrew's piracy. Wealth prevailed upon the Killigrews, allowing Lady Killigrew to be Lady of the near-completed Arwenack Manor: a building that was to go on to be Cornwall's most expensive and grand historical house. At this point the fairy tales should cease with, "And they all lived happily ever after."

However, there was the untimely inconvenience of Edward VI expiring. The Killigrews had been fervent supporters of Protestantism, and now they were stranded outside royal favour. With Queen Mary intent on imprisoning those ill-disposed to a Catholic leader, Lord Killigrew ensured the Protestants' safe passage as they sought refuge in France. This got the *Ladycross* indeed. Furthermore, his tendency to acquire and retain treasures and troves not meant for him availed him to his new Queen not one jot. Hence, John Killigrew, and his erstwhile son, John, rested up at Her Majesty's Pleasure in separate cells awaiting their fate. I imagine there was a passing thought of "*Feock*".

Oddly, he was released three weeks later having not so much as sniffed a noose. Incidentally, there was a plethora of justices of the peace amongst the Killigrew clansmen. Then Mary I passed away, so one could argue this is a story of *Come-to-Good*.

John Killigrew departed this life of natural causes leaving his son, John Killigrew, to be the named beneficiary of his conglomerates. Conveniently, Arwenack Manor was substantial enough for the dowager Lady Killigrew to remain unhindered by her widowhood. It is oft-stated that she was a shrewd and astute businesswoman. One could just as easily make the counter-case that wives were simply *Minions*: nothing but simple, obedient wives, pledged to support their husband's public lives, because that is what marriage wrought on a woman according to the legal mindset of her era.

Nonetheless, her son, John, went on to marry Mary Wolveston, and subject to the laws of aristocracy, she also became Lady Killigrew. Historians sometimes conclude that Mary and Elizabeth Killigrew are one and the same woman. Mary's John Killigrew was a feckless fellow, earning and squandering vast fortunes. At least once, he sojourned in a debtor's prison. When not being a spendthrift, Lord Killigrew was also a rarely-attending Member of Parliament, a diplomat, an active naval serviceman, a local magistrate, and of course, havener, or harbour master. One is inclined to use the *Catchall* of him being 'an industrious man'. Indeed, obituaries would attest that he was very much a respectable one. Less was made of him partaking in the hobby of cattle rustling, which must certainly have helped him wind down after a day's work plundering passing ships and making sweet deals with officials and customs men chasing revenue for their Queen.

Most ignored of all was the labour of the wives. Their roles seemed mostly to be confined to bearing new Johns without anaesthetic and secreting their husband's ill-gotten gains, even if *Flushing* and *Looe* were yet to be invented. Perhaps by complying, the Killigrew wives could ensure that the family, who were forever teetering on the brink of ruin, kept the wolves from the door of the lavish home they could ill-afford. Nonetheless, historians have a tendency to record that both wives relished their role as buriers of commandeered goods.

Old Lady Killigrew died in 1583, not but before the birth of her grandson, John, leaving the Younger Lady Killigrew, Mary, mother of John, to take the helm. With her husband largely absent on various expeditions on behalf of Queen Elizabeth, and no mother-in-law to usurp, it is said she took command of the home and the hunting of the watery *Playing Place*.

One dark and stormy night, the Marie of San Sebastian sought refuge in the harbour from the fierce Atlantic winds. Awaiting favourable weather with which to depart to Spain, the owners of the ship were courteously invited for a sumptuous *Merrymeet* in the Arwenack Manor. While they bloated their bellies, it is claimed that Mary ordered her men to raid their anchored ship. A sailor was murdered by whose hand we do not know. And By Golly! Would you believe it? The ship vanished! Naturally, this was reported to the local law-makers, most of whom were Justices of the Killigrew Peace.

It is unlikely, as host, that Mary would have abandoned her guests as some historians claim in their endeavours to shoe-horn women into the corruptions of yonder year. To my reading, it is little but a cack-handed modern-day quest to prove that 'women can do bad stuff too' slotting us into the histories of men in a way that makes the world seem more egalitarian, or equally as unfair, than it really was.

It would be more accurate to say that Mary was a fence. It was as a fence, despite being a married woman with no legal rights of her own, that she was brought to trial, and along with the two men under her employ, she was sentenced to death following a complaint from our Spanish cousins. Again, it seems odd that just two men were able to take hostage an entire crew, but that is recorded history for you.

Mary's staff were summarily executed although her son, John, secured her release from prison eighteen months later, complete with a pardon from Queen Elizabeth: a woman the family had served most devoutly. It left her free to play Grandma to her grandson, John.

Grandson John continued the family legacy of wanton profligacy, and quiet piracy, frequently plummeting the household into near ruin just as his forebears had. The Debtors' Prison was a seasonal second home. In between stints, he married a girl called Jane, who was thought to be all of twelve years old. No doubt she came with a handsome dowry, no doubt it went astray too.

Jane was largely left to amuse herself, and amuse herself she was rumoured to do. When the Lord of the Manor discovered an affair, she was denounced as a prostitute and divorce proceedings instigated forthwith. It appeared to be quite the torrid separation, given one day she simply upped and left Arwenack on horseback, taking nothing by way of value with her. John's legacy, as written in the local obituary, sees him described as, "a good and sober man".

Oxymoronic Oxfordshire

Inside the stall with the swing door, I placed the shampoo down by my feet and set about scrubbing my hair clean. There was a plastic mat beneath my feet making it painful underfoot. Here I had the privilege of using conditioner to help detangle my long tresses. Still the stench of chlorine lingered, as it always does in swimmers. There was nothing to hurry off for. Dinner wasn't for several hours, prep after. I was still grasping the rigours of the unfamiliar day and carried my note-laden timetable about my person. There was an overwhelming amount to familiarise myself with and the responsibility of timekeeping was just the first thing.

In an adjacent stall was a girl whose name I didn't yet know. A few others loitered around the changing room in different states of dress, hair still damp, chatting. Someone plugged in a hair dryer – her own. We had finished our swimming lessons and we were free to conduct our ablutions with no one supervising: no matron yanking our hair as she doused it with shampoo, no prefects shouting at us to hurry along, scalding us off for complaining about the water being too hot.

"We mostly have boys here, at least three times as many as girls," the grey-haired man had explained the evening before. "Even though it's been ten years since we allowed the girls to attend, we still seem to attract more boys." The smell of cigarettes from my new housemasters' quarters was all-pervading. My father was a smoker. The room was gloomy, typical of the small-windowed Victorian establishments, even though the man himself was ebullient. "We believe in second chances," he'd said, "We believe in accountability."

I remember staring at the girl squirming in an armchair opposite, shrinking behind her long, brown hair draped across her face. She peeked out, looking quite livid. Later, I learned her mother had just commenced her fourth marriage, and the current husband staunchly believed in a public school education. It was her first experience of the system, and now with adult eyes I realised she'd have been terrified. I was an old hand, albeit a novice old hand at this particular establishment. We both sat mute as the adults gibbered away about matters important only to them.

We had both been allocated to the same 'house' and the man was our Housemaster. It is not a 'house' in the architectural sense, but a social construct designed to give us a sense of kinship. It existed to provide us with an identity; a group to whom we belonged; a tribe. In reality it was meaningless. There were six houses and ours was named after the founding father of the school, a man who believed in a robust Christian education for boys.

Our housemaster finished up his speech making, just as our housemistress rapped on the door to introduce herself. The two of us were to live in the same residence, one set far from the main impressive building, several minutes' walk away. Our housemistress escorted us there in the dingy evening. We had missed supper, we were informed, but if we wanted some toast and tea, we should just ask. There was a kitchenette available for us we were told as she led us toward a brown-bricked building of modern amenity.

Only the boys resided in the large gothic manor. The place seemed like a megalopolis. There were buildings amok: a science block separated from the language block by a broad lawn; a church; a small sanitarium of three wards, a sports hall; an indoor swimming pool; a cricket pavilion; fields and fields; bridleways and stables too – although no horses were kept. There was an art block, tuck shop, book shop and cafe, and of course, several accommodation blocks. All of the latter were allocated to the girls who were divided by year group, then subdivided again into factions. There was an entire street of masters' houses. It was the only place, aside from outside the school's boundary and the boys' dorms, that we were forbidden from.

I was glad to have someone to be lost with. Starting a school mid-year is always a daunting affair. With no bells and few adults to barrack us, we decided when to get up and when to shower. As long as we turned up for breakfast, which started at six and finished at eight-thirty, and made sure a prefect ticked our names off a list, the rest of the day took care of itself. Eating was optional, but on offer was everything from cooked to continental, hot or cold, fresh or processed, sweet or savoury. After, it was to church for assembly. There was always something mandatory: learning, sports training, or playing toy soldiers with the cadets.

Our house was a purpose-built residence containing four dorms, a small living room containing a sofa and a television. Oddly we only ever watched 'The Waltons'*; Sunday re-runs of the saga of a wholesome American family and their homely escapades. We mimicked them mercilessly. There was indeed a kitchenette if one wanted to get all culinary – I doubt anyone ever found the time. As long as one was where one was supposed to be and when, then no one would bother. I was as free as the frontiers of the school – even though the grounds were in the middle of nowhere.*

****

At first glance, Oxfordshire is a county of rogues and miscreants, but it might be more accurate to say the county is nothing but a collection of sites that sound like punishments for the criminally-inclined. Let us begin at *Cane End*, the old masters' weapon of choice for recalcitrant children.

It may make one's hair stand on end to learn that corporal punishment remains legal in England in 'certain settings'. English lawmakers, in their bonkers circuitous manner, made the striking of adults unlawful in 1967 yet waited until 1986 to outlaw the hitting of children. Although this restriction was confined only to those attending the free-to-attend state schools. Fee-paying, independent schools, otherwise known oxymoronically as public schools, were only obliged to snap their rattans twelve years later. In 2005, no fewer than forty Christian schools took the government to court to demand back their rights to, "help form godly character", arguing the law had breached the teachers' rights. They lost.

Late one afternoon, I pulled up to photograph the sign pointing to *Littleworth* in the village of Wheatley, only to have my attention diverted by a pyramidal structure with a very sturdy, but firmly bolted door. It was a lock-up. A very locked-up lock up. If I wished to peruse the innards, it would require me to commit the crime of 'breaking and entering' so it stands there doing very little but be a pointy object balancing a ball. One might claim it once served as a deterrent, but that would be a bit of a stretch.

Typically, lock-ups, where they have survived, are round, hence their name in bygone literature as 'roundhouses'. Built largely in the Victorian era, these short-stay residences were exclusively occupied by men who had indulged in a little drunken debauchery or petty theft. Ironically, this lock-up sits on the corner of Holloway Road. 'Holloway' means sunken road, which is especially sardonic, given the word is most synonymous with London's former premier prison for women. HMP Holloway, closed in 2016, was the former abode of at least three-hundred Suffragettes, the last woman to be hanged: Ruth Ellis in 1955, and Britain's most famous female Nazi: Diana Freeman-Mitford.

Better known as Lady Mosley, wife of Oswald, she probably would have been hanged for treason, but for the fact that the pair were immensely chummy with Oxfordshire's most famous Prime Minister,

Winston Churchill. Instead of a cell-based existence, our esteemed WWII leader arranged for them to be interned together in matrimonial bliss in one of Holloway's private premises – segregating them away from the 'proper crims'. Prior to the war, they had 'lived in sin' until their wedding at the home of Joseph Goebbels, the act witnessed by none other than Adolf Hitler himself.

Hanging, like that which would have taken place at *Gallowstree Common,* was the mandated punishment for high treason at the time of their gallivanting. It was abolished completely, along with corporal punishment, in 1998. Once upon a pre-Victorian era, the gallows beckoned if one romped with the wife of the king; killed one's legal superior – be he employer, father or bishop; counterfeited; stole, or hung about with gipsies, among a myriad of other reasons. Hence, the phrase one might as well be hung for a sheep as a lamb.

Until 1814, men had the ignominious prospect of being hanged, drawn and quartered. Corded to a gibbet by the neck until nearly dead, the condemned man would be brought down for a disembowelment and penectomy then pulled apart by bolting horses. All that *Goring* just to be certain of his demise. It fell out of favour long before it was banned. For women, there was all of the above, plus the additional crime of matricide. Given the husband was deemed to be her legal superior, it seems superfluous for the separate crime to be so titled. Hey ho. Of course, hanging would not be befitting of any maiden, fair or otherwise. Thus, women convicted of matricide, theft, treason, adultery or generally found guilty of harbouring a vagina, could not be subjected to such bodily destruction lest the crowd be exposed to their unbecoming nakedness. Instead, they were burnt at the stake, which perhaps explains the origins of *Pyrton* and other "Pirs" about the lands.

So, if anyone ever asks, "What did the Victorians ever do for us?" one can safely answer, "They gave us women enough rope to hang ourselves with." Even today, women committing adultery has, in some parts of the world I have lived, a very separate punishment than that faced by men, as I was starkly reminded as I drove through the quaintness that is *Stonesfield.*

Aside from sparing us the flame, the Victorians did quite the remarkable job of criminalising the females of the species. The Victorian-built Holloway Gaol was mostly populated by women and girls who were dirt poor or somewhat occupied in the trade of prostitution, even if only on a part-time basis. One might say it was a matter of *Begbroke.*

Elsewhere, to avoid a series of near-revolutions threatening to dismantle the once-idealised nineteenth century, property-owning men and male workers who paid rent in excess of ten pounds per annum, were finally permitted to vote in 1867. This greatly disappointed the remaining forty percent of the male population who continued to be denied suffrage on the basis of their impoverishment. By 1918, all men and a proportion of women, were given the ability to have a say in their own country, although nearly a third of women had to wait for a further ten years before all women were given the equal privilege.

Still, it was not all bad news for everyone: The ennobled Victorian leaders of the time felt it necessary to repeal a previously existing law requiring men to pay for their illegitimate offspring. From 1834 onwards, unmarried mothers were given the sole responsibility of caretaking up until the child made sixteen, and, funnily enough, that included providing for them financially. The so-called Poor Laws had previously guaranteed sole parents an income, not unlike today's benefits system, and demanded the woman name a father. It gave mothers the choice of going into a workhouse and being separated from their child; paying a 'baby farmer' to bring their children up for them; or finding someone to marry them. Options anyone would find themselves *Baulking* at. Little wonder for most it became a story of a walk along a *Horspath.*

Middle-class Victorians with education and means supposed those of the female persuasion should assail to the impossibly high bar of 'house-angel'. Thus, the parliamentarians of the day conveniently deigned their women to be the sole upholders of social mores and matters of morality. Should any misfortune befall the woman, rest assured Victorian laws made it somehow her fault, before labelling her a 'fallen woman'.

Victorian reforms encouraged women into the state of house-boundness, presumably for their own safety. Limiting excursions to visiting other women's homes for afternoon tea, or accompanying their husbands to the play house, which was a theatre, and not a brothel. Life for a Victorian woman of a husband with means was somewhat humdrum.

Working class women's employment 'opportunities' were typically restricted to that of lady's maid, seamstress or work hand. Being dismally-paid, a fraction of that afforded men, female employees might dabble in a little sex work to bolster their finances. Earning a quick buck for very little enterprise was tempting, but most women found themselves practitioners of the world's oldest profession as the consequence of corruption, abuse and exploitation. Working in male dominated environs, or tenured to a household not of their own, women were seduced or raped, and once their virtue had been obliterated, their marriageability rolled down *Pishill.*

Not that this flourishing trade in vice was of uppermost concern to the upstanding Members of Parliament of the Victorian day. Instead, they were preoccupied by the rampant venereal disease wreaking havoc amid the workforce; hindering her majesty's military capabilities. The goings on between the sheets was a real *Nettlebed*, so the Contagious Diseases Act sprung into being in 1864. If that was not sufficient, a second act was passed in 1866, and a third in 1869.

There was a growing medical demand for the treatment of sexually-transmitted infections. Regardless, the bed-hoppers could not be contained, and so the policies saw fit to detain any woman at any moment upon the suspicion of having engaged in non-conjugal matters with non-conjugal men on a paid-for basis. It was thus she, not he, who was locked up for months while undergoing treatment. Such respite from life sounds just marvellous until one recalls that penicillin was not discovered until 1928. Hence the hospitals are probably best described as *Grimsbury:* The borough of the furious.

Thankfully, all these matters are heartily in the past. Since the demise of the Victorians, we have had the Elizabethan era mark II. A time period which saw men and women placed on an equal footing with the passing of the Sex Discrimination Act in 1975. This act has made it illegal for marriage, or the lack of, to be prejudicial to one's interests and it promotes the equality of opportunity. Naturally this has given women untold freedoms. Freedom of the city too!

So I was curious to learn that prior to Victorians passing the Municipal Reform Act of 1835, only those designated 'Freemans' could conduct business outside the boundaries of the city of Oxford. Unless he was a privileged tradesman having matriculated from its world-renowned university, earnings were restricted to city limits. To be a Freeman, one had to be the son of a Freeman or in apprenticeship to a Freeman. Contemporary Freemans are the beneficial owners of council meadows and rivers beyond the perimeter, giving them sole use of the pastures for their cattle and horses, and the right to fish without permit in the river Thames. It is all rather stupendously English – steeped in history and tradition, and completely disregarding any sagacity. Hence, I thought it a matter of *Oddington* to read that first women to be granted the Freedom of the City of Oxford occurred twenty-three years after the passing of the Sex Discrimination Act.

This admission of women ended five hundred years of ineligibility, because hangovers aren't just borne by drunks.

Warmongering in Warwickshire

It was the prefects who were tasked with inspecting us, checking our uniforms: tie straight? Skirt too short? Shoes clean? Hair neatly pinned back? Boys, of course, had long trousers, but the blazers and shirts kept us uniform. Only our ties that distinguished us – informing the observer to which house we had been assigned. Mine was plain, dark blue with a small crest. It had been a job just to learn to knot the menswear correctly.

Already the summer months were beckoning, permitting the boys to shed their blazers to swan about in pristine, white shirts, tie-less with their top two buttons unfastened. Girls were afforded no such privilege – remaining in the noose throughout the year. I queried one of the masters as to why this should be: "We couldn't be trusted," he replied. We'd likely select the two buttons around our breasts to create a gape, a window to our bras. It would be a distraction for masters and boys alike. Such a notion had never occurred to me. Was I the peculiar one; the one with the warped mind?

There were invisible rules everywhere; observable differences that controlled a person but were never made explicit unless they were contravened. The worst rules were those that were made up on the spot. Whenever incongruent anomalies were justified, I disguised any reaction and nodded my comprehension. At least, one could enquire, I supposed. Arguing was a fool's game. It was the school's job to prepare me for adulthood, and it was my role to be prepared for that eventuality. Once upon a time, it was to prepare us as fodder for war and to be commanders fighting for a realm that had long since crumbled away. All the while our founder's legacies trickled on, peace continued to reside across our lands.

Our institutor had decreed that religion was salvation and so we shuffled daily through the chapel's vestibule to receive our fill of religious education. The prefects yelling out boys' names punctuated the clattering and chattering of the assemblage. The unfortunate nominee, often the same one over and over, presented themselves meekly to their superiors with a sigh of dread combined with resignation. My ears would prick at the quips; the sniggering and snorting that commended a fellow comrade's wit and wisdom as the captured child stood dolefully before them awaiting admonishment, instruction or further ridicule.

The girls, irrespective of their age, were largely forsaken unless the senior had a crush on them. On this day, an eleven year-old was amidst our coterie, scrambling to make her way through the throng. Cute of features, blonde of hair, with exceptionally large doe eyes. Delicate, almost.

"She's mine as soon as she's sixteen," the head of house declared to bawdy laughter, clearly oblivious that he would have left the school before four months had passed, let alone five years.

The girl I had started with seemed to be called out frequently, until one day she wasn't. She was a raven-haired beauty for certain, and yet so fragile. Obsessive almost about trying to hide her face with her fringe getting it to sit 'just so': wetting it, drying it, styling it, wetting it again. Her compulsion would have her late for chapel, and that would attract her authorities' wrath. Even when she coaxed her hair to her satisfaction, she drew trouble for it not being fastened back. She quietly faded into the routines, absenting herself from meals, from any form of participation until the day she was officially withdrawn from school having had a 'bit of a to-do'. She was 'just' not able to hack it, someone said. Just flawed.

To our collective benefit, there was only one female prefect so, by default, she was also the head girl. It meant we couldn't really be patted down, or have our clothing tugged at – sometimes ripped. Half the time she barely attended the church or the dining hall herself. I had struck doubly lucky: as the only female prefect assigned, she was also part of one of the other five houses. Our seniors usually selected younger boys from their own houses to do their bidding. 'Sprogging' it was called, more universally known by the Etonian name of 'fagging'. There was no peace for the junior ranks, simple foot soldiers always skipping back and forth, running errands or sending messages.

Relief surged through us once we departed the narthex into the wonder that was homage to times mediaeval. The pews in our chapel ran lengthways along the nave, bisected by a deep red aisle framed by black ironworks. The scent of wood polish leached from ornate, carved benches and the high-arched austere ceilings amplified the din. Over the vestibule, the organ pipes spread the width of the church. It was a formidable space – gothic stone columns, chiselled granite, gripping stained-glass trefoils depicting scenes of cherubic boys comforted by gentle women. An oddity, given that there were so few women even counting the teaching staff. This was not a cherishing place.

Three houses sat to the left, three to the right. Mine was located on the far right, closest to the apse. Eventually, the hubbub of children was hushed by the smacking of masters' shoes, and the rare click-clacking of high heels. The masters' intimidating black gowns swished as they strode along the aisle up, peeling off at the stairs separating the houses taking to their fine wooden benches. Their mortar boards and stoles, denoting their academic accomplishments, were reserved for special occasions. As they settled themselves, the organ would grind out something teeth-curlingly woeful.

The silence that followed brought with it the first sermon, a passage read out from the bible and then exemplified usually by a master. Occasionally a favoured peer could be trusted to invoke the days' seminar. A friend had been nominated for a fortnight hence, and we spent time sifting through the King James Bible looking for something slightly evocative, or better still, provocative. Ecclesiastes 7. A chapter on wisdom and rebellion would be ideal. Perhaps, 7:25 - 28: "I applied mine heart to know, and to search, and to seek out wisdom, and the reason of things, and to know the wickedness of folly, even of foolishness and madness…[That] which yet my soul seeketh, but I find not: one man among a thousand have I found; but a woman among all those have I not found."

If I am not good enough for God's representatives, will I ever be judged good enough for anyone?

****

Looking like a sperm whale vomiting out Gloucestershire, the county of Warwickshire sounds like England's most warmongering region. Wick, in old English means 'dwelling place', so it is of little surprise that this county is also host to the violent-sounding settlements of *Rowington, Arrow, Shotteswell and Kinwarton.*

Turning into the commoners' carpark of the cemetery, mist swirled in its ominous way. The trees, seemingly bare of life, stood as if a sentry of skeletons. The place is a wonder on a winter's day, ideal for spying avaricious hawks circling rare prey. In the hush, one might accidentally startle grazing muntjac nibbling at boggy ground, or inadvertently terrify squirrels into darting up the nearest trunk. At this time of night, when the clock was about to strike midnight, it was just the owls that were out scavenging. Perhaps there were foxes too, but no eyes glinted back at me. I expected to hear their irksome carping as we settled in for a peaceful night.

Later in the year, bulbs would herald in a new season and bluebells would smother the woodland floor, reminding us that life goes on even as the dead sleep. Flowers brighten even the dingiest of souls but presently the ground remained barely thawed. I left The Shitron idling momentarily, watching via the side mirror the usually invisible exhaust inflicting its ill will upon our environment before twisting the key and plunging the van into the pitch. I have come to love cemeteries and crematoriums, and this one had no bar on the peripatetic making nocturnal use of it. By day, the dedicated visitor car park welcomes guest after dog-walking guest hoping to lose themselves within its woodland and wildlife. It is one of those rare places whose stillness seems to repel those requiring sexual relief. Perhaps it is the dead who deter, even if they are only represented as ashes, decaying flowers and plagues.

I unplugged my phone. The Admirable Nelson had already bounded his way towards the van's cocoon, knowing the promise of food was forthcoming. Miaowing his frustration that I was taking so long, I could only remain stock still as the beam of a torch bore down through the drivers' window, burning my retinas. I was as transfixed by, as I was blind to, the holder edging closer and closer to me. The van's keys were already lost to the depths of my carelessness. My fingers grappled for them. I needed keys in my hand, for they are women's best defence. I had foolishly tossed mine to one side thinking I was safe enough going from the near side drivers' door to the opposite side door, just some twelve steps away.

I could not recall how to lock the drivers' door. Was there a button besides that found on the key fob? Was there one for the door? All I did know was that I was alone, and there would be no protection from the dead, nor from the living, for this was a twenty-acre woodland surrounded by farmland. My fingers explored the door, perhaps something to hang on to, to be a barrier against the person who undoubtedly at any moment would make for its handle.

"Can you help me?" A voice muttered. My fingers crept up to the switch that rolls down the glass.

"Can you help me?" She asked me now more clearly. Eastern European, I guessed, distracted as I was by my body rapidly trying to rinse itself of the adrenaline.

"I've lost my dog. Can you help me look for him?"

"Sure." I say. "What kind of dog am I looking for?

"Alsatian," she replied.

I think the only less appealing answer would have been 'Rottweiler'. I spent an hour traipsing amongst the departed looking for a dog in the middle of a winter's night safe in the knowledge that danger, like wisdom, is never found where it is thought to be.

****

It just so happens that Warwickshire was instrumental in forming the country that is now recognised worldwide as England. Once upon a Mediaeval time, Warwickshire formed the western boundary of the imposing region known as Mercia and it was a time when the Norseman, but mostly Danish ones, came a-pilfering.

From 865 onwards there was a great deal of warfare as these Great Heathen Armies set about dismantling many of our monasteries in their atheistic quests, amongst other acts of effrontery. The invaders were certainly persuasive about putting people *Offchurch.* Led by Ivar the Boneless, these Vikings, as they are better known, crossed the Midlands into Northumbria, before capturing York. In 871, they joined forces with a second Danish wave of battalions, those ones called The Great Summer Army, led by Guthrum, whose name meant 'Battle-snake'. The Boneless wonder and his posse marched north and the Danish summer holidaymakers, led by Guthrum, headed south where the weather was said to be much more favourable. Following Ivan the Boneless' demise, the wooden helmet-headed Halfdan took command of the northern armies.

Many of the northern regions capitulated, leading Halfdan to claim a good chunk of the country-not-yet-known-as-England for himself. Elsewhere, Guthrum The Battle Snake, slithered southwest where he came a cropper, or as one could say, he met his *Wood End.* His dastardly ambitions had been out-thwarted by Alfred the Great, then King of Wessex.

Rather than fight the good fight until the bitter death, the two noblemen carved up the land yet to be known as England into two halves. Danelaw controlled the east and north, and Alfred the Great, anointing himself King of the Anglo-Saxons, took charge of the West and South. This put an end to the merciless warmongering.

It was a veritable Brexit-Sexit-Vexit and similar to recent times, a trade agreement between the two emerging powers was hammered out. Of paramount importance was Guthrum submitting to a christening. That way he could oversee the virtuously religious trapped within his realms just as capably as he had done his pagan brethren.

The treaty put the Kingdoms of Wessex and Mercia in close alliance. To strengthen the Anglo-Saxons mutualised opposition to the Vikings, Alfred the Great of Wessex had his eldest daughter married off to Æthelred, Lord, some say King, of Mercia. In between scrimmages, Alfred the Great fathered five or six children: no one really knows beyond one of them being called Edward the Elder, which has me presuming there was an Edward the Younger. Still, it was the Elder Ed who survived to adulthood, becoming the succeeding King of the Anglo-Saxons upon his father's death in 889.

Thus, we have yet another pretty ordinary pattern of how history is recited: a story of one man slaying another, claiming the crown and then procreating a lineage. Thereafter, the rest of men, calling themselves historians, write about it – often many years after the fact. We then absorb it in our school years so that we can promptly forget it all the day after the coursework is submitted.

Students who retained their book learning, might recall that this era is most commonly referred to as the 'Middle Ages'. It is the time period during which a woman is suddenly struck invisible. It commences when a woman enters her forties and lasts until she becomes elderly, whereupon she dies. Most report this global phenomenon of female dematerialisation has occurred by the ripe old age of forty-nine. This significant decline in womanhood just so happens to coincide with the ceasefire of a women's menses: an event which also occurs at the mean average age of forty-nine.

Having started careers, just like the other half of the population, by the age of forty-nine, most women will have battled through a world mired in discrimination, sexism and harassment, whilst simultaneously acquiring the very skills necessary to knuckle down and do the job that they were employed to execute. It almost goes without saying, the arrival of the middle ages is the period where women are finally left to get on with it, whatever 'it' is, without any distractions. Except for children, who can be a tremendous distraction when the mood takes them. But commonly, many offspring are in the process of escaping the home for quests of their own by the time their mothers hit their middling years. It is just unfortunate that a woman's time to shine coincides with the moment they go 'poof!' as they, metaphorically at least, find themselves banished to *No Man's Heath.*

Naturally, it is women who ultimately decide whether or not to partake in the baby-making requirements of the role of human being, albeit government and religious policy both home and away sometimes overrules this pragmatic reality – and has done since time immemorial.

Women's contribution to maintaining the human race sometimes has her exit stage left from the world of work as well as marketable shag-ability. Men traditionally, and often still typically, remain to do the working aspect of the work; assuming that work is something that one receives remuneration for. Likewise, men remained in the world of work to record both quantitatively and quantifiably any work that is done before placing value upon it.

The Mediaeval period was no different from any other period in that regard. English Annals such as the Anglo-Saxon Chronicles, written in the late ninth century, refer only to King Edward's sister. To our Welsh and Irish cousins, she is recorded as being the most renowned Saxon Queen. Their accounts have not only named her as Æthelflæd, but they also revere her for her courageous, capable leadership and defence against the Vikings.

It was she who oversaw the establishment of the fortified town of Warwick: one of thirteen she conjured up into being. Incidentally, in most Mediaeval towns, men were required to practise archery each and every Sunday at 'The Butts'. This explains why so many towns of the region formerly known as Mercia still have lanes and streets of Butts. This means all self-respecting towns can claim to be the arse end of somewhere. Alas, I seem to have inadvertently drifted into men's matters as is so often the way.

Æthelflæd was a prolific urban designer: founding churches; granting swathes of lands to kith, kin and religious bodies from as far south as Gloucester to the north of Chester. She maximised cooperation amongst the Anglos and the Saxons to face down their mutual Scandinavian threats. She promoted book learning heavily amongst the gentrified elite, just as her father had, considering it essential for both girls and boys. In between policy-making, she managed to find time to pop out one child, as well as maintaining the guardianship of her father's first-born son from the age of three. Her father had married his second wife, wife number one's whereabouts being uncertain. Clearly, wife number two felt no duty to bring up the youngster herself.

Æthelflæd also oversaw the construction of a string of fortifications along the entire edge of western boundary of Mercia, using them to reclaim Derby and Lincoln. Leicester simply rolled over, thought of England, and acquiesced without much further ado. Her most robust defence took place in northern Mercia at the fortification of Chester. The Northman, or Norwegian pagans, had been ousted from Ireland. Their leader, the Viking Ingimund, requested land for his army to build barns and dwellings for refuge - a request she acceded to. Quietly, he was eyeing up the flourishing town of Chester.

The Viking leader had numbers on his side, and Æthelflæd became wise to his ingratitude. Rather than hiding behind Chester's formidable walls, Æthelflæd's army opened the gates of Chester and welcomed in their foe's leading brigades. Then the portcullis dropped, his men trapped in a *Shuttington.* With nowhere to flee, Iguimiud's soldiers fought for their lives and all to a man they perished. Showing no mercy, their bodies were left to wrox, which is old English for 'rot', demoting the castle to a *Wroxhall.*

Nevertheless, Ingimund's army remained vast. Next, she wrote to the Irish fosterlings accompanying the Vikings. *"Life and Health to you from the King of the Saxons, who is ill, and from the Queen, who holds all authority over the Saxons, and they are certain that you are true and trustworthy friends to them. Therefore you should take their side."* (as quoted on www.hefenfelth.wordpress.com) With that, the Irish switched axis to assist her in blindsiding her Scandinavian nemeses.

Ingimund's army, although much depleted, remained sizeable, albeit possibly incensed by Æthelflæd's unwillingness to yield. They staged an attack on Chester's walls aiming to destabilise the outer shell. To protect the invading infantry, his footsloggers erected covered defences to stave off the rocks, javelins and arrows pelting down upon them. Undeterred, the Mercians boiled their ale, their water, and probably their piss too, before tipping it over the walls to peel off the skins of Chester's terrorists.

Still Ingimund refused to relinquish his ambitions, so the Mercians moved on to the source of their mead: the bees and their hives, lobbing them down to force a retreat. Hundreds and thousands of very pesky, very irritated displaced swarms savaged the Norsemen. The little twerps of the insect world scoured their way through the crevices of their soldiers' armour, condemning them to a period of *Long Itchington.* Fleeing could not spare them their anguish.

Æthelflæd's husband, Æthelred, ill for most of their union, died in 911. He was thought to be much older than his wife, who was somewhere in her late-teens when they had been betrothed. So how in English history is she remembered? Well, it is like discovering that Warwick is home to *Willey* and thereafter becoming instantly taken with learning more about *Willey* than about Warwick's considerable contribution to mediaeval times. My bet is if you have not yet googled *Willey*, you are about to…

I was fascinated to read that the first time an Englishman recognised her role in history, the historian claimed she declined to have sex after the birth of her only child because it would be, "unbecoming of the daughter of a king to give way to a delight!" Believing she sought chastity due to the painful consequences of having a bit of 'how's your father'. Yup, according to William of Malmesbury, England's foremost historian of the twelfth century, writing some three hundred years after her death, Æthelflæd was a coward who could not, or would not, take the pain of a second child. At least he recognised a portion of her not insignificant legacy in England's history, which is more than the Saxon writers of the Anglo-Saxon Chronicle did. In their tomes, she was merely King Edward's sister.

If one wishes to learn more without first becoming well-versed in Old Irish, Welsh or Gaelic, there are just three podcasts available dedicated to her. All inform the listener of Æthelflæd's attitude to sex, with significantly less time dedicated to her considerable career accomplishments. Radio 4's documentary podcast includes her wedding night depicted in gloriously dramatic detail. Apparently to maintain the audience's attention, it was deemed essential to insert an entirely fictionalised scene with the husband accusing his wife of putting it about a bit, and her distressingly affirming her perfection. Eventually, after much cogitation surrounding Æthelflæd's affinity towards sex by its two male presenters, a woman broadcaster points out in a manner most unsentimental that for much of her marriage, Æthelred was near death's door. The male co-hosts quickly changed the subject. Quite frankly, with whatever her husband had, Æthelflæd probably wished to preserve her own life: after all, no one likes lying back, thinking of England whilst being *Coughton.*

Æthelred was, in all likelihood, just too unwell to perform the job. For all anyone knows, the Lord of Mercia could well have been a *Gaydon.* Typically historians are averse to speculating about men's sexual orientation unless it emphasises their virility or proclivity for being unfaithful and hedonistic.

Æthelflæd, the radio hosts summarised, is probably the most influential woman that English history has forgotten. Continuing to rule Mercia after her husband's death, she was also the first queen to be succeeded by another queen. Yet, to the BBC broadcasters' collective bafflement, no one could fathom why instead of being a mediaeval myth, Æthelflæd became nothing but a middle-aged ghost.

It is said she died at the age of forty-nine.

The san, or sanitoria, to give it its proper name was equidistant from the manor and the chalets that housed the girls. Staff wore pristine nurses' smocks with thick waist belts with striking buckles, rolled-up sleeves and white caps. Inside, it was always stiflingly hot. Kindliness was in good supply, for they dished out care and free painkillers, as well as titbits of gossip.

Once school had commenced, and the masters were all safely discharged to their classrooms, the nurse on duty would wheel in a television, proffer hot water bottles and bring in a hot cup of tea, even some biscuits. Free tuck! Girls always outnumbered boys in the early morning queue to see the matron in charge, for it was girls who needed the chit to prove they were on their period and couldn't, or wouldn't, be playing sport later. I had very irregular periods (especially on the occasions when a 'vigorous run' was the rumoured activity).

I was less keen on the doctor: a disgruntled man who, the nurse let on, was deeply opposed to girls being in the former boys' school. He thought I was making a fuss about the monthlies, and that I should knuckle down and get on with it – just like the other girls did. Perhaps he just saw us all as work-shy. Perhaps, like many men, he was just plain squeamish – who can say?

Confinement. Weeks and weeks of confinement at a time, the promise of the forthcoming freedom was signalled when the expatriate children received notification that cholera and typhoid jabs, as well as prescriptions for malaria pills had been arranged. I dreaded the Cholera vaccine, for it was the mother of all jabs. Not because of an oversized syringe, nor a thicker-than-normal needle, but by it rendering agony across the entirety of one's limb for at least three days thereafter. One could nominate butt or arm, left or right. Within hours the limb would dangle immobilised, a quick glance even on the hand could induce near-tears. The butt was safer, albeit you had to sleep on your stomach for several days, shuffling from place to place. Sitting on the loo was an absolute improbability, and it altogether brought extraordinary complications to the execution of a day. Even then I had to apply for a chit excusing me from swimming. I always opted for my right arm until they got wise to my right-handedness.

Years later, I learned that the vaccine itself had little-to-no protective qualities and was subsequently discontinued. An irony that was especially astounding because the following term, all and sundry discovered that I had never had any childhood inoculations whatsoever. No MMR, no measles or rubella, no BCG, no Hep B, no tetanus, not even polio. Nada. I had simply returned to school with a sore throat. Two days later, one side of my neck was competing with my ear to stick out the furthest.

"You have the kissing disease," the nurse announced: glandular fever. Only the doctor declared it to be mumps and that was me restricted to the san for several weeks, along with a handful of children whose parents had similarly neglected to have their children vaccinated. I was a metaphorical pin-cushion for the rest of the term.

****

When asked why she refused to move hospitals, Sister Dora replied, "I am a woman, not a piece of furniture!" These days the immovable one can be located in statue form in Walsall's Town Centre. Erected in 1886, Sister Dora, or to use her christened name, Dorothy Pattison, was the first non-royal woman to be monumentalised in our lands. Her personification in alabaster took place some time before those of her more eminent fellow practitioner nurses, Florence Nightingale (1915) and Mary Seacole (2016), whose legacies, albeit after a battle or two, have been similarly sculpted.

Less than a fifth of the UK's statues depict women, and even fewer, just eighty of the eight-hundred and twenty-eight effigies are identifiable as women of renown. The remainder see us represented as nymphs and nudes. Such news does leave one to ponder how Sister Dora might feel about being immortalised as a piece of street furniture.

I learn that sister Dora never went to war, instead she was flung into the realms of the Black Country, then a novice, to cover for a fellow nun who had contracted scarlet fever: a prevalent disease of its time, leaving its hosts *Gravelly Hill.* Nurse Dora found herself overseeing an infirmary on Deadman's Lane, overwhelmed by sufferers ridden with smallpox. It was another highly-contagious lumpy infection that competed against those other sources of Victorian demise: tuberculosis and influenza. Spread through water contaminated by sewage, cholera thrived amidst the teeming conurbations to induce quite spectacular *Brown's Green* emissions.

Another time, another outbreak, saw Sister Dora treat nearly sixteen thousand patients almost single-handedly. Shortly after, she complained, somewhat underwhelmingly, that she felt, "quite exhausted". Within the year she passed from breast cancer. Her funeral was delayed by the hordes mourning her, paying their respects for her devotedness to their communities. Her life of steadfastness was commemorated in marble just six years later before being replaced with a bronze replica in 1956.

Up until this monumental moment of my arrival in The West Midlands, I had believed that the 'West Midlands' was simply a region of landlocked counties, notable for having the highest entanglement of canals, known as cuts, in England and a much-mocked accent. Its centrepiece, Birmingham, was once lauded as the beating heart of the manufacturing drum, driving an industrial revolution from south to north and back again. Such intense urbanisation and industry had birthed 'The Black Country', the boundaries of which no two Black Countrymen or women can ever agree. That said, they do all agree that it stretches across to include the epicentre of ostracism: Coventry.

Coventry, formerly and briefly, was the capital of England. It is much older than the more famous Birmingham, and it used to be home to Ikea's UK flagship store. Alas, too few people visited, which is odd because Coventry is *the* place to be banished to. 'Being sent to Coventry' is a phrase whose roots can be traced back to the English Civil War when Parliamentarians relocated Royalist prisoners of War as a way to demoralise and disenfranchise. Once abandoned, they were studiously ignored by the local inhabitants. If Coventry was a person, she would probably be a middle-aged, cat-owning woman.

Despite its cultural contribution to English history, yet pertinently ironically, Coventry was not even considered for nomination as the County Town to the West Midlands. To form the county as an administrative entity, entire districts had been excised from Herefordshire, Shropshire, Staffordshire, Warwickshire and Worcestershire. The previously contented cities and towns of Coventry, Wolverhampton, Birmingham, Dudley, Bromwich, Solihull and Walsall were bundled together to form this most artificial of England's counties. Laughably, the newly established West Midlands County Council set about governing this hotchpotch of a region on April Fool's Day, 1974. If only they'd thought to nominate *Chuckery* as its premier city, there would be some apt logic.

Unsurprisingly, the residents of this cobbled countydom lacked the historical roots that bind peoples together to form a regional culture and collective identity. Instead, the enforced relocation pitted townsfolk against townsfolk. All feared the council would favour Birmingham, leaving the previously thriving towns relegated to the status of satellites and suburbs. Envy, conflict and obfuscation abounded and administrative budgets and expenditure swelled four times over. Perhaps the counsellors of *Acock's Green* were as likely as the next to suggest that ratepayers' contributions were being used for political gain, rather than social development. It was not long before the favourite child, Birmingham, was put forward as the site for England's bid to host the Olympics…

In a rare moment of conspicuousness, Coventry's Member of Parliament decried that The West Midlands Council was, "as useful to local government as the appendix is to the digestive system. Its presence is unnecessary and it becomes noticeable only when it malfunctions." He might also have suggested its leaders be exiled to *Berkswell*, but that was an opportunity lost. The council disintegrated twelve years after its conception.

Today, the county of the West Midlands is run by the West Midlands Combined Authority. Quite how this changes matters is beyond my intelligence, although by endeavouring to fathom it, I was mildly amused to learn that the region is classified as NUTS. The NUTS is a hierarchical system for dividing up the economic territories of the UK and the EU, and the West Midlands is deemed to be NUTS 1 – the highest level of NUTS a region can be.

Winding up my somewhat perplexing exploration of the West Midlands, I received an unanticipated summons to Coventry. A letter arrived, via email, informing me that I had had a recent brain scan. I should have been nonplussed by this revelation, except for the fact that I could not recollect having had one. Two days later, a text pinged demanding I show up four days' hence at University Hospital Coventry & Warwickshire for another brain scan. The text implied my failure to do so would squander several hundred of my pre-paid NHS pounds. Thus, I saw it as my national duty to comply.

I was not unwell, not even a bit *Illey.* I was even more befuddled two days later when a consultant rang me to discuss the results of the brain scan I was due to have the following Friday. "I'm ringing to talk with you about the brain scan you're having on Friday, even though today is Wednesday…" he trailed off, himself slowly realising this was absurd to the both of us.

The following day a chipper nurse rang me to say the reason I was muddled was the result of her writing "MRI" instead of "CAT Scan". I assured her that this was not why I was so bewildered, even if Nelson was being dragged, curly whiskers and all, into this perplexing investigation of headspace. The timing, however, was impeccable: that

I should be in the West Midlands, a county I never knew existed, the very same week that its hospital demanded my presence.

Subsequently, I am now the proud owner of an NHS document whose opening line states: "Ms 'Person Irresponsible' is a bit confused." I shall keep this most accurate diagnosis for immortality and probably at some time get it framed to be placed in a downstairs loo. Rest assured, the brain scan showed no significant changes since the last one, which itself had shown there was nothing eminently life-threatening beyond my proclivity for general idiocy.

Thus, I arrived at a most nuts conclusion: if asking a person from Coventry why they were sent there is England's lamest and most predictable joke, Radiologists will say that, "Oh, I'm surprised that I have a brain," is their nomination for second place.

The County of Deliquesced Fish

"What's that bulge in your blazer?" It was a rare day that I was pulled aside by my head of house. "Sanitary towel," I answered, glancing him dead in the eye. He blanched and quickly flicked his wrist, dismissing me as if I was repugnant. It was twenty Benson & Hedges. Besides, I'd already graduated to Tampax. They were easier to smuggle about the person, quickly but silently slipping them up the shirt sleeve before pelting off to the nearest toilet. My periods had started when I was still at the Girls' School. One day I had turned to flush the loo, and noticed a pool of brown and red sludge beneath the water. There was more in my knickers. I remember folding in a tissue. It was many hours before I could return to my dorm to retrieve the box of sanitary towels shoved into the back of my allocated drawers patiently waiting for 'when the time comes'. Aunty Flow, The Curse, 'It', call it what you must, had made her first visit and I told not a soul about it - not least because I had been ousted from my dorm to live and it wasn't yet their time for sex ed.

Now in the mixed school, things were different again. It had been quite the ordeal learning to insert a slimline Tampax from the diagrams supplied. After many unsuccessful prods, with one leg resting on the toilet seat, the other firmly on the ground, I tilted the applicator backwards and forced it in. It felt wrong to even attend to that region of my body in the isolation of a toilet cubicle in a place where privacy was otherwise non-existent. It was not a thrilling experience. Regardless, I had promoted myself out of towels and into Tampax. It was always going to be Tampax because they came with the applicator.

The other option, Lil-Lets, on the other hand, were considered a little bit slutty, forcing hands to be a little bit too invasive.

But God forbid we repulsed the boys with talk of menstrual matters. We barely talked about it among ourselves. Yet, we were all so desperate to be adults already. Girls who opted for sanitary napkins were childish, we'd tell each other. "You walk like Farmer Giles, you do". We'd mock those junior if we suspected that they were off to change a towel. That is how each year inducted the next into the ways and means of feminine self-consciousness. I supposed some just learnt to hide one's preferred method. No doubt many more probably kept a decoy box of Tampax stuffed in their closet.

****

Precisely two hundred years after William Perrins and James Perrins dissolved their business partnership freeing the former to enter into a dissolving business with Mr John Wheeley Lea, The Shitron, Nelson and I lumbered into the county of the sauce of deliquesced fish – a veritable bottle of *Grimley* to my fish-averse taste buds.

I had anticipated that The Admirable Nelson, given his penchant for fish, and no other flavour, would have been full of gleeful dribble. He was only mildly intrigued when I gifted him a rechargeable flopping fish toy stuffed with catnip. The toy routinely detonated itself in the middle of the night, usually after it had been kicked off the bed, falling down the gap between the bed and the rear doors, often landing in the laundry basket. Despite several thorough dowsings, the damned thing would still bat itself silly. Alas, the cat did not bat it once.

My first observation in Worcestershire was how so many towns and villages had retained the Anglo-Saxon suffix 'ley' rather than using the 'ton' or 'don' as is typical for English settlements. It raised my suspicion that the county had played a definitive role in English history and I set about enlightening myself.

'Whee', means 'to express excitement', 'ley' is archaic English for a clearing in the woods, and 'lea' historically refers to 'a straight line'. It is also history that recorded Mr Wheeley Lea set things straight and clear with Mr Perrins on January 21st, 1823. Combined, they would go on to thrill the culinary world, albeit not before the 'Wheeley' portion was consigned to the wheelie bin.

Known globally as 'The English Sauce', Worcestershire, pronounced WUSS-Stuh-Shur-Sauce if sober, is also the site of the third and final battle of The English Civil War of 1642–1651.

Curiously, there have been many English civil wars, yet scholars usually choose to dismiss any competing conflicts as if they were nothing but an inferior brand of Worcestershire Sauce compared with the condiment produced by Kraft Heinz.

Like the Royalists of the seventeenth century, Lea & Perrins fought valiantly, albeit in vain, to protect their recipe from imitators clamouring instead to be the king of flavourings. Going so far as to sue for legal protection, they lost not once, but twice. Regardless, their recipe remains the best-selling rotting fish relish worldwide, even though it holds no stall in my fridge.

Similarly, the Royalists, led by Charles I, lost the English Civil War. It gave England her first taste of republicanism, as parliamentary power fell under the lash of Oliver Cromwell. Cromwell remains a Marmite character in English history, but he is still admired for rising from court obscurity to Head of State on merit, rather than aristocratic primogeniture, as has always been the English way. That said, assigning his son England's next political leader was not Cromwell's cleverest move and it caused Charles II, son of Charles I, to be invited back after just eleven years of republicanism. England has remained steadfastly sovereign up until the present times of Charles III. The royal family is similarly a Marmite subject among her denizens; coming into flavour following fits of festival pageantry, and falling away when youngest sons serve up heaps for the media to relish.

The most noted English Civil War was not solely fought to undermine absolute regal power and combat the excesses of the ruling elite, as I had presumed. Rather, its purpose furthered the quest to worship in ways not ordained by the Church of England. Some protestants feared the now well-established Anglican Church was imitating too many Catholic practices. After the King had married a French Catholic and appointed Catholic Lords into key political posts, the Protestants, once unified against Catholicism, fractured in their response. Still, there was an increasing will for religious leaders to be elected from within the ranks they represented, rather than by ordained as ministers via the royal court. Divided, the protestant opposition found themselves overlooked by royalty but also denounced by non-adherents for their puritanism.

As with all wars, the true battle ground was for control of the rhetoric. Words become currency to buy people's loyalties, and if it cannot be bought, it shall be coerced through shame, guilt or threat. In such times, to silence the religious opposition to royal rule, the leaders of Puritanical movements were summoned by the King's Bishop, and promptly had their ears lopped off. At least their tongues remained intact, thus avoiding a *Lickey End.*

History has repeatedly shown that stifling others views only entrenches the mindset. I wonder if any ideologues have ever changed their point of view on the infliction of a slight, a slur or a wound? In seventeenth century England, war was inevitable as the country split into two. One was either for or against the monarchy, with no space for indifference or compromise. The English Civil War saw more fatalities, in proportional terms, than the First Great War, and brought forth two new pejorative terms: 'Roundheads' and 'Cavaliers'.

The Roundheads, Cromwell's men, promoted themselves as men of merit and valour, committed to a fairer world. They denounced the Cavaliers as swashbuckling, rapscallion, womanising scoundrels of corruption and unearned privilege. The Cavaliers, in turn, demonised the Roundheads as dour, joy-killing, bible-bashing prigs. In between these two groups sat the majority of people: twiddlers, fence sitters and in-betweeners quietly going on with their lives as best they could. Nowadays, rivals simply label one another 'bell-ends'. Such vernacular is not at all helpful for determining one's voting preferences, views on the royal family, nor for any other contentious issue that might cause the nation to huff and puff.

Bell End was polled to be the funniest place name in the UK. This, the Holy Land of Rude Place Names, is rumoured to be found in Worcestershire. Popular television shows, such as 'The Last Leg', as well the press, often nominate despised political leaders, usually Putin, but also the odd home-grown political minister, a royal or two, or a general pillock as 'Bell End of the Year'. An effigy of the winner is placed next to the *Bell End* road sign and photo snapped for posterity.

Except *Bell End* does not actually have a road sign. *North Piddle* does, however. It pains me to piss on everyone's chips, but I simply must inform all and sundry that not a single post, advert nor parish council noticeboard has the words '*Bell End*' etched into it. In fact, there is nothing to indicate *Bell End's* existence beyond 'The Bell Public House' and the 'The Bell Service Station', both of which have clearly amputated their ends, if indeed they ever had one.

If one ever spots a picture of the road sign, it will have been taken in the neighbouring county of Staffordshire, where a road called *Bell End* feeds off the B4171 and leads drivers towards Mincing Lane. Bell End Road is located in the village of Rowley Regis, whose name means 'roughly cleared royal meadow' It has absolutely nothing to do with Worcestershire. The award-winning 'Village of Bell End' is laying claim to a crown that does not exist and anyone asserting that they live in *Bell End* is telling a very fishy tale indeed. I was as gutted as a Lea & Perrins anchovy to happen upon this pertinent mis-fact of English life. In fact, Worcestershire ranked thus far as the poorest county with just four 'awful-sounding settlements'. The last one, aptly, being *Suckley*.

No Sex Please, We're Herefordshire

I marched into the dorm, my hair still wet from the day's swimming training. A gathering of girls sat cross-legged on the floor munching on a picnic of snacks. Since I started smoking, I rarely had money for tuck, for phone cards, for stamps, or birthday cards. My finances were limited by my parents, whose own finances were limited by their children attending expensive educational establishments. I knew that this school cost more than the last one so I didn't feel I could ask for more. "She never stops talking about her old school," I heard one of the girls say. I assumed she was talking about me and the cavilling stung deep within. In this closeted existence, observation and criticism had become notions interchangeable.

There was a new girl starting mid-term and no doubt she would soon be attracting all of our attention, a hiccough in a routined world. Until she set foot in the dorm, there was a choice of where to sleep. To mix things up, we would whimsically switch our sleeping positions, new bunkmates brought new opportunities for bonding and gossiping, to be strategic about one's friends.

"Do you want to change beds?" One of the girls yelled across to me as I put away my sportswear and towels. Ours was a twelve-bed dorm of six bunks. For the most part it was a fairly mellow place. There was an identical dorm at the end of the corridor for the younger years. The girls there always seemed to be having smarts about something. The older years lived in houses elsewhere, doubled and quadrupled up in bedrooms, but a smattering remained in two four-person side dorms within our building. They could stay out later, but that seemed to be the only advantage. The front door was never locked in any case, and being on the ground floor, you could escape in at least a dozen ways if you truly wished to go for a midnight stroll.

On occasion, boys would knock on the door, enquiring after one of the thirty-two occupants, placing themselves in jeopardy. Their presence was all it took for tongues to wag about romance.

Sex. We talked about sex frequently. Who was having it? Who wasn't. How was it done? Who was doing what to whom? What was gross, what was not. No one ever mentioned their own doings, but confiding in a room-mate left her duty bound to inform another, who told another. The story would be embellished in its rotation so privacy was fiercely guarded. Regardless, the rumour mills crushed out tale after tale. How well the boys were developing, who'd started fingering, kissing with tongues, going the whole hog. No one talked about masturbation or self-soothing unless it was to condemn the outrage.

On rare occasions the housemother stalked the corridors to check if we had settled for the night. After lights out, we caught up on the days' mores and once in a while any chatterboxes might find themselves hauled into the corridor, left to stand there, sometimes all night. Not as an act of cruelty, but because the housemistress had forgotten to tell the miscreant to go back to bed.

So we were at liberty to swap beds within the dorm but we never shared them. That would be lesbianism, and that would be an indignation. For all our gossip of who fancied who, never did we mention someone of the same sex. Gay was a slur reserved for the boys. No one was ever gay – I mean no one dared tell their truth.

Nor did anyone care upon which mattress we slept so long as our parents paid the bill. All the beds were as hard as nails. I shook my head to the offer of a bed change. I had a top bunk in the centre of the room, behind the door, leaving me unsighted from the prying eyes of the houseparent. At least twice per term, her drunken husband would take to trawling up and down the corridor with a hockey stick – something only he found amusing.

In the bunk below was a weekly boarder; she was among the first to take up the option. Her parents lived in a nearby town and she had previously been a day-schooler. Those who couldn't or wouldn't resented the change in policy. There was a sense that it wasn't part of the 'espirit de corps'. Yet another classification or differentiation, something else to envy. She soon opted to become a full-time boarder: I suspect our hierarchies had its influence. I had appreciated her being my bunkmate, not only for her amiability, but because her absence gave me more privacy. More privacy for getting changed. More time to stuff contraband away on the rare days that the housemistress barged in. Fewer tremors from her rolling over or getting up to pee. Our single bunk bed was behind the dormitory door, giving us a tiny illusion of solace. The remaining five bunks were cast side by side, with gaps of a mere metre, and very visible.

At the end of the year, our little communities were beginning to fracture. Next term we'd move to four-bed dorms or other houses with smaller two-person bedrooms. Here, they liked to keep friendship groups together but I wondered who my friendship group was deemed to be now that the girl I had started with had been withdrawn. I got along with most, but it only ever felt peripheral, and life had taught me that vulnerability was the heel of the achilles.

The smokers and the non-smokers. The academics and those less so gifted. The musicians. The sporting types. The artists and dramatists. The fashionable and the frumps, the pretty blondes and the nots. We all had our roles to play. "You were good at swimming until you started smoking," one of the boys from my 'house' remarked. My smoking hurt our competitiveness for the sporting accolades that were frequently fought for between houses. My house had come second, perhaps we should have won. I shrugged. I hated being near-naked, especially when there was an audience cheering us on. Having to bend over on the blocks waiting for a whistle that couldn't be blown fast enough. I still turned up five or six days a week for training along with all the other boys and girls but only because I had to.

I liked smoking. It reminded me of family. Of freedom. Of adulthood. I liked being able to go for a random walk, to congregate with fellows we'd not ordinarily interact with – our sexes, our houses and year groups setting us apart. I liked belonging to a tribe of vagabonds who had a common sense of anarchy, and no adults determining who I must connect with.

"One day you'll regret starting smoking," my housemaster boomed at me as time after time I was ordered to appear before him. He confiscated my cigarettes, arranged for my housemistress to search my cupboards and bed, then sentenced me to a week's litter picking around the school's grounds. I was so used to it now, I'd even nabbed some of the cleaner's marigolds and stuffed them in my locker for next time. There would always be a next time.

****

Herefordshire was the filthiest county I had visited thus far, not that this is the fault of Herefordians, some of whom claim that nothing ever happens around these parts, but it was January and everything was smothered in thick brown sludge. Verges, brand new cars, hedgerows and road signs all defied the county's claim to black & white fame.

If the internet is to be believed, one is never far from sexual proclivity. Peculiarly, in England, sexual dalliances in public toilets is a criminal offence, whereas sex in public places is not, unless, of course it is witnessed, or has the potential to be, by two members of the public. Why two is anyone's guess, but as one of life's singletons, I am clearly not to be believed no matter what I attest.

I have it on good authority that it is usually men's cubicles that are modified to incorporate a *Hole In The Wall,* otherwise referred to as a glory hole. I remain clean ignorant on such matters, believing it to be boy's stuff. All I ever aspire for from my public toileting experience is some loo roll, a clean toilet and ideally no one else in the vicinity. A highlight would include some intelligent graffiti to amuse me. Perhaps something along the lines of, "Here I sit broken-hearted, came to shit but simply farted".

Outside of public conveniences, especially when parking up in the middle of nowhere, the proliferation of wet wipes rather than used condoms are the typical tells that come dusk, men (for it is almost always men) have a preference for combining fresh air, exercise and random encounters under the stars. In the proceeding six months, I had become accustomed to turning a blind *Eye* to sharing parking spaces. There was little one could do aside from snapping shut the curtain between me and the cab, and velcroing a blackout screen to the kitchen window. Never have I been bothered or harassed, beyond one gentle tapping on the driver's window just once before the hopeful left, ignored and rejected.

What does abduct my proverbial goat, however, is how the Vanlife communities are blamed for all the littering. Park4Night contributors are pretty good at recognising the conflict between the three types of outdoor hobbyists: dog walkers, doggers and van lifers, but keeping these fair isles pristine is a job for all of us. I only wish more councils provided litter bins. Nonetheless, the tensions surrounding the appropriate use of public places are far from black and white, and Herefordshire is no exception to the wider issues facing England and those who make use of her very sparse outdoor amenities.

As day follows night, Herefordshire's beauty is most striking during its waking hours. Wibbly-wobbly, oak timber-painted, black-framed and white lathed (traditionally a concoction of straw and dung) buildings dominate the county. Hamlet after hamlet brought an eye-watering enchantment to this otherwise sleepy rural community of brown and white Herefordshire beef cattle and mud-splattered sheep.

In fact, so little is known nationally about Herefordshire that, according to its local rag, Herefordshire is frequently assumed to be part of Wales and that its inhabitants spent an enormous amount of time pointing out that Hertfordshire is at least three hours' drive away and near London. It might be useful for locals to know that such a trip would only occur on a pertinently good day: like one where everyone else was restricted to their homes, had a flat tyre or skidded off the road. According to www.herefordtimes.com, Herefordshire's traffic is an abomination and the county is dreadfully in need of a bypass, although I thought that judgement was a little harsh myself.

That said, googling 'Interesting facts about Herefordshire' may well be Britain's best tonic to insomnia. Top fact, according to The Hereford Times: Yoda's voice was supplied by a man who was born in Herefordshire. He did not remain in the county long though, did he? He buggered off to Hollywood at the first opportunity. Second fact of interest: the storyline of 'Jesus Christ Superstar'' was thrashed out in a Herefordshire Hotel. Almost immediately, its writers high-tailed back to London to do the melody making. Herefordshire's other famous 'celebrity' was the Bishop of Hereford: he was one of Robin Hood's victims in a fictional story written in 1791.

It came as a relief to learn that Ellie Goulding was born in the county in 1986. Despite a string of songs including 'All By Myself', 'Don't Need Nobody' and 'Worry About Me', Ms Goulding is probably best known for singing 'Love Me Like You Do'. For the unfamiliar: it was the soundtrack to the film 'Fifty Shades of Grey'. If one has been asleep for the past century, or possibly confined to Herefordshire, Fifty Shades of Grey was the fastest-selling paperback of all time, probably because it made mainstream the practice of BDSM: bondage, domination, sadism and masochism. E.L. James's bonkbuster certainly involved *Much Birch.*

These days, according to Google, Ellie Goulding lives in Oxfordshire or London. Herefordshire, I can only conclude, is a place that one rushes away from as fast as one's steer will take it. This, I think, is a travesty because when not being brown and slushy, Herefordshire is truly a beguiling county.

Despite all this blandness, it came as quite the surprise to discover that Herefordshire was the county that supplied the nation with its most commented upon sex scandal of 2021. Herefordshire's best state school for the last decade, one with an 'outstanding' Ofsted rating, is, like every other school nationally, required to be LGBT-inclusive and to instruct pupils in the protected characteristics of the Equality Act and healthy relationships. Schools in Britain are not usually secular, and this particular one selected the programme 'A Fertile Mind' to supply their educational curriculum. This resource imparts the belief that marriage can only take place between a man and a woman, and that women should remain chaste until they can 'gift' their body to their husband. Men, on the other hand, are created to initiate sexual relationships, whereas women are 'receiver responders'. All this is at odds with the intentions of the Equality Act of 2010.

The last time I recall knickers being twisted so vigorously regarding sex education took place back in 1988, when Section 28 of the Local Government Act expressly forbade councils from promoting homosexuality. It had begun as a private member's bill which was not aimed at 'responsible homosexuals', but at 'sick homosexuals' who were suffering the symptoms of promiscuity, exhibitionism and were considered nothing more than "reservoirs for venereal disease". In other words, the bill was some old bore talking some *Old Gore*.

The government mandate fuelled rampant homophobia. Incidentally, and just as an aside, it is for this reason that, whilst they are certainly 'out there', I elected not to visit any places of the gay slur variety simply because I believe that unless one is in 'the club', one does not have the privilege of using specific terms.

One of the very many shortcomings of Section 28, however, was that no one could truly decipher if one was 'sick' or 'responsible' so all male-to-male attraction was branded by the same reductive stereotype. The deplorable doctrine galvanised the gay rights community, whose concerted efforts to be seen, heard, recognised and respected saw the Act being repealed fifteen years later. Their extraordinary exertions also led to the invocation of the Equality Act of 2010 for which all minority groups now benefit. Bravo!

Interestingly, as is the bizarrely unfathomably British way, only men could be homosexual. Lesbianism has never been illegal in England. A banning was considered in 1921 but the MPs and peers of the day rescinded from making it a prohibited act on the grounds that it would encourage women to try it. Thus, lesbians with a penchant for fornication al fresco coming together for an open-air cuddle, say in the outskirts of *Titley*, are presumably, absolutely welcome to do so provided no men get involved.

Likewise, what the authors of 'A Fertile Mind' failed to recognise was if there is one way of guaranteeing that teenagers try something, it is to tell them not to do something. After all, they probably have the most fertile of minds. All jokes aside, it was with some sadness that my arrival in Herefordshire coincided with the Church of England rejecting demands to conduct same-sex marriages. Once again England is having to examine her beliefs and question her authorities on matters of sex and sexuality.

"Fear is the path to the dark side. Fear leads to anger.
Anger leads to Hate. Hate leads to suffering."
Yoda (1999)

What about our priesthood? Don't you see that we could fall?
If we are to last at all, We can not be divided.
Bingham, B & Yaghjian, K (1973)

"Those fears we'll blow them all away, we'll blow them all away."
Golding, E (2019)

Hysterically Stressful Shropshire

Exeats came and went but this interlude of school routine came to bother me very little. Those remaining within grounds were crammed together into multi-year classes for Saturday school and revision was usually the topic. Some of the better teachers put a little fun into the curriculum on such days, but most absented themselves, leaving the class to best muddle its way through the day. On an evening we might be compensated with a cinema night or some other pity-soothing excursion, but usually we made do with nothing. The preternatural weekends compelled us to hang out with people outside of our usual spheres while we waited for the return of those fortunate enough to leave the premises for forty-eight hours twice per term. With pupils spread throughout the grounds, no longer did one have to watch on with envy as someone came along to claim a child. I appreciated the change in tempo that an exeat brought, and truth be told, I was content to remain within the school's parameters.

With my guardians now gone, half-terms were a whole other matter to be navigated. A full week plus one day trying to assimilate myself into yet another stranger's home. Working out what was permissible, and what was not. A simple walk along a lane – would it be too big a request? What about a bath? Did they even have a bed for me, or would the sofa do? A whole week and a day to deduce the ebb and flow of someone's home, only to forget it shortly after.

It seemed I spent half-terms with whomever would take me. Initially, a paternal aunt I barely knew became my designated responsible adult. Her six children, one born every two years, all carried on going to their state school whose half term wouldn't be for another week or two. She jollied me up and out during the day; taking me on my first bike ride in eight or nine years. I had learnt to ride sufficiently enough to go without stabilisers but had had no opportunity to cycle since. I lagged far behind my aunt, terrified by the speed, the wind rushing through my hair freaking me the hell out. I gripped onto the brakes as she careered away down hill, whooping all the while. I was hopeless at it, got off and walked the remainder of the way, resolving not to cry and cringing at every inch of my ineptness.

The following day she took me to a zoo where we watched a panther pace up, then pace back, then pace up, then pace back. It had worn an L-shaped groove into its pen, never breaking stride as it swayed mindlessly. "That repetition is how they show distress," my aunt commented. "It's not right to be cooped up like that. They call it zoochosis." It wouldn't help to give it a break, or a change of scene, or would it? I wondered. Only it would still be imprisoned just in an unfamiliar home, patiently doing the time until it could return to all it knew. I resolved never to return to a zoo again, and I never have.

My aunt was a warm-hearted woman, one with a sense of fun and joviality, and a deep commitment to indulging me with some light entertainment. There was no doubt that she cared deeply about my welfare but she was also ingrained in the ways of the Jehovah's Witnesses. For this reason she was much despised by my mother. My aunt had written about my week to my mother mentioning that I sang like a bird at the Kingdom Hall, and I had been enthusiastic about the door knocking on a Saturday. In truth, I had loved the change of scenery and the walk, the glimpses into what I might hope were normal people's lives. By now with no supervised letter writing, my efforts to keep abreast of my parents' lives had fallen by the wayside. That holiday, I listened as my mother scoffed at my attendance at church, telling her friend in my very presence that I most definitely could not sing, before launching into some vitriol about Jehovah's Witnesses in general. It would be best I didn't go back there, she decided, just in case I fell in with the cult.

The next time, I was to be collected by a woman called Susan. To this day I have no idea who the hell Susan was, nor indeed how she came to be my guardian for a single half-term. She was probably in her mid-thirties, frumpy and had a preference for floral clothing, floral curtains and floral bedspreads. She lived alone, pet-free, in a house that was sparsely furnished. I couldn't even tell you where that was. Beyond showing me how to get breakfast and lunch for myself, and to enquire what I wanted for dinner, there was little to squander the time, given the absence of books and television in her tiny house. She went to work during the day, after which she barely conversed. I do recall her soaking in the bath for four long hours one afternoon. I remember that so vividly because I desperately needed the loo for three of them. "She's got a psychiatric condition so you won't be going there again," my mother announced the following holiday. That was a relief.

Then came the psychologist-in-training. Her children were also at boarding school, their father remained overseas, where he'd recently moved his mistress into their former family home. Upon the revelation of the extra-marital affair, she had returned shell-shocked to her mothers' house to rebuild her life; changing career while in the throes of a divorce and dealing with the shock of an enforced relocation on top of her subsequent heartbreak. Into this, I arrived with my attitude, my hormones and my cigarettes. Her sons attended two different schools: one was still in prep, boarding school lingo to mean confined to a preparatory school. I found such places an oddity: given they are the just primary version feeding its commodities into a better-known boarding school. Just another way of keeping siblings far apart, breaking bonds for life. Her eldest was at the more senior establishment, and neither his half-term nor his younger brothers' week-long break matched the timing of mine. Besides, she didn't want me leading them astray. She refused to take me after the second or third visit. I couldn't have been more glad. I couldn't stand the woman.

Then came a new girl whose father lived in Wales and whose mother lived in Cheshire. We spent half with him, and half with her, and both lavished their time and energy on us, treating us to pub grub or cooking special meals, arranging for us to go to shopping malls, and giving us the run of their extremely substantial homes, one very much a mansion. We went feral with fags, drink and parties, pot and poppers galore, living the rebellious teenage dream. The week culminated in me losing my virginity. Although I didn't actually lose it, I deliberately gave it away. "She's a bad influence on you," my mother complained. I was just thrilled that she had taken to blaming someone else for my actions for usually I was the problem child. She asked that I start taking the pill to calm my raging hormones in some forlorn hope that it would fix me. Soon enough the school's doctor scrawled a prescription. Then my thighs ballooned.

I was finally relishing half terms; seeing them as something to anticipate with glee. With no one else to look after me, having a fellow wayward best friend was magical, and it seemed, despite the threat of separation, that the convenience was insurmountable.

****

"If you've got a lot on your mind, go for a walk," is oft-given advice in the event that a 'steadying cup of tea' fails to do the trick. Apparently, no one associates a long walk in a forest with stress. How I snort derisively. Clearly, anyone who asserts this has never disturbed not just one, but two, bears simultaneously whilst taking a lengthy perambulation from Mexico to Canada on one's own.

I was reminded of the recommendation, though, as I commenced my journey through the barrenlands of the heathery Shropshire hills. As we lumbered up the dales and plunged down through the valleys circling the *Long Mynd*, The Shitron and I fended off the gusts blasting hither and thither. With a ferocity so severe, the winds seemed determined to rush us over the verges to plummet us to who knew where. I swerved haphazardly from the airwakes of the lorries whipping by. While it may have been a feast for the eyes, the day's journey was complementary medicine ensuring swift digestion. Nonetheless, my search for *Myndtown* had proved to be an exhilarating thrill and true sustenance for my self-esteem.

Historically spelt *Mindtown*, the hamlet epitomises the tranquillity of the moody, windswept Shropshire valley in which it nestles. Hamlets always nestle, as opposed to urban zones, which always sprawl. Some say the latter are nothing short of incubators of mental distress, given their increased association with anxiety disorders, depression and schizophrenia. If that is the case, Shropshire is a tonic: offering much wilderness to appease the disturbed soul.

Shropshire was rumoured to be home to one of the two *Bedlams* found amidst our lands, *Bedlam* was once the nickname for the London-based Bethlam Institution: dedicated to the care of the mentally unwell. Its name has gone on to be associated with pandemonium, disorder and chaos. Best yet, England's two eponymous settlements are located far from the capital, which no longer has a *Bedlam* to call its own. For a time it seemed that Shropshire had forsaken hers as well then I happened upon a road sign, quite by accident, as I pulled up in *Bitterley*.

Bitterley had made my list of 'worst places to live in England' because it is a word more commonly associated with women than men, just like the word 'hysterical'. Alas, Shropshire has no place for hysteria, nor has anywhere else in England. The search for both settlements had mellowed me as I lost myself in the first of England's northern expanses. The breath-taking beauty of the *Long Mynd* prompted me to look at research on the differences between urban and nature walks. All thanks to the gloriousness of the *New Invention* called MRI scanners: we see what advice is sage, and what is nothing but glorious old wives' twaddle.

Like everything else in science, hypotheses are formed, then hopefully tested accurately, to provide provable, reliable and consistent results. The world abounds with incongruencies and half-baked ideas. History even more so. Women's matters especially so. Even now, findings from MRI scan research screeches across newspaper headlines in ways that the research conclusions did not intend. Women having smaller brains, for example, assumes an engendered stupidity: a sort of *Little Ness* in comparison with men's. It can take decades to unravel the adverse impacts of such tittle-tattle.

In the fifth century, Hippocrates, the father of modern medicine, was the first to use the word 'hysteria', believing as he would, that the cause of this womanly disease lay in a restless uterus. One's mental health was thought most grave if one's womb was prone to go a-wandering around the torso. Agitating womanly innards would, he claimed, produce toxic fumes, and any build up would lead to anxiety, a feeling of suffocation, paralysis or visible shakes, even convulsions and *Fitz*. He cited that the 'cure' for such disorders was a lot of sex of the heterosexual kind. Thank goodness then, that Shropshire has the wonderfully named *Willey Village.* Although, if fornicating there does not provide one with satisfactory results, one can always decamp to *Willey Moor.* But of course, this remedy was not appropriate for virgins, widows and bitter women who had been abandoned by their menfolk. For them, it was recommended they instead try re-marrying.

In Greek Mythology, the founder of psychiatry, Melampus, is said to have abated the hypersexuality of the three wild women of Argos. Rumours swirled of the women's carnal attacks on male shepherds in the woods, heaping embarrassment upon their king. Demanding a fee of two-thirds of his kingdom, Melampus hunted down the three nymphomaniacs, inadvertently killing one, before trapping the other two in a cave. He boasted he had healed them of their madness through the worship of the Goddess of the Wilderness, Artemis; a few baths and an abundance of Hellebore flowers. Incidentally, he married one and gave the other to his brother. I suspect this kidnapping, enforced betrothal and subsequent curtailing of their need to roam was responsible for obliterating any desire whatsoever. I rather hope the couples lived in very *Cross Houses* ever after.

European history's first female doctor, albeit she could not legitimately be one, was the magister Trota of the 12th Century. Recognising that the societal rules regarding women made them especially vulnerable, innocent and prone to condemnation, she could get to the heart of the matter just by being a 'she'. For women, sex and shame were an entangled mix. 'Per fornication' was a true *Wem* upon one's character, and self-pleasure was a delight most dubious: yet another dribble of moral stain upon one's womanhood. Trota was permitted into confidences that could not, should not, and must not be revealed to one of the male persuasion for they would surely be damned by the prejudices and principles of their minds. Trota too believed that abstinence was likely the cause of much illness, secretly prescribing relief in the shape of solo indulgence. Probably too, she flogged concoctions of musk oil and mint on the side to aid with the placating of their sexual thirsts.

By the sixteenth century, advancements in medicine meant that not much had changed for women. Although by now hysteria, and its close cousin melancholy, was thought to be a consequence of too much internal fluid and not enough ejaculation. Doctors still prescribed marriage and child bearing as the cure, but acknowledged the act of intercourse would be of most benefit if the woman could be brought to her moment of ecstasy and *Pant.*

In times unrecognisable, and in the absence of a husband, it was deemed appropriate for the local midwife to provide some manual stimulation. Now does the hamlet of *Knockin* not conjure a whole new interpretation for "Midwife Calling!"? Given their medical training, no doubt these nurses would also offer some purging oils and floral scents to hurry the process along. Compounding matters, however, was a mandate by the religious authorities to impress upon its clergy the need for celibacy and chastity. By taking even more eligible bachelors out of the suitability pool, the era became a simple case of *Cockshutt.* Midwifery was surely driven into a roaring industry.

As ever, it was convenient for the physician who was unable to identify the cause of a disease, to nominally assign women's symptoms as the work of the devil. Thus, science and religion were forever wed in holy matrimony. The only cure proposed for persistent hysteria was, in the absence of all other remedies, an exorcism. When all else fails, it is eminently human to *Betton Strange* to provide the therapy.

These days, science on a good day overtakes myth on a bad day. Scientists recently concluded that walks in nature do indeed greatly reduce stress. Unfortunately, the very same scientists, Sonya Sudimac, Vera Sale and Simone Kühn, went on to elaborate that this is not the case for those dwelling in urban settings. There, walks result in an upswing in anxiety and stress, and over time this deteriorates one's sense of wellbeing. Let us take a moment to consider our poor London-based Prime Ministers whose entrapment in the capital's confines have one by one turned them lunatic.

Alas, it is with regret that I inform the dear reader that the Shropshire Hills are also very short on Hellebore flowers, mint and musk deer. I did, however, spy the heads of dainty snowdrops so at least Spring was a-beckoning and from the sounds around my van on an evening, nature was very much taking its course without any medical or moral intervention whatsoever.

Body Matters in Staffordshire

I made a beeline for the music block, a nearby convenient hideaway for the smokers. It was heaving, the inevitable fug could be smelt a half-mile away - but safe to say, we rarely encountered our authorities. We were familiar faces, more than a little band of brothers and sisters from the first years to the sixth form. Two of the boys, in the year above, were leaning back against the brickwork giggling inanely at the entrance to the recess. They greeted me by name with an unusual exuberance. I said my 'hi' and immediately lit up, turning my back to catch up with my best friend who'd been to a different lesson. If I was more astute, more hypervigilant, more aware, perhaps I would have detected that they only animatedly greeted the girls. And perhaps, if I had looked down towards their groins, I would have noticed they'd pulled out their trouser pockets. I would certainly then have noted their penises hanging out of their zippers. It was called 'pulling the elephant', I have since learnt. I simply hadn't clocked anything and yet felt excluded from the joke. The butt of it, perhaps.

I flew to Johannesburg. The flight was an eleven hour one and I was glad there was no one in the middle seat, giving space between me and the straggly-haired stranger in his thirties. He looked slightly grubby in that cool heavy metal way that I secretly hankered for. We prattled on for a bit about why we were travelling 'home'. The stewardess pottered over about an hour after take-off with a tray for the vegetarian. The man indicated he wished to accept it. I told her that I also ordered a veggie meal but she informed me she only had one onboard. I pulled a face of disappointment and slunk back into my seat, no doubt my bottom lip giving away my feelings. The man gallantly offered me his tray. Flights are more bearable when not hungry, and I just adored aeroplane food: an effective distraction from the running thoughts that the plane might descend abruptly at any given moment. The only in-flight entertainment was a television dropped down from the ceiling with just one pre-selected film shown after dinner to the entire cabin.

"You owe me now. You can pay me after!" he asserted in his South African accent, accompanying it with a wink. That flight became an especially long one, and trapped by the window, I didn't dare leave my space to stretch my legs or use the facilities. I was still not yet sixteen, the age for consent.

I returned to school. I walked across the fields to the oak tree in the centre of the fields during one of the longer breaks, accompanied by two of my dorm-mates and a classmate. He started to pee against the tree: that annoying freedom that men have. When he was done, he spun around still grasping it exclaiming, "It's big, isn't it?" My friend snapped at him to put it away. We carried on chatting as if the whole event never happened. None of us was yet sixteen.

The same dorm-mate was a very regular visitor to her housemasters' private quarters at least once mid-week, and often weekends. What went on there was very much speculated upon, yet she evaded any queries. Silence tells no stories. She was oblivious to the fact that her housemaster had once threatened me, demanding I keep my nose out of matters that simply weren't my business. I wasn't sure there was anything untoward going on. I just thought he was smitten with her. I watched him once from the music block recess early one morning as he pounded away at the running circuit, his blonde-haired wife, a rare visitor to the school, cheering him on. A week later, a former student, and now rumoured lover of his, sat on the embankment whilst he completed his laps, heedless to my observation. The mill of hearsay had it that they got together during her tenure at the school. She looked very similar to my dorm-mate, who was not yet sixteen. A thousand stories, but just four for today.

****

It was the fabulous hamlets and villages of Staffordshire, like that of *Prospect Village* that had me shining a light on some of life's quirkier differences between gender and perception. I remember when, in 1999, the media fell apart at the seams as the iconic Pretty Woman raised her arms to wave at fans who had gathered to get a glimpse of her delightful self in London to promote a film called 'Notting Hill'. By doing so, she revealed armpit hair. From that moment on, it seemed all and sundry would *Talke Pits* as soon as the woman's name or her films was mentioned.

Twenty years laters women's razor's are still between ten and twenty percent more expensive than men's despite the blade not being any sharper. One way of boycotting the pink tax is to do away with them altogether. If one does, however, it is best if one doesn't read the comments below any article that highlights a celebrity with underarm hair because 'gross', 'smelly' and 'disgusting' seems to crop up from anonymous people with nothing better to do than judge the bodies of women they are likely never to meet, let alone smell.

Women's bodies have always been public property, and what precisely we should do with them is the stuff of real debate. *Tittensor* used to be the hilariously-named location for a maternity hospital in Staffordshire. No doubt it was a place where women discussed the pros and cons of breastfeeding as well as all the pains and pleasures. It was only in 2010 that it became legal for women to breastfeed in public. Even now women frequently report feeling a need to take responsibility for others' feelings and minimise their discomfort as well as 'keep themselves safe'. At least so says the expert in the field: Amy Brown. Beneath all that is a hungry baby whose needs, apparently, are of little consideration. The Guardian states about one third of women returning to work have expressed milk in the toilet, and far too many think breastfeeding in the toilet is acceptable. *Hints!* It is probably time to rethink that notion, or one should consider eating their meal while confined to the lavatorial cubicle.

And if it is not boobs, then it is beauty. A 2016 study by Christina Peters and her male sidekick revealed that pretty girls receive the best marks. If you look like you come from a witches' *Coven,* it may be best if one does courses online or via distance learning. Unsurprisingly, they found that physical attractiveness in men matters not one jot when it comes to assessing their academic vigour.

Most people are familiar with the stag-slut dichotomy, but as I travelled around my mind wandered back to a comment that had irked me for quite some time. A new organiser of a local chat group had just been appointed. "I'm only inviting pretty women to do the talks," he informed me. Perhaps, I was having one of those legendary, 'women have no sense of humour' moments. All the same, I frustrated myself by just nodding and not fecking reacting!

Wall is a very good place for banging one's head. Like most women, I have a conditioned response to conflict. Mine is to 'play dumb, stay shtum'. It irks me considerably, especially later when I explode from the indignity, usually long after the object of my chagrin has left the arena. I secretly envy women who can combust within the moment, calling out those who perpetuate an unfair world, and not keep it confined to academia. It is worth remembering that it is supposedly good to *Talke.*

"Women talk too much!" Who has not heard this observation? A former Prime Minister of Japan, Yoshirō Mori, plunged himself into terrible hot water when blaming women for meetings going on too long in 2021. There were five women executives in the forty-six directors of the Japanese Olympic Committee that he headed up. Ultimately, he lost his job which no doubt shut him up for quite some time, hopefully giving more time for the five women to contribute.

Several studies in recent decades have focused on the time men take talking versus the time women consume. Almost all concluded that if duration is the winner, women will not take home first prize. Some studies even posit that men talk up to 75% more when women are present than when they are in single-sex groups. It seems that women's integration into the corporate world has turned some men into gibbering wrecks.

However, my nomination for the most irritating recent findings from research: the phenomena of the *Hammerwich.* If women CEOs talk excessively they are seen as domineering, presumptuous and less competent. Verbose men, on the other hand, are perceived as powerful and in control. I guess then, it is best all round if women just shut up, put up and go away. I kid.

Another spectacular moment of *Hammerwich*-ing saw Arianna Huffington, the first female executive at Uber, explaining how data indicate that once one woman had joined the board of directors, then a company was more likely to hire a second. Only she was interrupted mid-speech by David Bonderman stating "Actually, what it shows is that it's much more likely to be talking." Now, strictly-speaking, given the above, this is true, but neither of them would have known it would be as the result of his presence and not hers. Cue him also exiting stage right to commiserate with Yoshirō Mori.

But it all balances out because, "women are better writers than men". Fabulous! Great news! All those academics, all those keyboards and all that pounding away led to Britta Glennon, Julia Lane and four other blokes to conclude that, "women in research teams are significantly less likely to be credited with authorship." Not that one needs to be in academia: Joanne Rowling, not even a scientist, and somewhat cancelled by universities and pressure groups, was obliged to use the term "JK" just so that no one knew she wore knickers. Does that not introduce the wound to some *Salt*?

We are now in times when gender is seen as a social construct and sex is obliterated. If the latter continues to be the case, it would certainly solve a great deal of problems: not least it might avert the forthcoming climate disaster as our population eradicates itself. Only it is sort of making things far more complicated while those for and against such binary divisions remain at *Loggerheads*.

For some time, our thought-leaders have been subsumed by a row between two groups loosely, and somewhat offensively, derided as the 'The Alphabet People' versus the 'Transphobic Bigots'. Proponents on either side are claiming to be on the right side of history, which is laughable, given that history has been kind to neither. It remains a present tense matter, and for politicians and individuals alike, an exorbitant amount of time is spent trying to be *Above Church* on the contentious issues, whereas our banks, charities and high-street conglomerates threaten to ban anyone not of the correct mindset. More and more judges are being brought in to sort out the resulting mess of sackings and hurt feelings at crowd-funded expense.

Many who have attested that 'Transwomen Are Not Women' have generally found themselves being marched off stage to queue up with all the other people who hold beliefs which may offend. Presently, it is not so much the time of 'Reds Under The Bed' but 'Terfs Under the Berth' so one must tread extremely carefully when discussing matters of women and men. Nonetheless, there is one space where the issues are mostly hotly contested: The place where one must go when in dire need of a *Leek*: the men's and women's; the 'ladies and gentlemen's', the rooms which separate 'people with incredibly straight legs' from 'people wearing knee-length skirts'. Hence, I was delighted to stumble upon some recent research into lavatorial matters of paramount importance: A £50,000 grant was issued to the Arts and Humanities Research Council in 2015 to look at the way public toilets are designed, ostensibly to determine if they are still fit for purpose in these transitional times. Two years later, in a fit of trying to please all the people all of the time, The Barbican Arts Centre, London, deemed 'Mens' and 'Womens' toilets to be an outdated convention and instead labelled their loos: 'Gender Neutral with Urinals' and 'Gender Neutral with Cubicles'.

It used to be a restaurant myth that women went to the loo in pairs so that they could talk about the meal, their men and the menu. I was certainly informed of this "indisputable fact" by a male professor at university. If one wanted to know what customers really thought of their dinner, he claimed, one should put an observer in the ladies' loo. Once a place of *No Man's Heath,* not even a male attendant would be allocated cleaning duties there, so how could his hypothesis be adequately tested? From the professor's assertion, one could deduce that men do not talk in loos at all, and if they did, it was without reference to the food. Regrettably, following up his declaration, I spent many an hour sitting in a cubicle conducting a piece of research. Turns out I spent many an hour sitting in a cubicle discovering that women really do not talk about very much of any significance whatsoever. They pee, sometimes fart, mostly wash their hands, and then they vacate the area.

Where they might talk, it seems, is while they are queuing for the sodding loo. It is a globally observed phenomena that the queue for 'The Ladies' is always a slow-moving, patience-zapping, frustrating test of one's pelvic floor muscles. Airports are the worst. Safe to say, then, that trips to the loo are not the result of us wanting to concoct gossip about the men, the menu or the meal, but simply because our bodies are urging us to keep things flowing.

It took a woman, Caroline Criado-Perez, to reveal why women's visits to the water closet are quite the expedition. In the UK, the toilet footprint is equally dedicated between the two sexes: so far, so equitable. Only, men can avail themselves of urinals, which take up significantly less space. Women use cubicles. One must wrestle one's way in, usually with a handbag or other. Then one must balance said belongings on the sanitary bin or circular toilet roll holder. (Note well: if going to 'some disabilities are invisible' single-unit toilets, sometimes the only provision, one might drop one's handbag conveniently in the hand wash basin. This activates the infra-red tap which then drenches one's most useful possessions. In my much-repeated experience, this has me taking significantly more time than is optimal). Following the careful placement of said accessory, women will whip down their clothing, or up depending on what they are wearing. Irrespective, most women wear a minimum of two layers to undress in order to 'do the do'. If they are under fifty or so, as over half the female population is, and at that grumpy time of the month, women will use this time to do what needs to be done there too. About fifty percent of women, particularly after the child-bearing years, will struggle with incontinence issues at some point in their lives, compared with just five percent of men. And it will not be so much as a dribble, as a proper *Weeford.* Of course, once matters have been attended to, it is a reverse engineering job: Whip up/down clothing, gather belongings, wrestle one's way out with the cubicle door and charge off to the mirrors, check facial matters, wash hands before drying hands. Only then, can one hurl oneself out of the amenities, jostling past the crush of women patiently waiting, mostly in silence, for a recently vacated cubicle.

Men, on the other hand, zip, flip, shake, flop, zip. It is all over in a *Flash.* Not even an utterance to delay them.

Recent studies indicate that women are more likely to wash their hands and dry them using the hand dryer, making men even more time-efficient. Come to think of it, it is the constant roar of the air dryer that is probably the reason why many women find the toilets a terrible space to hold a conversation.

If only the Arts and Humanities Research Council had waited for *The Barbican* to conduct an actual, real-time, and poorly conceived human social experiment: they could have saved the taxpayer £50,000. By decommissioning 'The Ladies Loo', the management simply gave men twice as much access to toileting amenities than women. On the plus side, at least these initiatives give us much more opportunity to stand around and do all that talking we have been deprived of elsewhere. It is a real shame, however, if one lives in a stranger-shy country such as England.

Out of Bounds in Derbyshire

The flight time on South African Airlines was two hours longer than that of British Airways. It was the first thing I noticed – that I was not on British Airways. I then learnt it popped into Cape Town prior to bouncing to Johannesburg. Two take-offs and two landings. My fear of flying was in its infancy, but I thought this an unnecessary antagonism.

I rang my mother to complain on one of the two telephones available for pupils' use. Access to telephones was a recent, legally-invoked provision in boarding schools. There were just two handsets, both with slots for a pre-paid phone card. They hung adjacent to one another, barely a half-metre apart, beside the foot of a staircase leading up to the boys' dorms. It was a clamorous place at the best of times as several hundred boys legged up and down, and at its most cacophonous in the early evening. The poor, but perhaps deliberate, choice of location forced the speaker to yell at the receiver.

I told her I disapproved of flying with South African Airlines. We'd all just watched a Free Nelson Mandela concert. South Africa was a bad place, with bad people, doing bad things. Everyone knew that.

"Where are you from?" I was still asked regularly.

"Lesotho," I'd reply.

"Where?"

"Le-su-tu," I'd enunciate.

"Oh! Le-so-tho" there was always someone to correct me.

"Yes, Le-su-tu, no 'th'" I'd correct them back.

But to most, I would explain that it is a tiny landlocked country within South Africa. And with those two words, disgust followed – guilty by association. But it was cheaper to fly with them, so that was that. The first thing I noticed was the absence of segregation on the plane. A couple of black people dispersed across the seating, along with a smattering of Chinese and Indians. If anything, the demographic was similarly representative of life at public school. The other thing I noted: there was an abundance of spare seats.

On my first experience of SAA, the check-in agency had allocated all passengers seats on the left-hand side of the plane. The captain announced that half of us must be re-settled on the right before he could safely take off, delaying us further. I wonder now about that quizzical anomaly of aviation seat distribution – a subtle provocation from the ground staff, perhaps?

I found the cabin crew, who were all white, much more amiable despite their strident accents, and was thrilled by their willingness to rustle up something tasty and vegetarian, because hardly ever did British Airways flights remember the pre-booked meal request, let alone do anything to alleviate my hunger .

The system of Apartheid, the Afrikaans for separateness, was barely detectable in Jan Smut Airport, except for the toilet facilities. Welcome to a military state: the place where all white men talked of their enforced two years' national service with a shudder. Sent away from home shortly after their eighteenth birthday to defend themselves and their families from the ever-present danger, as they saw it, of national insurgence. All of them bragged of it as if they had survived something hellish and yet none of them openly questioned why. When we are children, we do what we are told. We believe what we are taught. Is it not safer that way?

The next time I would call my mother would be the following September. Waiting in line at the foot of the stairwell, the din most deafening at the start of the academic year: a time of friends reuniting, expressing their joy or discontent with their new dorms or bragging about their summer exploits. But that wasn't the cause of the din.

The older boys, hauling two or three trunks towards the top step, hollered to get as much attention to the impromptu races that were about to be staged, as much as to warn those below of their impending peril. On the count of three, they would shunt the chests on their merry way, kicking them forcibly to maximise velocity, and all around spectators would cheer and jeer. Down the trunks hurtled and clattered, sometimes spinning and thumping into the walls. Inside each trunk would be a first year, all of eleven years old. Upon landing, bruised and disorientated, they'd drag themselves out of their tiny prisons, catching their breath to suppress their humiliation at the feet of those forming an orderly queue waiting to let their parents know they'd arrived back at school safely.

****

Drowning in rugged moorland and vast wilderness, this 'County of the Deer' is an aptly-named bountiful supplier of roadkill for those carnivorously-inclined. Nelson is not a convert to raw food, never has been, and will, most likely, always dry-wretch at anything that is supposedly better than the 'cheap supermarket crap' that lands in his bowl periodically throughout the day.

As for the vegetarian: she can feast her eyes on the moody heath-laden hills rich with coarse grasses. Spring was now springing all about with fresh colour beginning to creep back in, cracking open the wintry gloom. My exploration of this county, capturing its signage, had me treading mindfully, dodging the assortment of shortly-to-be flowering bulbs renewing their journey through life. One careless foot placement and *Whatstandwell* would be bent over awaiting its demise.

During the lengthening daylight hours, the cat and I would spy birds of prey circling over the fields as we cruised along. Not for a long time have I had a burning desire to run up a hill, tampon-advert style, to bound around in white clothing and pelt out, 'the hills are alive with the sound of music'. But Derbyshire's gloriously peaked district certainly invoked a yearning.

Alas, many of its open air car parks have height barriers restricting entry to car-dwellers only, so on we would trundle. Such a *Boundary* makes it clear that the travelling communities are not welcome here, nor seemingly is the 'man with van and sandwiches for lunch'. I briefly wondered if this is lawful. It is the local authority who decides whether there should be fees and height restrictions.

Although the Equality Act 2010 stipulates clearly that anyone of a nomadic lifestyle cannot be discriminated against, it is hard to justify the existence of open air barriers which prevent the 'admission of undesirables' to parking zones. Yet such barriers are prolific across England both in towns and rural communities. The topic is probably ripe for a good *Rowland* but it remains untested in the courts of the Kingdom. After all, the discriminated against and the impoverished are the least able to assert any rights they may have been assigned. Justice has always been, and shall always probably be, the territory of those who *Hasland*, or at least exceptionally good house insurance.

In England, unlike in Europe, the travelling communities are differentiated by their heritage: Irish, Welsh, Scottish or Roma (those from Eastern or Central Europe). These are the sets that are most likely to be wished good *Riddings* and remain the most disenfranchised, even when they have chosen a static lifestyle. As a result, Gypsies (as some prefer to be called) and Travellers (a term others find less offensive) tend to be absent from surveys. They have the lowest educational attainment as a class and they are twice as likely to struggle from bad health compared with those who ticked 'white British'. They have significantly shorter life expectancies and one in five travelling women will suffer child bereavement, compared with one in one hundred white British women. Our government observes that contemporary racism is largely indirect or underground, there is a communal tolerance for overt discrimination towards the travelling communities.

Such grouping includes those of the New Age, the boaters and the bargees, as well as the 'travelling showpeople'. For now, I probably fall into the latter category but my British-passport holding expatriate existence has made me a citizen of the world with no place to call home. I am not from here, nor I am from there but I am always from somewhere because the interlocutors seem to need to know, so I often invent it. I still smile about the times I replied that I was, "two days' walk away from Oxford". It made sense to the American hikers enquiring. Rest assured I now have acquired a few hundred place names for future use. Ask at your own peril.

It was in Derbyshire that I received a phone call from my doctors' surgery informing me that I had been delisted as a result of the new tenant from my former abode returning mail scrawled with a brief "not known at this address". If I needed medical help, I should seek it elsewhere. Quite how, or where, the receptionist did not seem to know but just not there. I could only hope I stayed in good health now I too felt the travelling communities' sense of disenfranchisement.

Aside from the minor shunning, it is safe to say that my tour of the county of Bakewell tarts was indeed a pleasant one. My favourite morning saw me spend a lazy hour observing a banditry of blue tits dive-bombing a leaf-festooned verge deep within the woodland we were hibernating in. Zipping up and down, they scoured for twigs, worms and other matters of nest-hood, much to the delight of The Admirable Nelson and the perplexity of yours truly: I had thought such birds were ardent and fierce competitors, and not in the least bit interested in operating in tribes.

February proved to be the ideal time for careering around the region that The Derbyshire Telegraph claimed as the birthplace of Sociology: the study of how human actions and consciousness shape, and are shaped, by our surrounding cultural and social structures. Alas, this is not strictly true – Sociology was born in France, and the forefather was Auguste Comte. Aside from that minor act of mis-parenting, Herbert Spencer, the second-proclaimed forebear, was most certainly born in Derby in 1820. He would go on to be admired for writing a best-selling book called 'Social Statics: The Conditions Essential to Human Happiness Specified'. It did not involve *Clownes*.

Just like most self-help books, seemingly it failed to change the world. In the first edition, he fervently supported amending the law to provide for equal freedom to both sexes. Years later, some say as a result of a growing personal resentment that women had repeatedly rejected him, he concluded that women were, after all, the doltish sex. More circumspect explanations attribute his volte face to his discovering that women as a class were more likely to vote for statist policies, especially if those laws promoted humanitarian causes. He decried them as 'low fools'; susceptible to *Foolow* principles that he himself did not agree with. Therein lies the problem of freedom of thought and speech: what to do when one deems the other plain wrong.

I found it a matter of ironic timing that Ms Sturgeon, First Minister of Scotland and avid supporter of gendered self-ID, resigned on the very morning that my womanly principles were rocketed into self-righteousness at my passing of *Lady Manners School.* For those spared the mortification, the sole purpose of the classical 'Finishing School' was to teach young women social graces and upper-class etiquette as a preparation for marriage and entry into high society. It would not do that we could just be. Instead girls were hen-pecked into terminal perfectionism.

It was inconceivable to me that in this day and age Finishing Schools were still in existence. Having recovered my eyebrows from the van's ceiling, it brought back the horrors of deportment lessons for someone whose gait is naturally clunky and the foretelling that I would never make a graceful bride walking down the aisle on her wedding day. Truth be told, I am more of a 'shlepper'. Given that I have scoliosis and somewhat mangled feet, it took a marathon walk across America to make peace with my afflictions.

The other suffering placed upon ladies-in-training: the brain-deadening elocution lessons. In our case, each week we commited to memory joyless poems not even of the amusing, 'How now, brown cow' kind variety. How I would have loved to recite ditties about Spanish precipitation trends. Instead, we rehearsed pertinently dull poems, only to have the elocution mistress despair of us multiple times per stanza.

Thanks to the God that is Google, I learned UK's finishing schools floundered in the 1990s, with just a handful surviving to teach cordon-bleu cooking to all, regardless of whether one has hot dog buns or sausage in the nether regions. Just as rapidly, I discovered that Lady Grace Manners was an actual human being whose passing circa 1670, bequeathed to Derbyshire, not only the aforementioned endowed school, but also a truly terrifying death mask.

Concerned with her own legacy, Lady Manners established the educational institution for boys in 1636. Two-hundred and sixty years later, to ensure its financial survival, the school's board invited girls to attend. New rules were quickly implemented to make sure one would never forget one's differences. Girls must always be permitted to enter and leave rooms before boys, and boys were expected to hold open doors for girls. Traces of this practice are still visible today. I only like it when I am the beneficiary, naturally, so in the unlikely event that men are reading, please do not let the door slam in the face in the pursuit of egalitarian progress or I might *Unthank* you quite loudly.

I admit that parking up outside *Lady Manners School* to educate myself on matters of Derbyshire's contribution to humankind was not me at my most brilliant best. It was, above all, particularly unthinking given I drive the stereotypical vehicle of choice for kidnappers, bank robbers and people with dubious sexual intent towards children. In my defence, your honour, it was one of those particularly stunning Spring days, and the more than adequate street parking facilities also availed me of high-speed internet; something that much of Derbyshire sorely lacks.

In between my research and note-taking I glanced towards her pupils as they milled around their expansive school grounds. Across the road, attendees indulged in a few acts of *Gamesley.* It got me to pondering about women's sports. Statista found in 2018 that nearly six and a half million men participate in sporting activities of moderate intensity for at least two and a half hours a week. On the other hand, just four million women get their arses in motion, and nearly two-thirds of girls have quit playing sport by the age of sixteen. One commonly cited reasons is that once upon a teenaged time, athletic-style sports might break the hymen: making a girl less than marriageable. This mentality still exists notably those where religion demands a woman's *Netherseal* is reserved only for her husband.

Secondly, by the time a woman has turned sixteen, her body has changed considerably. It is no longer comparable to the pre-pubescent curveless ideal that is projected by the press and modelling industry. Girls become very self-aware of what jiggles, and what ought not to, in their 'mind's eye'. Comparisons are almost always unfavourable, particularly when studying images that have touched up any 'flaws' such as cellulite, scars and birthmarks. Who wishes to swan about in a swimming costume if one is not yet 'summer body ready'? Our drastic change in proportions causes us to become unbalanced in our teenage years. I do not mean emotionally (but then again…), I mean we do become rather bockety.

There are also those pesky myths that sport induces body 'deformities': horse riding causes fat thighs; swimming makes for bulging, masculine shoulders; working weights has the tummy protrude and hockey will break your ankles. The last one is true.

There are also additional expenses: girls require special sports bras to avoid unnecessary pain and discomfort in the *Breaston* region. These cost around £20 each and will need replacing regularly, with wear and body growth. Following that, there are the really hidden costs: exercise means changing in and out of clothes, causing girls to rotate through a sanitary pack quicker. A realistic budget for a normal period is around 80p–£1 a day, some paying as much as £5 per day to access top-quality products. In 2022 top-flight sports clubs finally recognised that sportswomen declining to wear what was often obligatory white shorts was not girls simply trying to make a fashion statement or be just plain awkward.

Most infuriating of all is sportswear being sold as 'unisex'. In other words, they were designed for the default male body. For girls with curves, it means one's intergluteal cleft munches away at the fabric for much of the sports time. Chomp, chomp, chomp. Not only is it uncomfortable and unsightly, it might also be thought of as unbecoming of a lady to be snatching at her nether regions in public…

Then there is period pain: it is true that sports really do help alleviate it but who the hell feels like pratting around when one's innards are being clattered to smithereens as if at the centre of a grown man's rugby scrum? Around 10% of women globally have the excruciating agonising endometriosis, but around 80% of women report having menstrual cramps. One week in every four, one's womb is nothing short than a walloping *Kniveton.* Some bright spark, who I would love to see knighted, has invented a period pain simulator for use by men. I think it should be made mandatory for any male showing aversion to women mentioning periods – even the hills would resound with the singing!

If resources are not ploughed into getting girls active, society does not benefit from sustained long-term participation. These are usually cited as fewer stress-related illnesses and better health.

Since the 2012 London Olympics, government policy, led by the Tories, has shifted funds from council-funded sports initiatives to a national redistribution of wealth. Cathy Devine suggests that local councils are more focused on equal access and will disperse resources in the direction of the overlooked, the discriminated and disadvantaged. In short, this is a fancy way of saying there is a current trend towards allocating money to high-profile, highly-competitive, very elite sports.

In the UK, the top three by revenue and participation are football, cricket and rugby. This 'top-down' model of growth aims to have success seep down through to a grassroots level, via emulation and inspiration. Each time England sporting heroes do well, it creates more demand, which nourishes those supplying the infrastructure. It all combines to make robust ranks for the athlete to rise through in order to acquire the very knowledge, skills, and experience necessary to participate as a professional. Of course they, like all experts in their field, require coaching staff and scientific specialists to support their endeavours. Often such scaffolding comes from former players who can ensure knowledge will *Cross o'th' hands* via imparted wisdom and newly discovered findings fed into coaching decrees. This is the trickle-down economic thinking that saw the last, and third, female Prime Minister, Liz Truss, handed her arse on a plate.

Football, rugby and tennis all attract men, and tremendous wages are paid to those who succeed to their upper echelons. Top performers go on to become media megastars, and are recruited to influence the next generation. The hype and attention sells magazines and instagram promotes their glamorous lifestyle. Household names then collaborate with ghost-writers to produce self-help books which inform us on how to adopt their ways of thinking, being and behaving so that we too might experience all the trimmings of their success.

The hidden side is that women's sports are given short shrift. The view is sometimes taken that women demand funds that will deprive England's top three sports of future opportunities for further success. Women's sports have to be allocated resources, sometimes under duress, and so the economies are smaller and the press attention less. No matter how well women do, the breadth and depth of competition is often stated to be feeble by comparison. Women win, but they *Winsick.*

England's top three sports are also ultra-competitive. This can be ideologically incompatible for girls, who are more likely to be conditioned into 'playing nicely' and 'sharing is caring' by parents and educators alike. I think the current phrase is 'be kind'. Conversely, boys are more likely to be given a free pass on shoddy behaviour. "Boys will be boys" is an age-old means of dismissing consternation, as well as a song by Dua Lipa. She, via the medium of music, asserts that girls grow up to be women, yet boys seemingly have a special licence to behave immaturely for the duration of their lives.

Little wonder, then, that so few took heed of Derbyshire's foremost sociologist, Herbert Spencer's 1897 very strong views on the Englishman's favourite past-time:

"A nature which generates international hatreds and intense desires for revenge – which breeds duelists and a contempt for those who do not seek to wipe out a slight by a death, is not a nature out of which harmonious communities can be molded. Men who rush in

crowds to witness the brutalities of football matches, who roar out ferocious suggestions to the players, and mob the umpires who do not please them, so that police protection is required, are not men who will show careful consideration of one another's claims when they have agreed to work together for the common good."

Traditional girls' team sports are the lesser-spotted team sports, usually sighted every four years in the Olympics. Success in hockey, netball and curling drives a brief resurgence until the television wilderness kills them off again and we all return to *Youlgreave* with nothing but memories of the halcyon days. Exercise is typically sought via aerobics classes, yoga sessions and pilates. For many women, it is simply a case that the less sweaty the recreation is, the more appealing it is. Such activities are more costly overall, being privately supplied, as opposed to football and rugby which might be subsidised by their national associations. Cheapest of all would be to go for a run or a bike ride, but girls have been inculcated into a mindset of 'stranger danger' since they were able to fathom rhyming couplets. Riding on one's own while female in skin-tight lycra? Why, that is just asking for trouble!

Since England Women's football exploded onto mainstream television in the last decade, it has gone on to become the most revenue-making sports for girls. In second place? Tennis. Wimbledon has had parity of pay in the UK since 2007. Thank you Venus Williams and the Women's Tennis Association for taking up space in the arena, by speaking out and obtaining the acknowledgement that the work of being a professional athlete is what happens off the court rather than being relative to the speed of the serve or the number of sets one plays in a game. Because when it comes to the differences between men and women, sport and sporting institutions, it is almost always a case that women get *Shatton.*

And on the Sixth Day, God Created Manchester

That few girls made the head of house or deputy rank was just because boys made better leaders – at least that appeared to be the common consensus. Next year's prefects' list had been revealed ahead of the forthcoming academic year, but it remained to be seen who would get the top job: Head Boy.

We girls lacked the necessary skills for commanding others. We lacked a certain authority or gravitas. We lacked a depth to our voices – undoubtedly a useful skill for hollering and barracking. The latter point was about the most observant remark I ever heard. I never asked what good leadership was, nor how one obtained it. It was, perhaps, just something one had rather than one learnt. If only we'd thought to get a little militant about matters, to stage some kind of coup or act of vandalism. To speak up, shout out or otherwise conduct ourselves in ways unbecoming of a lady, but, of course, this would not serve us well. Complaining was so tiresome and so very pointless. Besides, were we not all sick of Margaret Thatcher already? Oh, and God forbid we should ever forget Edwina Currie, she of the egg industry-smashing shenanigans.

Many girls' battlecry was starving their bodies, but to speak of such matters would be a betrayal of the girls' code. "You'll fade away," my housemaster once informed me as I skipped lunch, preferring to go and walk about in fields. Hardly. I remained a self-conscious chunk despite a restricted diet, although perhaps my teenaged eyes deceived me.

The final farewell for the summer terms always closed with the public issuing of awards and commendations. Usually, they came in the form of the school's half and full colours: alternative neck ties representing a sporting or scientific achievement. I think they could only be worn on Saturdays and high days. Why Saturdays, a day we still went to school, I have no idea.

All I remember is that in order to receive an accolade, the incumbent was forced to walk awkwardly to the Headmaster with three hundred pairs of eyes observing one's every step. I was determined never to get one and I very nearly succeeded but alas, I let myself down badly by achieving a school first in outdoor swimming; the only one of the group who did. The master responsible for training us wasted no time in informing me that I almost failed even in my moment of sole success – I just scraped through, rather than shone, it seems.

Still, with the end of year ceremonies and awards over, we could rush off into our summer holidays. To reacquaint our beings with the goings on in the outside world. To discover new fashions, new music and new identities. Long reign the summer holidays, a time when we could familiarise ourselves with our real lives. With the illusion of real life. To just be free.

****

The county of Greater Manchester is yet another ceremonial concoction formed on 1st April 1974, although, unlike Avon, it endures. For the most part, the county is five hundred square miles of concentric, and very compact, settlements mostly melded into one vast urbanisation best known as England's second largest city. The region is famous for its ubiquitous Victorian two-up, two-down terraced homes rammed together and best depicted in the soap opera 'Coronation Street'. That is not to say there are not any attractive green spaces, it is just like moles on a body: they are randomly dotted all about the place.

Upon superficial inspection, Greater Manchester is arguably the most toxically masculine of the English counties. Chester, it is posited, derives from the Roman 'caestrum' meaning 'encampment'. *Greater Man Camp.* I am undecided which word ought to be emphasised, but no matter which one is stressed, it has an indelible impact on one's imagination. However, the 'Man' is not 'The Man' whatsoever. This particular syllable most likely correlates to the Celtic 'Mamm' as in 'mammary', meaning 'of the breast'. 'Greater Boob Camp' has it sounding akin to an exotic bra for the ample-chested.

I had anticipated that any research undertaken on this region would result in article after article citing its football team: Manchester United. Indeed there was quite a lot to battle through but traces of women, like the county's green parks, could be found lurking everywhere. One just has to be tenacious enough when googling for pertinent facts about the county.

Like most tourists, I liked to immerse myself in learning more about the hamlets, villages and towns that I visited, to glean a little of their heritage, how they came to be named and what, if anything, they have contributed to their county, if not the land at large. Later, when I sought inspiration for writing, my eyes might scan all the way through looking for a mention of a woman or matters of feminine persuasion.

The settlement of *Horwich* must surely have an abundance of women who made notable contributions to the history of this fine county? Alas, eight men were mentioned by name. No women. Sixteen men in the second offering, but no women. I did not bother counting the third, but skimming alone revealed no women. That was me done with the top three suggestions powered by Google.

It took just two articles on the settlement of *Failsworth* for me to become greatly excited at the mention of a 'Daisy Nook'. Alas, further interrogation revealed that Daisy Nook is a place and not a person. With a bit more digging, I discovered that the MP for the region was currently Labour's Angela Raynor. She once hit the headlines for calling the incumbent Tories, "A bunch of scum, homophobic, racist, misogynistic, absolutely vile…pieces of scum."

She later added that she had, "held back a little". Her dear leader, Keir Starmer, a man who had won the leadership mantle beating six other candidates, all female, defended her sentiments albeit demonstrating a modicum of decorum by stating it was, "not language I would use." Shame, it would make me find the man mildly more interesting.

Thankfully, instead of politics and football, I could turn instead to Manchester's other significant contribution to English culture: its music scene. The city was once delectably encapsulated into the blended 'Madchester'. For those that missed the era, either as the result of boarding school; too many psychedelic drugs or a lack of timely conception, Madchester was a period that commenced in the late 1980s and declined in the early 1990s. It brought to public consciousness some tremendously iconic bands who hashed together acid-house with melodic pop. The most renowned of bands were the four-man group, The Stone Roses and the five-man set: The Happy Mondays. Together, they brought a cheeriness to the otherwise melancholic indie scene previously dominated by two male quartets: The Smiths and Joy Division. Other notables included the Inspiral Carpets (five blokes); The Charlatans (four blokes); James (ultimately seven blokes, with a woman being admitted briefly in 1996) and 808 state (three men). That is pretty much the era concisely summarised. It appears, to Google at least, that no British women contributed to the scene whatsoever. Just try Googling "Top Bands in the late 1980s" to see if there were any women active in your part of the world.

Not that the era was an absolute tragedy for womanhood, after all it supplied us with baggy trousers. The baggier, the better. It was heaven sent for those like me sporting a *Broadbottom*, as one could drown oneself in layers of drapery. *Broadbottom's* current claim to Wikipedia fame is that firstly it does, finally, mention a woman on its webpage. Albeit one does have to scroll to the bottom of the site to locate the heading 'Notable People'. There, 'Millie Gibson' is listed as the sole entrant. In case, like me, one does not have her down as a person of note, she was once a Coronation Street actress, and is now a Doctor Who companion. Doctor Who ranks at no. 66 in Britain's most popular TV programmes of all times, with Coronation Street finding itself in 352nd place. Incidentally, Millie Gibson's bottom is enviably slim. It can also be observed on Google that she seems to be comfortable accentuating her substantial *Higher Folds.*

Higher Folds is a settlement some fifteen miles from central Manchester. Wikipedia wastes little introductory wordage before informing the reader that Shaun Keaveny grew up there. Assuming one will need to google Shaun Keaveny, I can spare you the bother. He was a presenter on Britain's 47th most popular radio station. Radio, not television. What I found more fascinating was that *Higher Folds* once registered as the divorce capital of Britain, with one in six marriages ending in acrimony back in 2001. How times have changed. What happened to all the marriages one might ask? They folded.

With that insight into the cultural phenomena contributed by Greater Manchester gleaned, I left with just a little sadness: absolutely no one with so much as fifteen minutes of fame originates from *Hunger Hill.* Nonetheless, the village reminded me that it was only after I left formal education, one supplied to me at vast expense, that I came to learn of Manchester's most famous women: Emmeline Pankhurst, and her daughters: Christabel, Sylvia and Adela.

These four women are our forewomen: the igniters of modern women's leadership in England. Their window-breaking campaign is no longer judged as an act of wanton anarchy, but rather a movement towards national salvation. A very womanly example of the cliche: one man's freedom fighter is another man's terrorist. Their smashing strategy was born out of the failure of peaceful protesting: their slow moving marches saw multitudes of women sexually assaulted by the very police force tasked with upholding the nations' mores. Apparently, being out, loud and about was simply 'asking for it'. Following the realisation that arrest for criminal damage was far less brutal, less humiliating and much more swift, the women turned bellicose, giving the chattering classes much to chatter about. Eventually, their indignance could no longer be ignored. The Liberal Party's Lloyd George, then Prime Minister of Britain, remarked of Emmeline Pankhurst's eldest child, "talking to Christabel Pankhurst was like going to a lunatic asylum and talking to a man who thinks he is God." I suppose we should all be glad he did not just call her scum.

Finding sympathy among the grass-root readers of the Daily News, its editors asked, "By what means, but screaming, knocking, and rioting, did men themselves ever gain what they were pleased to call their rights?" Conversely, their mischief was condemned by the Tory paper, London's The Morning Post. Their take on the women's vandalism was roundly put down: "Nothing could indicate more plainly their lack of fitness to be entrusted with the exercise of political power". And so, the women set off to walk towards equality in 1928, albeit at times the journey they started seems far from finished.

That Cheesy Cheshire Cat Grin

"Sis!" I said. I can't even remember why. It is the Afrikaans for 'disgusting' and all of us teens were saying it randomly and wantonly. I was learning a lot of new lexicon in my new homelands. My favourite so far: Slaghuis. Every South African town seemed to have a slaghuis, but it was not a place I would be seen dead in. I was, much to my mother's frustration, still a defiant vegetarian, a phase that I stubbornly refused to grow out of no matter how inconvenient it was.

I had made a new best friend, via a woman my mother worked with. She was her step-daughter and she was my age. She and I spent much of our telephone conversations trying to decrypt one other's accents, and arranging to escape our confines. English was her second language, although she was fluent in my mother tongue and indecipherably fast at speaking it. Afrikaans was her first. She was Namibian by birth but she spent her summer holidays with her brother, her father and his second wife, returning to live with her mother and her much detested step-father during the school terms. Perhaps it is embarrassing to admit that your parents had to find you friends to hang out with, but in an international life what else can one do?

It is with great heart that I could say that she and I hit it off extremely well despite the accent barrier and parental micro-management. Red Martini with lemonade aided me to overcome my linguistic incompetence, as did Taboo and Cinzano. Of all the people the adults insisted I befriend, she is the one I have the fondest memories of.

My return to yet another Michaelmas term did not diminish the friendship. Via letter, her mother invited me to Namibia for the Christmas holidays, to a remote seaside town far up the western coast. There, to earn my keep, I would work in their casino. I left England with her denizens shivering through the festive season to broil in the Namib desert, desperate for darkness to bring coolness. I ate a Christmas dinner of salads and sandwiches on the beach, quaffing sparkling wine and puffing away on Peter Stuyvesants. On Boxing Day, we traipsed around a penguin colony avoiding the jackass' shit; their scent permeated our clothing for days after, and had us sniffing one another in paranoia.

Daytimes were idled away watching the Atlantic pound the shore from our bedroom windows, each time dragging away fractions of millimetres from the sandbank on which the houses rested. In time, the tarmacked street would be washed away completely, like the previous one had been, the erosion rapacious. By night, we'd make fast friends in bars chock-full of vacationing teenagers, they too trying to escape stifling family holidays. We would skinny dip, sing along to ghetto blasters and snog all sorts. We did all the things our parents warned us never to do. Unbeknownst to me, back at school, my best friend was in the throes of falling pregnant. She didn't fall as much as lie down willingly.

A carefree existence can also be a careless one. I had traded the expense of driving lessons for this holiday of a lifetime long before I was even eligible to learn. It was a price I freely paid.

****

That cheesy Cheshire cat grin is rapidly induced just by saying the word 'Pussy!' out loud in the vicinity of a heterosexual man. I have no idea if this is a universal truth because I have yet to go around screaming the homonym at random men I suspect of being straight.

Cheshire's name, on the other hand, is woefully boring: the shire of the camp, a tribute to our dearly departed Roman visitors. How very literal. How very direct. Nonetheless, it was in Cheshire that I happened upon a ranking of the nation's favourite 'vagina' substitutes. The English are loathe to use perfectly clear anatomical terms even with people who have studied such matters intensely during their studies at university. Instead, on the pretext of sparing everyone's blushes, we find creative alternatives. I thought it most tragic that no one uses the euphemism *Secret Bunker.* It transpires it is one of Cheshire's most famous visitor attractions, and one that is tremendously, but incongruently, well signposted across the county.

I suspect it was no coincidence that Dr. Sameer Sanghvi of Lloyd's Pharmacy published his findings of the Englishwomen's preferred word for their nether regions on the International Women's Day of March 8th, 2022. Pussy landed at no.6. Further abreast, the ostensibly snicker-snacking 'private parts' is chosen by our Scottish cousins; a very pragmatic 'lady bits' is favoured by the Welsh, and 'Nunny' was our Northern Irish neighbours' nomination. Back in England, one can pretty much pinpoint where in the country one hails from by their proffered surrogate. If one opts for a 'foo-foo', then one likely originates from the East, although the more conservative Yorkshirewomen keep it short and simple with 'vag'. In the North East it is a 'foof', whereas in the West Midlands, it is all just 'down there'.

In the actual regions of down there, Londoners jazz it up as a 'vajayjay', although those coming from the South East opt for a bit of 'minge'. The vagina is an absolute 'Noo Noo' if one is rooted in the South West. As for Cheshire? There, residents make use of England's no. 1 genteelism: Fanny. The UK's fanny, much to the astonishment of our American counterparts, is not to be confused with what they might call a 'tush'. Tush, in British English, is an expression of contempt or disdain. If you want to see the reserved Brit expressing contempt, one must surely pop across to *Tushingham* to talk loudly of fanny packs.

Tushingham's proper name is the much more grandiloquent: *Tushingham-cum-Grindley*. It is a small village located in a southern district of Cheshire. The county's welcome sign proudly proclaims that Cheshire just so happens to be, "Home of England's Finest Gardens". This reminds me that, my favourite term: 'lady garden' sadly, does not rank amongst the top ten of euphemisms, nor does *Wigland*.

Disappointingly, there is no equivalent survey conducted by Lloyds Pharmacy, or any other for that matter, so I cannot tell you where on a list of penis alternatives *Wincle* ranks. And with that observation, I swiftly departed Cheshire, the home of England's finest euphemisms.

Culture Ranking (Cranking) in Merseyside

Life had definitely taken an upswing in my second school. No longer was I perennially hungry, dreading slops that had to be forced down. It astonishes me now that no matter one's age, there was a choice of just two sizes: ordinary or small, and decision-making was limited to how distasteful you found the sole offering.

With sport only played twice weekly for no more than an hour or two, an excess of calories probably wasn't required. Even 'tuck', the selection being between a bag of crisps, two biscuits or a roll of sweets, was limited to Saturday afternoons, following the successful completion of a run around the school grounds, or an in-house game of hockey or netball. Of course, there was always contraband, albeit the mice in the cellar fared especially well, and opened packets of biscuits were nothing but petri dishes for mould.

But at this former boys' school, I lived in a world of feasts. The canteen was a wonder of carbs and fried food, of cream horns and jellied fruit, of rice and pasta salads. The tuck shop was available seven days a week, with only finances limiting one's options. Sport or some form of physical activity was mandatory daily, but after opting for a specialism to be practised four days a week, one would then try out other activities: hockey, tennis, lacrosse, orienteering, cricket, athletics, netball, weight-lifting and gym, water polo, softball, basketball, martial arts and even climbing. I am certain there was golf too but it might have been a case of gentlemen only, ladies forbidden.

Largely it was the powers that be who decided exactly what one would be dipping one's toes into. No longer was horse riding on the menu, which would have been my only selection were it permissible. There was also compulsory cadet training in preparation for careers in the RAF, the army and the navy, as well as the Duke of Edinburgh awards. One of the girls in my year suggested we might enjoy something less physical on one of the days of the week; I recall the suggestion was similar to a book club or discussion group. Another girl proposed a more sedate art and craft focus, like crochet. Alas, they were deemed not to be beneficial to our welfare. My expertise in embroidery, learnt at the girls' school, dissolved into gnarly threads.

Notwithstanding that, the problem for some was our growing sizes. To my mind, my body had become a source for others to consume. I never seemed to stop widening in all the wrong places. "If only girls could play rugby," one of my boys had quipped at me.

There was another campaign, this one led by boys, to start a football club. The school, like many of its ilk, had contempt for England's national sport. The saying "Football is a gentleman's game played by hooligans, whereas Rugby is a hooligans' game played by gentlemen," is long held as an observation by Winston Churchill, Rugby vied with cricket to be considered as the elite sport, and tournaments took its teams far and wide, to face off against other schools of good repute. Girls, of course, could play neither – although if we wished to stand pitchside to cheer, that would be most welcomed.

Football was viewed with discernible suspicion that it was unbecoming of a public school boy. Nevertheless, in the footsteps of progress, a football team was established. Soon after fellow schools were sought out for them to compete against and it involved interacting with the local comprehensives. Another win for the boys.

I carried on swimming, it was better than practising hockey, netball and rounders badly against my peers. They were sports with no competitive leagues and no bus rides away. Then one of my seniors asked if she could earn the Royal Life Saving Society badges. She was sick of stomping around a parade square playing toy soldiers, practising for an enemy we were unlikely to face, and careers we didn't wish to pursue. To everyone's astonishment, her wish was granted. Only it meant we'd have to skip Thursday's prep to be bussed to a local amenity for specialist lessons. A whole gaggle of us willingly forewent the homework hours, pledging to make them up another time. It really wasn't a challenge to find recruits: the fun we had pretending to drown rather than swim, just bobbing around in the water waiting to be rescued. When not in the water, we'd be beating up a Resuci Annie. Never should we forget, though, that any form of play must always have serious undercurrents. Always.

****

To an American, a *Crank* is someone in a foul mood; to a Brit, it is an eccentric individual or one behaving in a manner most odd, and to a Scouser, she is a bunny boiler.

It is almost impossible to research Merseyside without getting a ton of facts and stats on Liverpool. Google searches seem to present it as being one and the same place: a sort of reductionist 'London is England' type of mentality. For the record, London is London, the rest of England is the presumed enigma. Thus, stereotyping's primary purpose is not to offend but to help make sense of things that are potentially analogous. Needless to say, I can only apologise in advance for any and all the clangers that I might drop.

The Liverpudlian accent, otherwise referred to as Scouse, was once a Norwegian Stew. It was nominated as Britain's most untrustworthy accent in 2012. By 2020 though, it had climbed up to second-worst place, losing the mantle to Birmingham. Quite what occurred to cause this shift is anyone's guess. After Scottish, Scouse is the most identifiable dialect across the United Kingdom, which is quite an accomplishment for a nation of just over 90,000 square miles containing forty-plus official manners of speaking. We seemingly have nearly one accent per county. I should, however, caveat this by saying that to a Merseysider's ear, it is easy to distinguish if one is a resident of St Helens, Widnes, Southport or the Wirral. What is a confirmed phenomena is accent bias. It can lead to unequal access to employment opportunities, housing and education. Disadvantage is exacerbated if using 'working-class' or 'ethnic' rhetoric.

I would argue that outside of London, Liverpool dominates the culture wars: *The Grand National, The Beatles, 'Our Cilla'* ("the most despised national treasure," so say British Airways Cabin Crew).

Liverpool also boasts the highest number of museums outside London with over 2,400 listed buildings, according to the Liverpool Echo.

Most of Liverpool's iconic buildings were largely constructed and financed during its maritime 'heyday'. The Mersey estuary was once the site of 80% of Britain's slave-based economic activity, which of itself comprised 40% of the world's economy. The mass exploitation of primarily African nationals drove an employment boom within the shipping industry, and at the time established Liverpool as Britain's second-most important city. Consequently, Liverpool boasts the oldest and longest settled black community within the UK. Combined with the influx of Welsh and Irish communities seeking work in the docks, their presence ostensibly altered the local dialect, giving Merseyside its distinctive voice.

The 1970s and 1980s saw global economic restructuring, with Liverpool becoming a macrocosm typifying England's woes: extortionate levels of unemployment, urban decay, increasing social unrest, escalating crime rates, growing distrust of authorities and abject racism. None in Merseyside suffered more than the informally segregated black inhabitants of Toxteth. The Toxteth riots of 1981, kicking off national condemnation, were triggered by the police pulling over a black motorist for, "loitering with intent to commit an arrestable offence". To my innocent ears, this sounds awfully quite like being arrested for thinking, pondering or daydreaming. Nearby, sensing unfair treatment, his best friend remonstrated with police, and that too saw him carted off. It led to a six-week long uprising and resulted in the death of one man who was run over by a police Range Rover; eight hundred injured policemen; five-hundred and forty-two arrests; and the destruction of seventy buildings.

Margaret Simey, Merseyside's County Councillor as well as Chairman of the Police Authority for the region, remarked of the confrontation, "They would be apathetic fools…if they didn't protest." From then onwards, she was parodied as Liverpool's greatest crank by the national media of all echelons.

It took a Tory, Michael Heseltine, then the Environment Secretary, to campaign vociferously for Liverpool's rejuvenation and resurrection. He had the ear of Britain's first woman Prime Minister and much maligned crank, Margaret Thatcher. In the other ear was her Chancellor, Sir Geoffrey Howe, who implored her not to commit scarce resources to futile causes. Instead he suggested the manufacturing regions, known for their ardent Labour voters, be managed through to decline. He cited Merseyside as being, "the hardest nut to crack," firm in his belief that the capital should give up on it.

Thatcher sided with Heseltine. The media were brought in to assist in restyling Merseyside. Its inhabitants were rebranded as the nation's most natural comedians, complete with an easy-going charm, quick wit, with true depth and breadth of culture. The enduring legacy for locals has been their lampooning by Harry Enfield in *The Scousers*. If one really wants to offend someone from Merseyside chant, 'Calm Down' to them: twice, and in quick succession. After all, the television series was only cancelled thirty years ago!

I left Merseyside with just one burning question. I enquired of Google if I could buy 'The Sun', Britain's premier paper-based newspaper, in Merseyside. From the Liverpool Echo, I discovered that Sainsbury's in Liverpool stocked it under the counter if one asked, I presumed, nicely. The campaign to rid all of Merseyside of The Sun began on the 19th April, 1989 and it remains as vehement as ever. Following the overfilling and subsequent crushing of the penned-in football supporters at a match in Hillsborough, The Sun's editors published the headline, "The Truth". It informed a nation in mourning that Liverpool fans were overwhelmingly responsible for the tragedy. What should have otherwise been a typical premiership football game saw seven women and girls, along with ninety men and boys, perish unnecessarily thanks to poor policing. Twenty-three years later, the former editor of The Sun, Kelvin MacKenzie, admitted that the headline should have been, "The Lies".

Margaret Aspinall, a figurehead for the families' fight for justice, was forced to accept £1,200 pounds as compensation for the death of her eighteen-year-old son. Along with the other relatives of the victims, she used it to pay the fees necessary to hold the first inquest. The Goliaths they were up against were the institutions under investigation: the Police, the Ambulance Service and Liverpool's own County Council. Only these organisations could avail themselves of lawyers funded by the tax-payers' purse. Three inquiries came and went, as well as a third of a century, before the Liverpudlian fans were exonerated. Comprehensively exonerated. The deceased were, to quote the justice system, "unlawfully killed".

Speaking to the Liverpool Echo after the 2016 tribunal, Mrs Aspinall was forthright: *"Let's be honest about this – people were against us. We had the media against us, as well as the establishment. Everything was against us. The only people that weren't against us was our own city. That's why I am so grateful to my city and so proud of my city. They always believed in us."*

The one thing I know as a fact is that Merseyside has just one rude-sounding place: *Crank.* It casts no aspirations on its inhabitants: the only way to leave the region was with admiration for their collective and enduring tenacity in the face of systemic oppression.

The Omnishambles Surrounding Lancashire

Two years older than me, he passed his driving test at the first attempt, although he was yet to finish his school. We rarely stayed at the villa together. Either he or I preferred to spend our time exploring the beauty that is Southern Africa, sometimes together, mostly apart. Sometimes on horseback, sometimes on dreadful family holidays. On this occasion, we had a fortnight together and no planned adventures: the punishment for a disastrously chaotic week in Cape Town on a previous visit. Our teenaged reticence to leave our beds provoked our parents into flouncing off, locking us in our hotel room with nothing to do until their return late that night. The rest of the holidays crawled by at an excruciatingly slow pace. Us versus them. Upon the termination of the vacation, our father once again retreated to work and mother maintained her relationship with wine.

Trapped at the house we lived in, and dependent on parents to ferry us to and from friends, in a place where it was not especially safe to use the local Kombis (the bus transport), my brother was keen to take the family car out for some post-passing practice, a milestone towards fully-fledged adulthood. My father was equally as averse to relinquishing his use of the family car, even though he typically walked to work. The male adult in the family had needed the car for four petulant days. It never usually left the garage and was kept spic and span by the gardener, except for shopping trips or other outings. Finally he caved, much to everyone's astonishment.

The road to Bloemfontein was, for the most part, straight, with just one long hard shoulder. It was a familiar journey as 'Bloem' was the nearest large city for good groceries. In South Africa, they drive the English way; on what 65% of the world might call the 'wrong' side of the road. Cars pulled into the hard shoulder, even if it was gravel, to let faster cars speed past unhindered, rather than forcing an overtake by crossing to the oncoming side. At least, that was the theory, but the minibuses, jam-packed with commuters, would pull over and stop wherever and whenever they felt like it, so some trips were more precarious than others.

There were other advantages and anomalies too. Fuel prices were set nationally, changing on a monthly basis, and were quite affordable. One always informed the attendant how much one wished to spend on fuel, never leaving the comfort of one's car and the transaction was conducted in cash via the window. The attendant wiped down the windscreen, hoping to earn a tip for their diligence. Parking always came with a pestering child or ten, offering to guard a car as well as wash it, in return for a few coins. Other tiny children badgered to carry bags from the store to the car, huffing and puffing under their weight. I hated that most, the debate on whether to encourage them in their child labour, or to refuse, knowing full well it meant less food on the table. Our lives couldn't have been more stark.

There were robots too. Traffic lights to the rest of the world, although it was always made clear: never stop at a red light come dusk. The night was the cloak under which carjackers made their earnings, defying the laws that had them curfewed in their townships. But daylight brings new rules and we were pulled over by the police for failing to stop at a "stop" sign during daylight hours. Apparently, one could crawl past it at a snail's pace in England as long as one was cautious and clear-sighted. "In South Africa, when the sign says 'stop', you STOP!" the officer asserted in no uncertain terms. We were let off on account of us being white, young and foreign, although I suspect the complication of paperwork was a matter of assistance too.

On return, my brother had forgotten to obtain fuel, causing all sorts of outrage. "I can't wait for you to turn seventeen," my father barked as soon as my brother had swept off to his room, "Once you can drive, I will never let him use the car again." Not wishing to be a pawn in his feud with his own son, I silently swore never to oblige him. Morals are difficult things to contend with.

****

If one ever desires a visit to the hamlet of *Cockerham* and one does not reside within the confines of Lancashire, one will undoubtedly journey along a part of England's longest motorway. With typical English logic, England's first motorway was called the M6. M to denote "Motorway", and "6" to account for the five motorways that did not exist. Construction took two years, plus the unheard of phenomena of 'project overshoot'. This one exceeded its deadline by five additional months.

If England is ever to be accurately accused of deluded optimism, it is in her ability to deliver any feat of engineering on time and on budget. Although, I can attest that this country is not remotely unique for floundering on project delivery. Seemingly within days of commissioning, reports headed '*Cantsfield*' land on the desks of those paid handsomely to deliver Britain's large-scale construction pursuits. It is almost as if those who deliver projects live in an entirely different nation than those who conceive of it; and the two only meet for a brief period while on holiday having over-indulged in the free bar.

What is just as perplexing is the unique cultural phenomenon that is the Englishperson's propensity for saying 'sorry' for the most trivial of reasons: such as the weather. Yet, it is seemingly unheard of for any institution to say that very word when it is authentically appropriate. In true English spirit, the delayed completion of the M6 was not attributed to any particular brand of human incompetence; instead the overseers blamed the delay on the predictably unpredictable English weather. In this instance, it was of the type typically found in the rain-infused Pennine region.

The first photograph of a motorway took place not on a bedazzling summers' day, as had been hoped for exceedingly bullishly, but rather in a grim and grizzly December in 1958 near Preston. Given almost all photography was of the fuzzy black and white variety, it is safe to say nobody noticed and almost all present will probably have forgotten by now.

The original M6 was a glorious eight and a half miles long. Within minutes of its opening, it became the ignominious host to the first motorway bottleneck as a log-jam of journalists, town planners and celebrants tailed the motorway's first journeyman: Labour's British Prime Minister, Harold MacMillan. Within six weeks, it was closed down because of weather-induced road damage of the *Much Hoole* variety.

It was while I was heading towards the aforementioned *Much Hoole,* full of blissful appreciation of the free-flowing aspects of the civilised M6, that I too fell victim to a project-threatening misfortune of the expensive kind. Labouring away at a steady sixty miles per hour on the inner lane, I was startled by an hitherto unheard siren emitting from the Citroën's dashboard. I had not realised the van was so sophisticated that it would make noises to accompany the red oil light that had flashed up abruptly. It signalled something to the effect of, "stop – terminal engine failure!" Relieved it happened right before an exit road peeled off towards some services, I rang my usual repair shop for advice. "Shit! That's bad!" was not the kind of the optimism I was hoping for. Then my recovery services informed me it would require three separate tow trucks to take us back to that ultimate oxymoron: a trustworthy garage. A very good friend was, at the time, its delightful owner.

The exhausting overnight journey back to glorious Cotswolds was delayed further by one of the recovery vehicles breaking down in sympathy, leaving the pair of us to spend several hours twiddling digits waiting for two additional trucks to arrive: one for his vehicle and a second for mine.

Thankfully, The Shitron was saved to survive another rainy day so back up the M6 we trundled, one budget-busting bill later. If there is anything I have learnt from this journey, it is that I did not factor in things going amiss, mechanically speaking. I still joke that my very good friend was able to escape the wintry gloom on my account. But all is fair in love and business, and between my mistakes and the van's age, we certainly kept her mechanics in paid work.

The M6 was the initial poster child of British road transport, so it is a wonder another fifty motorways have since been built: nine in Scotland and forty-one in England. Wales and Ireland have sensibly not bothered. England's highways engineers have proceeded to create smart motorways – supposedly designed to hurry the driver along and ease congestion. Alas, they have proved to be expensive to run and far more risky for drivers. Not so jeffing smart then.

Fascinatingly, or not as the case may prove to be, the M6 takes a person, should one wish, from the West Midlands all the way up to the Scottish border. One even has a choice of going the 'long way round' on the M6, or paying an additional surcharge over and above road tax to save twenty-five minutes by taking the M6 Toll. This appears to be a very attractive feature for motorists: generating a whopping £55 million in revenue per annum. Unfortunately this averages around £25 million less than is required to break even. The good news, however, is that England does not actually own this particular road - the M6 (Toll) is Australian property.

On arrival at Scotland, the M6 morphs into the M74, despite it not being disrupted by so much as a roundabout. Alternatively, one can opt to take the M1, whose route is just east of the middle. It starts at the outskirts of North London and terminates at Leeds, where it simply becomes the Byzantine A1(M). Once again, I suggest that two Brits met in a bar…

Logically, one would expect the motorways to be numerical: starting with M1, proceeding to M2 and all the way up to M50. However, this would be too sensible. Instead they are named after a nearby A-road. Hence, there is no M7, because the A7 has never been replaced by a motorway. That is the first clue as to how our convoluted motorway numbering system came to be so peculiar. It also explains why London, which would normally claim all and every prestige, is not circumnavigated by the M1, but by the M25. What it does do, however, is beg the question as to where does all this tarmacked numerical omnishambles come from. History is obviously the first place to take a gander.

Once upon a time, a very proper task force was set up in 1923 to classify Britain's roads. They divided them into an unimaginative: Class I and Class II. Class I were major trunk roads connecting our towns and cities to one another. Class II did not. To add some spice to the classification system, they named Class I roads "A" and Class II roads "B". Having selected a letter, they then allocated between one and four digits. The fewer the numbers, the more significant the road. Thus, the A1, connecting London to Edinburgh, was deemed the road of greatest importance. The Welsh were given the A4 just to keep things spicy.

The major roads also demarcated a zoning system, carving England into six zones, conventionally naming said zones from one to six; Scotland into three (zones seven, eight and nine). Somehow, they omitted to section Wales at all, instead allocating a fraction of North Wales to Zone 5, and the remainder to Zone 4.

Shortly after, the cartographers of British roadmaps deemed this quite a useful concept and added in the numerical references in order to assiduously assist the road user in taking shortcuts: the ultimate euphemism for 'getting lost'. Even more pitifully, the classifications went on to spawn that most mundane of conversation openers, "Which route did you come by?" This is usually the cue that the question-asker is about to launch into how one came the wrong way and one should have saved minutes or money going an alternative route. They will then bedazzle the listener with their knowledge of British road systems and road numbers, whilst one stands there vacantly nodding abjectly to this wannabe *Whalley* of Top Gear.

Nonetheless, the task force's endeavours created clusters of road networks each starting with the same digit. Except, this did not always pan out either. Take Lancashire as an example, a place where one could, if one wished, drive along the A666 from *Whalley* all the way to the M6. Alternatively, one might prefer the slightly faster A59, which, confoundingly, is actually entirely in Zone 6. Elsewhere, even more anomalies can be found such as the A303 in the South West being a far more populated route than the A30. It certainly does not aid one whatsoever in fathoming why there are two A594s – one in Cumbria (Zone 5), the other in Leicestershire (Zone 6). Then there is the A66, which starts in Middlesbrough on the East Coast (Zone 1) and terminates upon meeting the A1. Of course, there is that other A66 which joins the A1 further south, and terminates at Penrith (Zone 5). One might have presumed the A66 was one continuous road with not a single driver noticing the great sodding great motorway, with its distinctive blue signage, in the middle. Applying logic to our road networks simply serves to be a *Staining* on English civil engineering pragmatism.

One might reasonably assume that all those little piddly B roads are the teeny tiny country lanes, often narrow enough to require passing places to be gauged out of the hedgerow. The sort of country tracks which typically get your otherwise serene white van driver swearing like a *Docker* as she meets something unexpected on-coming. Something like a very large passenger bus stuffed full of eyes glaring at her delaying their journeys home. The encounter forced me to slowly reverse backwards for several miles along with everything else that had previously been shuffling behind. Most memorable was the incident that saw me inflict some damage to my right rear lighting panel: one of my rear lights ended up with a sodding great big hole in it, forcing yet another trip to a garage.

The transport system was once considered flawless, and much celebrated by those in the know. And it truly was worth celebrating, right up until Britain's actual drivers came along and utilised their steering wheels. The road to *Weeton* is a great example of this. According to the UK road planning classification system, there are no C roads, just M, A and B. Bear in mind that it took a Road Traffic Act to be passed through parliament just to add the M, I was astonished to discover there were the planned works on the C270 between Wesham and *Weeton*. I rest my case on the omnishambles that is the English vanlife driving experience.

And what has any of this got to do with Lancashire? Not much, except Lancashire was home to Britain's first female Transport Minister, Barbara Castle (nee Betts). In 1966, she declared war on reckless driving. During that time, there were approximately 7.7 million cars registered on British roads, which were responsible for 7,500 fatalities per year.

She was widely rounded on by politicians and journalists alike for being a killjoy, and even once publicly rebuked by a BBC journalist who derided her policy as rotten and misguided. The policy was for the introduction of the breathalyser. Denounced for being a woman who did not drive, it was posited that pedestrians and passengers should not have an opinion on road matters. The number of deaths dropped 16% within twelve months. She also permanently ratified the 70mph speed limit on motorways, cutting deaths by 20%, then made it mandatory for cars to be fitted with seatbelts. Wearing them, however, remained optional until January 1983.

The Right Honourable Mrs Castle had her seat in The Cabinet removed by the replacement leader of the Labour Party, James Callahan, on the pretext that she was too old. She was only eighteen months older than her boss. Barbara Castle's contribution as Transport Minister remains significant and far-reaching. Currently, there are 1,500 fatalities per annum from nearly 33 million registered cars on the road – a reduction of eighty percent, despite four times the number of road users. That is all down to reduced speed limits, strong drink-driving deterrents and seatbelts, as well as motorways becoming the safest roads for travelling across the country.

Cumbria is in the Eye of the Beholder

The grassy sweet-smelling rugged steppes are what I remember most fondly. Miles of valleys, gentle rolling mountains, kept apart by rough pastures, themselves cracked with icy-cold rivulets. The clanging of sheeps' bells occasionally chimed through gentle winds, and the rhythmic drum of horse hooves arrested the silence. Briefly, here and there, we'd holler "Dumela" and "Le Kae" back at a herdboy, whose life I presumed to be either most tedious, or most philosophical. I suspected we were their only interruption in days identical except for their weather systems. "What does one dream of when one's life is so unadorned with materialism and consumerism?" I pondered as we plodded along atop our Basotho ponies for a week-long trek across the tiny country. My horse, like that of my fellows, was stocky, sure-footed and almost slumberous. The little bay was to carry me, and my saddle bags crammed with teenaged desirables: Walkman, tapes, spare batteries, a week's supply of cigarettes, changes of clothes (almost all unworn) and no sun cream. A regrettable oversight: my neck bubbled up with fat blisters.

We were three teenagers: two girls, one boy, alone in the wilderness except for our guide, a reassuring but commanding horseman. He implored us to not push our horses hard, for the days were long, and the horses unaccustomed to anything pacey. It was a wonderful world away from the constricting routines of boarding school intertwined with the repression of a family system gone awry. This was my initiation into a life filled with yearning for constant adventure; to salve my troubled mind.

Each night was spent in the luxury of an immaculate sleeping bag on a frizzled mat placed upon the ground of the mokhoro: a rondavel, for those more accustomed to the South African word. These circular stone houses, rarely with any form of heating or lighting, were little more than enclosed shelters. Rickety wooden doors kept the worst of the night's freezing temperatures at bay. This is how the Basotho lived outside of the capital, and in a way of life largely unchanged for millenia. It was harsh and simple and yet in other ways, so enviable.

Each evening, our string of tiring horses would stagger into the villages, small huddles of a few mokhoros. A gaggle of children would rush to greet us, trying to grab our hands to hold, helping to unload and unsaddle our weary beasts and taking them to graze elsewhere. The commotion would be shushed away by an ageing woman who would make a smattering of conversation via our horseman. Typically, within moments of our arrival, we'd be ushered off to greet the VIP: the ventilated improved pit latrine. Only the more salubrious hamlets offered a VIP. Usually, they were a one-person small wooden shack, with much gappage, and a precariously-placed plank of wood upon which one would rest one's rear, as one's hands gripped its fragile walls for safety's sake. They were the pride of every village: a symbol of their accomplished aspirations.

"VIP a hokae?" I asked the woman swathed in a blue Sotho blanket, brushing away at bare ground. It was our fifth night out in the remote mountain kingdom.

"Hohle, hohle, hohle!" she gestured with her hands as a broad smile flashed across her face.

"Everywhere," our guide laughed as he translated her words. Grabbing our plush toilet paper, we ventured off to find a discreet spot, far below the mound that the village squatted on. A site, hopefully, far from the prying eyes of its residents. Having marched a respectable

distance, we dispersed ourselves suitably apart from one another. Only once I was done did I observe the gathering of herdboys studying our every move on the adjacent hill. They bellowed a collective "La kae?" (How are you?) as I stood up to retrieve my trousers.

Even if my teenage mortification was not at its worst, I certainly did not have either the Sesotho, nor a guide, to quip back, "About half a pound lighter than five minutes ago, thanks!"

****

If Scotland and Wales came together to make a baby, Cumbria would be the gushing result. The county idles, rather than wanders, lonely as a cloud in the uppermost eastern corner: a melange of shallow meres, bracing tarns and deep verdant vales hidden amidst rugged mountains, interspersed with squares of tamed wilderness in the shape of camping sites.

I had arrived in Cumbria somewhere between post-winter and pre-spring. Further south, in the rest of England, the decaying remains of previously fluttering daffodils had toppled, and frolicking lambs were careening round pastures green readying their limbs for the dinner plate. Whereas, atop Cumbria's hillsides, smiley-faced sheep, many with the famous blueish fleece, still bore the livid orange and pink staining: the hallmarks of the rams' rogering. They waddled, fat and round, nuzzling at frosted lowlands or tiptoeing along faint paths cutting through the snow-speckled ranges. My criss-crossing along well-managed single-track, stone-walled narrow lanes, up yonder and down dale, had me and the cat hollering our hellos to striking white-banded black Galloway cattle. They blinked slowly back at us while standing resolute on the roads, gently snorting out wisps of misty clouds, knowing full well that I was the interloper and they were in charge. The pathetically bleating of the Citroën's horn did little to dissuade them from their road-hogging contemplations, and their delinquent propensity for standing inert beyond gentle bends in the road certainly kept us on the *Beckfoot*.

The bare murmuring of the words 'lake' and 'district' can rapidly induce in England's womenfolk, as well as its Romantic poets, a collective sigh of wished-for contentment. England's largest area of outstanding natural beauty, smothering one-third of the county, is indisputably heart-breaking, eye-watering and jaw-dropping; the landscape artists' utopia.

Despite what might be inferred from local signs, it smells divinely of geosmin for much of the year. It was just unfortunate timing, of course, that the farmers were out doing what farmers do with second-hand manure. "How was your trip to Cumbria?" my nearest and dearest were inclined to ask.

"It not half *Stank*!" was my retort.

Outside of muck-spreading season, its sheer cinematographic marvellousness is what makes the county the ultimate destination for retreat and rejuvenation. At least, that is the enticement supplied by its Tourist Board, whose role it is to beckon visitors to its resplendency as soon as England's summer months hint at introducing themselves.

What is perhaps less idyllic is the single cloud under which Cumbria lies replete. It casts a vast shadow across the region, creating a lexicon for precipitation that is not typically heard elsewhere in the country. Cumbria is sprinkled by seventy-two inches of relief rainfall per annum, whereas the rest of England makes do with just thirty-nine. A fusion between Ireland, the Atlantic, the Irish sea and the wizardry of meteorology gives the region twelve unique seasons, rather than the usual four.

The Cumbrian seasonal year commences with Spring, followed by Syling Spring. Then comes Winter Resumption; Fool's Spring; Winter Reditus; Spring's-Stotting-Non-Stop; Summer Hossings; By Jove! A Summer's Day, which is abruptly demarcated at the arrival of Mizzling Autumn, swiftly followed by Hoying-Down-October. That one is kicked out by Winter Presumptuous and closed down by Winter Proper. It is for these reasons of seasons that Cumbria is predominantly ignored for nine months of the calendar year by the general populace. However, as soon as the first English heatwave bounces in, the nation is hit with a slew of advertising campaigns encouraging one to decimate the tranquillity that is Wordsworth's county.

Via a quickie marriage between hill-ascending winding lanes and caravans, sixteen million visitors are sucked in per year, and very much at risk of never getting out again if their sat nav packs up, or diverts them down a lane best used by a horse and cart. All come intent on seeking out the promise of rural idyll deep within the region, but few enjoy the rare day that the sun casts a shine on Cumbria's unique and numerous visitor attractions, such as the glorious towns of *Cockermouth* and *Slackhead,* or the heady heights of Scafell Pike.

Scafell Pike is England's highest mountain, peaking at 3,209ft, or just shy of a kilometre for those better at comprehending logical maths. There is no universal definition of a mountain: England has subjectively classified its lumps to include all hulking great land masses greater than 1,000 feet, or 300 metres. On the other hand, the Americans require their upwardly smashed formations to be at least twice that. Thus, to those over the pond, Scafell Pike is nothing but a mere hillock, at best a gentle mound. Nonetheless, climbing it is a heart-bursting endeavour undertaken by over a quarter of a million hikers per annum. Presumably, during prolonged periods of wetness and muddiness, one descends on one's *Beck Side,* particularly if one is Southern African or Australian in origin.

Best known, of course, is that Cumbria is host to The Lake District – a region of outstanding national balderdash: the beauty spot only boasts one lake. Apparently, all the rest are eye-watering mimics, and are better denoted as meres, tarns, reservoirs and waters for reasons of depth, temperature and other combinations necessitating a geography degree. It is best to simply accept they are called lakes for those who are, like myself, lacking in relevant scientific credentials. This would include that most unappealing of oversized puddles: *Cocklake*, which is in fact a hamlet.

Least likely to be mentioned in Cumbria's tourist brochure is Sellafield, the world's first commercial nuclear power station. Once upon a commercial time, nuclear energy was thought to be so cheap to manufacture that it would be deemed 'unmeterable' by English householders. Britain's leaders were as keen as mustard to have the nation's power needs met, long before the era of rampant technological advancements made us the spawns of Gadgetman.

It turns out that Sellafield currently ranks as one of the most complex and hazardous facilities in the world. It will cost the taxpayer up to £260 billion to decommission at current estimations. Notwithstanding that, it will take one hundred thousand years for the radioactive material to deplete. Most astonishing of all: the engineering has yet to be devised to safely dismantle all its component parts. With the benefit of hindsight, and a lack of scientific insight, one does wonder whether it was the most sensible of ideas to build a concrete nuclear monstrosity adjacent to the salt-corroding seaside air - even if at the time of conception, it was out of reach of German bombers. No doubt one will *Unthank* me later for putting that worry into one's head on top of the other climate concerns that abound in the news media.

How, one might ask, did it even come into being? *How* is actually an Old Norse word meaning mound, so if in doubt, we can at least in this instance blame the foreigners. As for Sellafield, I can offer no great wisdom on where to spread the blame. If it does go up England will be nothing but one large burial mound. On the bright side, this newly-developed oversized cemetery will be a bounty for future expeditioners to explore.

If that thought was not depressing enough, in the event of a nuclear war instigated by foreign foes, or a catastrophic episode of 'friendly fire', the tik-tokkers of the future: the clip-cloppers, filter-faced-notepadders, you-screeners and whatnot, might sell the virtues of Cumbria as being the only English county viable for escaping nuclear fallout. I have no doubt they will bring gravitas to their assertions by citing the cartographical evidence supplied by the now defunct Estate Agent Emoov – indicating the fallout zones from a strike on any of our major cities. Assuming the wind always blows east, Cumbria would be unaffected.

Bizarrely, in Emoov's keenness to sell Cumbrian real estate: their agents had presumed that the necessary provisions and resources would remain available to continue decommissioning Cumbria's most dangerous beachside commercial property. I thought it a peculiar oversight to not factor in the anticipated liquidation of the rest of England's taxpayers. One can only infer that the members of Britain's seventh-least trusted profession had not done their research all that thoroughly. Nonetheless, in the event of any nuclear strikes on England's main cities, *Crooklands* struck me as a particularly pleasant place to relocate to as did *Killington*.

Despite being England's second largest county, fewer than one percent of Britons rightfully call Cumbria home. By rightfully, I mean they are council-tax paying members of the community, rather than the consequence of a misfiring sat nav stranding a van with kitchenette-cum-bathroom-cum-bedroom far up yonder. Perhaps this steadfastness explains why Cumbria's placenames are the least affected by the many invasions from the Romans, Anglos, Saxons, Normans, Danes and pretty much anyone else who endeavoured to annex these fine lands.

The *cum* in Cumbria is likely a remnant of the old Brythonic word for compatriot or kin, meaning countryman, just as the Welsh word for Wales is Cymru *(Kum-ree)*. 'Wales', incidentally, is an old Germanic word, oddly meaning foreigner. The Cums that once spread far and wide across these now united lands, pre-Roman times, are more commonly referred to as The Celts. Some say it with a soft C, most with a hard K. *Whassett?* The C or the K is a fashionable thing! It is subject to change at a moment's notice, but do get it wrong at one's own peril because one is only ever six clicks away from a pedant. Nonetheless, 'Celt' is a word which simply never existed. Nowadays, historians use it to describe the diaspora of tribes who once wandered in from both northern and southern climes in the very dim and distant past. What is slightly less vague is that our European cousins dubbed the occupants of these green fields the 'Pretani', meaning the Island of the Painted People. Perhaps this also explains *Stainton*.

No matter what titles our ancestors may have used, the Romans rebranded our little island 'Albion', meaning white land. Such a title leaves one to presume that they likened Great Britain to an oversized chalk pencil. I sort of wish it had stuck: "Great Albion!" sounds like an exclamation of surprise, wonder or disbelief that could potentially outrank the barely-ever uttered "Great Scot!".

Albion fell out of favour as a result of the Romans tendency to personify their colonies as Goddesses. The Goddess of Britannia was depicted as a helmet-headed, trident-wielding, single-boob-exposing woman with a fierce, yet submissive, character. Her image, forever cast into coinage, welcomed the Roman Emperor with, "Veni Expectate", or more the more everyday: "Come, O expected one." I think we have all politely demanded that once or twice although perhaps not as eloquently.

Once the Romans departed, the name 'Britannia' remained all the rage right up until it was discarded. Some suggest the island briefly morphed into Bretwalda or Brytenwealda during early Anglo-Saxon times. However, upon England being unified, her maiden name was all but eradicated. Then dropped the English Renaissance in the 16th and 17th centuries but too few royal sons. Subsequently, buxom-sporting queens joined English and Scottish royalty together in holy matrimony, albeit now with both boobs firmly packed away. By the eighteenth century, the name 'Brittania' had been resurrected as her nom de rigueur to gird the loins of patriotism, to meld us as an island. 'Rule, Britannia!' soon topped the charts for jingoistic chanting. It began as a ditty, until the composer got carried away. Then it exhorted our seafarers to conquer and colonise the wider world and protect our kelly lands from foreign invaders, promising we will never be enslaved.

I finished my Cumbrian days beside the murky-brown seaside contemplating times past after a jaunt into *Nethertown*. Cumbria's waters are still and shallow, a giant cove shielded by Ireland and Scotland, who take the brunt of the buffeting Irish Sea on our behalf. These seas I have intimate knowledge of as I once attempted to jet-ski around the UK at a time when no woman had succeeded in doing so. I have absolutely no recollection of how I came up with this grand plan but suffice to say it involved a colossal amount of Bacardi with a dash of Diet Coke. The following morning we discovered we were the proud owners of two three-seater jet-skis. Shortly after, I learnt only three men had successfully accomplished the task: two royal marines and the pee-drinking, scout-leading, former SAS reservist, Bear Grylls. Just for context, I am not, nor have been, suitable for military service as I am overwhelmingly allergic to hardcore exercise. Moreover, I had never once ridden a jet-ski, not even pillion.

"But how will I pee?" was a much contemplated question. It is remarkable just how many people: bosses, friends and countrywomen have asked me over the years how one combines jet-skiing with the craft of outdoor urination. 'Shewees' were not the solution for me despite a thorough try. Many assume we wore wetsuits, but pragmatically, they are too cold for prolonged exposure in the northern waters.

I had, in a rare moment of great wisdom, sufficient forethought to ask for a specialist drysuit to be tailored. Thick rubber cuffs and collars would have me hermetically sealed, preventing any watery discomfort except to our faces. The hefty piece of baggy neoprene permitted many internal layers of underclothing and had the added benefit of trapping in body heat to ward off the blasting north winds and stone cold sea water. The outfit was so roomy I looked like a deflated hot air balloon. If I accidentally tipped myself into the water, I looked very much like an inflated hot air balloon.

I had asked that they situate a large waterproof zip so it dragged deep into the space between my legs. A tug on the cord would open up the region, allowing a quick side-swipe of one's undergarment. Then with some contortionism, I could tug the zipper back in place, sealing me until I could return to the land of dry and flushing toilets. In my mind's eye, my design was flawless: keeping it all discreet, and yet permitting gravity to do its thing. I could deflate the inner balloon whenever sea conditions were sufficiently calm to safely idle the jet-ski and maintain balance.

Imagine my despair when just days before I was due to set off, I unpacked my drysuit to see that the zip was, in fact, better positioned for a man's, shall we say, erogenous zone. Furious, I rang the tailor in an attempt to explain that without the prerequisite manhose this design was as good as useless. I was even explicit regarding the engineering differences between men and women. Alas, it was too late to change anything, and the man on the other end of the phone assured me his design, identical to the significantly cheaper off-the-shelf suit purchased by my husband, was far superior and suitable for my needs. Mansplaining at its finest.

There is just one thing one might be ignorant of regarding jet-skis: when the engine idles, the contraption slowly but gracefully pirouettes, ultimately giving the rider several 360° views of one's land and seascape. Thankfully, back in those days, I had quite the robust pelvic floor: that enviable trait that permits young women to stop and start the flow at whim. Not noticing the three Cumbrian fisherman minding their rods, crouched on the nearby cliffs, I demonstrated, whilst wearing a drysuit suitable only for men, how one pees using a plastic cup purloined from McDonalds. They were decent enough to give me a round of applause when I had finished.

I left the vicinity destined never to become the world's first female circumnavigator of English waters on a jet-ski, albeit I gave it a very good go. Moreover, I will not be the first woman vanlifer to visit all of England's counties bar London. Quite simply because two days after I left Cumbria, the government dismantled it and created two new counties: Cumberland and Westmorland & Furness. The move was opposed by the Cumbria County Council. I can only hazard a guess that two bureaucrats in a bar have been hammering the Bacardi again.

No One Goes to Northumbria Anymore...

We resided at the far end of what might be fancifully called a cul-de-sac. In reality it was nothing short of a dirt track, a dusty little street of deep potholes, set well back from the main drag carrying heavy-ladened trucks and overfilled kombis to and from the border. Behind us, the Mohokare river, a stream of never-ending brown sludge, kept the two countries divided. Ours a kingdom, the other a republic, both transfixed with their own inner turmoils.

Surrounded by a chain-link fence, several metres high, with three gnarly rows of barbed wire, the villa kept the world at bay with a rusty warning sign informing only the literate that guards operated onsite, a claim that wasn't true.

By day, our street could be a pleasant place with few disturbances beyond the occasional horse-riders clip-clopping along or some other odd innocent going about their business, igniting our dog, a Rhodesian Ridgeback with squiffy eyes, into a feverish frenzy. Rare was the car that drove by. If the gate were opened, the dog would lunge at the attendee and persistently try to lick them in the nether regions. No one was spared the humiliation: guest, staff or resident.

Beyond two bored sojourning teenagers, the other presences were the gardner-cum-groom and a housemaid, Esther, who was in fact the same age as our mother. Perhaps she dreaded our return in case it upset her domestic routines, but she never let it show. I often caught her chatting back at the cat, who pestered her for extra treats. I loved her for giving him attention. She had six children, having brought them up single-handedly, and who sometimes helped her out – the girls in training for domestic service, the boys for company.

They were our defences when the sun splayed across the capital, and it was they who reminded us to never open the gates alone. In these days of low technology, we only had eyes, ears and fears to protect us. It was a typical ploy for gangs to turn up on the pretext of being called by the landlord to fix something, to somehow charm their way in, only they would pull a gun the minute the padlocks were released. In an instant, they would have the staff taken hostage and frogmarched to the main building. Their safe release could only be assured after the property had been ransacked.

By the creaking, flimsy metal gates, sat a guard's kiosk. During the day, it served as our smoking haven. Behind it was the 'servants' quarters; in effect two simple rooms with a shared outdoor cooking area, adjacent to the garage. We had already fired one gardner for bringing prostitutes back, earning himself a little extra by renting his room out for a fee. Once he had double-booked himself, creatively evicting the placid Esther from her room, and that was how the truth outed. His replacement, Samuel, was a former shepherd, a young man both taciturn and radiating an enviable calmness, who was raising a two-year-old son. He much preferred the caretaking of our horse, taking it for long daily treks, rather than attending to the gardening. In fact, the few crops he did manage to cultivate, were only offered to us if the horse had rejected them. The lawn never needed mowing, simply because the horse was diligently guided around the place, tearing away at any sizable tufts. The two had a better bond than I was ever able to muster up. Too many farewells does that to a person.

At night, at fifteen minute intervals, one could hear an unarmed guard marching around the boundary, a third hand on a clock. He would sometimes stop to greet the amiable, but neurotic, former racehorse stabled in the backyard with his battalion of flies for company. Sometimes, one might hear him shuffle off to see what had provoked the dog into the midnight kerfuffles, carrying only a small truncheon with which to defend himself and us. Every fifteen minutes, religiously, he turned a key on one of five mechanisms hung around the property, leaving a little stamp to prove he was alert throughout the night or be fired. In the summer months, he might close my bedroom window as I lay awake listening to distant gunfire: a rush of abrupt popping. Seldom was the darkness not shattered by it. All the windows had bars running lengthways, rather than mesh. I left mine wide enough for the cat to come and go. Next door had purchased six chickens, and so far we had found four of them underneath my bed, quite dead come morning. Our neighbour, an American man inclined to fury, was quite perplexed as to how his chickens were vanishing. He could oft be heard hollering the blame at his dog.

****

"Where are you off to next?" my friend had enquired of me.

"Northumbria!" I replied excitedly. I knew precisely no one that far north so I deemed it daring to be so remote and exposed, a true exploration of the nation's hinterland. On the Park4Night app, I had spied a little hilltop parking spot and anticipated it would boast clear panoramic views of mellowing fields as its trees were bare of leaves. England's northern climes were still idling their way through the barren wintering months. I wished to soak up the weak sunlight and glorious frosted mornings, drinking in its contemplative isolation with just the cat and a hot chocolate for company.

Two days prior, I was bemoaning to an attending gathering of strangers how my electrics had packed up again, this time drawing down no energy from the running of my engine. I was perilously close to having no heating or lighting. This is the hardest part of being solo: no one to turn to when one is out of inspiration and ideas. One cannot demand the recovery services redeem one's vehicle when its inners are acting up, and there were few commercial operators willing to assist. I say 'few', I mean none of those that I rang. One garage had kindly checked my alternator as a goodwill gesture, clear that they were too swamped with work, like all the others in the area, to actually be of any tangible use. I watched on as the mechanic diligently connected a cord from his voltmeter from the alternator, before pressing a second against the wall of the van, confirming a healthy reading. Despondent as to the diagnosis, I shuffled off, contemplating my lack of options.

"I'm a senior aircraft engineer," one of the participants had sidled up to me after the event, "Do you think I could help?"

The following day, I could be found doing his domestic tasks in exchange for him rewiring my van. I washed, buffed and cleaned, putting stuff away in unfamiliar cupboards, whilst he poked and prodded electrical gubbins around the internals. My understanding of, "check the engine," is to lift the bonnet to confirm it still has one in situ. With my new-found mechanical knowledge, I could point at the cylindrical object and proudly assert that it was, "the alternator" before exclaiming that it was working, "just fine".

"That's the air filter," my newest friend smiled. Without any further input from me, he determined that one of the copper coils that earth the power pack had snapped, probably as a result of the sub-freezing temperatures. By mid-afternoon, he had brought my batteries back to life and I took him out for dinner, having left him enough clean plates to last an entire fortnight.

What I had not anticipated was a drenching in snowfall as I wended my way towards 'Destination Hilltop'. Beneath me my tyres drifted, slipped and slurred trying to maintain a grip against the incline. The Shitron threatened to come to a complete standstill frustratingly close to the top, the first gear wailing out its distress. Reversing back down the several miles of winding, narrow lane was a terrifying prospect, and one unlikely to be successful, given the snowstorm doing its punishing best. Pushing my right foot into cramp, I pressed the pedal harder against the footwell. Any euphoria from earlier in the day swiftly evaporated as toxic adrenaline zipped through me. New prayers were composed to thwart the impending jeopardy of skidding off into the hedgerow, or worse, further downhill into a slew of parked cars. Beneath the seats, the cat was overcome by sudden car sickness and could be heard chundering out God knows what.

Just as the van was about to expire, to slink back south, one wheel found a teeny bit of grip and the road levelled out. It was sufficient to generate another head of steam so we could tackle another ascent. Two mounds later, I despaired it would never end. It was close to midnight, before I was finally able to engage the handbrake, knowing full well sleep would be lost to me as I relived the idiocy of my decision. As I opened the rear door, Nelson hurtled out to take refuge under the tinkering van, his eyes ballooning at the wonder at the falling flakes, glistening in the full moon. "Welcome to Northumbria," I muttered to him as I set about decontaminating the van from his regurgitated dinner, crunching the fresh snow beneath my feet as I traipsed backwards and forwards to a much appreciated dog poo bin.

It turns out that Northumbria ceased to exist in 927. On the modern day map, Northumberland is a fairly sizable blob situated in England's north east corner, just south of Scotland. Fascinatingly, it has no cities. It seems even Royalty has blithely ignored its existence now that the Romans, Picts, Barbarians and Vikings have ceased breaching the peace.

Bafflingly, the welcome sign for Northumberland confoundingly claims it is, "England's border country" as if it were a sub-nation of this nation, which of course is a sub-nation of a bigger nation. Like a Russian doll, I simply keep discovering new layers of realm. The reason for this assertion remains an enigma to me and to Google, and I can only assume it is a glorious typo. That said, two of its hamlets are called *Once Brewed* and *Twice Brewed*, implying there are other plausible explanations. Nonetheless, one may reasonably conclude Northumberland's sole purpose is to be a buffer between Scotland and England proper, but given the last incursion took place in 1513 by James IV at Flodden, it might also suggest the civil servants in charge of concocting road sign slogans have taken an overly-defensive stance.

Just in case one is oblivious to this monumental moment in Scottish-English history, a clash which is largely ignored even by reenactors, the battle at Flodden was an unmitigated disaster for the Scots. Out-flanked, out-weaponised and out of good fighting terrain, nearly ten thousand Scotsmen and four thousand Englishmen's lives were sacrificed along with that of King James IV in the boggy valleys of Northumberland. The leaderless men hightailed it back to their lowlands and highlands. From thence, the Scots sensibly kept themselves confined within their own borders; not daring to lift so much as an eyebrow until the invention of tourism in the 19th century.

That learnt, it came as quite the surprise to discover that Hadrian's Wall does not follow the Scottish/English border whatsoever. This is very much contrary to what my Geography teacher told me back in the day of hard wooden chairs and Welsh desks with inkwells. It would also be fair to allege that I just was not paying adequate attention.

Hadrian's Wall lines up quite far south of the imaginary line that bisects these two countries cohabiting, usually amiably, within the shared sovereign state of the United Kingdom. The Wall used to be, in its heyday, a complex system of fortifications, roads, ditches, mini-castles and turrets spread across seventy-three miles, from coast to coast, rather than a boundary made of bricks as my mind's eye had constructed it. It is a veritable series of *Wallish Walls*.

Its explicit purpose was to repel any lawless land grabs common in the second century by The Picts coming from the north. The Romans had denounced the Picts as illiterate, uncivilised, barely-dressed, horny heathens. Scottish historians, on the other hand, would prefer them to be referred to as distinguished gentlemen, with intimate knowledge of the bible and classical literature. Well-read though they may have been, the Scots regularly foisted many an insurgency upon the occupying Romans loitering around the region.

Hence, the wall was built some eight-hundred years before England and Scotland came into existence. Although quite why Hadrian needed a wall is anyone's guess: the area has sufficient omens to daunt many an invading army: *Slaggyford, Cottonhopeburnsfoot* and *Deadwater* as well as war-threatening gore: *Beltingham, Choppington, Kilham, Carterway Heads* and *Chopwell Woods*.

Mind you, neither the wall nor the place names prevented the raping and pillaging by Vikings who wrecked lamentable havoc on the glorious hills following their capture of the monastic island of Lindisfarne in 793. They, wrongly depicted as helmet-wearers of *Woodhorn*, slaughtered the majority of the monks, who presumably, were more accustomed to peacefully worshipping their Christian values. The few surviving monks, and those safely contained with the mainland, decried it a sign of God's wrath on their collective guilt, beseeching followers to be more chaste, less garish, and more devotedly vestal. The Vikings simply rolled their eyes heaven-ward before romping on to other holy sites to ultimately dominate England's eastside. These annexed lands went on to be archived as Danelaw.

Northumbria's history on Wikipedia records that between the years 737 and 806 the region cruised through ten kings whose reigns ceased upon them either interned or interred. The latter massacred with levels of gruesomeness not typically shown before the watershed. The Northumbrian rulers who survived were suddenly enchanted by one of the region's monasteries and checked themselves in permanently.

Northumberland's history is thus one long legacy of invasion. Most legends recite much slaying and ravaging by the Picts from the north, Vikings from the East and from pretty much everyone else from the south. This is probably why, despite its lack of citizens, Northumberland has the highest number of castles per hilly mile compared with any other county. If one is feeling depleted of ruin, then Northumberland is the place to come to recharge. Except do be careful of the wild *Chillingham* cattle - no longer domesticated, with horns a mile wide, they are believed to be so dangerous, they are not even handled by a veterinarian.

Perhaps, however, it is not its gruesome history, nor its terrifying towns and villages, that has Northumberland stand out from its country cousins, but the fact that its signage is blue lettering on a white background. This flies in the face of the national system which gives us green signs on primary routes, and black and white ones everywhere else. Brown, denotes a site of historical interest or a tourist attraction, whereas blue is mandated for motorways and HGV drivers.

Once upon a time, a mid-to-dark blue boundary on a sign indicated local information, but any existing examples are typically the battered remnants of yonder year awaiting a student pillaging, like that indicating the direction of *Crookham*. Normally, conventions on shape and colour will conform to those prescribed by the Worboys Committee's publication: 'Traffic Signs: Report of the committee on traffic signs for all-purpose roads'. I can attest that it is a profound cure for menopausal insomnia, albeit I was mildly amused that signage has its own font called, somewhat unimaginatively: Transport. I personally would have preferred the precursor to emoticons: Windings or, at a push, Comic Sans just to bring some light-hearted *Snitter* to the region.

Still, as with all matters legal, I was interested (I confess that is quite the stretch) to discover that Part I, Regulation 11, paragraph 1 of the UK's Statutory Instruments issue No. 362 (2016) states that, "The colours prescribed for signs must conform to British Standards BS EN 12899-1:200". But then it goes on to say that Paragraph 1 does not apply, "to the extent it is provided that part of a sign may be of any, or any contrasting, colour". This, I argue, is nothing but legalese for what a load of *Low Cocklaw*. Nonetheless, one might be reassured to know there are legal requirements on signage except when there are not.

Much to my dismay, the only place without adequate signage was *Nunnykirk*: best translated as, 'The Church of the Northern Vagina'. Aside from that, Northumberland is, for the most part, terribly well sign-posted. Of particular note was that of *Shilbottle*, whose roadsigns are frequently tended to by marker pen enthusiasts instigating a war against peoples wielding industrial-grade Tippex.

Despite all that, Google informs me that Northumberland is the recommended destination of choice for those with mild anthropophobia or people otherwise contently introverted. With just one hundred and seventy citizens per square mile, Northumberland compares wonderfully with the national one thousand and seventy people per hilly mile elsewhere. Safe to say then, as a protecting country, Northumberland is woefully short on fighting folk in the event of invasion. Moreover, its misplaced defensive wall has largely sunk, or worse, had its stone requisitioned for use to construct newer properties, notably, the very straight, and yet heavily unguarded, Military Road. In short, the border has next to no hurdle for incomers to surmount, and there is very little traffic to dodge.

That said, Northumberland remains a place of outstanding national interest if one has a curious penchant for naked men who are, for whatever reason, called Lee: *Barelees* is quite the heaven-sent rural idyll. Disappointingly for some, perhaps, I must report I saw no one of that ilk in these parts, not that I have never had any ambition to encounter random naked men swanning about now or in the past.

It is not atypical for women to have the fear of men inculcated into them from quite the young age, and school lessons play their part. History, as I was taught at school, is ordinarily a long recital of men's violence towards other men, and as a brief aside, we are also told they do unspeakable matters to women. Indeed, one might regard history as a sort of subliminal advertisement indoctrinating its youth that the world out there is indeed big, bad and especially dangerous coming with a brief caution for women to continuously 'watch out'.

Death Features in Tyne and Wear

I cannot tell you what time it was. I can only tell you I awoke startled but unsure why. A tepid evening, I lay there, blinking in my double bed of red sheets, sensing something amiss. Then I heard the telltale crack. Then another one. It was close, a few scores of feet away, by the gate. Attuned now that a gun battle was underway, I could hear the horse stampeding in his paddock. I fretted for our cat as I rolled out of bed, flopping on the floor, anxious for the dog, who oddly was not barking. Flattening myself hard against the floor another bullet ricocheted off the roof above me, I crabbed towards the door, grasping for the handle. In the distance I heard the yelling of a woman's voice – perhaps Esther's – shrieking. More cracks.

Light spilled from the corridor, rebounding off my bedroom window: I had not drawn my curtains the full distance and my window faced the scene of ongoing crime. Whomever was last to bed had failed to turn off the hallway light but I couldn't recall if I were the miscreant.

"They'll see we're here!" my father screamed at the oversight. He tried to shut the door on me, trapping me in the room closest to the

shootout, as I resisted his pulling, desperate to join him and my mother already congregated in the centre of the house. I heard the click of my brother's bedroom door and him creeping in with them too. This set my father off again about light escaping from the house, but the distraction helped me make my escape.

"They will see we are awake and come for us!" my father raged pointlessly to us all as the gunfight at the gate rattled on just metres away. I would not dare to suggest that it probably would be the light that would alert them to our presence, but rather his own loud terror. I always hold my tongue in fear. A few more minutes waxed by, before a ceasefire seemed to break out, and no more shots trilled forth. "Out of ammo," my brother determined using language popularised in films. The only thing that made these gunshots so remarkable was that they were so close.

We slunk back to our bedrooms, not bothering to investigate the commotion, fervently hoping that Esther, Samuel and the nightguard had too managed to find safety. Come dawn, we discovered it was two drunk policemen. One had perished at the gate, his blood pooling in the dust around our entrance, and a scattering of shells the only evidence of the to-do. We had all survived it, yet for days after, my father vented his fury at the scandal of the light at whomever's ears were available. It was the most we'd heard from him this holiday, so rarely sighted he was in our lives. Back to boarding school I went. I doubt I told anyone of the incident, I did not suppose anyone would understand a day in the life of a tiny African kingdom.

****

England's fifth smallest county offered me little to write about. With just four little places of disgust to remark on, the world should have been a bed of slimy oysters. Instead, the opposite was true, I could find nothing to fire my imagination whatsoever in Tyne and Wear despite it being home to *Spital Tongues.*

That was the prompt that had me discover that women have a reduced tongue strength reserve compared to men. Who knew? In fact, who needed to know? Nonetheless, that our muscles are weaker than men's is hardly headline news, but if it comes to blowing raspberries, men can be presumed to do it much more forcefully. Men's tongues are also longer, by about half a centimetre on average. Conversely, women have many more condensed taste buds. All the better to taste rancid milk with. Is it a genetic throwback to ward off imbibing rotting food, perhaps? A third of women can be classed as supertasters compared with just fifteen percent of men. This had me wondering whether I was indeed a "fussy child" as my mother woefully insisted. It may be that I experienced taste much more evocatively than my older male sibling: my oral organ and my sex made it all the easier to despair at her dreadful cooking. Suddenly, I was all fascinated by my tongue and its role in shaping my parents' perception of me.

I then discovered that *Tyne* in obsolete English means to become lost or to perish. Welcome to death, or rather *Killingworth.* Death is oft said to be mankind's number one fear. It turns out that is only true if one is young, full of the joys of spring and male. Women have a second spike of morbid anxiety in their fifties. Undoubtedly, taxes and lousy government policy will do that to a person. Curiously, once one knows one's life is in terminal decline, one becomes much more upbeat and positive than when living under uncertainty or youth!

That led to me pondering what was the number one killer for men and for women. It used to be heart disease for both sexes but then women started living longer, so these days, it is dementia that does for us. However, if very old age does not beckon, the leading cause of death amongst women aged 50–79 is cancer of the trachea, bronchia or breast. For men, it is still heart disease. Alas, despite having a greater life expectancy, women spend more time suffering ill-health or experiencing disability when compared with men.

Perhaps one will be interested to learn that the gaps in the prevalence of disease, outcomes or access to health care varies from region to region. Globally, men are more likely to face greater health risks, so finally at least, us women are getting the benefit of access to a health system that in the UK, like in thirty-two other countries, is pre-paid for. That is until one learns that the UK bucks the trend: the UK has the largest female health gap in the G20, and the twelfth-largest globally, according to the statistics generated by our own government. In short, women with dementia receive worse treatment than men with the condition. Women make fewer visits to the doctor and receive less frequent health monitoring, when treatment during pregnancy and for menopause is excluded. Women also take medication that is not adequately tested on women because men make better guinea pigs. Embarrassingly, women are still finding it, "slightly awks," talking about menstrual and urinary matters with their health practitioners. As for matters maternal, twice as many black women die giving birth in comparison with Asian women, who themselves are twice as likely to die compared with white women. Reasons explaining this disparity have yet to be adduced.

Despite the medical profession being less enamoured of women's matters, women are most likely to opt for non-essential surgery. The top five cosmetic surgeries are, in order: breast augmentations; breast reductions; tummy tucks; liposuction and finally, eye-lifts. Of the recipients of such acts of *Chopwell*: 93% are women. It is a wonder how we are outliving the men at all.

Located on the outskirts of Newcastle, I discovered that the *Tongues* in Spital Tongues refers to two tranches of land given by Edward I to St. Mary Magdalene Hospital For The Incurables. Approximately five hundred years ago, it became St. Lukes Private Lunatic Asylum. Later on, it became a hospital, and with the Tynesider's propensity for a glottal stop, they excised the Ho, leaving just the Spital.

If one is oblivious to what the revoltingly-sounding glottal stop is, keep the mouth *Wide Open*, but use the throat to block the airflow. The sudden restriction of breath through the vocal cords gives a perceptible pause after the sounds 'p', 't' or 'k'. That is what makes the Geordie and Mackem accents so uniquely wonderful and yet so impenetrable for the hard of accenting. Take the word 'Spital', someone from Tyneside is most likely to say "sp'i….tul'"

Spitting, of course, is largely a male pastime, and one which is universally condemned by women as gross. Unfortunately for the gob globullers, there is no biological evidence to support any assertion that men produce more saliva, nor can this be attributed to their tongues being marginally longer and substantially stronger. Men who spit are, to borrow a phrase, nothing but drooling delinquents who were not chastised out of the practice, as girls might be.

Anyway, back to Spital Tongues. About one hundred and twenty-five years ago, the once hospital for the incurables, then asylum for the lunatics, was reassigned as a retiring soldiers' home, after which it became a clothing factory. It seems that is an appropriate, if not ironic, ending for the delectable Tyne and Wear.

The Englishwoman's Home is not her Durham Castle

"You need to see your housemasters," our housemistress grimly intervened as the two of us traipsed towards the doorway to our residence. We whipped around and slunk off towards the manor,

perplexed, before separating off down different wings to our individual housemasters' quarters. Clouded by that sinking feeling that something was up, yet not quite sure what exactly we had been caught doing now. Whatever it was, we were to be interrogated apart, and await our punishment.

We were old enough now that our dorms had just one roommate, and for a while, I had shared a space with a new girl. She was pleasant enough but not someone of my own choosing. She had swiftly been adopted by a different friendship circle, one of whom occupied a room with my best friend. Somehow, we finagled the authorities into believing we would behave if we exchanged dorm-mates, I think on account of my best friend failing miserably at exams, and me shining in them. I have a vague recollection that I vowed to coach her in maths and science, that this might pull her up into a passable place. After all, what are we there for if not to make the school look academically brilliant to the next generation of parents?

Instead, we dyed our hair purple, moved in some pet rats, and spent much of the 'prep hours' smoking cigarettes out of our bedroom window, on occasion inviting some of the boys to join us. Admittedly my logic baffles me in the present day, but we also concluded by extinguishing our cigarettes in a jug full of water, and storing it under our bunk, no one would notice, not even the cleaners. If intelligence was supposedly my strong point, it was probably the only reason I had not yet been permanently excluded. I had been suspended a couple of times, once with my best friend, so we spent the exclusion at her father's house, where we dyed our hair green and black, our lesson clearly not learnt. Apparently, when they rang to inform my father, he simply asked for his money back, then chastised them for failing to do the actual 'upbringing' part of the contract. When I was suspended the second time, I was sequestered to the San for the week, and frozen out of all school activities including lessons and sport. A whole week lying around 'revising' in between television programmes.

In recent weeks, there had been increasing talk of a spate of thefts, just small sums of money going missing here and there, from all across the four girls' dwellings. To catch the culprit, some wallets had been left lying around communal areas with five-pound notes in with their serial numbers recorded. That afternoon in the tuck shop, some bars of chocolate were exchanged for one of them. It turns out it was another of my friends, an act particularly baffling because her family were truly well off. That is what we were interrogated about – did we know she was the resident kleptomaniac?

While we were learning of the thief in our midst, our housemistress took to searching through our belongings and permanently confiscated all of our now legally-purchased cigarettes, chewing gum and other forbidden possessions. To my astonishment, there were several bottles of beer, which my best friend truthfully admitted ownership of. Although I had no prior knowledge of them, said to be a birthday present for her father, no one believed either of us. The housemistress, who was in all aspects a lovely woman, also discovered the jug of butt ends, and back on suspension we were placed. This time, I was sent back to the bloody psychologist's house who insisted I give her my cheque book and card. I lied and said I had left them at school.

****

The phrase, 'The Englishman's home is his castle,' was born of the notion that no authority had the right to enter one's abode for any reason. In the event of being formally summoned to a place of inquisition, the occupier was at liberty to remain unmolested in the sanctuary of his dwelling place. He might even ask his neighbours to support him in this endeavour of remaining steadfast, pleading for them to *Pity Me* whilst in his self-imposed home-confinement and possibly the earliest known bouts of agoraphobia. They may well not have all been out to get him, but why risk venturing out into the big, bad *Cockfields* just in case?

It was Judge William Standford in 1505 who made this conflation between 'the home' and 'a future ruin for tourists to gawp at'. The phrase spawned a belief that the home-dweller, or preferably his servants, was licensed to inflict any amount of painful deterrence upon those intent on invading, pillaging or otherwise finagling about a property, thus, making the surroundings a fair *Wackerfield.*

Such times ceased to endure, although some might be inclined to regret this, particularly in County Durham, the home of *Quaking Houses.* This county is currently placed tenth in a ranking of England's most-frequently burgled houses. With such rich pickings for practice, it may not be too coincidental that County Durham's constabulary claims the bronze medal for national burglary detection. Placed third out of the forty-three constabularies, Durham's residents might even deem that achievement as worthy of a round of applause. On the other hand, one might rush to cross one's arms in resigned defiance upon learning that Durham's police solve just under twelve percent of the received reports of breaking and entering. Probably most would think it a *Straindrop* in the ocean of home invasion clear-up rates.

It is little wonder then how many security companies opt to scream out, usually via their advertising, that there is a burglary every one hundred and six seconds. More responsible anti-theft organisations have updated their website to claim there is one every hundred and sixty-four seconds. That is nearly an entire minute to relax for every three strikes past twelve of the burglar's extremely hot watch's second hand. Only it turns out such stats are *Cockerton.*

London, as expected, has the most home burglaries, with around one-hundred and ten break-ins per day. That works out at around one every thirteen minutes, or if one prefers: one every seven hundred and eighty seconds of a genuine fake Rolex.

Perhaps, then, the most shocking revelation is that half of all home robberies are committed by a person who is already known to the victim. Added to the fact that seventy percent of burglaries are committed by the same person, I am going to suggest we should all start talking about whom within our friend and family groups we think this might be. I realise this is inciting a lot of gossip, but it might be worth it if it drives down the burglary rates in the neighbourhood, especially given the police are not likely to manage it.

It behoves me to draw attention to the fact that in sixty-four percent of burglaries there is someone present in the property. By this, I mean there is a legitimate entitlement for someone being there in addition to the transgressor. This is a very intimidating fact. Mind you, this statistic includes all those swift burglaries where someone has simply swiped a wallet, watch or handbag, rather than a full swagbag of electronic gubbins, before going on their merry way. Missing a wallet the day before pay day? Then one must simply report it stolen, get a crime number, before claiming from one's insurance policy. The police will not investigate it either, but nonetheless the stat will later be included for maths bafflement by a marketeer happily flogging blue-tooth activated burglar detection systems at a later date – conflation of the *Merrybent* kind perhaps?

Happening upon such casual stats such as those illustrated above might surely leave the average Englishperson to ponder where and what in the house would be most strategic for keeping one's limited supply of suitable weapons for repelling the home invader. Incidentally, one in seven burglars are said to gain access by walking through an unlocked door, which seems to suggest that the friends and family kleptomaniac delinquency theory has some merit. It has long since been a well-known criminal offence for the Englishman to protect his castle, unless of course, the victim can prove he used reasonable force. Either way, there is a trial involved, but any victim of burglary may well be prosecuted in the event of *Killerby.* Knives obviously belong in the kitchen drawer, which in the average English house, is located downstairs. Said kitchen typically has a back door, which is the second most popular means for gaining access, with one in three respectable burglars waltzing in via this convention. Just one in five clamber through windows, but only six percent smash them. So happening to have taken a knife upstairs is an unlikely defence. Moreover, very few of us own a pitchfork as a matter of convenience. Combined with the fact that we are a firearms-free country (for the most part), and also one which does not really play baseball, it really only leaves us to contemplate keeping an upstairs *Broompark.*

Nonetheless, this is usually unsuitably located under the stairs or in a futility room beside the kitchen. There are, however, many more reassuring facts to discover. About half of all burglaries take place on the spur of the moment. This implies that in half of burglaries, the *Crook*, or family member, is aware of one's comings and goings. The reality is that one is either having a marvellous time on holiday, or one comes from a household that requires all and sundry to go out and earn enough to actually pay for the abode and its commodities.

In other good news, burglary rates in the last twenty years have plummeted from nearly 900,000 per annum to around 400,000 pre-Covid. Lockdown certainly had its benefits: with over 220,000 fewer break-ins in the years of 2020–2022. This suggests the average English adult would benefit from a bit more home-working and a lot more agoraphobia.

More contemporary protections of national importance are supplied by UNESCO. The convention was set up in 1946 to conserve enclaves, be they breathtaking wildernesses; evidence of intellectual history or because they represent a remarkable accomplishment of humanity. Such an invocation ensures the host government is tasked with safeguarding selected heritage sites from exploitation and ruination from those with enterprising ambitions, or just plain neglect.

Durham Castle, the brainchild of William the Conqueror, was among the first in England to receive the esteemed protection. Ironic, given it was from this seat that his soldiers harried the northerners into capitulation in 1069 by ransacking their villages and igniting their homes, leaving us, possibly, with the origins of the villages of *Burnt Houses, North Bitchburn and Sockburn.* Without doubt, his legacy has put some proof into the pudding that, 'An Englishman's home is his castle'. For students at the University of Durham this is truly the case, with their lodgings situated within the UNESCO World Heritage Site.

Upon graduation, Durham's students splurge into society: erudite, empowered and equipped with potentially a lifetime's supply of indebtedness for the privilege. Welcome to *Blanchland!* One can only purport that their education has made them all the better at reading and comprehending the latest articles discussing the state of Britain's housing 'crisis'. For matters of national residencies, talk is always of a 'crisis', it is never just a bit of a to-do or folderol.

If globally, 'shelter' is the first in Maslow's hierarchy of needs, in Britain, this might translate to securing the largest possible mortgage just so one can occupy one of Europe's smallest homes. Alas, Britain's stock of housing cannot keep up with demand: England's population in the last one hundred years has grown from around thirty-six million people to nearly fifty-six million today so sometimes it seems there is *No Place* to go except back home.

It is a typical British endeavour to own one's home. Alas, twenty percent of politicians have enterprisingly worked out that by owning buy-to-rent houses, they safely can glean consistent return on investments. Hence, rents are costlier than mortgage repayments for houses and there is little to no incentive for this to change, crisis or no crisis. Incidentally, home ownership is now around 35% for those under forty, but around 75% for those over 65 years of age. The current reality condemns educated Englanders to spend less money and time acquiring life skills, hobbies and other methods for personal development than previous generations. It is almost like generation after generation is sliding back into the *Ruffside.*

Durham, incidentally, does not offer a single stately home for perusal. This is because the term is simply not used by historians. Instead, they speak of castles and abbeys, historic houses of halls and manors, and country estates. England's stately homes are facing a uniquely British housing crisis of their own. It is estimated that somewhere between a fifth and a third of England's most glorious houses were established via wealth generated from the slave trade. The theft of people and the mass displacement of culture and community might render such a place as an uncomfortable *Crookhall*: nothing but a monument to an elitist past built on the souls of innocents.

County Durham has some of the finest examples of regret. *Coxhoe* would be one such example: rebuilt in 1725, as a gothic castellated Georgian three-story hall, it was once considered the grandest in County Durham ultimately falling under ownership of two Jamaican plantation-holders. The emancipation of slaves in 1833 near-ruined the family's prosperity, forcing them to shed themselves of not one but two country piles. Initially sold to a mining company, it was requisitioned for use as a prisoner of war camp throughout the war, and then came to be the prized possession of the National Coal Board. They demolished it in 1956 to curtail expenditure.

Nearly forty percent of England's five thousand mansions have now been razed, with demolition peaking in the 1950s. Most of England's stately homes were requisitioned in the war effort, their spacing useful as hospitals, prisons and shelter. At the end of the war, the cost of restoring these to their former glory was prohibitive; to cover the expense of maintaining them required the owners to sell the vast tracts of land that were attached; that is how so many came to be converted into boarding houses, prisons and hotels. Eventually, The National Trust was formed: permitting the nations' residents to finally comprehend how the other half cannot surmount the repeated cost of living crises either.

EASTER TERM

The coming of age and frequently answering the question:

"Aren't you lonely?"

A Few Days in the Life in the North Van-Ridings

"I have this spot on my neck," I turned to my best friend, "can you take a look at it?" It wasn't like your typical teenage acne, more of a dry spot that suddenly bubbled up before ejecting watery dribble, then scabbing over.

"It's like a polo mint," she observed. By the end of the day, more had made their mark. "We will have to call you Ringo Starr!" my roommate fell about at her quip. Within two days, I was polka-dotted. Defeated by the fact I could disguise the lurgy no longer, I popped across to see the sister in the San. The doctor was promptly summoned. I had Lyme's Disease, a diagnosis that delighted the usually cantankerous physician. Ordinarily, he was someone I suspected had overslept, or just played hooky, when lectures on 'bedside manner' had been taught at medical school.

Lyme's Disease had become a named illness a year prior, and for that reason, there was a fear it might be contagious, bringing forth more isolation, self-study and television gawping. Thankfully, I didn't have the symptoms of fever, headache or joint pain. I was no more lacking in energy than any other of my peers. In fact, it was timely – we were in the run up to mock exams. With nothing else to do, except sink myself into the textbooks, it probably raised my grades higher than they would otherwise have been, even if they were, to quote the masters, "pretty dismal" for someone with my aptitude for learning.

****

I pootled into England's largest county at a time when the great moors were at their beige best and the wintry heather smothered the land in a caramelised crust. Not that I would realise the gloriousness of the yonder before me, for I had cruised into these blustering lands late in the pitch. The van shook, rattled and rolled on its suspension long after the parking brake had been applied, as the gathering storms pelted the sides. The turbulence certainly made cooking dinner an especially exciting affair, not a great deal of *Heck,* just a *Little Heck*. Nonetheless, the reverberation kept me, but not the Furry Imbecile, up til the wee hours.

Despite it all, the bleatings of newly-birthed lambs, with dangling umbilical cords, woke me early as their mothers huddled beside the van. Typically, each morning saw me greeted by Nelson. Overnight, he kept himself comatose down by my feet, only staging the great trek north upon the first rumblings of his stomach. On arrival at my head, he would proceed to gobble at my hair. For anyone who is unfamiliar with the anatomy of a cat: their tongues have velcro-like rasps on them and I have tremendously long hair. What usually follows is a series of sounds not dissimilar to a hairball being regurgitated in the general direction of my ear lobe, although he reserves the actual ones for the rugs. Mostly, several hours post-dawn, I rely on him to be my morning alarm clock. I hit the snooze button, albeit not literally – I simply reclaim my hair, and roll over to face him. In reply, he turns around to give me a close up of his anus. According to the cat experts, this is cat-speak for, "Hey!" and "I love you!" I have my misgivings. Nelson might then join in with me gazing out at the panorama via a small side window behind my pillows. We might cuddle as the world came to life: fuzzy birds flying high, out of focus grasses fluttering away and a horizon that was mostly just a blur. There might be sheep, but they could just as well be blobs of stone. Unless they waddled forth it was impossible to tell. At some point, I would reach over for my glasses, click on the heating and then proceed to make the five foot dash to the loo for a much needed *Weeton.* But not on this first Yorkshire morning. For I was disturbed not by the sounds not of dribbling saliva, but dribbling rain coming through the ceiling of the van, rattling off the toilet seat. A form of rhythmic torture that could not be smothered out with a pillow.

I had been keen to explore England's largest county, and were it not for the constant meddling of administrations from as far back to the tenth century, these lands of the wild boar would be half the size of Wales and referred to as the 'Yorkshire Ridings'. Alas, the boar was extirpated in the 13th century and the Ridings in 1974: yet another example of English *Killinghall.*

Subsequently, the region was carved up into the counties of North, West and South Yorkshire, with only the East Riding of Yorkshire defiantly clinging on to its heritage. The 'riding' has no association with horsemanship, albeit Yorkshire supplies the best in hacking country. Rather it derives from the Olde Danish 'thridding', meaning 'a third', hence there previously being no such county as South Yorkshire, or South Ridings.

After years of boundary-meddling, and in typical nonsensical English governance, North Yorkshire had been allocated the largest of the quartet, over three times the size of the second-placed East Riding of Yorkshire. If this was a piece of 'Yorkshire Parkin', a sickly-sweet coming together of cake and bread, someone was always going to feel very ripped off. Yet, to the locals, Yorkshire, in all its component parts, remains 'Gods Own Country', home to fat rascals, curd tarts and yorkshire puddings: three of England's beigest but loveliest yet most calorific foodstuffs topping the *Sinnington* lists. Only two of them are sweet: the pudding, unfathomably, is savoury. Whilst the rest of the world derides my mother country for its bland, tasteless, soggy, fat-laden dullness, I can only conclude that Yorkshire appears to be responsible for the invention of much of it.

Yorkshire grub is the origin for much of Slimming World's list of 'syns', those obstacles that prevent us from arriving at the hallowed ground of *Skinningrove*: Wensleydale Cheese, Liquorice Allsorts, Seabrook Crisps, Party Rings, Jelly Babies, Smarties, Kit-Kats, Polos, Terry's Chocolate Orange (which he was good enough to share), Quality Street, After Eights, Fruit Gums, Pontefract Cakes, Aeros, Jelly Tots, and Whittaker's Chocolate. Basically, if it is hanging around on racks next to the service station cashier, and it is trying to sabotage one's teeth, weight or blood sugar levels, it comes from Yorkshire.

For those trying to maintain some kind of diet, Yorkshire is revered for its production of asparagus and rhubarb. Unfortunately, both of these have extremely high levels of asparagusic acid: the ingredient that has one's pee smelling incredibly funky within minutes of ingestion. Undeniably, this is something one has to bear in mind if one is living in a Shitron. Moreover, neither of them can be eaten *Raw.*

What I yearned for most during my stay in the Yorkshire Dales was the 'bits' that can be sprinkled over the country's national, but beigeist, dish: fish and chips. I forgo the fish for dietary reasons, as well as the mushy peas and curry sauce (I would like to attest that it is my international travels that have refined my taste buds but I may just be fussy after all). I opt instead just for the flakes of batter to dress the chips, before rinsing the lot in vinegar with a smattering of salt. If such a phenomena as, "Chips wi' Bits" exists outside of Yorkshire, I am oblivious to it.

Allegedly, the nation's favourite food is Italian pizza, at least according to a survey undertaken by Just Eat, although Poultry World claims it is Chicken Tikka Masala. According to YouGov, England's true culinary champion is the chippy supper. Following very closely behind is, 'The Roast', preferably one centring around chicken. Irrespective of the main meat, no self-respecting roast can be considered complete without a bowl-shaped pancake. The primary purpose of the Yorkshire pudding is to mop up the vegetable-infused gravy dregs of England's second-best dinner. Without the pudding, it is just a chicken dinner and not a roast. I will brook no *Bickerton* to the contrary. In third place of meals that constitute the English cuisine, also known as dishes that make one fat, is none other than the *Fryup.*

The globally-recognised icon of breakfast is a mammoth feast of pork served two ways accompanied by various unappetising accompaniments. These typically include fried eggs with snotty tops; over-boiled baked beans; greasy mushrooms; black pudding (which is coagulated blood); cold toast and a single grilled half-tomato for colour. It is customary to push the tomato to one side to avoid accidentally imbibing a nutrient before smothering the lot in ketchup. Note well: potatoes should never feature, not even hash browns.

Usually given the constraints of time, it is a weekend indulgence. I started each morning with cornflakes, pretty much every day as shelf-space was a premium in a van and I was having a 'no bread' year. Besides which, the travel toaster guzzled up electricity and threatened to overload the inverter. Following the most important meal of the day, I would usually write, or research, undertake some marketing, or plan a journey. Despite my hamster wheel of routine, I was greatly anticipating my time in the wilds of the Yorkshire Dales, being free to indulge in its magical ruggedness.

Because of Nelson, I had taken to driving for just two or three hours at a time, pausing only so he could snack. He was now of the opinion that his wet food must come with a smattering of dried biscuits on top. Not separate, nor underneath, but sprinkled so some tinkered against the metal rim, leaving him to revel in his *Pickering.* He usually nibbled at about half of the contents before loudly announcing his food bowl was near-empty. I took to going for a walk in the hope he might polish off the remainder, but that short walk was often into a service station garage to treat myself to something moreish. The weight that the Shitron lugged was becoming appreciable: by now we were a right pair of *Blubberhouses.*

Lonely Yorkshire roads criss-crossed up and over its valleys, and caused the contents of my fridge to rearrange themselves of their own accord. Thoroughly shaken, not stirred was how my ketchup was served, and all across the floor was how my risotto rice ended up having been improperly secured in an overhead cupboard – once two days running. Bringing forth even more exclamations of *Heck!*

To top it all off, I lost a day of travelling trying to find LPG once again. The first service station advertised it but had removed it years previously. The second had it, but claimed that on the grounds of health and safety, I could not refill my canister. The third also had it, but unfathomably the dispenser would not kick in. No one is empowered to help these days because, and I quote directly, "they might get sued". A fellow caravanner volunteered himself but had no success. Eventually, a kindly attendant decided I was not the litigious type and assisted. He was chatty, and cheerful, and soon enough discovered the rig just needed resetting at the inside terminal.

Two days after, I was drowning in a head cold, or Covid, following these anonymous exchanges with mankind. My mobile van was very much a *Sicklinghall.* I was so utterly food-averse, even the delightful thought of Yorkshire's finest cuisine turned my stomach.

The leaking vent was still tap, tap, tapping away all times of the day and night. I had procured some silicon gel, but it had been too rainy to affix, and so on I suffered the mental torment, now hogtied by insufficient energy to help myself come rain or shine. I was as floored as my arborio, and as restricted to the van as the contents of my fridge. Even the most basic of tasks, such as loo attendance, mine and the cats', had become a chore of such magnificence that it overwhelmed me. I cancelled two speaking engagements, unable to coherently chat to the cat, let alone actual people.

By the fourth morning, the external sealant surrounding the fan above my bed was as crumbly as the Wensleydale cheese the region is famed for. To wake me, the cat had to circumvent a large pool of rainwater. Admirably, he patiently withstood the boredom. It was the only time I worried for his welfare since the initial few weeks. He revels in the driving hours, cuddling up against my thigh in the middle seat that is kept especially clear for him. If it is a long day, he might tentatively drop down to his bed below the gear stick for a full snooze. He had taken to leash-walking with surprising equanimity. In the evenings, he would often curl up on the stove top cover, still cooling from a boiling pot, to peer out at the nightly void, legs tucked like those of a trussed chicken. Then the sealant on the third, and final, vent, the one directly above Nelson's preferred evening recline, ceased its only duty: to prevent water ingressing.

It was fair to say that with so much confinement, the occupants were more than ready for the *Sykehouse.* My inability to stay awake long enough to tend to Nelson's every need meant he suffered. In the midst of my delirium, high up in the moorlands, I recalled a red grouse designated the roof of the van as its home. Each time it waddled the length of our ceiling, it set off the cat most *Cray Cray*. I could only be grateful that at least some form of entertainment was provided. Once I was back on my feet, albeit stuffed full of laryngitis and a chest infection, I mustered up enough energy to drive a few hours, clear out our respective toilets, obtain a shower, and most importantly of all: replenish the van with toilet rolls. I had reached the point of severe rationings – the true indication of an acute illness. Times such as these were, without doubt, the toughest to be alone, lonely and isolated.

Notwithstanding it all, I managed to fall in love with the region. It captured my heart then pissed all over it because it certainly rains a lot in April. My stay in the Yorkshire Ridings coincided with my embarking on my final term of Van Life. The typical inquisitions had shifted over time, having begun with a plethora of, "Aren't you scared?" before transitioning into, "Aren't you cold?". In this final term, the most commonly asked question was, "Aren't you lonely?"

The season of public holidays rushed in, plunging me further into reclusivity. I now needed to find spaces that were best suited to sitting out such periods far from the madding crowds. For that reason, I avoided the coastlines and the renowned beauty spots. Winter had me accustomed to immersing myself in many a sweet spot alone and untethered. I could appreciate every ounce of England's wilderness from my desk, my loo and my driving cab, but a crop of Spring Bank holidays had me competing along with all the other caravans, campervans, car campers and motorhomes. All of us tussling over narrow country lanes and patiently awaiting flickers of headlamps to permit us to right-turn onto busy A-roads. Frustrated drivers careered dangerously past or followed so closely that, were there not a shadow from their vehicle, I would have no idea they were on my tail. Come a long weekend, it was nothing short of *Bedlam.*

The spring weather stirred up the wildlife and my secluded night spots were regularly interrupted by Volkswagen Polos thumping out a din that most parents would call, 'shit for turning off'. Having successfully, but usually not, executed their rituals of hand-brake induced tyre-squealing doughnuts, along with the mating calls of revving engines, the teenage occupants might proceed to explore the boundaries of their unbridled passion. I just wished they could avoid accidentally discharging their horns as the lucky scorers grappled with one another and their unyielding car space as they fathomed *Sexhow.*

In some ways, we are all one another's nuisances on this tiny island, even in the vastness of North Yorkshire. One memorable evening. I parked up to admire the glorious sunset that the open vales permitted, simultaneously chatting nonchalantly to a friend during a rare spell of phone reception. A man in a top-of-the-range Discovery drove by to tell me to be gone before dusk. Other mornings, I was awoken by the long blaring of a car horn. In my sick bed, I had happened upon an anti-van life Facebook group and learnt that the crack of dawn beeping is all a part of the hunting: a means to repel the vanlifers. Apparently it is also fair game to throw bread crumbs on the roof of vans. Perhaps in Yorkshire, they throw cake. It left me suspicious as to why that red grouse took a shine to my van, and why all three of my vents failed within days of each other. But then, it was probably just the isolation turning me into a paranoid *Crackpot.*

After my illness shifted, and my sinuses were restored to their glorious best, my sense of smell returned. It was then I discovered I had had a gas leak and discharged almost all the LPG. Sometimes, I wonder how come I do not walk around with my death certificate stapled to my toe. I decided, for the benefit of my own mental health, to return back to the folds of Warwickshire and Oxfordshire, to be with my kith and kin. To be nurtured, cared for, listened to, sympathised with and understood. A quick hiatus away from this year of adventure, to restore myself to sanity, or at least a variation of it.

As the van sniffled into life, I tugged down the right-hand knob to wipe away the latest downpour blurring the windshield. The two wipers shrugged momentarily before dropping back into slumber, their motor expired. *Great Heck* was not the phrase I chose. The recovery service remembered us from the previous phone call. A few hours later, we set off again another great trek southbound, the van safely secured to a series of truck beds. As I clambered up the cab to sit on the passenger side of the second truck, my rear was delighted by the discovery that the seat was heated. Albeit my mind had momentarily erased the fact I had placed a toasted cheese sandwich there just seconds before.

The Uncomfortable Fashions of West Yorkshire

It had all been getting out of hand of late, and suddenly we'd all been refused entry to French by a rare woman teacher. Thus, we were banished from revising the subjunctive on the basis of wearing too much makeup. Generally speaking, no one objected to a thin coating of foundation, sleek eyeliner and mascara, perhaps a dusting of eye shadow. But the fashion had struck bold o'clock – a smudge of rouge, a blast of eye shadow, thick eyeliner and metallic lipstick. Back to our dorms we trudged, sharing the multitude of sinks dotted about the place. We stripped our faces naked. Some smeared a thin layer back on, borrowing a lighter shade from a friend. Others dotted blemishes and zits with concealer, despite the fact that every pair of eyes was about to descend upon us as we dribbled back into class. I went for the concealer option, hating my freckles, but glad that the days of knicker inspections, a weekly event at the previous school, was never on the agenda here.

Elsewhere boys de-bagging one another appeared to be the latest craze. One moment they were minding their own business, standing in the corridor awaiting the arrival of the master, the next a gang of contemporaries tore off their uniform, although ideally only the trousers and underpants. Judged on their ability to laugh it off, all eyes scanned for signs of weakness. Timing is everything, and never ever did a master appear to turn up in time.

****

The West Yorkshire market town of *Penistone* is perhaps, after Shitterton, England's most excruciatingly and embarrassingly-named settlement. One might anticipate that its moniker has filtered down from the Town of Penis. Alas, it does not follow the logic. The town initially appeared as Pengeston, town of the penge, in the Doomsday Book. Penge is the Danish for money, yet unusually for the region, it is not thought to derive from the language of our Viking cousins. In later years, it was recorded as Peningston, meaning 'town of the head'. Perhaps, then, it was always destined to become a notorious place name of smut.

But money is what rules our waves: Penistone's history replicates a wider national story of how England obtained her capital. By the 17th century, Penistone was acclaimed far and wide for its cloth, and textiles are what established it as a thriving market town. On its outskirts, Penistone Sheep prospered within the rugged moorland. The moors are a *Foulby* zone of discomforts: harsh winters, exposed terrain and a dearth of good sustenance. Neglect is what the Penistone sheep thrived on and that may well explain why its wool is notably robust and enduring. Alas, it was also itchy, scratchy and prickly.

Unsurprisingly then, the average Englishwoman wantonly, and unpatriotically, availed herself of cotton, particularly the affordable commodities that were calico and chintz. This cheaper material permitted the emerging middle-class women to more readily emulate the fashions sported by their uppers. Somewhat understandably, it was not long before the region's farmers, shepherds, shearers, spinners, weavers and dyers, whose very livelihoods were imperilled, called on Parliament for protection of our native industry.

In 1700, Parliament swiftly passed the Calico Act, blocking the importation of cotton cloth from the east, specifically India. As public policy went, banishing cotton backfired spectacularly among consumer groups, who wished not to return to the days of irritation. Not to be pushed around, our parliamentarians passed further legislation prohibiting the sale of almost all cotton cloth, be it domestic or imported, with the exception of raw cotton. Those caught wearing cotton could expect a thorough shunning.

It remained for the women to watch and to wait until the Industrial Revolution could bring turmoil back upon our lands. The abolition of cheap cloth from the east drove the demand for refining machinery to process raw cotton. Inventors invented, pencils snapped, heads banged, and shortly after, the cotton-weaving spinning jenny spun into prominence. The honing of production ensured that cloth became both cheap and plentiful, and quickly Englanders returned to a scratch-free existence. The ultimate consumer was, however, far removed from the horrors of the production fields. The demise of Penistone wool would have been a near-certainty, except a new market was found: it was now sold as coarse cloth to be worn by the enslaved persons handpicking the cotton fields in western lands under the lash of the white immigrant man endeavouring to provide wealth for the now rapacious English economy.

By 1770, the mill owners changed stance – heartily campaigning to legalise the sale of pure cotton cloth now that the illicit second-hand market was burgeoning. Deregulation swiftly occurred in 1774 and England's demand for cotton was free to balloon: bulk went vogue. Wide skirts, kilted up with loops, ribbons, buttons and tassels, formed fold after fold. Others went for the full curtain drapery, from shoulder to floor, pinched in at the waist. Some, daringly, exposed a mass of underlayers. This trend expanded women's rear ends in every direction and broad bottoms became the rears of the year.

Until this finery arrived, Englanders had not been of the knicker-wearing persuasion, having abandoned wearing any form of underwear: snappily called 'subligaculum' since Roman times. The next 'must have' addition for the wardrobe was drawers. Not the boxy containers for storage, although they too became essential, but undergarments that were pulled up and tied. Hence, their laconic name. Necessity being the mother of invention, women required something to protect their plush outer garments from themselves or else the nether regions would be a veritable *Stainland.*

In the absence of Tena Lady, knee-length billowing cotton smalls were added to the catalogue. Of course, no one would know what was going on down there, fabrically-speaking, as the glory of the knickerbockers were discreetly covered by a football pitch's worth of material. Then came the women's rights activist, Amelia Bloomer. The American owner of the feminist publication, The Lily, demanded that women's costumes better suit her wants and needs, rather than being an adornment seeking man's approval. With that outrageous stipulation, she shortened her skirts and lengthened her knickers. Her 'bloomers' truly bloomed, giving birth to a new range of lingerie. Shortly after, clearly exposed from beneath knee-length dresses, bloomers became the undergarment of political statement for suffragettes world-wide – one suspects the usual slurs of *Horwich* rang around.

Thus began the trend of women wearing alluring underwear to attract attention, from causes célèbre to fast cars. From the early 1900s, titillation via ankles and arms was sufficient, but then the novelty wore off and so knickers got shorter. Knickerbockers became knickers, which the more politely-inclined called 'smalls'.

By the 1930s, men were increasingly contemplating how and where they should *Laycock.* Coopers Inc of Chicago, designed the world's first briefs, with the now infamous Y-shaped access hole keeping it all snug and tidy when out of operation. By 1938, 'jockey pants' arrived on these shores, and sold like the proverbial hotcakes. Within ten years, some men preferred a little less of a *Netherbridge*, and so adapted the sportswear Boxers as undergarments.

Absolutely no one anticipated the birth of the *Netherthong.* Thongs came into being after Californian legislators in 1974 voted to outlaw nude sunbathing, demanding that in the interests of common sensibilities, women should wear bikinis. Quite literally, the Austrian-born American fashion designer Rudi Gernreich spotted a gap in the market.

That brings us to the top half of the story: the *Upperthong as* one might say. Once upon a time, there was no such thing as a bra. Instead a band of cloth or leather, called a strophium or mamilare, was bound around one's breasts to flatten them if necessary, particularly to quell their enthusiasm during physical exertion, especially if one had been gifted an *Eccup* or larger. It was not until the 14th century that the corset encapsulated women and its purpose was to deny the breasts any freedom whatsoever. By the 16th century, its many iterations were increasingly crushing women into cages as they aspired to change their body shape to trends of the era. Womens' enslavement to fashion was sealed: demanding forevermore that their gowns accentuate the décolletage and diminish the waist.

Things took a radical turn when the French women's rights activist, Herminie Cadolle, along with the support of men from the sphere of physicians, successfully focused on the anatomical damage done to women's chests as much as their midriffs. Ms Cadolle split the corset in two in 1889 before filing for a patent for the first bra. This she called a corselet-gorge. Elsewhere, in America, the press preferred the term 'Brassiere', meaning 'child's undershirt'. Soon enough, in the interest of verbal expediency, the 'siere' was stripped away.

Combining the nethers and the uppers, the bikini was the invention of a French car builder in 1946 whose legacy is to forever link together buxom ladies, bras and bonnets in the marketeers' eye. The rest, as they say, is history.

Except for Penistone's eponymous sheep. To better suit contemporary times, they have been rebranded as Whitefaced Woodland Sheep and are classified as an endangered and vulnerable rare breed with fewer than two hundred breeding ewes nibbling away at their near-barren lands.

Slavery was, after a battle royale, abolished in England in 1807. Although the slaves held within her territories were not freed until 1838: they were only reluctantly released from their servitude upon the payment of substantial compensation for loss of income foregone by their bearers. The emancipated workers were not given a penny to assist in their transition from owned stock to human beings. The compensation paid to the plantation owners remains bound up within many of England's upper echelons today, upon whose inheritors we look to inform our fashion consciousness.

The Ostentatious Effrontery of East Riding of Yorkshire

"You're not going out dressed like that," my father declared to us both as we prepared to set off in the vicinity of the town to gather with the other teens of the expats. 'That' was dressed in ripped jeans – deliberate tears revealing the allure of one's patella, the mandatory outfit for a teenager of the 1980s. "Not in this country, not where torn and grubby clothes are the uniform of the poor." It was a point, difficult to counter, even during the era of arguments being the

preferred medium for all communications. Instead, we left them trodden into the floor, waiting for Esther to gather them up and wash them by hand, kneeling on her worn knees beside the blue bath, swilling them around, laboriously rinsing them out under the tap. With home help, there was no point in owning any of life's electronic household goods beyond a fridge and a freezer. Buying a microwave had seemed like an act of ostentation, a rare form of collective family entertainment. How we had all gasped at it scrambling some eggs for dinner. No one could think of what else to do with it.

****

A friend informed me that they had spied a washing machine at their local Sainsbury's and wondered who the hell would possibly consider washing their dirty laundry so publicly. Then he remembered me and my little adventure, hence the phone call. I too had noted the rebirth of the public launderette slowly seeping into the country. Unlike times of old, no longer is the launderette a regimented line up of top-loaders squaring off against ginormous tumble dryers in a town centre mall, run by a stereotyped fag-ash-Lil busying herself with folding linen in one corner. These days, there is a choice between a large and small washer beside a huge drier, all formulaically contained under an outdoor shelter. By forsaking the deposit on a house, you can wash to your heart's content, passing the time by supping on an overpriced latte and a slightly stale croissant. I also learnt that public amenities are also a very practical way of acquiring a collection of random odd socks.

"Yes, they are very popular with citizens who use them to wash their dogs' beds," I told my friend. "I've wasted many an hour, and met a few charming engineers repairing them while trying to locate one that doesn't smell; isn't likely to contaminate my clothing further, and permits me to get the wash completed before the car parking restrictions kick in." A wash takes around forty-five minutes, and if one opts to machine dry at heart-breaking expense, then a further hour is needed at a minimum. This leaves just fifteen minutes to load, unload, reload, run back to the van and exit the car park all before the Eyes In The Sky activate the parking charge invoices.

I had packed a clothes horse, but so far I had refrained from using it lest I attracted unwanted tuts from passersby. Moreover, a clothes horse is pointless in winter for drying. Instead, I became that person who sits in car parks watching their laundry intently and frets whether the local homeless might avail themselves of it should I turn my back for a moment. It had already taken me years to accept that hanging my smalls on the outside washing line was a perfectly decent thing to do in my own backyard. Being flung further afield, with fewer friends in my vicinity, I frequently ran low on my vanlife uniform: baggy tops with leggings.

To spare time, I restrict myself to owning black socks of all the same size. This life hack will probably permit me at least an extra night in bed during the course of my anticipated lifetime. My choice of simple attire had me eking out around six weeks between the laundry chores. When dry, my clothes were easy to roll up and store so I deliberately selected fabrics that did not need separating into light and dark, that were multi-seasonal and capable of hiding a dribble or two. Sheets would only last so long between washes, especially with a cat. Finances and my conscience do not permit replacing old with new. Although once, after Nelson had a fit of the hairballs, right after I had changed linen, I did succumb to doing exactly that.

It is customary in literature to write a page of acknowledgements usually at the book's starting pages or its final ones. It would not be in my nature to swim with the tide, and so I shall position my thanks here to those who endeavoured to keep me presentable for public consumption: Claire in Kent, Shemeam, Dominic Green, Ewelina Szulc-Barnsley, Gill Boyles, Jacqui Lewis, Fiona Grainger, Bex Kilby, Jayne Fairbairn, Tanya Canetti, Virginia and Richard the Nut.

Now please do confess: which one of you is responsible for the red, and very skimpy, lacy knickers that somehow arrived in my life via my laundry basket?

****

It was on coming to the county that is the mealy-mouthed East Riding of Yorkshire that I found myself in need of a recap on exactly how England's most disgustingly named towns and villages came into being. Let us start with the assumption that the effrontery that is many of the East Ridings of Yorkshire towns' names began some time between 5000 BC and 4500 BC.

One argument is that naming conventions may have commenced, seemingly not at great speed, by the nomadic Mesolithic stone-aged peoples. It was their realisation that hunting large animals as a pack was a somewhat arduous occupation, not to mention incredibly time-consuming and dangerous. Would it not be far better instead to maintain a hunter-gatherer way of life, but from a central spot of convenience?

"Let's stay in one place. We could call it 'hom'". This was probably not quite how the suggestion came out. Instead, there was probably much guttural grunting in what I am sloppily describing as Old English as the tribes weighed up such a volte face in their way of being. My best guess is that a pregnant woman finally lost her shit and went on strike, having had enough of waddling up and down dale (even though the East Ridings of Yorkshire are notably flat and fen-like). Back then, however, the county was little more than vast tracts of bog and marsh, a thorough *Skidby*, making the waddling even more incommodious.

Given almost all collectives harbour at least one detractor who is the unofficial prophet of doom, I am presuming that a number of naysayers screeched out, "It'll never work!" or, "But that's not how we do things around here!" I reckon it was quite the delicious drama to partake in. Despite the myriad of objections, the age of permanent settlements may have begun with these avant garde stone-aged folks. What remains unaccounted for is, who was the trendsetter and how did all the other tribes catch on to such a revolutionary concept?

It is this quandary that leads to that other nomadic proposition: that agricultural workers from Europe drifted this way before intermingling with the locals, who seemingly just laid back and thought of England. Their migration also had them importing England's first domesticated cows, sheep and goats. Pigs already existed in the shape of boars, so they merely required taming.

The European settlers are said to have introduced the annual sowing of crops such as wheat and barley, stripping the land of its natural ecology, and replacing it with managed swathes. This furnished the legacy of tending to land in order to feed, not only the populace, but also their now captive docile *Swine*. Even today, The County of the East Ridings of Yorkshire remains the pig-farming capital of England.

The ideal residential plots needed to be situated adjacent to all-year-round supplies of fresh water: once also called swine! Thankfully, this was not challenging for the incumbents of the East Ridings of Yorkshire, the county being a gentle swampy buffer between the Yorkshire Dales and the coast. In fact, the primest of sites were located on the many small islets that proliferated in the fens. These not only maximised a sense of protection but also thwarted any of the animal's wild ambitions for absconding and reduced the need for fencing. In Old Norse, such micro islands were called ‘Holmr’ which have become modern days ‘Holms’. Naturally, as groups settled far and wide, dialects did their thing, and ‘homs’ bifurcated into ‘hams’ or ‘holms’. Thus, we have the beginnings of a north-south divide as well as the invention of ‘hamlets’.

This clustering of dwellings solved many difficulties and yet a whole host of new conflicts spawned: pertinently around capacity, ownership and entitlement. Not least, was the small matter of fencing, not the kind involving swords, but those regarding boundaries and barriers: perhaps even originating in *Rimswell.* Naturally, livestock needed to be penned in, but by doing so, such visible partitions conferred spaces as ‘ours’ and ‘not ours, but perhaps one day’. No doubt such an invention as fencing also instigated the very first neighbour boundary dispute.

Incidentally, in bygone days ‘swell’ meant much the same as it does today: to grow bigger; and without doubt, the radical change from a-wandering to a-staying stimulated a population boom. The hams expanded in every direction, with multiple houses gathered together in less than holy matrimony. “We’re bursting at the seams,” many a hamletter might have decried in now slightly less grunty tones. And if there is one thing that humankind always agreed on: size matters.

Societies thus needed some way of distinguishing themselves from the paltry simpleton hamlets of yesterday to reflect the multi-occupancy, multi-generational, multi-hutted megahams they now inhabited. ‘Wicks’ was the Germanic solution, loosely coming to represent more sizable villages such as *Burstwick.* Later on, the word would come to denote a dairy farm, probably found on the outskirts of the hamlets and villages.

Then, just like now, every village needed to harbour its very own idiot. The now Neolithic wicks would likely also have an accuser bemoaning that the rest were not pulling their weight; a micro-manager nit-picking away over work production while achieving little themselves; an overblown show-off making phallic monuments; someone to gripe about the quality of the harvest or the food (likely both) and, of course, someone else to complain about the stench of the fly-ridden animals. Before long, a group of renegades thinking they could do better would up sticks and sod off to establish themselves a utopia elsewhere. Thus, came the ‘thorpes’, or wick-ships, or side-hamlets for want of a better term, like that of *Bugthorpe.*

Other communities, in their quest to maintain or otherwise impose peace, would call on the spiritual to remind all and sundry that morality, cohesion and harmony ought to be sought, lest God smite one's crops or flocks. Failing that, it left the senior leadership teams to conjure up the much-derided, and very squirmy, concept of team-building away-days. Only, they called them harvest festivals – gatherings of enforced fun and frivolity involving a maypole, some jingly bells and a few drums. All arranged, I presume at great expense, in the vain hope that everyone would just collaborate nicely thereafter. Naturally, in the event of that not harmonising the team, one could always fall back on blaming the messengers of God, which may well explain *Nunburnholme.* In the interests of historical accuracy, it is oft-reported that the 'burn' in this instance is derived from the old English meaning 'stream'. The nuns came much later, when there was a shortage of eligible bachelors, and a beastly patriarchy, which permitted little by way of women's autonomy. That said, the nuns were largely burnt to death at the hands of Henry VIII so the *Nunburnholme* nomenclature was more of a foretelling than a recollection.

Over time, the thorpes and the wicks pursued their relentless expansion. Somewhere down the line, lords of the manor were born. Of course, the more wealth one has, the more one hankers for it. But it is equally true that the more one has, the more abjectly one fears loss. Thus, it was the engorged manor houses that came, by hook or crook, to dominate the ebb and flow of life of the surrounding settlements.

On occasion, the hamlets, wicks and thorpes all needed to be distinguished from one another and where one hailed from would dictate how much swing and sway one had. Some folk truly thrived, in part through favour, and yet others through an abundance of crops or simply because of their fortuitous location. Through these elements, fiefdoms rose and fell.

Thus, it came to pass that some of the villages morphed into little towns with little markets: thriving little micro-economies of supply and demand. In turn, this generated the need for the efficiency of exchange. With that came the invention of hard currency being valued as much as the honed skills of bartering, negotiating and contracting. The more urbane the deal, the more one required the services of an educated elite. Of course, with the educated elite, came the need for better remuneration. And that is how such enclaves of early commerce evolved into gloriously small towns, such as *Weeton.*

However, with population growth comes struggle. The powers that came to rule thought it best to insist that, like stock, human resources be confined within a given proximity. Thereafter, man was beast: fed, watered and exploited. The epoch of totalitarianism was upon us and who heralded from where suddenly became of paramount importance in the hierarchy of life, and allowed hamlets to proliferate. Oftentimes, it was simply enough to name a new dwelling place by relating it to a notable feature. Many Yorkshire hamlets adopted the very simple suffix 'by' to denote an abode or hamlet. That said, plenty of others argue that 'by' is a remnant of Old Norse for 'law' or 'rule', whereas others still claim it is Old Norse for farm, the Vikings seemingly having tired of ham.

Naturally, the towns, villages and hamlets required much by way of food, production of which required much by way of cultivation of land. Such cultivation demanded much by way of its man, woman and animal power. And with so much man, woman and animal power, came much manufacturing of manure. All this leads to the near-obsolete Yorkshire-ism of 'where there's muck, there's *Sewerby.*'

So this is the tale of how it came to be that England's sleepy little settlements became cultured. It was humans doing what humans do that led to the accretion of settlements across these fair lands and no place more aptly demonstrates our relentless march towards civilisation than the ostentatiously-sounding County of the East Ridings of Yorkshire.

And if all of that fails to impress, then one can always claim they hail from *Wetwang,* arguably so-called as it was a field where a legal dispute was settled. Who'd have thunk it? There really is nothing more straightforwardly Yorkshire than naming places as a result of their surroundings.

Spouting Rubbish in South Yorkshire

Half the class plonked themselves down in the computer room, the other half were milling about doing maths revision in the adjacent room. The screens were already lit up with mouldy green characters. We were to tap in our names, dates of birth and sex before answering, to the best of our ability, a series of questions about our interests, our anticipated grades and our impressions of our own aptitudes and mindsets. I enjoyed history, was reasonable at maths, disappointing at English literature, slightly better at English language, abysmal at French, hopeless at physics and fairly indifferent to the rest of my chosen subjects – most of which had been subtly chosen for me in any case. Did I like order, routine and precision, or was I more artistic and creative? God only knows, I was so indoctrinated into 'right thinking' that I couldn't be trusted with my own opinion. Whatever it was I inputted, within thirty minutes or so, the printer replied by spitting out a series of potential career paths. I do not recall the implications. In response, the master pointed out that the data indicated I would not thrive in the military. Here endeth the lesson on careers: public school style. I barely knew anything about the working world beyond managers, teachers, pilots, air crew, check-in staff, cleaners, administrators and nurses. Besides, university was the expectation, was it not? There was time a-plenty surely?

****

Wending my way down the east coast of England, me and my two bags of rubbish on the front seat came to roost in the birthplace of governmental recycling policy: *Barnsley*, South Yorkshire.

It is said that the average person generates just over two kilograms, or four and a half pounds, of waste per day, although that figure would not include the human matter that goes down the loo. I produced around twenty to thirty litres of disposable detritus per day if I claimed the cat's share for myself, although our production included some substances of the *Dungworth* kind. That said, since compostable woodchip cat litter had returned to the menu, our contribution to landfill had reduced significantly.

One of the restrictions of vanlife is the futility of dedicating time to sorting rubbish into paper, metal and plastic because I simply do not have the space, nor access to, suitable receptacles. Instead I have to happen upon public amenities, usually at service stations or roadside, and then discreetly chuck the lot into their bins. Vanlifers encourage one another to tap into one's inner womble: it is in our interests to leave an area tidier than when we pitched up in the battle to retain access to spaces, but how universally this is applied, I cannot say. All I know is that once a week, I collect up an additional fifty litres – usually wet wipes, cigarette packets, drinks containers and fast food wrappers.

Alas, I had nothing made of glass with which to commemorate my arrival at the location of the nation's first bottle bank because, unlike in 1977, milk, fizzy drinks and cosmetics are barely ever sold in glass containers. Thus, it can be said that South Yorkshire is the birthplace of recycling but one does have to overlook that in the 1950s, housewives had to be taught how to generate waste. Back then, the marketing extolled how time could be freed up by using plastic cutlery, plates and disposable wax-sheened cups, and women were cajoled into buying pre-packaged meals. The Second World War had reduced our rubbish to near zilch, and even prior to that, we were incredibly efficient at recycling – with many bulkier items like glassware being subjected to a deposit-based benefit. It is odd now to think that women once required demonstrations on how to use cling film rather than Tupperware and that we had to be convinced that plastic carrier bags were better than linen shopping bags.

These days, there are fifty thousand bottle banks of varying colours dotted about the country dedicated to collecting glass. They encourage the environmentally conscious to sort their vessels into brown, clear or green matter and approximately one-fifth of the nation uses them. Many of England's councils allocate separate bins for glassware to each house. Such a provision does not demand sorting glass by colour. Except one must never put Pyrex in, no matter how brown the glass is. Nor should the bins be used to discard lightbulbs, spectacles, some drinking glasses, vases, mirrors or empty nail varnish bottles. And that is just for glass matter. One practically needs a GCSE in recycling to cope with other substances such as cardboard boxes, plastics, compost and cooked food, all of which is localised to the county's policy. It is a good enough reason alone to never move house!

It is possibly for this reason of county-generated policy that England is said to be the laggard of Europe when it comes to manufacturing glass: a substance that is 100% recyclable and requires forty percent less energy to smelt than mixing it from sand, soda ash and limestone. This is in part attributed to too few councils providing dedicated glass collection bins. Even fewer ask that glassware be colour-coordinated, unlike in Germany, that bastion of comparable efficiency. Around ten years ago, we were recycling around half of what our German cousins did, the undisputed kings of European glass recycling. Then Covid happened. Suddenly, the glassware was taken away from the hospitality industry and put into the homes of humans who were restricted in their movements. And bam! Our glass recycling targets were shattered: reaching a rate of recycling of 76.5%, which is 3.5% shy of the government's target of 80% by 2030.

Not that the government gave any credit to the people, of course. The government at the time was too enamoured by their own very private cheese and wine parties. The cabinet, it seems, got smashed more than once at the time the rest of the country was doing the environment the greatest-ever rehabilitation service. Their parties, I have no doubt, were serviced by professional caterers. Commercial victualers are less likely to recycle than your average householder. Glass is, as I have already said, 100% recyclable: yet interestingly, only household glass is weighed, assessed and analysed or otherwise obliterated into data.

Old glass windows and greenhouse panes simply end up as landfill each year, albeit a small quantity is crushed down to make aggregate in road construction. The remaining two hundred thousand tonnes is simply made into mountains because there is absolutely no financial imperative for demolition companies to recycle it. To put that in perspective: each household throws away around one-eighth of a ton of glass per annum, which is the equivalent of 1.6 million households not bothering to recycle their glass on top of the approximate six and a half million households who prefer to send it to landfill for reasons of confusion, lack of suitable bin, sheer exhaustion, incompetence or laziness – delete as appropriate.

In over half of British households, it remains 'a 'man's job' to take the bin out. It is also the man's job to change the lightbulbs, remove spiders, mow the lawn, dust the windowsills, mop the floors, hoover the carpets and stairs, sort the recycling, scrub the toilet and change the bed linen. Although this is only typical if he lives alone and does not hire a cleaner*. In the event of a female partner, just 22% of men say they do their fair share.

*It almost goes without saying that this assumes the household is very traditional and very heterosexual, but once upon a time, taking the bin out was classified 'a man's job'. Unsurprisingly, this all changed with the advent of recycling. Women, it is reported, are twice as likely to comply with a myriad of guidelines surrounding recycling.

In true English nonsensical fashion: while it was viewed as the man's role to remove the household waste from the receptacle indoors to the wheelie bin outdoors, it was the woman who was responsible for heaving the outdoor bin from its usual position to the kerb to await collection. She was also responsible for returning it too.

The advent of multiple bin management systems being incorporated into the kitchen meant the kitchen bin was no longer a fetid, heaving mess, patiently waiting for the man to swoop in to rescue incumbents from their rancid peril just before bin collection day. No, these days almost all plastic, glass or tin has to be put through the dishwasher first then crushed before being sorted into appropriate piles, which vary according to one's postcode. Only then, is it taken to a larger receptacle to await collection once a fortnight. Somehow all this complexity utterly turned the tables.

Not that it is all bad news. I was heartened to read that the waste management sector is just one of three industries where women out-earn men – by a whopping seven percent. The other two? The industries of sewerage and water treatment. Otherwise career women earn four-fifths of what the menfolk do as a general rule.

This rare piece of economic reality is largely attributed to the fact that the calculations are based on the median hourly rate of all workers at all ranks, rather than being role-specific or hierarchical. Indeed, almost all 'binmen', nowadays called 'waste management operatives, are men earning a couple of pounds above minimum wage. The women employed are more likely to be in junior management roles and their earnings warp the statistics quite considerably.

That the job of binman fits around childcare so well is the burning attraction of such a position; it readily lends itself to part-time hours and by walking up to nine miles a day one would save a fortune in gym membership. Given women have become so adept at driving wheelie bins to the kerb, combined with the fact that there is no heavy lifting involved any more, it is a wonder that the work remains spectacularly male. But then again, with English society functioning as it does, not really.

The Homestead of the Snot People

I leafed through a magazine, it may have been 'Just Seventeen' or 'Take A Break' or 'Cosmopolitan' or something equally as appealing to my teenage self, while biding my time for an appointment to see the dentist. Taken alone by taxi, periodically having my braces adjusted was nothing but a brief blip away from the routines of school life. Waiting to be called, sitting unaccompanied in my uniform on a hard-backed chair I was enraptured by an article on foster children and their feelings of loss, abandonment, rejection and helplessness. How they grow up too soon, and struggle to connect with others. How their expectations for life were shaped by their experiences. It was heartbreaking in its transparency, and I was agog.

"I think like that," I whispered to myself. "I feel like that," I murmured to no one.

"But you're in boarding school, not state care. You're privileged. You're special. You're lucky." I silently overrode my thoughts before the receptionist called out my name.

****

I only knew two things about Nottinghamshire before the Shitron, Nelson and I swanned in. First, that it was the location for England's most gravest personal insult, although in order to keep it suitable for the children, *Newark* had it disguised in anagram form.

As for the other fact: it was the birthplace of England's most tenacious, most virtuous paragon. The one who had taken on power in all of its corrupted forms, exposing the cruelty of churches, charities as well as the establishment. A pertinacious seeker of redress on behalf of their victims. The true hero of Nottinghamshire needs no epithet.

Margaret Humphreys says of this City of the Snots, "My home town boasts many attractive features, but the evening rush-hour traffic is not one of them." I was inclined to agree with her as I skirted around what may well be Britain's most iconic council house.

I have never lived in one myself; being a child of two stately homes, and a myriad of rentals, you can imagine the sort of contempt I held for them. In my defence, I maintain that this is not exclusive to the elite nor the fellow boarding school pseudos; the media of all classes loves to portray council estates as squalid, crime-ridden ghettoes, suitable for only the most despairing of people. More typically, these agglomerates are denounced as nothing but havens for the workshy, those whose efforts to obtain fulfilling employment is depicted as little more than a sop to further their benefit claims. The nemesis of the *Worksop.*

It is an oft-held myth that one does not leave a sink estate, one escapes. It is also a classic example of 'she who controls the rhetoric, controls the mind'. Conversely, Teresa May MP, former British Prime Minister, called our national social housing schemes, "the biggest collective leap in living standards in British History," and it is hard to debate that assertion when contemplating the squalor that was Nottingham's slums in the 1920s.

Families, penurious and enervated after the First World War, and their menfolk having been compulsorily enlisted into combat, were out of ideas, innovation and options. By mid-1916, thanks to the meticulous work of Notts Heritage Gateway, I learned that over twenty-four thousand men, a fifth of Nottingham's entire male stock old or young, had volunteered for battle, twice the current population of *Warsop.* Still, it was insufficient to meet the burden of war. Following the introduction of conscription, a further twenty-five thousand, the bulk of Nottingham's eligible men aged between 18 and 51, were dragooned into military service despite over fifteen thousand demurring the mandate. Their wishes and feelings were first ridiculed, then overruled by martial courts, and any conscientious objectors were subsequently shunned for cowardice.

By 1918, nearly five and a half thousand of Nottingham's menfolk, over ten percent of those called to fight for His Majesty, had perished. It is telling that three years after the ceasefire, Nottingham's General Hospital, place of *Owthorpe,* was still treating in excess of eighteen thousand permanently disabled former servicemen.

While war is held as the ultimate failure of social and political responsibility, from an adult woman's perspective, conscription was the state-sanctioned abandonment of family life. The passing of The Military Service Act in 1916 forced children to grow up without fathers and mothers to supply for them without their primary providers, antagonising the belief that the woman's role was in the home and that to aspire otherwise was unnatural, or the fanciful chatter of the radical suffragette. Only men could be lionhearts, only men were placed in a position that recognised their sacrifice in the *Mansfield* of Flanders and beyond. Only men's names would be recorded on the monuments erected in almost every hamlet, town and village, lest we forget their sacrifice.

The women's job was to put up, shut up and get on with it. For the designated heroes fortunate to be reinstated back to civilian life, they returned to decimated cities struggling to accommodate them, let alone resolve the trauma that war had inflicted upon the psyche. Women's mental health goes unrecorded. Much lamented, however, was the men's lack of employability and resettlement. It was a national scandal in the brewing, and radical shifts in public policy were only convened under the threat of revolution.

Perhaps, in this instance, a more kindly view is required. In the race to care for the survivors, prefabricated high-rises of concrete and steel were thrown up. What is less well known to the world at large is England's clay-riven lands make for a weak base, requiring more concrete reinforcement than would be needed in the rock-basins than underpin the larger continents. It is why we avoid building high wherever possible.

Nevertheless, high-rises were the initial means for Nottingham's councillors to resolve the pressures besetting the city's boundary, brimming as it was with impoverishment, sickness and degradation. They were soon denounced as brutal, sunshine-occluding eyesores, and their legacy sees them portrayed in the nation's psyche as concrete boxes infested with crime, vandalism and piss-soaked stairwells. Consequently, any city of tall buildings, like that of Nottingham, is depicted as a modern-day *Gotham*... much in need of a Batman to save the day.

Enter Nottingham's Chairman of the Housing Committee; following a trip to Scotland, the construction baron conceived of the archetypal council house. Typically in Nottinghamshire, homes came with outdoor privies in small courtyards, suitable for keeping one or two livestock or for storing coal. Identikit front doors opened straight onto the narrow streets, across which Monday's laundry hung, weather permitting. But building more of such idylls was hampered by a shortage of skilled labour, building materials and time. Thus it fell to the Batman of the Housing Committee to introduce to the county the concrete-walled, metal A-framed, prefabricated home – known as 'prefabs' in the wider rhetoric but 'Crane Houses' to local residents.

Within twenty years of the first world war ending, Nottinghamshire was the county most applauded for having the swiftest, most effective builders of state-subsidised living quarters. Many of the much-maligned, pebble-dashed prefabs are still standing today, having outlasted their ten-year life expectancy by one hundred years and counting. What also endures is the debate on whether some strata should continue to be housed for below-market rates, when other citizens are confined to a choice between a lifetime's debt or leasing from a private second-home owner, finance-backed corporation or aristocratic portfolio. Is the taxman just a modern day Robin Hood, taking from the wealthy to reallocate to the poor, or are the poor simply too workshy to pay their fair way in society?

Back in the city of Nottingham, on March 17th, 1927, eight years after the signing of the Treaty of Versailles, which formally ended the first world war, Nottingham's latest Chairman of the Estates Committee laid the foundation stone of the grandest state building to be commissioned in the UK in the twentieth century. Costing in the region of £500,000 (a cool £40 million in 2023's money), the controversy was smoothed over by the City Councillor's very public assurance that business taxes, rather than any increase in housing rates, would keep it solvent. Quite what the entrepreneurs of Nottingham had to say about that is anyone's guess, but regardless, Nottingham Council House was erected in three short years. The final stage of construction was commemorated by the placement of a *Little John* within its striking dome.

I was somewhat dispirited to find that *Little John* was not a public convenience, but rather England's fifth-heaviest bell. Weighing in at ten and a half tonnes, it was quickly, with typical English wryness, dubbed *Little John* after Robin Hood's most favoured and somewhat over-sized lieutenant. With deep resonance, *Little John* reminds the city-dwelling denizens of its existence every fifteen minutes, and when the technology fails, all through the night too.

Nottingham's Council House is now a grade II listed baroque edifice and the envy of many a market square. The centrepiece is its eight Portland stone columns, holding aloft a façade depicting the town councils' twenty-one divisions who had pledged to serve the merry folk of Nottinghamshire. What those twenty-one faculties were remains a mystery to me, but typically a town council's duties are restricted to managing public amenities such as parks, washhouses, cemeteries, bridleways, bus shelters, rubbish bins, village halls and war memorials. These days, most of the departments have been relocated for fiscal reasons to Loxley House – clearly the businessfolk of Nottinghamshire failed to keep up with the councillors' aspirations!

County Councils, on the other hand, tackle wide-ranging social issues and needs affecting a region and devise policies for addressing them. They are funded both through local taxation (council tax) and government grants for which they must compete. They are less concerned with the management of amenities, but instead concentrate on the provision of services such as housing and highways, environmental protection, the promotion of arts and culture, planning and development, as well as facilitating children's and adults' services.

The latter assignments are collectively lumped together as 'social services'. It was they who employed the Nottingham born and bred, Margaret Humphries. Her role required her to interact with parents who, for various reasons, were not well equipped to raise their own children. No doubt it is a thankless task that most would baulk at if given the responsibility. In her spare time, she voluntarily ran a group helping adult adoptees and looked-after children talk about their experiences and world view, helping them to make sense of their lives.

Life is full of remarkable, upending events and then there are those moments that are so unremarkable, one does not realise the significance until later. Just before I departed for Nottinghamshire, I enjoyed a coffee with a friend in one of those fancy boutique places. The kind that set themselves apart with Farrow and Ball paintwork; a hotchpotch of antique chairs and tables, all with wobbly legs; faux-stained vintage pictures and a feature wall to contrast the rest of the decor. This particular one had opted to re-home the unwanted, oft-rotated books found gathering dust in high street charity shops.

Several hundred examples of such fodder had been recycled to create a homely feel. One of the books, a hardback, screamed out 'Empty Cradles' along its spine in bright red capital letters. It caught my eye. For a quick donation to charity, it was mine.

Nobody just puts children on a boat and sends them halfway across the world without their parents – that was Margaret's initial disbelief when meeting a woman who claimed her brother had been sent to Australia when she was aged just four.

As a social worker, Margaret's role was to make decisions on behalf of children. "What will she think years from now?" she asked herself in the opening chapter, having just removed someone's daughter from the family home, "What will she think about the decisions being made for her? What will she think about being separated from her mother and father?" at the behest of the county?

'Empty Cradles' tells the stories of children being shipped overseas. She, and they, went on to discover that almost everything they were told as a child was a lie. Not all were born in Nottingham, but many were told that their parents had died, or had not wanted them, before being transported to Australia, *Rhodesia* and Canada. Their role? To populate them for the purposes of protecting England's former colonies against the threat of multiculturalism, for the expressed purpose of keeping those countries white. Those children grew up, and yet were never offered citizenship of the host country and had seemingly no ties to this one. A lifelong legacy of asking themselves, "Who are you and where are you from?"

England's taken children were, at the request of the Australian and Canadian governments, and complicit with ours, removed from their country of birth, to be assigned to charity-run Christian institutions – to serve the Commonwealth as farmhands, domestic workers and breeders of the next generation. Only those children relocated to *Rhodesia* spoke positively about their experiences – little wonder given they were to join the white ruling ranks of the colony, and were largely adopted into host families. The remainder of the migrant children talk about hellish institutional life, without reprieve, at the mercy of cruel or cold caretakers; far from anything familiar.

"How could they? How could they?" It is a common refrain among the adult-child survivors to the woman who had noticed them. Margaret Humpreys, Nottingham's most authentic hero, went on to set up the Child Migrants Trust and write the book 'Empty Cradles'. Later, the essence of the book was fictionalised into 'Oranges and Sunshine'; the royalties from which fund the charity. Like many, it struggles to get sufficient income to complete its primary objective of tracking down surviving relatives for the discarded, abandoned children who forever will ask, "How could they?"

How could the boarding school elite, many themselves abandoned to an institution as children, go on to put in place such a devastating policy of *Scarrington*? I have since learnt that many boarding school children, at the polar end of the scale and having survived similar institutional abuse, go on to ask the same very same question of their own parents.

A wise woman recently told me, "there has to be a pre-existing dysfunction within the family to force the conclusion that boarding school is a viable option for bringing up children." To extrapolate that outwards: there had to be pre-existing dysfunction in our public school-abandoned leaders for them to have rationalised robbing the children of the poor, to serve the rich far from home.

The Yellow Peril of Lincolnshire

"... the world's mine oyster" are the actual words. Apparently. I am free from the perils of Shakespeare's impenetrable plots, from homeostasis, exothermic reactions and the particle model of matter. Free from exams, and hothoused elitism. I have an out from the boarding school way of life: I had met my obligations grade-wise, gifting to the school their proof of purpose by passing all my exams apart from French, for which I was in receipt of a 'D'. Perhaps it was the subjunctive that did for me after all.

According to my mother, the school would not welcome my return unless I agreed to sign a contract promising to behave myself. Otherwise, I would have to go local. There was implied shame and risk in this: that I will forgo the mysterious training that will ensure I could stand on my own two feet, to develop 'life skills', to be more socially adept than my day-school peers. I would eschew the chance to obtain a true sense of independence all while being kept 'safe'. All the usual brochure guff that makes the parent the customer, and the child the commodity. Despite my so-called superior education, I could not have articulated it in such a way at the time. I felt so estranged from my peers despite my friendship group, and how much more adult did I need to be? To travel the world unaccompanied, to befriend stranger after stranger, all while being housed amongst bullies and the odd paedo with few opportunities for respite?

I had a choice, and the world was my oyster. I thought the school was my prison. That I was somehow missing out on a real life but now I could choose to be free, with the blessing of the headmaster, a man I had never spoken to, who did not wish for my return. My best friend did not have the same choice. Again with child, this one would be allowed to come to life, hopes were that I might just grow up outside of the shadow of her influence.

Trouble must be afoot if my father was taking time to join me intermittently in the smoking hut to let me know he felt great responsibility for my habit, while giving me permission to help myself to his cartons. We went horse riding together and he seemed more at peace than previously known. I had put it down to him taking time away from work, just the Saturday mornings, but that was better than nothing, right? Perhaps, on reflection, it was the consequence of my brother hitting the heady heights of lawful adulthood, and refusing all invitations to visit the family. He headed off for a Russell Group university, fully supported financially by my parents. For now, I was the only child in their orbit.

What to do? What to do indeed.

****

The Admirable Nelson, like all cats, has a plethora of quirks. I had duly noted his preference to chill in his cat bed beneath the gear stick when I was absorbed in a podcast. However, the minute I opted for music, blasting out via a six-inch thick speaker sitting on the passenger seat, he jumped up and settled down, smothering the stereo. Eventually, I deduced that the furry imbecile presumed the contraption was purring in response to his cuddling.

England's most yellow county whizzing by had me warbling along to Miley Cyrus' *Flowers.* Glances, further afield, the vista conjured up an even stranger notion to download 'Yellow' by Coldplay. Lincolnshire's air was already saturated with pollen, and Nelson's eyes sprung leaks as we cruised past floccose verges, already mottled with clusters of glowing dandelions and shimmering puffballs. As far as the gaze permitted, Lincolnshire's vast blankets of fields were *Steeping* in flowering oil seed rape, setting the land aflame as the first of glimpse of the beckoning summer splayed across the land. Between the dramatic illuminations, resting meadows sat sprinkled with huddles of yellow-belled cowslips. Even the lichen was yellow.

We skirted around the delectable Scunthorpe, bound instead for the capital of Lincolnshire's most awful-sounding places to live: *Grimsby.*

Falling deeply in love with the aptly monikered yellow-bellied county of Lincolnshire, I discovered it to be a place where the locals are just as perplexed as to why they came to be referred to as 'yeller bellies'. What is certain, however, is the phrase in the East of England has nothing to do with cowardice as it might be perceived in lands far beyond her waters. Indeed, how pusillanimity came to be associated with yellow remains a mystery all of its own. The delightful colour of sunshine has oft been used to persecute those who we revile. It seems that *Tongues End* will always wag, but that truths will not always out.

Once upon a time, Lincolnshire's heavily cultivated fenlands billowed with the autumn-flowering mustard plants. Interspersing weeds would be munched away by the field-fertilising Lincoln Longwools playing their part to yield the next season's crop. Their ever-growing fleeces brushed up against the dark yellow pollen. Subsequently, Lincolnshire's puffs of wool sported a distinct underside of yellow, offering us one plausible 'yeller-belly' legacy before they were exited stage right in the name of progress.

Polyculture has a limited role in the expansive agricultural practice that is modern farming. Nowadays, it is more akin to an industry dependent on sophisticated chemicals and generous grants. Together, they are combined to ensure England's most prominent growers can supply Britons with just over half of their vegetable consumption. The remainder is imported from fields of foreign yonder. Lincolnshire's flatlands are renowned for supplying the English dinner tables with their most cruciferous plants: broccoli, turnip, brussel sprouts, peas, cabbage and cauliflower. The genus whose by-product is most politely referred to as flatulence. Little wonder then that Lincolnshire is home to *Belchford, Farthorpe* and *Rippingale.*

It is claimed that as we age, we are inclined to become old farts. Although, one study of sixteen thousand participants, and the only one known to Google, refutes this. It turns out the young are more inclined to parp but a broader caveat for this unexpected turn of events is that old people are more likely to under-report their bottom belches. It is a phenomenon known as 'social desirability bias': the worrying of what others might think of us if we told the truth, even when clearly it is of paramount national importance that the truth be told!

An acquaintance of mine relayed the tale of her recent introduction to her son's latest girlfriend. There are mutterings that she is probably 'the one'. The scent of romance, like his pungent aftershave, lingers long in the air as he wafts dreamily from room to room in a heady bout of youthful fervour. It is the stark reminder that he is on the cusp of adulthood, and she on the cusp of obsolescence.

"I said 'hi' and promptly old-lady farted as I stood up to greet her," she whimpered. The *Old Leake* has started. The tale was all it took for my eyes to stream with tears as slippery as those of the hayfevering Nelson. I could only recommend she invests in a dog for use as an alibi.

The best advice is to avoid foodstuffs that cause gas, which is pretty much all the vegetables that Lincolnshire produces in abundance. Furthermore, if one is sensitive to obnoxious fumes, it is best to avoid the entire county of Lincolnshire in January, because that is *Muckton*-spreading season, a time of *Wellingore*. Slurry-spreading has fallen out of favour in recent times, predominantly because of the harmful ammonia it releases into our atmosphere. That said, the government's ongoing battle with inflation had them step away from banning the noisome of the countryside. It is hard to imagine now, but in the not too distant future, the pong and whiff of biosolids will be nothing more than a distant memory. Just a tale to bore the next generation with. "I remember when these green fields smelt of old farts," the old farts will reminisce. One can practically hear their unborn grandchildren rolling their eyes already.

But change is said to generate resilience: that mystical substance that has one successfully adapting to adversity, stress and life-affective experiences. I find this linkage odd – surely I, with my lifetime of instability, should sail through life with a mere shrug of near equanimity, no matter how severe the calamity.

It was the slowly farting tyre, a *New Leake*, that had me on the cusp of a mental breakdown. It was one of my pre-trip fears: I have not got a scooby doo about how to change a tyre, let alone repair one on a three and a half tonne van. Of course, it happened on the day I was feeling all 'she-man' because I had finally, I hoped, sealed the roof of the van – having attempted multiple times, only to be repeatedly heartbroken upon the arrival of yet another Spring shower.

To compound my self-admonishment, I had not got around to repairing the previous tyre after it had spontaneously deflated, causing the recovery service to be beckoned yet again. With no spare, there was little point summoning them. It was my right front tyre, the new one, that looked decidedly sluggish. It turns out it is surprisingly easy to deal with: simply pay a garage. First, ring to ensure that long-wheel vans are most definitely within their remit, being very clear that the van is a long-wheel base. Be confident about their assurances, and present oneself as scheduled. Then, wait two days for said garage to determine both front tyres need replacing, before placing a second order. Watch on as they break the mechanism that hangs the spare tyre under the van, and then suppress the inner 'Karen' (a term I deem utterly misogynistic) while listening to the repairman recommend one goes to another garage to get the actual fitting done because, and I quote, "the van might be too heavy". I persisted and somehow just avoided losing my shit. Several hundred pounds later, I gained two shiny new tyres and an operating spare, as well as some more character to add to my personality-building juice drink. No *Harmston*, I supposed. Despite the mental fatigue, it was not going to stop me getting to *Grimsby*.

"Grimsby named as one of the worst places to live in England, but it's not as bad as it sounds" was this year's tempered headline in its local rag: The Grimsby Telegraph. Apparently, from a low of twelfth place, the last few years saw it wriggle down the national rankings, from sixteenth to eighteenth. This year the seaside town, Lincolnshire's most dangerous, was skimming around in thirtieth place – cause for celebration one would have thought, but perhaps it just implies that other places in England are faring worse.

With just a marathon-length of motorway, Lincolnshire's road network is mostly dominated by single carriageways and country lanes. Criss-crossing the sunken fenland was the helter-skelter of cupboard-discharging adventure. It had me both squealing and cursing in equal measure. As frequently as night follows day, I found myself re-stacking the contents of drawers and lockers, and more than once supplied Britain's verges with dried rice and pasta laced with cat fluff.

One reality of Britain's environmental policy is that electric cars are hammering the tarmac, all the while its owners are benefiting from tax breaks worth up to £2,000 per annum for their supposedly green credentials. The poorest will always be those who have to buy the cheapest second-hand diesels, and yet perversely it is they who are charged with paying an excess of levies and tax to off-set their adverse contribution to the environment. The era of the pricier Electric Vehicle is upon us, but there is still much *Cockerington* about the wholesale benefits of this motoring iteration. One would hope that it will not be long before those exacerbating the nation's collection of potholes are coerced into underwriting their repair. Politics may yet intervene, but until then, its residents might as well continue to mutter about the government and their ambitious austerity cuts.

Yet, there is something about prolonged asceticism that seems to suit this region. Lincolnshire's leaders may just be better adapted for sustained impoverishment, having endured decades of painful economic retractions: dismantling steel works; misguided anti-English fishing policies, and Britain's withdrawal from the EU restricting the supply of European pickers available to tend its farming enterprises. That is a lot of change for any economic region to *Swallow.* Lincolnshire is a non-stop parable of 'when life gives you lemons, make lemonade'; although in this county's instance it might as well be, 'when one's fishing industries dry up, convert one's coastlines into Britain's premier seafood processing plants.' Grimsby's most recent innovation is to turn one's cabbages into protein shakes, which sounds to my ears like the 'cabbage diet' all over again, except with fewer lumps. Just more *Grimsthorpe* to be tackled by the digestive tract.

The on-going government decade-long policy to starve councils of funds has introduced swinging cutbacks far and wide. Unlike other regions, England's fourth-biggest county, despite being sparse of hedgerow, can only afford to strim its curbs twice per year as opposed to the more typical thrice per annum. This has inadvertently created superhighways and havens for our many rural-dwelling mammals. Deep in the tangles that was once a gap between the farmland and the asphalt, our badgers, moles, hedgehogs and shrews can better reconnect with long-lost relatives. This will ultimately strengthen their gene pool and expand their life-expectancy. Albeit, those dependent on agricultural yields may be less than delighted by the pests' regeneration.

The other loser of the grass-growing policy is the motorist. Blind to the roadside drainage, some occasionally swerve off too-narrow lanes to permit the white woman van driver to cruise by. It was twice that I bore witness to a lower-slung car driver tipping their vehicle on its side in their keenness to allow me through unhindered. In both instances, the motorists claimed to have a friend with a tractor to come to their rescue. In Lincolnshire, one can readily believe it.

One other benefit of taking a driving tour of Lincolnshire, the vegetation is slowly devouring the speed limit signs. Not that was a problem, the potholes did wonders for keeping the right foot light. Nonetheless, somehow I picked up a speeding fine doing forty-nine miles per hour in the middle of the night on an A-road. I suppose it is worth remembering the adage: that before one dies, life will always be a *Bitchfield.*

There are Cheesy Goings-on, but not in Leicestershire

The smell of smoked cigarettes combined with the pong of a recently-used toilet resumed being the only evidence of his existence in our daily lives. Usually he left the fag end on the miniature ashtray affixed to the wall just above the roll of toilet paper. He left early, and came back gone midnight. Weekends were no different. She, on the other hand, bombed back from work to pour out a slug of brandy, splashing in a dash of ginger ale, gulping it down before exhaling dramatically. Only after that would I be greeted.

Sometime later she would start on dinner, but I learnt to politely decline. Pasta was often overcooked, or raw. Vegetables were black, or still growing. I took to making my own dinner. Cheese. I loved cheese. Packet macaroni cheese. Cheese mixed with rice. Cheese-stuffed jacket potatoes done in the microwave. Alternatively, packet soups with added pasta shapes would sustain me through the cheese shortages. Adventurous I was not.

By eight o'clock she was conked out on the sofa. Rarely did we rent a video to pass the evening away as she was already several glasses of wine down before it started and we had no terrestrial television. The capital's bookshop was limited in its supply. We had a computer in the dining room where I could play endless video games. No prep: my homework was done by early afternoon. My evenings were my own to entertain myself with – there was just a shortage of things with which to entertain myself.

****

It is often touted that morning should start with a meditation, a time of quiet reflection, to ground oneself in readiness for a bustling day. Perhaps one might even partake in a chant or become absorbed in a short, morale-boosting motivational quote. Anything to separate the psyche from its *Grimston* innermost thoughts that run rampant the moment my anxiety comes to detect a new dawn.

Whoever comes up with such schemes has neither had a cat nor young children. May's five o'clock sun rises had the not-so-jeffing-Admirable Nelson yowling to go out first thing. This was always several hours before I became similarly-minded. With another month to go until the longest day, his demands for a brisk morning's perambulation had become quite the ear-sore, and were only quieted by putting the pot on the stove for coffee to stoke me up for the day, then harnessing him up.

For the most part, I kept him leashed. I called it a compromise on the grounds of health and safety – his. If he could speak English – he is selectively mono-linguistically Korean – I suspect he would call my decision an abominable decimation of his feline rights. In Leicestershire, I spied many a hawk circling above us as we explored several metres of countryside, and wished for him not to be breakfast.

For the benefit of the uninitiated, walking a cat is quite unlike walking a dog. Dogs follow. Dogs, well most of them, obey instructions, even as they skitter backwards and forwards about their walking companion, their excitable tails creating a small wake of turbulence as they forage. They mindfully take a few moments to pee or poop, then continue bouncing and sniffing along the bridleway. On the whole, the dog and owner keep abreast of one another, and both benefit from a bit of forenoon's exercise.

Cats, on the other hand, at least mine, will spend a minimum of five minutes scanning their environment before tentatively stepping forward approximately half a foot. In Nelson's case, this would take him from the side door to the footstool. There, he would perch for a while in order to contemplate his inner zen. Some indeterminate time later, he might bimble off in search of some grass, or he might trot off. Or bolt. There was really no predicting neither the timing nor the velocity of his departure from the stool. For that reason, his leash was three metres long. Cats do not follow. Cats do not follow instructions either. Cats do, however, sniff one blade of grass tremendously intensively before biting the head off it or turning around to spray on it. Nelson would then decide that a blade of grass about twenty metres away must now be inspected – immediately. Such an inspection might take up to ten minutes. When done, I would release the leash so that Nelson could gallivant straight back towards The Shitron: sometimes at breakneck speed, sometimes outpaced by a snail, and occasionally flourished with a roly poly. Usually, he tripped on the footstool as he launched himself back into the van before splaying out for an early morning snooze.

During this period of outdoorsiness, I availed myself of some gentle, non-cat-spooking, stretches. Sometimes, when I had moments of sufficient presence of mind and time to grab my phone on the way out, I checked out the goings on in the frivolous world. I never read the news before dusk, but I do like a modicum of flippancy to accompany my morning slurp. Of course, this is as whimsical as Google decides and very much driven by any cookies left over from previous wanderings around the Interweb. No other kinds of cookies in my life last as long.

As I was in Leicestershire, home of one of England's most recognisable cheeses, it was unsurprising that Google had felt obliged to inform me that a Canadian woman had won this year's cheese-rolling contest, despite splurging unconscious over the finishing line. This contest of calamity takes place annually in Gloucestershire, and has done since 1826, although it has been banned more than once on the grounds of health and safety. For the unfamiliar, it involves a large wheel of Double Gloucester cheese being sent spinning down an exceptionally steep grassy knoll, and for reasons of idiocy, approximately twenty-to-thirty twenty-to thirty-year-olds chase after it. It is not necessary to catch the wheel to win. At the bottom of the hill is a haphazard line of string to mark the end of the race, behind which stand fifteen burly rugby players serving as brakes, and an entire fleet of St. John Ambulances.

Most participants stagger downhill for four or five paces before gravity and velocity do their scientific thing. On this particular morning, YouTube thought I might also appreciate 'People Chasing Cheese Downhill To The Sound Of Ave Maria'. YouTube was quite correct and it certainly set me up for a decent morning's work learning as much as I could about Leicestershire's most striking cheese.

I had always thought England was world-renowned for its cheeses, especially given that we gave the world Cheddar, or rather, Somerset did. The Americans, just like the British, have cheddar as their number one flavour of cheese, although recent experience did teach me that our two nations might not agree on how that flavour should, in fact, taste. So it came as a tremendous surprise that not one of England's five favourite cheeses was ranked in the best one hundred cheeses of the world. In fact, England only had one nomination and it neither came from Somerset nor Leicestershire. It was even beaten in the rankings by Montenegro's unpronounceable Pljevaljski Sir, the dreadfully mouldy Crottin de Chavignol (from where else but France), and the almost-*Wartnaby*-looking Bundz from Poland.

It transpires that England's sole entry to the Eurovision Cheese Contest was: the Lincolnshire Poacher. Coming in at fifty-fifth place, I was surprised that I, a life long turophile, had never tried it, let alone heard of it. It seems that it is also absent from both Tesco and the Vanlifer's most favourite supermarket: Morrison's.

Thankfully, TasteAtlas, who conducted the survey of over twenty-one thousand cheese-eating sufferers of ageusia, qualified that their rankings, "should not be seen as the final global conclusion about food." Thank Goodness for that: it would have me *Stoke Dry* into a most outraged fit.

A good cheese should in my opinion be full of flavour, pleasant on the nose, smooth on the tongue and, in particular, should have the quality of *Bitteswell.* Cottage cheese, for example, finds no home in my tiny van's refrigerator. Nor does Leicestershire's most notable cheese, the one that comes with Protected Geographical Status: the utterly unsuitable for vanlife, and very revolting: Stilton.

Stilton used to be a village in Leicestershire. Alas, it was requisitioned by Cambridgeshire, so the village is no longer eligible to churn out wheels of its bromodosis-smelling namesake. To call a cheese a Stilton, blue or white, it must be produced within a designated region and involve the ruination of some perfectly adequate pasteurised cows' milk, which must be obtained from specified locally-grazing dairy cows.

Once upon a time, such cows would have dwelled in the pastures of Lindley Hall Farm, owned ironically enough by a certain Mr Farmer and his wife, Mrs Farmer. His first name is recorded as Stephen. Hers not at all. Sadly in 2001, Foot and Mouth disease ran rampant through their holding and the subsequent culling of their animals ended any hopes of them continuing to contribute to the Stilton cheese factories. Today the farm is mostly livestock or arable, and they are registered as a farm by the Department for Environment, Food and Rural Affairs (DEFRA). DEFRA deems the farm to be in Warwickshire, largely because of the farm buildings' erroneous CV postcode. These fields are, however, most definitely within Leicestershire's borders. This most emphatic assertion was clarified in 2002 when the Ordnance Survey, the national mapping agency of Great Britain, decreed that one of Lindley Hall Farm's Leicestershire fields was the precise centre of England.

For five hundred years previously, Meriden in the West Midlands had staked the claim and reinforced this assertion with a monument of sandstone shaped into a cross. Then along came Global Satellite Positioning and it moved six miles, permitting Mr Farmer to stake a railway sleeper on his ground before announcing to all and sundry he was the fine owner of middle England. This reconfiguration stoked the ire not only of the residents of Meriden, but also those of Morton in Derbyshire, and Midland Oak in Warwickshire, some twenty-four miles south, as well as, probably, the notoriously indignant denizens of Tunbridge Wells, Kent.

For the record, I think Red Leicester is Britain's bestest cheese and the vast majority who prefer Cheddar are plain delusional. That said, both cheeses do best when kept in the door of the refrigerator, rather than deep within its recesses. One should also avoid storing it in cling film and Tupperware, ideally wrapping it in parchment paper so that it breathes rather than sweats. Of course, that presumes it lives in one place for very long at all.

What was the Point of Rutland?

"We are separating," my mother announced.

"Okay then," I replied. If she was looking for drama, I was the least likely to have been knocked over by a feather. That night she moved into what had been my brother's bedroom.

"We're not telling anyone for now," she informed me, "so you can't talk about it."

"Okay then," I replied.

"I thought you'd be more upset," she provoked me.

"Everyone is divorced these days. You're the freaks."

"We will be staying under the same roof until you are eighteen, then we'll tell people and I'll move back to England."

"Okay then," I repeated.

Within a week, my father was marching about town on an evening with a girlfriend. At least that is what I heard. I also heard my mother crying herself to sleep at night. I moved in with my lover, who I had been seeing for quite some time. He was thirty-one, I was sixteen. My one true love, or so I thought. I still did my homework religiously every afternoon.

****

Rut, in modern English, refers to a period of the year when the males of the species, usually deer and sheep, are at their most sexually active. In rutting season, the males are more prone to fighting. In more modern parlance, it might be said they have the '*Horn*'. And it was the merry hamlet of *Horn* that I ventured here to seek.

Rutland, home of upside down horseshoes, and far too many magpies to salute, is actually, contrary to what is attested on most of Rutland's tourist websites, the fourth smallest county in the UK.

Granted, it may possibly be the third depending on the tides caressing the Isle of Wight or the water level in England's largest manmade reservoir: Rutland Waters.

Perhaps, then, it is no coincidence that Rutland Water is shaped like a horseshoe set sideways, by way of compromise between those who believe that the tips facing up captures luck (most of England) and those who insist the ends facing down drip good fortune upon the heads of those who pass by (the Raddlesfolk). Such positioning of horseshoes provokes much debate for the three-quarters of Englanders who are said to be superstitious, even if only a tiny bit. According to YouGov, 14% of Brits believe in the 'power of hanging a horseshoe'. In reality, I think Rutland Water looks more like a pair of discarded antlers pointing west.

Quite why anyone thought the miniscule Rutland, over and above any other county, had spare land to drown, is anyone's guess. Possibly, someone thought the river Gwash should have a silent G, or that it should be returned to its original name of 'Wash'. Perhaps a bureaucrat elsewhere thought, "I'll go one better, and drown out the entire stream!" Or perhaps, they had had no luck in Rutland and in a fit of the hissies inflicted their wrath upon it. Either way, it was a wretched fortune for those who called the valleys around Gwash home.

Suffice to say, the proposal to submerge three percent of the county was opposed by the Raddlemen and women of Rutland. But, thanks to a surfeit of clay with which to conveniently build a dam, Rutland Waters became a site that, according to the Rutland County Museum, has gone on to, "become a major tourist attraction internationally recognised for its wildlife". It is a contention I found fascinating simply for the fact that I had never heard of Rutland Waters until after I passed by despite all my global jet-setting. All those years of living overseas, and all that chatting to folk not of this country, and not once did anyone enquire about Rutland Water's wildlife.

The flooding of the region overwhelmed one of the earliest dwellings in Rutland, the mediaeval Beehive Cottage, and the entire hamlet of Nether Hambleton. But what did evade the county's plunging was Normanton Church, whose earliest recorded Rector preached from 1227 to 1235. It would have been him, probably, who oversaw the earliest iterations of a Rutland wedding ceremony.

Once upon a mediaeval time, it was sufficient for a man and a woman to turn to one another and be married without so much as a witness being in attendance nor an exclamation of 'I do'. Although the man going down on one knee, possibly pleading, was a thing even then. But that was that: they were betrothed. It did not require the head-wrecking complications of compiling a seating plan for friends, families and other feral members of the community.

All told, marriage was for the purposes of securing financial, as well as political, advantage for the family, and was typically at the behest of the bride's father. It was not so much a case of 'love don't live here anymore' as 'there's no such thing as love'. Undoubtedly, it was the time period for the cynic to reign supreme. Such beliefs began the tradition of the bride not seeing the groom before the wedding, then presenting her smothered under a veil, wrapped up like a Christmas gift: it all contrived to prevent an efficient jilting.

Then the religious shoehorned themselves into the party: our canons believed it to be preferable if the betrothed gave verbal consent to the arrangement prior to them sealing the deal, or rather unseal the deal if she was of virginal qualities. From around 1215 onwards, it was decreed that only upon formal consent, combined with consummation, would the invisible marital bind be sanctified, and such nuptials would require the blessings of a priest.

By the sixteenth century, our clergy demanded that notices be spoken aloud in one's local parish church, usually at least four weeks before giving consent to married life. The priest, now firmly wedged into the legal process, would persist upon the couple that there should be absolutely no premarital shenanigans between handfasting, as the initial engagement was called, and the formal ceremony. History also records that very frequently the preachers' preachings fell on deaf ears and even more history recites that they were most indignant about no one taking a blind bit of notice.

Over time, came the custom that the husband and wife might wish to exchange tokens of hospitality to one another: a sort of 'welcome to our humble marriage' enactment. According to Wikipedia, this might be a gold ring, a coin, a pair of gloves or a toothpick. Thus began the precarious tradition of inappropriate gift-giving: buying lingerie, a vacuum cleaner or some pointless gadget for the kitchen or other household object inclined to detonate the first marital row. Then came vows, bouquets, witnesses, celebrants, souvenirs for the guests, extensive shopping lists authored by the happy couple, bridal magazines, tears, tantrums, reality tv shows, and a house deposit's-worth of debt.

Throughout, the nation has hung on to some pretty odd customs. Lucky horseshoes, for example, being part of the bouquet. Brides could marry in any colour of their choosing – white is merely a two-hundred year old tradition – but never red. If one was of Chinese heritage, it must have been a hell of a dilemma. Then came the insistence of having something borrowed, something blue, an old thing and a new thing for reasons that make absolutely no sense. Others espoused the importance of putting a coin in one's shoe – presumably limping to the altar is a catwalk fashion statement. One also might wish to consult on whether the moon is waxing or waning, as well as be mindful of the day of the week. Saturday, according to Celtic heritage, is most unpropitious. That it is now the most common day of the week to get married may serve as an explanation for why forty-two percent of marriages end in divorce. Another reason for the rising divorce rate is, of course, ceasing the practice of lobbing worn shoes at the newly-betrothed for luck. We replaced smelly footwear with white rice until someone discovered it was killing the wildlife, so we took to chucking confetti about the place. Then churches banned that for being messy, so now it is dried flowers.

About four-fifths of Englanders who marry do so outside of church. The last wedding to be conducted at Normanton Church was in 1954. Thereafter, the chapel was deconsecrated so the building could be reconstructed to withstand the incoming reservoir. Later, it was reopened as a wedding venue for couples to pledge their love in civil ceremonies and without an attending member of the clergy. These days, one can bypass the marriage bit altogether and just shack up instead: just like forty-eight percent of the couples in Rutland do, and nine percent of divorced Raddlesfolk probably regret not doing so.

Fascinatingly, one-third of Rutland's residents say they have never been married nor in a civil partnership. Yet, frustratingly, within this epicentre of singledom, I had absolutely no luck finding *Horn*.

Separating Ideologies in Cambridgeshire

He smashed my heart into smithereens. I had gone on holiday, and he slept with another girl. A girl, not a woman. Right before my exams, and despite all my hard work, I bombed them and failed to graduate from high school. Any university ambitions were in tatters, although it had clashed with my hope for a marriage.

There was no reason to stay now. My parents announced their separation to all and sundry, and yet still pratted about as if they were still together when in public, leaving observers confused. I had kept their secret for eighteen months, and now the cat was out of the bag.

The actual cat, dog and horse were all rehomed. My father moved house and briefly moved in with another girlfriend. I noticed that he worked regular hours now.

Where do I go now? England? Perhaps I might go to university, after all, to do any course that would have me. Only to be told that I was eighteen, I was an adult and that I would have to pay for it myself. Moreover, as a foreign learner, the fees were horrific.

****

I love being part of stealth communities, with all their secretive jargon and covert behaviours. When I was a quad-bike rider, motorcyclists whizzed by with a bob of their helmeted heads, or a raise of a solitary index finger, joining us briefly in mechanical solidarity. With vanlifers, the clanship is less strident, unless one is a solo woman traveller greeting another fellow solo woman traveller, then the full beam of a wide smile binds us together momentarily across windscreens. We are not as rare a breed as one might suppose. A similar invisible camaraderie exists between us and the women bus drivers who wind their windows down to give us a quick 'howdy-doody' as we squeeze our vehicles past one another on calm country lanes. Our sorority evokes a sense of the avant-garde about it all, a *Trumpington* demonstrating we are just fine and dandy as we are, and perhaps above all underpinned by a presumption that she too has surmounted the invisible mental and structural barriers of her sex. Conquering her inner demons of *Needingworth.*

It should not be this way, of course, but fairy tale fodder promised our girlish imaginations that all would work out perfectly and, having obtained a life partner, we would live happily ever after. Those very same books with their noble ambitions to instil in me right from wrong, also taught me that only good-looking people find love and happiness, and that ugly, fat people deserve miserable lives.

Then came the magazines with their endless suggestions on how to be alluring, to lure or to somehow modify ourselves to fit with a stranger's expectations. A belief system that we were simply not good enough as we were, that we must somehow adapt, change, alter from our position of lacking, limited or lamentable existence. An incessant whine that, "nobody will want to marry you unless…" You rid yourself of acne, you have pearly white, straight teeth, you slim down, you wear long hair, ad infinitum according to your current 'nots'. It seemed to me that romance was, in reality, better depicted as a sport: a game to be won, a prize to catch and an event to train for; dating was a game of *Huntingdon.*

I harboured a sinister belief that the end game for a girl was to be married. That the worst thing that could befall a woman was to be a spinster and old maid. The Romantic diarists foretold all who read that to be single was an unpalatable disgrace and that was despite over thirty-percent of women of that era being exactly that – neither married nor cohabiting. By depiction, they became objects to look at, to ridicule or to pity. And yet, nonsensically it inferred that the other seventy percent were content, satisfied or otherwise fulfilled. These days, an estimated forty percent of the adult population is neither cohabiting nor married – hardly a small minority.

Certainly no children's book warned me that I might meet middle age with divorce, that my husband would call time abruptly, to have me a *Welches Dam.* His decision thrust us amidst the other forty-two percenters who failed to terminate the marriage by conveniently expiring, leaving me to weep *Graveley* at my inability to surmount one of life's biggest challenges. The *Ring's End* saw it flung into the back of a cupboard and it took a year before the indentation smoothed out.

No one ever told me that the union's demise would leave me dwelling on the 'why' for far too long. That the seeking to understand would simply distract me from focusing on how to rebuild a life just for me. The 'why' is a fascinating but endless pontification – a veritable *Six Mile Bottom*. It is only natural to do so, we are told. To permit oneself to grieve, to not bounce back in some faux demonstration that it never mattered to begin with. But when is it enough? When does trying to learn from past mistakes, of necessary reflection, cross the line into pointless rumination?

There is one aspect of divorce that is eminently enjoyable: the invention of the many slurs upon which to pour scorn on his very being, like *Prickwillow.* I confess, it took a few years before I permitted myself to use his first name again – and that was only on a good day. Perhaps, these days I am more consumed by the question, 'why did I not leave?' I knew on some level that our marriage was rotten to its core, but I had no courage to go, and conversely I called him the coward for leaving. I supposed I had always assumed that prior to the decimation of a marriage, there would be a lot of *Yelling.*

If the idea of divorce sends a shudder down one's spine, then one should avoid seaside towns. Bizarrely, it is these scenic locations, according to the Office of National Statistics, that become England's hotspots for the dissolution of marriages. Landlocked Cambridgeshire, therefore, would make for a very attractive destination for those who wish to remain within their unions. An exception is found in the district of Peterborough, the town topping the charts of marital demise in the absence of a seaside. Marriages there are currently disintegrating at a rate of eleven percent, nearly two percentage points higher than the national average. The rest of the county is pretty stereotypical – around half its residents are currently married.

One reason given for divorce is 'drifting apart'. Of course this is what happens to long marriages. One day, the children have gone, one looks towards the other, factors in the advancing years, then ponders what the hell is in store for them: *Dullingham?* I have often heard it said that one should 'cherchez la femme' when a man walks out, but an exit affair is a pretty common way to end a marriage, while it may also *Upend* the esteem of the one left behind. I pass no moral judgement, but at the same time, chuck the entire church at them. Then there are those couples harbouring wonderfully incompatible natures, like two people who have become inherently competitive. They would sooner tear each other apart in their need to be right, rather than focus on any demands for happiness. If I was tired, he was exhausted. If I was fed up, he would remind me that I should think about him for a change. And on, and on, and on we would go dwindling downwards, a pair of *Warboys*.

Or perhaps the mysticism just dies away. No longer are farts retained nor toilet doors kept closed. The makeup is off, the crack revealed and one, or both, is slowly creeping into their parent's skin. From fancying the socks off a partner, to barely being able to look in their direction without a mind full of *Gorefield*. Of course, there is always the sex. The lack of, the inefficient or the disappointment after the event – a mess of *Hardwick* that needed to *Stow Longa* or a simple preference to *Knapwell*.

Still, divorce is not without good news. Once the splitting up is done and dusted, and all has settled down into a new routine, it is worth reminding oneself that Mintel, a global intelligence gathering company, discovered that sixty-one percent of women cite being happy with their relationship status, providing they ticked the box that says 'single'. On the other hand, only forty-nine percent of unattached men state the same, which is perhaps why so many men are in such a rush to re-bond so quickly.

All told, there are just two things that I miss about marriage. First *Wittering*. Having someone to make brainless remarks to. And secondly? Having someone to panic with when shit goes wrong.

Nelson's County

I was back in the house I was born in. It was small, cramped and horribly foreign-feeling. Our country, to my eyes, was grey, gloomy and miserable. I secured a job in a pub, but I struggled to integrate with the others who worked there, let alone appreciate the leery attentions of some of its punters. I started night school too, but made few friends. I was awkward and distant and hostile. I had no points of reference for maintaining conversation, and felt a fool for not comprehending much of what my peers spoke of. I was worldly-wise, but pig-ignorant. I was exhausted, yet full of the flush of youth. An alien in the mother country.

Nelson Mandela had just finished his long walk to freedom. I felt excluded. Remote. Distant. I caught glimpses of joyous reports on the news. Back there, life had been a string of riots, bombs and teargas. Town visits had become heavy as men from The Afrikana Weerstandsbeweging, in a menacing air, mounted their resplendent horses in protest, by blocking the drags, at the looming referendum threatening to end Apartheid. I attended a concert and the band urged the gathered audience to vote "Ja" for freedom. Chanting a "ya-h, ya-h, ya-h", ambitious to engage with the fans. A whoosh of "ne-eh" hurled back at them. The music was enticing, but the atmosphere was terrifying. Politics and arts make for dangerous bedfellows.

It is just how it was. It was just normal. I had lived on a farm, carrying a gun on my lap if travelling at night. We feared ransacking gangs wrecking revenge after years of confinement to townships, poverty and repression. We were a part of history: up close and personal; witnesses to a regime change, hoping for the best, fearing the worst. The future was a raggedy uncertainty. Nothing was black and white. Was the change to be abrupt, vicious or gradual? In time, the streets would be renamed, commending the freedom-seekers still gaining momentum for a brave new world, obliterating the plaques and honorifics commemorating the white guard. Public conveniences were already de-colourising.

Back in England, a neighbour tried to explain how buses work to me, but all the landmarks she mentioned were an anathema, as were the placenames. I boarded the wrong bus too many times, and in my numbed stasis, I rode for hours trying to take in something of this place that I come from.

****

We whizzed into the County of Nelson. "You're home!" I informed the South Korean import who had never previously visited the region in any of his nine lives. It turns out he was not the star turn: that belonged to a certain Admiral Horatio Nelson, the much-battered, philandering naval commander. Nelson took the news with typical feline indifference, with a flash of great *Seething.*

Despite his global fame and substantive accolades, it occurred to me that I have never met anyone called Horatio, at least not to my ever-increasingly fallible knowledge, although I think it makes for a fabulous cat's name. It is fairly typical of the British public for children's names to honour family members or note-worthy characters of their times. Just ask all those men called Neil born circa 1969, or the many Dianas with birth certificates issued after 1981. The royal marriage brought the girl's name to the top ten, having languished in three hundred and somethingth place for several decades.

According to the website www.ukbabynames.com, as a boys' name, Horatio, Italian in origin, scores 52% in the approval stakes, whatever that might mean. It also transpires that in the last year alone, nine boys have been christened after the glorious leader. Horace, its Anglicised equivalent, has a popularity ratio of 0%, with absolutely no boys being christened in emulation in recent years.

Calling the cat 'Nelson' was indeed inspired: his name receives a rousing approval of 76%. That said, it is thought to signify that he is the 'Son of Neil'. It is highly improbable that his real dad was called Neil, nor was his once adoptive dad. The commanding puddle of overexcited fluff ended up so called because I had a dream. This sounds as if I should probably have called him Martin. I awoke the following morning, positioned as usual between the two irritants; one the husband, *Great Snoring,* the other the cat, *Little Snoring,* and informed both of the cognomen. Astonishingly, both males accepted it without so much as a minor *Barney.* That said, given the choice of whom to cuddle upon waking, having cats only contrived to manufacture a *Spooner Row* first thing, with much envy emanating from the husband.

Nonetheless, the name Nelson was a vast improvement on 'The Daft Twerp' which was how we initially referred to him after we observed him falling off, or headbutting at speed, the entirety of his home and for using the bed as a litter tray, leaving it a *Foulden* to be tackled just before lights out.

These days, Nelson has more panache. More, but not absolute – although he is now reliably using a litter tray. Alas, he is not the only daft twerp in my household of two. I failed to learn on the first occasion to never chuck his soiled wood chip litter directly into gusts of wind pushing towards me. *Ickburgh!* It was also me who sported cranial bruising week after week; my brain never quite mapping out exactly where the van's overhead cupboards were situated, despite repeated introductions. Perhaps this was no accident, given it has long been held that women have inferior spatial awareness. In fact, it was that thought that prompted yet another Google search.

Google duly obliged me with a 2019 study, by Li Yuan and others, which stated quite categorically that women, "are more susceptible to emotions and their parahippocampal gyrus worked less efficiently than males." A finding quite *Bittering*, even if I do not have a scooby doo what precisely it means. Take parking, for instance: it has oft been claimed that women are worse at parallel parking, reverse parking and parking generally, than men. I was thrilled to read that by spending five minutes or so playing Tetris on one's phone, a woman's so-called natural inability may be corrected fairly instantaneously – findings claimed by Lynn Okagaki. Mind you, it is a bit of a faff, and probably highly offensive to the Highway Code, to have to complete a game before reversing into a space at the local supermarket.

It has always puzzled me that boys are significantly more likely to pass their driving test at the first attempt, and yet, prior to the passing of 2010 Equality Act, a newly-licensed woman's insurance was substantially lower: sometimes more than half that charged for a newly-licensed man. The algorithm used to determine the legal requirement reflected the female of the species' lack of propensity for smashing up the car, before discrimination on the grounds of sex was outlawed. Thereafter, women's insurance rocketed in an upward trajectory in line with men's. Answers on a postcard…

I am of the view that if women are told frequently enough that they cannot do something, they will come to accept it as fact. It is like a form of Stockholm Syndrome, but without having to venture to Scandinavia. Somewhat unsurprisingly, I greatly enjoyed listening to 'The Gendered Brain' by Gina Rippon as I toured the northern-eastern pregnant-looking part of England. Her analysis of recent research debunked much of what has been said on women's capabilities over the aeons. For the unfamiliar, she is an occasionally-defined 'neuronazi' campaigning to correct a wide range of cultural 'neurofoolishness'. Or, to use more proper terms, she is a neuroscientist with a doctorate in physiological psychology. She set out to explore the differences between men and women, and found many conclusions sorely lacking in science. Her fascinating book outlines how much of what has been universally agreed amongst nations is nothing less than a prime opportunity for a good *Diss* on the female of the species.

Map-reading was a particular life skill that was once weaponised as a wonderful example of womanly ineptness. The University of Limerick published a study during the pandemic which indicated that women get to the right result, but overall it takes longer, and we rely on a different gazing technique. I personally use the technique of gazing at Google Maps because, first and foremost, it gives me something to blame when it all goes wrong. If I am to be abjectly truthful about it, I frequently take a wrong turn because I am gazing at something other than the map.

In Norfolk, it seemed that everywhere I went, Google Maps was telling me to turn on to "The Street". Every second lane seemed to be called that and it got me worrying about the levels of creativity amid Norfolk's urban planners. Upon thorough investigation, it was not a lack of road names, but rather that Google was simply having a quirky old time of it, banally renaming what was otherwise sensibly monikered asphalt.

My journey around England frequently had me deciphering why a place is so called. Typically, we have all learnt, a name comes from its pragmatic relationship to the land, or because of some other notable feature, like *Woodrising*. Oftentimes, original names have been corrupted over the years by the impact of the repeated invasions on our locutions; or the ever-changing enunciations of an accent affecting either spelling or the scribe's deciphering. It is why, for example, I can sing along to Haevn's song, 'Kites in a Hurricane', yet simultaneously worry excessively about how the felines fared during the stormy weather. Like most, I thoroughly enjoy a good mondegreen, although I never once believed that The Police wrote a song called 'Sue Lawley'.

All this historical reality of England and her language has given rise to some stupendously marvellous innovations over the years, even when spelling lets the side down, as '*Hoe*' does. What perhaps is surprising, is how many places survived the Victorian tendency towards Bowdlerisation. Bowdlerisation is what happened to

Opie St in Norwich, prior to it being Opie Street. It was, like Butts Lane, a commonly-found fareway in almost all urban zones, only it was previously called a very German sounding: 'Gropekuntelane'. The spelling varied across the regions, but I have opted for the politest variant. It literally was the road you travelled down to have a swift *Feltwell* of a ladies' nether regions, presumably for a fee.

Nowadays, Opie Street is, not that it is obvious, named after a woman: Amelia Opie, nee Aldersen. Quite what she would feel about becoming a substitute name for a road otherwise referred to as 'Shame Street' is anyone's guess. In 1833, this writer and philanthropist's name topped the list of 187,000 Parliamentary petitioners known collectively as the Ladies Anti-Slavery Society. It was an emancipation campaign organisation set up in Norfolk's capital town, whose acronym was, I presume, LASS! She is the very epitome of a contemporary socially-acceptable icon, and yet her legacy is obscured for the lack of a full name.

It was via discovering Ms Opie's contributions to womankind that had me pondering what proportion of street names are male in origin. The absolutely fabulously-named Ms Sankaranarayanan once had the very same idea. Unlike me, she also has phenomenal computer engineering skills, and used them to analyse some of the world's greatest metropolitan centres including London. From there, my favourite computer programmer-to-date came up with an approximation of 27.5% as a global statistic. A similar study of European cities by Alice Corona and Lorenzo Ferrai found that fewer than 9% of streets were named after female individuals.

Does any of it matter? Maria Pia Ercolini of Toponomastica Femminile, a movement addressing the male bias in tarmac in Italy, believes so. Sensibly, she argues that rather than renaming much of the roads, a practical and costly quagmire, the redress should come via new developments.

Should is a powerful word in English. A moral obligation, a duty, a call to compel. Norfolk even has a *Shouldham*. So I googled Norfolk's naming and shaming policy. It is very explicit: first up, all name(s) should, when possible, have a proven historical connection to the land intended for development. If no suitable historical name can be found for the land, then a historical name related to an adjacent area may be suitable. One would not need a degree in sociology to understand the fallibility of such a policy. The clue is in the word: history. Still, it gave me a fantastic opportunity to exemplify my very Britishness with a typical *Tuttingham*.

To pretend that tried and tested policies devised in yonder year do not have in-built partiality is nothing but a *Foulsham.* Schools, the very epicentre for imparting knowledge to young and very impressionable minds, are another subset of architectural male prejudice. A recent Schools Week investigation found that Multi-academy Trusts are six times more likely to be named after men, despite three-quarters of its profession being women.

Nonetheless, as Horatio Nelson might have said himself: good leadership is no laughing matter. It literally is the difference between winning a battle and losing it. Unfortunately, history seems to repeat itself, over and over, and with that, to Norfolk I said my *Bylaugh.*

Suffolkating these Lands

No grant. No fatherly support, and despite astronomical student fees, I scrimped and saved, then borrowed eye-watering amounts to snag myself a university place – not even for a degree. Within a year, I had come top of the class, and transferred to the Bachelor's course. I worked full time. I partied only after I had made my submissions. I found friends, but I lost friends too. I went through life mechanistically, fulfilling invisible expectations for invisible masters and yet never questioned why it was so important to get those letters after my name. I wanted respect. Self-respect, probably. I enjoyed some of my course – but it felt like hoop-jumping, and for what, I could not predict. A better job at the end of it? I wanted to travel, to adventure, to experience. I hankered for something 'other'. Not this, not that. Just other.

****

The first of the summer heat waves rolled around, bringing with it the ceremonial turning of the temperature knob on my dashboard from the red setting to the blue one. Nonetheless, warm air streamed out of the vents. It was not sufficient enough to prevent sweat plunging downwards to areas I would rather it did not. Around me, brilliant red poppies and stalks of purple lupins danced in the gentle breezes. Deer galore, seemingly fearless of the traffic bearing down on them, nibbled at plants below the poisonous hemlock suffocating the abundant verges. By mid-morning, fresh roadkill rotted in the baking climes, torn apart by crows tugging away at their innards, blood staining the asphalt. *Gipping* stuff.

Blood is part of Suffolk's traditional way of life: from as far back as the 14th century the fluids from beasts and berries were once used to dye its limestone-painted timbered houses a deep salmon pink. These days there are laws prohibiting the recycling of such matters as much as there are regulations on the precise shade of paint that can be used. Just ask Marco Pierre White, who used too much of his surname and not enough of the claret colouring on one of his restaurants, much displeasing the local councillors.

In the fields beyond Suffolk's exquisite hamlets, fat rosy pigs sunbathed the day away, their piglets gallivanting around readying themselves for breakfast. The farmer's objective eye waiting for the moment that they *Sizewell.* I adored the time spent journeying around the countryside, although less enticing is the foetid stench that permeates through the vents as we pass by the bacon farms.

The dusty pink pigs had me wonder when the colour pink became 'girly'. It turns out this association was formed as recently as the inter-war years of the twentieth century. Bi-colouration of children's toys was for the convenience of marketeers and manufacturers; prior to this, there was simply no correlation between child and colour. Still, between the age of two and four, girls are more attracted to pink items, and boys begin to reject them. Tellingly, this behaviour is not replicated within tribal communities with fewer children's commodities. As much as pink houses are the norm for Suffolk, it would not do, say, in the Cotswolds, for no other reason than tradition. This is how we do things around here and any questions will not be sensibly answered. We are, when it suits us, *Onehouse.*

In 1978, an experiment by Caroline Smith and Barbara Lloyds illustrated how adults deemed what toys are appropriate for children to play with, entirely based on the colouring of the youngster's attire. If the baby wore pink, fewer toys demanding physical interaction were offered, but instead they were given objects that encourage verbal engagement, typically a doll or suchlike. Blue-clothed babies were supplied with plastic hammers, and played with them more vigorously. Of course, unbeknownst to the adult participants, the perceived boys were, in fact, girls and vice versa. If the children had had *Naughton*, it is likely that they would have been offered alternative 'gender-appropriate' toys.

War is said to make boys into men, but the inter-war years turned women into girls. The Women's Land Army was founded in 1917, as the first of two devastating wars brought England to the brink of starvation. Prior to the onset of war, England had imported some seventy percent of her basic foodstuffs, usually by sea. Germany, wise to England's weakness, systematically cut off supply chains, damning the population to a slow and prolonged death by famine. By 1916, England's farms had mostly been stripped of their male labourers via conscription, leaving fields fallow and neglected. A veritable *Nayland.*

"In most other European countries women have traditionally worked alongside their menfolk, herding animals, digging and planting in the fields, harvesting and haymaking," claims Nicola Tyrer, author of 'They Fought in the Fields'. Not so in Britain, where farms remained steadfast *Cockfields*. The farmers' wives were only good for breeding and feeding children, collecting a few eggs and boiling up a bit of jam. The Women's Institute was set up to tempt them away from the drudgery, to gift them a social life and a modicum of education and information. Their lives were otherwise invisible, unsighted and unremarkable, leaving behind a perennial sense of *Lackford* to their lives. The management of land was a matter for men, and men alone. More *Wangford.*

Within a few short weeks of the Women's Land Army being re-commissioned, forty-three thousand women had volunteered themselves. Just over half of them were deemed to be sufficiently hardy to adopt the mantle of the farmhand and be initiated into the world of homesteading – tractor driving, ploughing, harvesting, milking, ditching, felling, animal husbandry and rat-catching. Many had sought freedom from inner-city confines and the mind-dwindling factory work typically done by the unmarried and unencumbered. Few women had any grasp of the wider agricultural world, of the birds and bees, when they showed up at the hostels for their month-long training. Perhaps lessons began with the questions *Whatisfield* and *Whatisham?*

By the end of the First World War, because of the women's endeavours, 1.75 million acres of land had been ploughed up mostly for the purposes of harvesting wheat. Whatever was learnt in those years, of the women's contribution in wartime, to agriculture and to staving off Britain's hunger is barely recorded. Within twenty years, not even the passing of a full generation, those very same fields returned to untended grassland. Farming had all but collapsed as a profitable enterprise except for low-labour intensive dairy farming. The women did not cause so much as a revolution as be a mere blip in how agriculture was done round these parts. Nothing but a ripple that died out before hitting dry land. *Barking* though that now seems.

Along came the Second World War and our dependence on foreign fields and factories for our sustenance was again our achilles' heel – by then sixty percent of our comestibles came from overseas. Unsurprisingly, Germany set out to starve the country into capitulation. No longer women, farmers required the 'land girls' back as the war consumed the male fodder. Soon enough, all the ministries needed 'girls' to do war work. The WRNS, or 'Wrens' and the WAAFs, are the acronyms that denoted the women's division of the Navy and the Air Force, respectively. Initially, they required women for cooking, clerking, telephony, radar and range plotting, and even on occasion to be electricians and mechanics. The Auxiliary Territorial Service, or ATS, had women become drivers, mess orderlies, butchers, bakers, postal workers, ammunition inspectors and military police. The only condition placed upon their service was that they should not fire weapons, and that they be paid two-thirds of a man's wage.

Amidst all these new-found working freedoms, the Women's Land Army (WLA) was resurrected, offering the 'Land Girl' even less pay, with board and lodgings deducted, longer working hours, half the holiday entitlements, fewer perks such as subsidised commodities and no direct employer beyond the farmer to whom they had been assigned. Led by the formidable Lady Denman, the affiliation was scorned for being a one-rank gaggle of girls, who were either anaemic or Amazonian. Their wishes to 'play farm' were derided from hamlet to Whitehall.

Undeterred, the women traipsed in from far and wide. Now sporting their allocated uniform of fawn breeches and green sweatshirts. With a modicum of basic training, they were dispersed occasionally in groups, but mostly as solitary figures, far from their county of origin. Some expressed a wish to nurture rather than obliterate, a quiet conscientious objection to war, and yet others saw farmwork as a freedom from manufacturing drudgery. Most espoused the desire to provide for their county's very basic needs. No doubt many were swayed by the Pathé newsreels depicting rosy-cheeked women sporting wide smiles and pitchforks, tending cattle and driving tractors in endless summertime scenes. "Be a farmer's girl" one advert suggested, above a beaming cartoon model of a female farmhand.

However, for one full year the government of the day procrastinated, leaving the women volunteers to languish around waiting for training, farmstead allocation and genuine tasks. Whilst on the wireless, two government ministers lamented the lack of available labourers to meet the country's food requirements in national broadcasts, both seemingly oblivious to the women queuing up to toil our fields. Typically bureaucratic *Assington.* On the cusp of a near-failing harvest, the WLA was finally deployed, ensuring an additional two million acres of land was fertilised and seeded, keeping Britain and her compatriots nourished.

By the end of the war, nearly a quarter of a million young women had taken to the farms: ploughing, muck-shifting, lambing, staking in fences, hauling around back-breaking sacks of grain, or simply managing the heavy machinery or imposing carthorses. Refusing to wallow in the hardships and the lack of provisions, these poorly-kitted women tended to all farm tasks, with only one week of holiday permitted each winter, and a half day off per week.

Notably, many women remained in situ during the rationing years of the post-war era, whereas their serving compatriots were demobbed to much gratitude and fanfare, and a £150 resettlement stipend to help them rebuild their lives. Yet, the Minister of Labour refused to issue any benefits to the WLA, including access to retraining grants and unemployment benefit. At the same time he insisted their efforts must continue. I suspect those first four years of peacetime were the women's darkest.

In 1949, it was announced that the WLA was to be dispensed with. The news came as a devastating blow to the National Farming Union and its representatives. The farmers themselves urged the government to find a means to continue the WLA. Unsurprisingly, given labour rates for women were cheaper than for men, but mostly the women were commended for being just as capable as men, and of being more amenable in attitude. A plethora of reports survive, which record that few of 'the girls' wished to return to their pre-war lives. They had thrived despite the scorn, the sexist put-downs, the atrocious English weather, the arduously filthy work, the dangers of the farm and the deprivations that come with war and the simple life.

Presenting the WLA's leader, Lady Denman with the Grand Cross of the British Empire in 1950, King George VI observed that, "the land girls were not well treated," in comparison with the serving women of the forces. Today, the CEO of the National Farmers Union is a woman and the agricultural industry employs a workforce that is almost one-third female.

Fifty-seven years after the last 'Land Girl' was dismissed, the women's contribution to the war effort was formally recognised with the minting of a medal for service. Many of the female farm hands had passed away and were thus unable to receive the honour thanking them for their blood, their sweat and their tears. As one would expect, the medal is a circular disk of green, red and gold. Our land, their blood and the encapsulation of their outstanding contribution.

Essex is another Way

I graduated from university, later than everyone else as I took a couple of years off to go and earn more money. There is safety to be found in having a bank account in the black. Box ticked, on to the next one: pursuing houses to buy, not that there were many that I could afford. One estate agent I went to see snorted at my innocent enquiry on how to get a mortgage. I slunk out, ashamed of my over-ambition. "Anything is possible," they lied. I put the idea on the backburner.

I had set up a little business. I worked hard at three different jobs. Life could not have been more dull, more predictable, more ordinary.

My father re-emerged after several years of absence. I had tried to have a relationship with him via phone, but often I interrupted him during office hours, riling him. If I called the home number, only the house worker was there to answer. I let the relationship dwindle away. He moved countries several times and was now in the Far East. He came across for a visit, and as I made cauliflower cheese, he snubbed my ingredients and bemoaned the fact that I had invited my brother to join us. Another relation whom I barely knew, truth be told. Returning shortly from a shop with better quality cheeses, we tried to play happy families, as our father whipped up a better cheese sauce for us to admire.

"I'm going to buy a house here – would you like to live in it?" he asked, quite out of the blue. I did not hesitate to say yes – it seemed like divine timing. I could restart the little business, I could get new jobs. I could start over. It is what I am good at. It is the only thing I am good at. Another relationship had recently fallen by the wayside. He had moved in quickly, and had been less proactive about moving out. It had become very ugly. Police got called more than once. There was nothing to stay for anyway. Jobs come and go. Free houses do not.

I moved: lock, stock and barrel. No pets to rehome. Few friends to say goodbye to. My brother hired a van to take me to my next abode, I was still too fretful to learn to drive.

A few weeks later, after I had unpacked, my father introduced his wife to me then announced we would be living together. He trotted off overseas again. There was nothing overtly wrong with her, except she was not my wife, she did not speak English, and I had not got a clue what on earth I was supposed to do with her.

I moved out. I had no job. My savings were paltry. My business did not easily re-start. I retrained, having to acquire yet more debt.

****

"Where are you staying tonight?" my friend had asked, freely offering her front drive as a possible alternative location. "Down by the estuary," I replied somewhat vaguely as I pointed in the direction of what I hoped might be south. The entire southern boundary of Essex comprises the northern shore of the River Thames, so my vague answer probably appeared quite obtuse. I have long become accustomed to relying only on the 'lat long coordinates' to guide me to my nightly destinations, rather than an actual place name, so "estuary" was about as specific as I could muster.

I had slunk in the previous night, exhausted after a four-hour delay idling by the scene of a motorway crash. With the blue lights of the emergency vehicles tearing at my retinas for the duration, I could do little but pass the time with prayers for the poor soul, or souls, who I assumed had just suffered a life-altering intervention. The night was already striking the wee hours by the time I pulled up adjacent to a motorhome. The choice of centre stage in a wide open arena of hardstanding left me feeling vulnerable. We were woken twice by yobbos intent on performing squealing doughnuts and inspired them to blare their horns into the void for reasons best known to themselves, making the parking lot a *Toothill.*

In the pitch, I had been oblivious to several smaller, more intimate car parks on the periphery. The following morning, blurry eyed on departure, I had noticed an encampment of vans by the picturesque waters. I determined I would insert The Shitron into this convoy of yet unfamiliar kith and kin later that evening. First, I was to spend a day catching up with an old pal from times past. We talked divorce, regrets, sadness and renewal. How being single kept us sane, got us our self-esteem back and injected a sense of pride into our lives.

Friend visited, laundry laundered, coffee quaffed and laughs guffawed, I said my fond farewell armed with eight litres of out-of-date orange juice and a kilo of dried pasta. One curiosity of this van way of life is having people offload things on to me. I appreciate the generosity, peculiar though that I find it. Over the last ten months, I had been gifted four boxes of tea bags, a litre of cranberry juice, at least eight half-eaten cakes, a ginormous soda bread, an assortment of fabulous leftovers and stews, a bag of frozen vegetables, gallons of milk, some ginger ale, a jar of decaf coffee from Lidl, a kilo of M&S quinoa, a half packet of red lentils, a wide selection of cheeses and two jars of apple sauce, one spiced with chilli. Most of the quinoa and lentils were now terribly well travelled somewhere in the back of the cupboard. I had reluctantly declined several bags of oats and oat-based products for reasons of *Shellow Bowells* - my innards becoming mysteriously allergic in recent years.

From waving my farewell to my friend of many years, it was just twenty minutes before I was vigorously shaking hands with two stranger-dangers I had never previously encountered. They had mobbed me as I tried to make my way from the driving seat to the other side of the van. "Marlon! I am!" the man beamed, tapping his chest. "And I'm Cathy." the woman chipped in, proffering her hand to shake. Both had opted to spend the afternoon together, lounging on two picnic chairs by the seaside, having just met and hitting it off tremendously well.

"Can we look in your van?" Marlon requested, "I want to know what it is like!" He was residing in a seven-seater and was trying to save up enough to upgrade to a van. He worked in IT, but wished to be an entrepreneur, and rattled out a series of app ideas to test on us. The woman was car-camping for a long weekend in a small five-door car. She was cheery in manner, although shy on personal detail. She had invested in a decent sound system, the music bringing an exciting inoffensive ambience to this most tranquil of destinations. Twice a day, the sea would creep in, lapping just feet away from our front tyres.

"Sure," I agreed. Fleetingly, the thought had crossed my mind that I was a fool for letting them inspect my internals, but post-divorce life has taught me that randoms are just friends not yet made. Besides, I had eight litres of expired orange juice to lob about if things got *Ugley.* I stood beside the van, slurping on a coffee as my new neighbours gave themselves the grand tour. The only thing I would change, I let them know, was I wished I had just one passenger seat, one that could swivel around so I could sit and watch television more comfortably, and not have to traipse around the van to get from the cab to the living quarters.

I did not use the shower anymore, either, I explained. Having cruised into East Anglia with its dearth of motorways, I had taken up swimming several times per week at the suggestion of an acquaintance, then rinsing off with a hot, soapy shower after, usually of the infuriating push button variety. It had taken time to adjust to meandering up and down the swimming lanes, tailing others like aircrafts trundling along a runway but without ever taking off. Unlike my teenage-self, I was not thrashing away for a personal best, nor perfecting the strokes of my arms or legs. I shed my self-consciousness of my wobbly bits and overcome that sense of defencelessness that is inflicted by focal short-sightedness. I soon ceased being distracted by the presence of splashier, sloppier or the other mildly-drowning practitioners. To just blob about without a care in the world, gliding up and down the lanes purposelessly: free from being trained, or timed, or corrected. To just mellow into the rhythm of my breast stroke. It was, as promised, a true act of purposeful mindlessness.

"I'd also like a porthole on the other side of the van," I interjected the gushing remarks from my two guests, "so I can look out in both directions whenever I hear unusual noises but aside from that, whoever designed this van pretty much got it right in terms of space and storage".

I thought about retrieving my own deckchair from the garage and adding it with theirs, but sleep deprivation was tapping me on the shoulder. I answered, not for the first time, that I travel and write, and write and travel. "Is that what brought you to Essex?" Cathy enquired. Yes, that along with *Fiddler's Hamlet* and *Thresher's Bush.*

It was already dawning on me that my year of living in a van was coming to a close. "What's next?" was becoming an all too familiar question, and I was devoid of a satisfactory answer, finding myself *Fobbing* the inquisitive off with a pair of raised hands and glance towards the heavens. I had not planned beyond this point, and I was well behind in my writing schedule. "Fuck knows" I answered Marlon honestly and he guffawed.

"It's the accent, man. I can't get past the posh swearing."

I had revelled in this life a lot more than I thought I might. I liked its unpredictability, its solitude and its randomness. I adored the beauty and the simplicity. I liked the hardship only after it had passed, when I got to bask in my she-manship. Most of all, I loved the rugged rural settings, even as I lamented that England does not vary much in its topography, unlike America. Hiking from Mexico to Canada has forever spoiled my vista: England is never sufficiently vast or epic, breath-taking or eye-watering. I still sought rolling hills or grey seas for extended stays for those days that I wrote, or feigned to write. I suspect I will always hanker for variety, for change, for nature and all of her healing powers. That vanlife, rather than cure me of it, has reminded me that I will always be an ex-boarder, and one who may never shake off the lingering dread of recapture.

As I entered the final furlong of my year of no fear, I was often asked what it was I missed most in this unconventional life. My answer surprised even me – I missed food. I still cooked from scratch, as I have always liked to do, but I had come to rely on the same few basic meals week in, week out, driven by my unwillingness to create too much washing up, and all the while being cautious of my gas consumption. My diet had become *Boreham,* in part, because I had also decided to abstain from bread for the duration. I worried that my need for a quick meal would make bread too simple a go-to. I missed being able to bung something in the oven before forgetting about it until either the smell tickled my nostrils or the fire alarm went off. I also wished to store stuff in a freezer, although I had an icebox, but one peculiarity of van life was that my fridge only worked when my batteries had a charge of less than eighty percent. On bright days and travel days, that was impossible.

In Essex I had noticed that, once again, my Renogy charger had packed up despite being less than six months old. It took nearly as long to get them to honour the warranty, and they never did send a replacement. I continue to battle for my money back. Solar, rather than engine power, was the only way I could run my electrical resources, and with the long summer days this was not a challenge. Although, now back in the season of heatwaves, my reliance on my solar panel prevented me from seeking refuge within woodlands to dodge the baking heat of the daytime.

I excused myself from Marlon and Cathy's company, and succumbed to a long nap, undisturbed by a caravan of fellow vanlifers arriving in dribs and drabs: some blasting out a variety of musical genres. The 1980s pop songs with singalong lyrics won out over all and roused me out of my slumber just in time for dinner. I wandered about our little encampment, shaking hands: some old timers, other newbies, some quaffing beer, others tea. "I've been doing this for three years," the man next to me announced. "I'll never go back. An amazing way of life. Just amazing."

"Third night of van life," another couple cut in. We all crowded around to let them know about the doggers and the nuisances, as well as the highlights. But it is the lowlights that we revel in surviving: retelling stories of dealing with egg-throwers and those who feel the need to relieve themselves against the van's sides under the cover of darkness. I pointed out a smear of poop that had slowly dribbled down the side of my van. I had no knowledge of how it came to be there and had simply hoped that the rain would deal with it. Alas, drought had poured across the lands instead, baking it to the side. Despite others' best efforts, nothing anyone had done had put any of us off, quite the reverse: it was a reminder to be kind.

Behind us, Cathy, Marlon and four or five others set to dismantling a fly-tip. Chairs, broken cupboards, rugs, children's toys, even garish makeup had been dumped down the embankment, as well as much soggy, mouldy cardboard, now rank and stinking. At least two van loads needed shifting, and the motley crew set to deal with someone else's *Mucking*.

"Can someone video this?" A man with marigolds demanded. "I will!" I had offered, quickly recording the wombling as they removed every scrap to a set of bins so that the council may one day notice it and then hopefully relocate it appropriately. Vans, of course, are prohibited from recycling centres, risking fines if we tried. Even if any of us could fit the garbage inside our garages, the stench would be a little bit too much to bear.

A local fox scampered around just metres away from around two or three of the wombles. One of the men grabbed his dinner and dropped it down for her. She was mangy and skinny, and, according to Cathy, this had been her patch for six years. She usually had at least one or two pups in tow. This year she had none.

Come dusk, I settled back into my home, the music still pummelling the air, it bothered me not a jot as the hubbub of fellows continued their party. I sank back into peaceful slumber, and was only detonated out of it by the starting of an air pump at the crack of dawn. In the expansive car park, with a good two acres or so of available unused space, a twenty-something, male paddle-boarder felt it essential to inflate his kit whilst directly alongside our line of vans. The air pump sounded like a rocket taking off. If it was his mission to show his contempt for us, he failed dismally to elicit any response.

If any of us could have been bothered, we might have threatened to douse him and his equipment with our tanks of *Weeley* and *Messing*, but perhaps that is just hypervigilant me always being on guard to thwart attack. In any case, he was three vans away from me, so I simply rolled over and went back to sleep as did the cat. Sometimes, of people, I despair but I suppose, like everyone else, with next to no information, he must also decide who is friend and who is foe. People who are not afraid have no reason to behave provocatively. And for some, van dwellers will always induce some *Feering*.

I stayed two more delicious days and nights by our coastal waters, soaking in every second of my sojourn by the sea. I decided, yet again, that wild swimming was an experience for another time and place. The Thames may have started in Kemble, but it travelled through nine counties and the poo-discharging had continued all year unabated according to the Guardian who have made it their mission to harangue the water companies. Finally, it was being addressed and for that the residents would have the bills increasing still further, when margins were already tight for Joe Public.

I wandered along the coast, inhaling the salty air, and reminiscing of times gone. Between tapping out paragraphs, I smiled at Nelson contemplating the wading birds, laughed at the cranes that had his eyes on stalks, and the gulls who pricked his ears with their merciless screeching. I glanced at the little boats resting on exposed sands, bobbing up as the sea meandered in. The ebbs and the flows of seaside life in their tidal routines. I felt a gentle sadness, as if I might never come back here again. An odd form of bereavement for a place that I have never called home.

Then came the moment to move off to pastures new. Packing away the little footstool before walking Nelson one more time in the marram grasses. He skipped around boggy marshes. If I could have stayed longer, I probably would have but a book will not write itself and I wished to acquaint myself with *Fingeringhoe.*

I released the handbrake and guided The Shitron across deep potholes. I slunk out and away from the car parks onto a rubbly dirt road that would ultimately lead us back to civilisation. Half way along the dusty track stood a woman alone. She hailed me as if I was a taxi, yet blocked my route by standing in the centre of the road. Instinctively I pondered: friend or foe? Or perhaps in Essex it is a case of *Wivenhoe?*

I slowed down gradually, then stopped. "Can you give me a lift?" she pleaded.

"Sure!" I leant across to shuffle things around: chucking the cat bed into the innards of the van, pulling the litter tray into its place and dragging the bin box to the centre seat, half mindful that my handbag was in striking distance.

"Are you okay?" I enquired of the flustered woman as she clamoured in.

"Not really. I got dumped here by some bloke I barely know. He just drove off and left me down here." Her phone rang and she answered swiftly with "Hi Mum!" There was talk of her having no money to call a cab or get a train home. "A woman's picked me up and she's going to drop me off at the bus station," she pacified her parent. I continued to trundle along the coastal road hoping she might signal when she wanted to disembark. There was a flurry of insults of what a cock he was and how she was never going to trust him again before she hung up and turned her attention to me.

She nattered about her job and her home, telling me little of the ordeal that had left her stranded down a dirt road. To fill the silence, I told her I was writing a book and travelling around England, learning about England's feminine culture and women's history as I went along.

"On your own?" she asked.

"Yup." I reply, anticipating the "You're brave" retort that typically comes with this territory.

"Men are dickheads; you're better off on your own," she stated quite emphatically. I refrain from giving the standard NAMALT: not all men are like that.

"I'm doing my best to avoid the dickheads," I smiled back at her, "but it is not like they wear badges." It reminded me that I needed to prepare for a gratis talk that I was due to give to Women's Aid – the charity that offers all women, 'The Freedom Programme'. Helping us to demand and expect to be treated decently by our relationship partners. Not all men are like that, but enough are for that course to be oversubscribed and under-provided.

I Name Thee Hindfordshire

Staring down the barrel of boredom, one day blending into the next, my feet were as itchy as they had ever been. I knew I could not stay here and set my sights on international travel. The world was back to being my oyster, although I had failed to grow out of the 'vegetarian' phase that had once provoked my mother's ire so abjectly.

I scanned advert after advert looking for employers who did not require a wealth of experience, but who loved enthusiasm. I rejected anything predictable or ordinary: France, Spain, Germany. Anything this side of the Urals, but then Serbia struck me as a fascinating region, once still piecing herself together after years of internal strife following the demise of communist ideology. I applied for a job and, to my astonishment, was recruited. I told everyone who might even be vaguely interested where I was off to, having completely overlooked quite a vital syllable.

Siberia had never been on the bucket list. To counter this drastic, yet very embarrassing, moment of cognitive dissonance, I hastily used up the dregs of my dismal bank account buying the thickest, most expensive coat imaginable. I was off to explore the big bad world once again. To live as I have always lived: using someone else's bathroom, sleeping in someone else's bed, fathoming out the rules of their ways, and just getting on with it.

****

Titmore Green and *Titley Green* topped my list of places to pass by, but nothing on my to-do list was being struck out. Instead, I was spending time seeking out insightful, fridge-magnet-esque quotes.

"But the more I reflect on events recent and past, the more I am struck by the element of the absurd in everything humans do."
Attributed to Tacitus; AD56–AD120

If one has a penchant for sitting idle for hours at a time on motorways, watching weak-bladdered men dive off behind the armco to fertilise the roadside banks, then Hertfordshire is probably a county of great appeal. Ahead of me, a sole parent, no doubt exasperated, had managed to persuade his toddler to pee in a shallow piece of tupperware rather than cart him over the barrier. I thought it quite an achievement: him expertly balancing the shimmering liquid out of the car before flinging it across the asphalt. What the women in cars around me did I cannot say, I did not witness a single incident. It is at times such as these that van life gives one a rare sense of sophisticated superiority as it morphs into one's own private service station, one with gratis coffee and snacks.

The only other form of entertainment apparent to me as I whiled away the delay was noticing the rumour mill in action.

"Viewed from a distance, everything is beautiful."
Attributed to Tacitus; AD56–AD120

Something out of sight would spark a sudden rush to re-ignite our engines. The noise of a fleet of diesels firing up, rather than the absurd panting made by the whining electric vehicles, would set off a hundred-yard dash among those who had taken to stretching their legs as a pretext for gandering at the scene of the crash, the helicopter and the attending crews. The lure of the illicit is a powerful pull. Despite the flurry of activity, not an iota of progress was made. Many hours later the police directed us to u-turn and drive along the motorway in the wrong direction lawfully.

The myriad of traffic jams afforded me an abundance of opportunity to learn a little of this county of the stags hanging out by the river. As is ever the case, I had to wade through a flood of stories of men and their antics in order to acquaint myself with the pertinent matters of she. On this occasion, of utmost distraction was social media being awash with the talk of a powerful television man from the third channel entertaining himself with an inappropriate but not illegal relationship with a lad substantially younger. It had been a brief national transfixation with a high-profile *Letchworth.*

Amid the day's weeping 'mea culpa' was the frequently observable tactic of the guilty: offence being the best form of defence. Deny, attack, reverse victim and offender – a cowardly act of *Wormley*: The DARVO. We are a nation at pains to apologise when we walk into lamp posts, but when it comes to genuine erring, an apology is rarely forthcoming. Step two: deflect by drawing attention to a presumed more guiltier party. Our subjugated iconoclast claimed that the press reportage was mere homophobia in action. That such condemnation would not occur if it were an older man taking up with a barely-of-age girl, implying this is the norm in the big, bad world of TV-dom. It does little but stage an argument that is nothing but a scraping of the *Trowley Bottom* in the games of 'whataboutery'.

Soon after, I was endeavouring to write about my travels around Hertfordshire, although in reality, indulging in another countrywide childhood re-enactment of the board game: 'Guess Who'. One of Britain's Red Tops refused to name, but still shamed, a married household-name for some unbecoming shenanigans with a male person of less than two decades. Another story of *Letchmore.*

On this more recent scandal, the behemoth broadcasting company had sat immobile for weeks following an accusation that its highest paid newsreader had solicited a relationship with a boy, who it was attested should have been studying for his A-levels. More allegations were surfacing, before the counter wave kicked in reminding us there is always a human being behind the headlines. Previously, the BBC had facilitated the reign of Jimmy Saville's terror for decades. Had the promised lessons really been learnt?

In order to make some headway in progressing this book, I had returned to the scene of one of my own failings: the negligent loss of my cat in Hampshire at the very beginning of this journey. The

Admirable Nelson, once panicked at being tethered and out of the confines of the van, had been startled by the arrival of a gasping cyclist. In response, he had flung himself deep into plants most thorny and *Bushey.*

Now, a year later, he pranced about the ground full of conquered bravery. Within a few hours, freed from the leash, I smiled wryly as he shot back to the van for cover as soon as another cyclist, heaving breathlessly, summited the hill. I left the van's door wide open, giving him the freedom to come and go as he pleased. He was indeed pleased. Less so was I with the dead offering that came back. If cats bringing in mice is said to be an act of love, the furry imbecile did not so much as offer me a toenail. I was even less delighted when he brought forth a live mouse which scuttled off into the garage area under the bed, leaving behind a smell most *Nasty.*

With panoramic views and rarely passing traffic, far from the madding towns, I had hoped this spot would be the prime location for getting my head down and reflecting on what I had learnt along the way. Hampshire, of course, was where I familiarised myself with this country's potted history. Of men, of war, of violence, of its leadership and their corrupting powers.

But I was not here to research all things Hampshire, but rather that of Hertfordshire. Just in case, I had missed any significance within English history, I googled the top-ten topics for A-level students. Only the Cambridge Exam Board supplied any information, and it was already a decade old. It remains the teacher's discretion which subjects to impart wisdom via. Seemingly Russian Dictators top the charts, swiftly followed up by an analysis of the US Civil Rights movement. Placing third is Germany: specifically the years 1933–1963, lest we ever forget to mention the war. English heritage introduces herself in fourth place with the offering of an in-depth study of Tudor times. Fifth, and very notably, old Winston Churchill comes toddling in. Forthcoming reformations in the syllabi meant students might become acquainted with Alfred the Great, Genghis Khan or British Prime Ministers from Pitt to Peel. More broadly, there was to be the introduction of two significant topics: African Kingdoms and the French Revolution. I could only comfort myself with cake.

If harts are male, and hinds are female, then Hindfordshire must surely be the place to rediscover the only women leader in English history that my formal education had made passing mention of. This most formidable of women, I was once told, had built a deep ditch called Devil's Dyke in Cambridgeshire: a commemoration of

Digswell. I had once taken a stroll along it in my early twenties, a time when I could not have cared less for ancient history. The seven mile, two-storey high piece of landscaping was carved out of her flatlands, enabling the Warrior Queen of AD60–61 to defend East Anglia from the Romans who were intent upon annexing our fair isles.

In Mediaeval times, the dyke was referred to as 'the dic'. Modern archeologists have generally fallen away from this supposition: artefacts recovered seem to date its mounds from the much later Anglo-Saxon times. My lips much in *Puckeridge,* I concede it is likely she cannot take credit for this remnant of our forebears.

Notwithstanding this inconvenient truth, it is claimed the flame-haired leader of the Iceni tribesfolk, Boudica, became the region's nominal ruler upon the death of her husband. She is oft-depicted with red hair splayed across her shoulders. Her fierce determination on show as she handsomely commands a chariot, its wheels spiked and horses rearing in defiant anticipation of war, her bosom firmly shrouded in a white smock.

The Romans, willfully blinding themselves to Boudica's legacy, believed her vulnerable and primed themselves for an invasion. At their first encounter, the Romans set about nihilating her: publicly scourging her as if a slave then violating her two child-aged daughters.

When a woman has lost her chastity, she will shrink from nothing.
Attributed to Tacitus, AD56–AD120

Queen Boudica set off for Colchester, Essex, known then as Camulodunum: a *Bygrave* retirement village for impaired and ageing Roman legionnaires. Fire-razing the settlement into dust, eliminating all those residing within the sanatoria, she headed off to Londinium to instigate a second, more substantial barbecue of its occupiers – a bigger *Cow Roast.*

Upon her second mission being accomplished, she high-tailed it to Verulamium to triangulate her fury at her and her children's degradation. Her rampage against the empire culminated in the woman warrior and her tribes being thrashed in battle within the year. Veni, vidi, vici. Where Julius Caesar had set out and failed, Claudius' army had succeeded.

This is the unfair thing about war, victory is claimed by all and failure to one alone.
Attributed to Tacitus, AD56–AD120

These days Verulamium has been renamed St. Albans, in honour of the first recorded martyr. The recipient of such loftiness was a man, beheaded around the same period that someone else was thinking of building a ruddy great ditch in Cambridgeshire.

Later identified as Albanus, he had provided shelter for a persecuted Christian priest. When news of his stow leaked out, the man of cloth was summoned to the feet of his overlords. To ensure compliance, Roman soldiers were dispatched to accompany him. In a moment of inspired subterfuge, Albanus exchanged cloaks, instead presenting himself before the judge, leaving the priest free to abscond. Continuing the deception, Alban refused to recant and was thus heartily flogged, although on Wikipedia it is reported that he bore his torments both 'patiently and joyfully'. Not having had the desired effect, Alban's head was reallocated away from his body, before being rested in *Graveley.* Possibly – Wikipedia is very light on details here.

Albanus' soul and courage went on to be venerated a few hundred years later. In the eighth century an eponymous Abbey was built adjacent to the hamlet he was rumoured to have hailed from. Today, there are well over one hundred churches globally honouring his sacrifice to preserve Christianity.

In reality, there remain no contemporaneous accounts to confirm either Albanus' nor Boudica's existence. All the sources heralding their contribution to history are nothing but elaborate scripts written long after the protagonists had perished. For as long as Hertfordshire stands, Alban remains immortalised as a cathedral city, whereas Boudica dissolves.

Boudica, an old English word for victorious, is probably nothing but a figment of Tacitus' imagination. Tacitus was a scholar renowned for throwing opprobrium in the direction of Rome's elites, and it was he who probably concocted the story of a woman beating back the English invaders in an attempt to eviscerate the reputations of the powerful languishing in Rome. His recordings of a Barbarian Queen is, in all probability, nothing but a means for him to warn of the perils of female power.

To make his narration palatable to the masses, to give it its happy ending, he had Boudica commit suicide – deemed then as the act of ultimate cowardice for a soldier. Tacitus never once set foot on our fair isles, and he would have been all of four years old if ever she did exact her revenge upon her family's abusers.

Greater things are believed of those who are absent
Attributed to Tacitus, AD56–AD120

I'm off to Bedfordshire

I would follow him to the ends of the world. That wasn't my initial thought. He was okay, I supposed. He was interesting, worldly, well-travelled. Funny. Very funny. He was ambitious and so much more well put together than me. He shared my politics, or at least he claimed to. He wooed, he wowed and he would buy me flowers. He was ten years older. We shared a mother tongue and a dysfunctional upbringing. He started watching Formula One with me, keenly adopting my passion. We went to foreign races together, cheering on anyone but Schumacher.

I had met him on a blind date, set up by his boss, eager to show him that a Siberian life wasn't going to be so glum after all. We were introduced outside of the women's toilets, my hands still dripping wet from the recess with no drying facilities.

He moved in swiftly. How we laughed at the typical Russian toilet that came with my flat. The water closet was contained in a mint-coloured cupboard separate from the bathroom, and was most novel for having a landing shelf to catch one's more solid matter. It was, my Russian friends assured me, a healthy practice to observe the innermost workings of one's anatomy. I just thought it permitted the full assault of one's own doings on one's own nostrils.

We bought what was to become my first car: a Lada Niva. Russia's own brand of family car, not updated from communist times, simply because nothing else could contend with the Siberian winters. I flew to Kent and did an intensive driving course spread across a week, passing at my second attempt. I passed the theory test with flying colours – the stereotypical woman driver. Of course, I was expected to drive on the left hand side of the road, and greatly amused my instructor by always ending up on the wrong side of the road following a left turn. Within a week, I was qualified to be unleashed alone, utterly terrified by the lack of a patient tutor commenting on my every manoeuvre: one who had gently assured me I was doing just fine.

The paperwork, written entirely in Cyrillic stated the Lada was green, but it was most certainly a drab blue. Bought straight from the production line, on its initial test drive, thankfully in the autumn, the driver's window had shuddered down, and refused to wind up. The windshield mirror spontaneously shed its mountings, and the two rear ashtrays pinged out in response to the crossing of any shallow pothole. It had four wheels yet five gears – the fifth ceased working within a few months. We were told it was a pointless repair.

Despite my swearing to never obtain a licence, I was all set to plunge into my fear of driving.

****

If the standardisation of English spelling is a fairly recent innovation, *Luton* has much to explain. The word 'loo' is a hand-me-down from our French cousins who would screeched, "Guardez l'eau!" prior to tipping the swill from the chamber pot over their balcony to splash across the street below, putting in peril any passing pedestrians.

The intrepid English anglicised it, and brought into English phraseology the 'gardy loo'. The greenbottomed natives then excised the 'gardy', leaving us with loo. As it remained my quest to find the lavatory that England was, metaphorically alleged, to be hurtling down, I had high hopes for *Luton*.

Alas, it is absolutely fine as a place as far as I can adduce. Particularly so if one googles the question, "What's Luton like to live in?" Scouring over 21,200,000 results in 0.48 seconds, the Google-o-randomator ranks answer after answer. The blurb beneath the top five suggested sites make use of the following adjectives: 'popular', 'ideal' 'fantastic', 'excellent' and 'good'. The sixth website listed belonged to the local rag, Bedfordshire Live, so one might wish to overlook any bias. Their headline notified its readers that *Luton* was the unfortunate recipient of the Bronze medal for Britain's worst place to live, proving the truism that one should only criticise a place if they hail from it. I will risk getting splinters in my rear by suggesting that one makes one's own mind up and pops over for a visit if one is not from the area. A sunny day, like snow, brings much daylight to everything one surveys.

"Where are you going next?" was another frequently asked question in my year of van life but I had not realised that, "I'm off to Bedfordshire," had previously been a popular colloquialism – particularly in the 1930s and 40s. Once upon a time, it was more common to mutter that one was 'going up the wooden hill to Bedfordshire'. At some point the staircase reference was dropped, probably as the result of the ageing moving into bungalows, the *Woodend* mountain had become difficult to conquer.

Nelson just sods off in some direction with not so much as a murmur. Now with the summer keeping the van beyond toasty, he indulged his preference for dozing away the wee hours in the driver's seat, far from my menopausal night burnings. When not driving, I covered it with a small square of fluffy rug. It is his Linus' blanket: an emotional support prop that has followed him from place to place, and accompanied him into various catteries. A true creature comfort, it is his equivalent of a teddy bear. In vanlife, like almost everything else, it has been multi-purposed, and I now use it as a barrier keeping his shed fur from sticking to my backside.

I awoke from my first nights' slumber in the county of Bedfordshire, puzzled to discover the cat asleep by my ankles. Later that morning, the anomaly was revealed to me as I clambered up into the cab. There had been an incident of *Great Barford.* There is nothing like encountering the redistribution of the digestive tract several hours after gurgitation to make one's *Souldrop.*

"You are why I can't have nice things," I told the indifferent Admirable, who retreated to his hideaway under the middle passenger seat – his little *Moggerhanger.* I have never fathomed until this moment why cats always disgorge their innards on the soft furnishings as opposed to the easier-to-clean hard flooring. In a house, this would quickly be resolved by recovering said item and throwing it into the gaping mouth of the washing machine before slamming the door, leaving detergent to do the hard work. In van life, such happenings interfere with my day considerably, as somehow I have to wrangle the item into a tiny sink and decontaminate it, or divert off to find a communal washing machine.

In the course of my year, Nelson has splattered both faux sheep fleeces and the floor mat three times. The bloody *Swinehead.* At times, I fretted that he might be homesick, in the truest sense of the word, before I realised he was just catting. Hairballs, like hayfever, inevitably accompany the warming months. For the uninitiated, it is a graphic, convulsive rigmarole with much hiccoughing to siren that the cat is bodily *Eggington* away to expel whatever it is that has caused its stomach such great offence. It seems rugs and carpets offer enhanced grippage for their tiny claws, ensuring a *Slip End.*

Nelson is acting purely on instinct rather than buffoonery or rebellion. He has a need for safety when he is at his most vulnerable. Quite like his owner-cum-slave, he likes to defy stereotypes, to test boundaries and to refuse to submit to expectations placed upon him. He wishes to tread his own path and, if denied, he continues to scream like the proverbial toddler. I would not have him any other way: he is my security blanket and I am his protector, and together we had nearly conquered a full year of van living. At times we have both positively thrived.

"A fish doesn't see the water it swims in," I once heard it said on a podcast, and perhaps for my cat, our lives are completely normal, not remotely deranged or wackadoodle. Then again, we are on the inside of a way being, not objective, just conveniently subjective. It is only when one takes a deliberate look at the lands we inhabit, its language and culture, that idiosyncrasies start to make sense. My mission around Bedfordshire complete, I pulled up next to an identical white van with its rear doors open to the elements, taking in the evening's breeze. A snapshot of van life in all its glory.

"Bet he's got flies for company already," I glanced down at the smug-faced cat beside me. He cannot help how he looks, it is in his genes. He extended one paw out, then the other before peering up and blinking at me groggily. He yawned, splitting his face into two, then jumped down to elongate his spine before vanishing into the tunnel to the rear of the van. I, of course, had to traipse around the outside of the vehicle to mindlessly put the pot on, retrieve Nelson's harness and prepare to get ourselves a breath of fresh air.

"Hiya!" I waved to a twenty-something man fannying about in his kitchen. On hearing a reply, the Admirable Nelson hightailed it back to the safety of his home, leaving me, coffee in hand, to introduce myself to the stranger.

"Are you up for a chat?" I enquired. The man nodded his affirmation so I edged towards his side door.

"Have you been on the road long?" I asked by way of breaking the ice.

"Two weeks," he replied, slightly bashful. "I'm just starting to get used to it."

"I bet you have a ton of questions," I smiled.

"Yes! So many! ...Where do you get water?" The quizzing commenced.

"Cemeteries" I informed him. "Or Morrisons!" I added only after he had processed the shock. "But always carry a rucksack with an empty two-litre bottle in it to top up wherever there's a tap."

I showed him how to use the Park4Night App effectively too. He explained the mystifying peculiarities of his abode: he had built his van himself, inspired by YouTube videos. He showed me his, I showed him mine.

I am an old hand at this van life malarkey now. With the summer months reigning over us, vanlife had become fleetingly sociable, and I dared to admit: I had slowly fallen in love with this way of being and I was not sure I was at all ready to say farewell to it just yet. I had my routines. Nelson had his. He still spent an unfathomable amount of time trying to bake himself beneath the windshield. What had surprised me most about van life was just how well he had adapted to it. He remains wary of strangers and is naturally happiest when we are in the middle of nowhere. One might not be able to teach an old dog new tricks, but at the grand old age of twelve, my cat had mastered meandering in ever-changing territory. That alone was the ingredient for our combined success.

I let my place-mate for the night know my intention was to write another book. How my journey had taken me around the worst-sounding of English hamlets, villages and towns. "If it's got a cock in it, I've been there," I said wryly. He threw his head back in humour as I told him how I had visited my final phallic-based destination earlier that day.

Along the way, I had taught myself a modicum of old English so I knew that 'ley' referred to a meadow or field and that 'hat' may well mean 'protected', but of the 'ayne' I was not sure. According to Google, I learnt it meant 'one's own'. I had come from a place that can be interpreted into 'one's own protected cock field'. It sounds to my ears like an especially imaginative alternative term for the patriarchy. When I set out on this venture, I had no firm idea of what I would be researching beyond a fascination of why some people call me brave, because it jars so hard against my internal anxieties. I knew I would spend time exploring why and how women's fear differs from men's. Whether it is socialised into us or is it just simply naturally occurring: a sex-based birth defect. Nobody knows for certain. What I do know is that it continues to harm some women in creative ways, limiting our achievements, preventing us from asserting ourselves. Yet I am not alone in thinking the word 'empowerment' is nothing short of irritating and sanctimonious. Still, for too many women, those voices in our heads prattle on that we are wrong for doing things outside of the norms of our ladyships.

Across the year I have waved, or chatted to, at least a handful of solo women vanlifers. We are a rare breed, but not one close to extinction. Our only known role model comes from the film adaptation of Alan Bennett's 'The Lady in the Van'. It sort of implies that we are irascible, grotty transients wearing knee-length stained overcoats freeloading on other people's front drives. Even that week, someone had made the inevitable joke and in reply I had asked her if she had watched the film. She shook her head. The day had not fully passed before I received a text. "I'm mortified. Beyond mortified by my joke. I'm sorry." I had declined to take offence because she is just lovely as a person. However, as I age, my unthwarted willfulness to live my life fully and unrestricted will be characterised more and more as eccentric or outlandish, even though I am still a while off the time for dying my hair purple.

I had long since finished my coffee when the younger man let me know he was a TCK. He did not himself use that acronym, but I know it denotes: Third Country Kid. He is not from here, but he is not from there either. A citizen of the world. His English has a slight lilt to it, but not an accent per se. It tells me that he was predominantly raised here, but the parental influence is detectable. His parents have since returned to their home country: they were not immigrants but sojourners of foreign countries. Just like mine had been. He flits between there and here. Ever restless. He loves the food from 'over there', but struggles to find the right ingredients over here. He tells me he fits better here: personality-wise, and thinks there are better opportunities. Regardless, he wishes to spend time exploring his host country. He has plans to spend extended periods of time in foreign places. Ever restless. Ever restless.

That is my greatest fear: stopping. Staying still. Being confined to one place, not even one I might like to dwell in. Doing the living routine, week-in, week-out. Having an authority wielding rules I find arbitrary, nonsensical or stifling. My year travelling has given me a deep insight into me, and it is all down to one hour spent someplace best kept vague. One of those towns that does not invoke a sense of snobbery, nor of any inverted snobbery. A nondescript kind of locality that I had only headed into in order to attend a meeting of Alcoholics Anonymous.

Not only are they great places for getting a few litres of water, they also keep me dry. It was a dank Saturday night in the wintering months and there were just six of us sat upon the arse-numbing chairs, slurping away from chipped cups and nibbling at cheap biscuits in yet another decrepit church hall. Often, once everyone has spoken on matters brought to mind, the meeting is closed and we all slink off from whence we came, having agreed to say nothing of who we have seen nor what we have heard upon departure.

At this meeting, however, the tradition was to remain open for an entire hour and a half. The man who had spoken first, piped up again. "I just want to say that I went to boarding school. I was never sexually abused there, but what happened to me was criminal." Those were not his precise words, that is merely the gist. Once he fell silent, the man next to him opened up,

"I went to boarding school too," he whispered. Time passed as he talked of his experiences before he too quieted, allowing the silence to swirl around the room. Only it was soon punctuated by a third man snorting, bringing the room's attention to himself.

"I went to boarding school…" he began. There was a fourth man sitting to my right. The room fell about as he introduced himself with his first name: "My name is John Barleycorn, and I am an ex-boarder…" mimicking the pattern by which all AAs indicate their desire to speak. I was the only woman present, and I figured I might as well mention that I went to two. Only the sixth attendee went to a comprehensive.

It was my 'slap me round the face with a kipper' moment. The realisation that boarding school, on top of teaching me a lot about stuff either I cannot recall or never truly fathomed, as well as quite a lot of men's history and cultural norms, had perhaps done more harm than good. I had always assumed that the reason the meetings I ordinarily attended had a healthy proportion of former boarders was because for years I have lived in the *lah-di-dah* Cotswolds.

After that wintry meeting, I discovered that just one percent of the English population attends boarding school. Worse, if one extrapolates out the foreign learners, just 0.7% of English adults are separated from their families, their comforts, their wider family, their friends and their pets in order to obtain 'the best possible' education along with similarly-minded children. All that expense in order to 'set us up for success'. I wonder how many people realise that AA, and I do not know about other addiction-based recovery systems, is incredibly over-populated with boarding school alma mater. At every meeting I have attended since, far and wide, I have mentioned my boarding school status and watched for others twitching. There are always twitchers. Perhaps, we are simply lured into twelve-step systems by the absence of rules, regulations, authority figures and attendance registers, which may make other methods of acquiring abstinence less appealing. That when I go, how frequently, or which room I settle in is fully determined by me and no one else. It is a place the ex-boarder can finally learn what it means to feel safe; that people are rooting for us to beat the odds; rather than setting us up in competition against our peers. That is finally okay to talk, to be vulnerable, to admit our suffering and to ask others for help. That it is okay to connect with others and to not hide behind a façade. It is a place where overwhelming fear goes to die, but it cannot cure us of the full effects of being brought up in an institution. I used to think that alcoholics were born and not made. Today, I have profound doubts.

The other thing I learnt soon after is that so many 'experts' and therapists who talk knowledgeably on such matters end their seminars with the caveat, "perhaps boarding school is good for people who come from dysfunctional families." Respectfully, I argue the precise opposite: the child has to learn to navigate their family life, no matter how challenging that might be. The boarding school child has to become fluent and capable in two distinct and corrupting sub-cultures. When all one's energy is spent surviving, there is little opportunity to thrive, we are left to carry that desire to escape for a lifetime.

Once, girls were admitted to keep the schools accessible to boys, now they are doing their recruitment drives overseas, particularly so in China, the Eastern bloc and the Middle East. The defenders of boarding schools have always, from generation to generation, starkly asserted, "it was different in your day. It's changed". I do not agree. In part to the increasing availability of drugs in our society, the youngsters are hitting rock bottom faster. Only the lucky ones stagger into recovery. What was different in my time was the absence of research: of MRI scanners and a wealth of empirical knowledge delving into 'adverse childhood experiences' and 'theories of attachment'. This literature exists now. Yet, given all the other ills of this world, the privileged child sounds spoiled if they should talk of rough childhoods.

It is only the cost of living crisis that is threatening the bottom line of boarding schools, rendering them accessible only to the most elite of elite: those with stately homes and mini-mansions. Those very people who are most likely to become our leaders in industry and in our governance. I think I finally understand why counties get re-named and obliterated at the stroke of a pen. Because, stripped of culture and a sense of belonging, and replacing it with something artificial and man-made, it is perfectly normal to just change spaces as and when the year moves on. We moved from bed to bed, from holiday to term, from dorm to dorm. No place to call our own. And home, for the third country kids, was never here, nor was it there. Home was always someplace else.

And now that I have been to Bedfordshire, I can truthfully say I once came from *Cockayne Hatley.*

Bucking Death in Mid-Summer

"You'll die by bandits," my colleagues pronounced when I let them in on my plans. "That Lada will never make it," my English fellows exclaimed, revealing two very contrasting, but equally pessimistic, cultural reactions to the same adventure.

Rather than leaving on a jet plane, we were going to drive from central Siberia, all across Europe, before parking up somewhere in central England. We hoped to do it in three weeks.

There were no Google maps. Instead we made do with a tiny collection of diagrams of Russian roads, all written in Cyrillic. It seemed the Russians had no equivalent to a Collins A-to-Z, or at least none that we could obtain. As best we could, we readied the car, packing away all my coursework for a half-completed master's degree, and wrapping precious souvenirs we had picked up during our years there. They prompted the inevitable, "Do you remember when..."

****

If one googles '15 things you didn't know about Buckinghamshire', one might find oneself lured into the county's official tourist destination webpage. Following a quick perusal, one may briskly absorb some vaguely interesting facts about the county. I say vaguely because it depends on whether one thinks that Milton Keynes being its largest town is a particularity of the compelling kind. Nonetheless, that pertinent piece of information made the number two spot. Being home to more National Trust houses than any other county came in first place. I would posit that one might instead be more taken by the fourteenth point, or rather the lack of.

I, on the other hand, was enticed into Buckinghamshire by the mildly saucy hamlets of *Lacey Green* and *Bakers Wood.* The former has a restored windmill which can only be visited during low wind speeds lest one is decapitated, or perhaps if it blows so hard, one's outer clothing is shed. The latter, *Bakers Wood*, is substantially more fascinating: it is a settlement so swanky that it has its very own residents' committee to serve the fifty or so mini-mansions that huddle around a small grove. It is strictly out of bounds to the common or garden human pest. If that were not pretentious enough, the hamlet has its own Facebook page and a terribly glossy website where one can learn a little about the wildlife trapped within the gated community. One might be tremendously thrilled to find that the area is home to a slow worm. A slow worm looks like a snake but is in fact a legless lizard. It must be all that champagne living. Under the threat of death, the small snake-like slow worm is astonishingly quick at making a getaway should its blood be warm enough. In colder times, its next preferred defence is to poo itself. Apparently the *Ickford* generates a smell so vile, it puts the hungry off its dinner. If that fails, it resorts to biting and shedding its tail. Quite the slippery character then.

But obscure wildlife aside, it was the fifteenth listing in, "Things you didn't know about Buckinghamshire" that was of particular intrigue: That it is the most filmed county in England, claiming for itself ITV's two-decade-long ongoing drama 'Midsomer Murders'. Ordinarily, it is set in South Oxfordshire. In short, it tells the tale of the fictional county of Midsomer and its tremendously overworked Detective Chief Inspector John Barnaby, successor to his cousin Tom Barnaby, who once sharply observed, "Every time I go into any Midsomer Village it's always the same thing: Blackmail, sexual deviances, suicide, and murder. How could you possibly expect me to go and live in one of them?"

Or expect anyone else to for that matter. Yet with typically mind-boggling Englishness, given that portions of the show are filmed in quintessential Buckinghamshire, the tourist-board-powers-that-be have proclaimed the programme for themselves. It seems that even our fictional television shows also succumb to the vanishing countyship syndrome that has struck me confused more than once during my time journeying across these lands.

Regardless, if Buckinghamshire wishes to sell itself as the real life Midsomer, it begs the question of why? Probably the most striking similarity between the county of Midsomer and that of Buckinghamshire is the number of recorded homicides – both cite around four hundred or so in the last two decades, a true place of *Soulbury*. But that is where the resemblances cease. By my calculations, the chances of being dead and female in the whimsical Midsomer are as close to parity as the 2010 Equality Act endeavours to obtain in all other aspects of humanity: work, sport, education and leisure.

Having spent a year travelling around England talking about fear and bravery to groups of women, I always ask what would scare a person about living remotely, far from the madding crowds.

Unsurprisingly, 'serial killers' or just plain 'people' (which is usually clarified to mean 'men') is nominated without any undue haste or prompting on my part. Incidentally, I ranked 'axe-murderers' quite high up my fear list that I wrote before I walked across America alone.

Later, the talk leads to our risk of being slain at the hands of people (by which we mean men). Almost all women nod when asked if they have heard of the statistic that, "two women are killed every week" but often that figure includes spree-killings such as that instigated by terrorists, be they bomb-based or similar ram-raiding atrocities. In reality, of the average one hundred and forty femicides per year, nearly two-thirds are murdered by their spouse, partner or boyfriend, past or present. That works out to around ninety women per year. In a population of thirty million men, I quite fancy my chances of avoiding crossing paths with a serial killer.

The Thames Valley Region, which includes Buckinghamshire, Berkshire and Oxfordshire, recorded forty-three femicides between the years 2009 and 2018. Using these metrics, at least twenty-seven of them were killed by someone they were previously intimate with. Nominally, one's chances of death in the Midsomer region converts to a rate of less than two women per million, which is about the national average for women generally. The greatest risks occur in the North East, Greater Manchester, Leicestershire and the West Midlands, all of whom record in excess of three femicides per million. For context, England as a whole has a homicide rate of nearly twelve per million if we bring male victims into the conversation.

What may give mothers nightmares is the next biggest threat to life: sons. Around ten women per year are killed by their male offspring, just slightly less than the eleven women per annum who die at the hands of a stranger. Sometimes these two rankings swap round. And if one is in any doubt, I obtained all this information from a dedicated team of researchers who meticulously track down the minutiae of every fatal wounding of women each and every year. Their annual publication 'Femicide Census' is freely available on www.femicidecensus.org. I highly recommend their ten-year report, which I believe is an insightful read for all women and not just those, like me, with a penchant for understanding women's lives.

As Jena Freidman once asserted: women do not watch true crime, we study it. Nearly two-thirds of women admit to engaging with podcasts, films or shows that recant vicious, gruesome and abhorrent slayings of their fellow human beings for reasons that make no sense whatsoever. I am one of them and even I can not possibly explain why

I feel a frisson of excitement when a new biopic of a serial killer is released, even though I already know who did it, why and how.

It is reassuring to learn that In recent decades there has seen a drastic decline in serial killing. One explanation for this is that the sexually deviant are more readily satisfied supplied via diversionary porn and webcam titillation supplying the need for a *Great cum Marsh.* Others assert quite the opposite: that it objectifies women and creates a perception that all women are gagging for it but the advent of sophisticated technology and the evolution of clinically-accurate forensic science acts as a deterrent.

Except that year on year, killing of women remains largely unaffected by such innovations because, again, the vast majority of women are killed by people known to them. Our danger remains in the home. What is odd is that when we are not living in fear, we are bringing it in via paperback, ebooks or websites – perhaps just to keep us continually mindful that 'out there' bad things might happen.

Women are much more drawn to crime fiction as much as non-fiction than men who prefer to read tomes of war. Perhaps once one has become addicted to the concoction of hormones that drive fear, worry and anxiety, they become a difficult drug to give up. It certainly will not help if we are inculcated into a mindset of fear from a very young age, and then we are continually reminded in our twenties that it is somehow our fault for being out and about, minding our own business when trouble arrives.

Probably the most perceptive writer on such matters is Julie Bindle. She is, and was, a woman who happened to be traipsing the streets of Yorkshire at the height of the terrors reigned down by the caricature 'The Yorkshire Ripper'. Historically, women victims have carried some of the blame for their own demise for being 'sex workers', even as recently as 2006, when an Ipswich lorry driver killed at least five women. The slayings of women residing in places of *Great Horwood* implies that one's job defines one's value, and that women who prostitute themselves are lesser beings. If one wishes to extend that notion further, it insinuates that serial killers are somehow ridding the streets of immorality, thus doing society a favour. Once again, women get *Weedon.*

Even though nearly half of the victims in the Ripper's case were not employed as sex workers, there remains a legacy that women who are killed are somehow complicit in their deaths. Moreover, as Julie Bindle herself observed, every time a serial killer is reported, it is the women who the police order to stay home: it is a form of unofficial curfew *Slapton* half the population and no one seems to bat an eyelid.

Making the point obvious, back in 1981, Ms Bindle outlined the case for women's freedom by reminding the other half of the population that, "there is a serial killer on the loose in the area. Out of consideration for the safety of women, please ensure you are indoors by 8pm each evening so that women can go about their business without the fear you may provoke by simply walking behind her."

Others set up similar campaigns, and eleven women were arrested for drawing attention to the idiosyncrasy of our national policing systems. Three decades later, in Ipswich, the police again advised women to stay at home to avoid putting "themselves" in danger. It is wilful and idiosyncratic blindness to the fact that what is putting women in danger is the serial killer. It also assumes that serial killers only go after women.

"The cleverest lies, Jones, are those we're already inclined to believe,"
DCI Tom Barnaby: Midsomer Murders: Days of Misrule.

Fear is what whispers loudest. I believe it was Margaret Atwood who first observed something akin to men being afraid that women will laugh at them, whereas women are afraid men will kill them. Women have been taught over the aeons that murder is something that happens in the great outdoors, like in the cases of Midsomer, or the streets of the cities – as is depicted in any of the docu-dramas made of true crime killers. For women, this is clearly not the reality. Home is where the heart is, and it is also where the killer lurks. By being single and childfree, and then ponying about England in a van, I dramatically reduced my chances of being unlawfully slaughtered. Let that sink in for a second the next time you call me brave.

Finally to paraphrase the great criminologist, Dr. Gemma Flynn, let us not forget it is we women who should be escorting the men home: reminding them to be careful of stranger dangers, telling them to walk with their keys in their hands, or indeed coldly conveying the statistics predicting the chances of their demise as they pop out for an evening being all sociable and such.

Sleep well one and all!

The dusty roads, brimming with potholes and neglect, the drunk-drivers swerving back and forth across the multi-laned motorways circling Moscow. Corrupt police forces pulling us over to insist we pay a fine for over-sized fog lamps (standard Russian issue) or for speeding – the limit being forty-four miles per hour. Probably the dashboard wasn't calibrated, or we were going downhill with a tailwind. The mosquitos. The sixteen or seventeen hours spent daily in a cab with a heater that could not be turned off lest the engine overheated. The dehydration and the indignity of using grass verges for toileting only for a passing lorry to honk at me.

To save money, my husband had de-studded the winter tyres – but his thriftiness had left me grappling with vibrating fingers, complicating the matters of eating, writing and sleeping. They only felt comfortable when holding the steering wheel. I was in charge of communications – organising hotels in my limited Russian, getting directions when lost, which happened a lot, as well as bartering and negotiating for supplies. I revelled in all of its trials, it was just the driving I hated, especially when my husband screamed at my myriad of driving mistakes, or mocked my novice incompetence. I missed the calmness of a driving instructor patiently guiding me around roundabouts, navigating the best way, keeping me at one with the vehicle. Mostly, I was astonished that despite my expectations to the contrary, I was now a licensed driver – something so normal, so adult and so everyday. I had broken my promise to my teenage self – and that felt okay.

We trundled up towards the border, the road forked off. The first had a long queue, cars rammed nose to tail, but the second was devoid of traffic – that was our route. Within minutes of skulking down the road less travelled, through no man's land, several soldiers sprang out, guns at the ready. "Koo-da veh yer-dit-cher?" the man hollered out, combatively (Where are you going?).

"Anglia," I replied.

"A-kuda-veh?" He demanded, unsmilingly. The question I dread most in life, "Where are you from?"

"Anglia, Ya Anglichanka!" I replied as I grappled for my passport to show the camouflaged man we were in the right place, even if the car had Russian plates. "Oh! Welcome to Finland," he

announced in English and beamed, "... please continue". He gestured towards the border buildings.

The car had made it out of Russia and, best of all, no one had murdered us. It broke down once in Finland, and another time in Germany, but not terminally. I drove along the more sedate highways and the byways of Europe, but always with my heartbeat hammering a percussion. I do remember we had the mother of all rows in the channel tunnel, and we were in full sulk as we pootled towards the English port.

"Blimey! Is that a Lada Niva? You don't see many of them to the pound," the man at Dover Passport Control chortled. Sweaty, grimy, over-tired and over-stressed, I basked in my pride at having driven it from Siberia, observing his disbelief that the car had made it! Impressed as I was with what I had accomplished despite myself, now on the wrong side of the road, cowardice crept in so I insisted my husband take control, opting to complete only the final few miles on quiet country lanes as we reached our destination.

I pulled up outside my mother's house, hitting the fencepost on the way in, once again setting the husband off stratospheric. Anxiety threatened to drown my insides for the umpteenth day in succession. I ratcheted up the handbrake for the final time, quietly swearing to myself to never again take a car's steering wheel into my hands.

It was a promise maintained until the day he left our marriage.

****

According to the Urban Dictionary, 'Northampton' is a severe insult that can cause major laughs. In the course of writing this book, I have probably done far too much of this. Just in case my laughs have insulted you, I apologise for any offence caused. In fact, if anything I have ever said has distressed you, I am sorry. I never knew how utterly terrified of people I was until I examined my less-than-perfect life. It is often said that, "hurt people hurt people" and I know now that to be a matter of fact. I endeavour to do better day by day.

I never set out to write a book about boarding school either. Until this year I have never talked about my experiences to anyone, anywhere – ever. Nor has anyone ever asked me about them. Needless to say, I do not think they are places that 'make us'. Having reflected on my experiences, I now consider that too many children's souls are sold on false promises. The ramifications of that are horrific. It is a sobering fact that currently one-third of current attendees have been extricated from their homes, their families, their communities and, most importantly of all, their culture. They were not born here, and it is not intended that they will live here as adults. Yet, they are to be educated in 'Britain's finest schools' just to keep such places financially viable.

In England, more and more parents have become aware of 'Boarding School Syndrome' (a phenomenon I only recently learned of) so opt instead to rear their children themselves. Once my foreign kin have been removed from everything that is familiar, isolated in an English institution, then I ask you: Where are they from?

I parked up at Pitsford Water, having succumbed to the temptation of a cooling ice cream from a merry little van holding forth in a largely empty car park. No overnight staying permitted, and several 'pay and display' signs prominently warned off any free-loaders looking to spend a lunch hour mesmerised by Canada geese, moorhens, coots and mute swans gracefully swirling about its shores. As I munched on a deliciously creamy ninety-nine cone, the furry imbecile set about stalking the milling wildfowl – all of whom were safely protected by the unyielding windshield.

I glanced across at an ageing husband and wife cosied up in a decrepit car beside me. I watched on as they pulled dry sandwiches from a shared Tupperware container, seemingly making no conversation, but oozing contentment in their silence. Perhaps this thought might see me *Slapton*, but I will take the risk. Outwardly, they had a look of the foreign to them, just as I have a feeling of the foreign in me. One world but a universe of stories as yet unheard.

"Where are you from?" one might wish I had asked by way of breaking ice. My bet is that they have been asked a trillion times, and they too might perceive the question to be loaded and inwardly wince when politely responding to what could be deemed a racist question. I laughed as my imagination saw them answering, "*Hanging Houghton*!" delivered in the most Midland of accents. I returned my gaze to the lake, trying to identify all those for whom it was home.

Pitford's website revealed that, some years, the rarer whooper swans visit from Iceland. Another time, a sole Berwick swan sojourned here, far away from its birthplace in the Russian tundra with its arctic winters. Now in the summering months, they would have returned from whence they came, leaving me to contemplate my anticipated return to the county next door: Warwickshire.

In the course of the last twelve months, I had set up a little public speaking business, organised and run over twenty-five events single-handedly. My largest audience was forty-four and my smallest only three. My fear of no one turning up had me cancelling two events, and sickness, two more. I had written just shy of three quarters of this book, and driven just over thirty-thousand miles alone, with just a little twelve-year-old South Korean cat for company. Not bad for someone whose husband once told her she had *Nobottle*.

'Nobottle', is a word I discovered that comes from the only place I have not visited in my quest to better understand the Englishwoman's culture: the land of the Cockneys. In Cockney rhyming slang, 'bottle' derives from 'bottle and glass' and means 'arse', and to 'lose your bottle' is to lose control of one's bowels. Not an ideal happening for a van dweller. I always used to say that the best part of London was Heathrow. Today, I am not so insensitive to maintain that. For much of England's population, London is home.

On the last official day of "Van Life", I discovered a little hideaway down a dirt track, beneath a small copse, content for it to be my resting place to sit out the dismal summer's very rare warmwave. Behind me pulled up a similarly aged couple. They made their living at weekends attending festivals, directing people into parking places, bagging freebie entertainment when off duty. They saved up their income to fling themselves far and wide across Europe in the winter months, when demand for festivals fell. "They can have me when I'm *Old,*" the woman remarked defiantly. "They can have me when I'm weary and useless, then they can give me my twenty-two days holiday to do with what I like." I don't know who 'they' are, but these two made for charming van fellows. The following day they departed, and a different man, open about his struggles with Social Anxiety Disorder, made wonderful conversation about his newly acquired rescue dog. "He's rescuing me," he nodded. Everyone needs a second heartbeat, and the skittish Jack Russell was his.

My time was spent catching up on my writing, which had fallen by the wayside as I endeavoured to finish the journey within the one designated year. It had taken a full three months longer than I had planned. My regrets remained unchanged: that I did not avail myself of the pleasure of the moment. That I should, somehow, always be 'over there' or 'not here'. That life was a race to cruise through, to beat, to compete, to succeed. It is difficult to shake my belief that stasis is just a fanciful term for laziness, and laziness has always been *Badby.*

I went to yet another self-help seminar. Randomly I was given a card that says, "Time you enjoy wasting is not wasted time." No longer must I viciously castigate myself for my failings. No more

Scaldwell about my tardiness. I recognise that today I have never fully re-learnt how to play: a childish pastime that ceased the day I was taken away from the only place I have ever called home. One day, I might return there, but it may be better if sleeping dogs are left to lie.

I had started this adventure in *Shitterton*, Dorset, ignorant of much of these kelly lands. Now, quietly and without fanfare, I terminated my trip pondering about poor *Weedon Lois*. According to my trusty informant, Wikipedia, her waters cured the blind and the leprous. I had presumed that the *Weedons, Bec* and *Lois,* simply meant 'West Towns', but it seems I was wrong. In fact, their names derive from the Anglo-Saxon for a 'shrine' or 'holy place'. An ending I think apt for a book called, "Everywhere I Never Wanted To Go".

Thank you for travelling with me, I am very grateful that you have joined me. It has been one hell of a ride. If you could kindly play your part by helping me restock the finances - a short review, a recommendation or a simple rating, my gratitude will be boundless. Best of all, if you could follow the instructions given on page 58, tagging me in, I would love to play the game 'Hide and seek' on the Internet with you.

I will also express here my deepest gratitude to Clare McNulty: the wonderful perfectionist who helped edit this book; whilst fundamentally disagreeing with some of it. For starters: she thinks Stilton is the best cheese in Britain. She is also a woman who loathes me using the word 'whilst' rather than 'while'. I may have passive-aggressively changed a few back. If you do spot any errors, they are almost certainly mine – although I will probably blame Nelson who has a nasty habit of jumping on the laptop when he wants attention.

Talking of whom: To the Admirable Nelson: Thank you from the bottom of my heart for the happiest year of my life, and for being a warming cuddle on the tough days. I am tremendously sorry about all those objects that fell on your head.

And finally, to England: It has been a pleasure getting to know you at long last.

****

Everything You Ever Taught Me

"If you've got a lot on your mind, go for a walk…"

In 2020, the world went to hell in a handbag. This isn't exactly headline news - although it was then. I went from perfectly locatable in the Cotswolds to utterly baffled in the American wilderness when I embarked on a quest to walk from Mexico to Canada for reasons that escape me. It was most probably nothing more dramatic than a mid-life crisis.

Perhaps I should have come 'home' but I lived in the deluded optimism the pandemic would be all over by the summer. Besides, I'd given up my place: shoving my belongings into storage, persuaded someone to take care of my cat and someone else to look after my car. I did think about returning but each time I popped into civilisation to top up my supplies, I discovered a new reason to run for the hills. So "home" became a tent, a mere flimsy bit of fabric to protect me from every conceivable terror that exists in the wilderness - bears, rattlesnakes, deserts, avalanches and other human beings. Most dangerous of all was the racket inside my head.

Everything You Ever Taught Me is my journey, relying on nothing other than the twelve steps of recovery, teaching me to take it one day at a time, one step at a time and one bloody ginormous mountain at a time as I staggered my way along the Pacific Crest Trail. As midlife crises go, I remain clueless why mine took me from my sofa to the Canadian border via the fridge, powered as I was only by two chubby legs and a fart arse.

Authentic, not paid-for and untampered reviews…

"Best hiking book ever. Best book on being a human I have read."

"...had me feeling emotional, followed by involuntary snorts at various points throughout."

"I cannot put it down. It's one of the best books I've read for ages."

"…keeps you hooked with her entertaining narrative throughout the pages"

STUFF I READ TO WRITE THIS BOOK -

Besides hours of Wikipedia and Google!

A History of English Place Names, Moss J (2020); Pen & Sword History
The Book of English Place Names, Taggart C (2023); Ebury Press
A Dictionary of English Place Names, Mills AD (2011); OUP
Invisible Women, Criado Perez, C (2019); Chatto & Windus
Empty Cradles, Humpreys, M (1994); Doubleday
The Gendered Brain, Rippon G, (2020) Vintage
They Fought in the Fields, Tyrer N, (2007) The History Press

Dorset
www.dorset.live/news/dorset-news/went-shitterton-rural-dorset-deserves-7158231↠www.bereregisparishcouncil.co.uk/↠www.bereregis.org/village-industries-history.htm↠www.theworld.org/stories/2013-08-19/piddle-or-puddle-curious-little-english-river↠www.nationaltrust.org.uk/visit/dorset/cerne-giant↠www.megalithic.co.uk/article.php?sid=7527↠www.history.co.uk/articles/when-womens-football-was-bigger-than-mens↠www.historic-uk.com/CultureUK/Pioneers-Womens-Football/
Hampshire
www.bucklershard.co.uk/about-us/↠www.british-history.ac.uk/vch/hants/vol4/pp525-530↠wwwagathachristie.fandom.com/wiki/Alibi_(Michael_Morton_adaptation)
East Sussex
www.edition.cnn.com/2021/01/26/health/swearing-benefits-wellness/index.html↠www.greatbritishlife.co.uk/homes-and-gardens/places-to-live/22573642.15-things-know-midhurst/↠www.evvy.com/blog/censoring-vagina↠www.jstor.org/stable/3813705↠adrienguille.github.io/publications/swearing.pdf↠www.journalijdr.com/nature-types-motives-and-functions-swear-words-sociolinguistic-analysis↠www.keele.ac.uk/research/researchnews/2020/june/traditional-swearing/tolerate-pain.php
West Sussex
www.english-heritage.org.uk/visit/inspire-me/origins-of-english-place-names
Kent
www.theguardian.com/environment/2021/apr/19/sewage-island-how-britain-spews-untreated-waste-rivers-sea↠www.kfhs.org.uk/kent-history↠www.bromley.gov.uk/local-history-heritage/history-bromley-area/2↠www.kentlive.news/news/kent-news/exact-borderline-kent-london-changed-3781612↠www.mytailoredtours.com/news/what-is-a-man-of-kent-and-a-kentish-man/↠www.kentlive.news/news/kent-news/rochester-was-kents-second-city-546170↠www.bbc.co.uk/kent/content/articles/2008/05/21/garden_of_england_nature_feature.shtml
Surrey
www.bbc.co.uk/news/uk-england-surrey-18118309↠www.getsurrey.co.uk/news/surrey-news/donkey-town-called-donkey-town-13936503↠museum.chobham.org/village-history/by-era/18th-century/
Berkshire
www.getreading.co.uk/news/berkshire-history/broadmoor-hospitals-youngest-patient-10-23559199↠www.chcgra.co.uk/about↠thejournalofantiquities.com/category/rebeccas-well-at-wargrave-in-berkshire/↠www.ampcleanenergy.com/blog/how-the-ukraine-crisis-caused-a-global-wood-pellet-shortage
Wiltshire

www.wiltshire.gov.uk/article/1622/White-horses→www.history.co.uk/shows/alien-files-unsealed/articles/top-ufo-spots-in-the-uk→www.whatdotheyknow.com/request/ufo_sightings_19→www.abandonedcommunities.co.uk/snap.html→www.smithsonianmag.com/arts-culture/crop-circles-the-art-of-the-hoax-2524283/→www.amazon.co.uk/Crooked-Soley-Crop-Circle-Revelation/product-reviews/1906069174/→wiltshireweb.co.uk/summer/lacock-the-well-preserved-village→www.cotswolds.info/places/lacock.shtml→www.visitwiltshire.co.uk/whats-on/lacock-scarecrow-trail-p2964103→www.ilivehere.co.uk/swindon-wiltshire-britain-in-microcosm.html→www.swindonadvertiser.co.uk/news/23311493.swindon-residents-fume-town-labelled-one-uks-worst-live/→www.roads.org.uk/articles/the-magic-roundabout→news.bbc.co.uk/1/hi/england/2782039.stm→www.theguardian.com/uk/2003/feb/19/britishidentity.johnezard→www.bbc.co.uk/news/uk-england-wiltshire-23239341

Isle of Wight

→www.spellingsociety.org/history#/page/1→www.ruf.rice.edu/~kemmer/Histengl/spelling.html→www.omniglot.com/writing/runic.htm→aslanhub.com/2018/07/wihtwara-isle-wight/→chaucer.fas.harvard.edu/pages/great-vowel-shift→www.discoveryuk.com/mysteries/what-was-the-great-vowel-shift-and-why-did-it-happen→guernseydonkey.com/english-language-history-what-caused-the-great-vowel-shift→www.espacoidiomas.com/why-is-english-spelling-so-irregular/→www.wightlink.co.uk/blog/the-dark-side-of-the-wight→www.yourweather.co.uk/news/trending/where-is-the-sunniest-place-in-the-uk-sunshine.html→www.islandcottageholidays.com/guides/isle-of-wight-garlic→www.dailymail.co.uk/tvshowbiz/article-9853933/EDEN-CONFIDENTIAL-Cowes-Week-throws-Ladies-Day-overboard-woke-yachties-rule.html

Gloucestershire

→www.theguardian.com/technology/shortcuts/2016/mar/06/miserden-cotswolds-village-worse-internet-mount-everest→www.loc.gov/item/lcwaN0004130→www.iema.net/articles/thames-water-fined-4m-after-sewerage-discharge→www.bbc.co.uk/news/uk-england-london-60046320

Bristol

→www.bristolpost.co.uk/news/bristol-news/what-county-is-bristol-in-189099→localhistories.org/a-history-of-bristol→www.independent.co.uk/news/uk/home-news/new-jubilee-cities-benefits-costs-b2083862.html→www.centreforcities.org/blog/lets-not-pretend-that-the-winning-of-city-status-will-bring-with-it-an-economic-boom/→commonslibrary.parliament.uk/what-makes-a-city→citymonitor.ai/government/when-does-town-become-city→www.gov.uk/guidance/process-for-the-appointment-of-lord-lieutenants→www.telegraph.co.uk/women/work/peaches-golding-descendant-slave-first-black-female-lord-lieutenant/→www.bristol.ac.uk/university/history/→www.thehistorypress.co.uk/articles/11-little-known-things-about-elizabeth-garrett-anderson/→www.womenshistory.org/education-resources/biographies/elizabeth-blackwell→victorianweb.org/science/health/eganderson.html→www.medicalwomensfederation.org.uk/our-work/facts-figures

Somerset

→www.soakology.co.uk/blog/bathing-habits-of-the-world/→www.healthline.com/health/beauty-skin-care/how-often-should-you-shower→assets.publishing.service.gov.uk/media/5a8213c7e5274a2e8ab57610/1967_House_condition_survey_of_England_and_Wales.pdf→localhistories.org/a-history-of-baths-and-showers/→www.bigbathroomshop.co.uk/info/blog/clean-streak-men-vs-women-shower-habits/→www.phrases.org.uk/meanings/cleanliness-is-next-to-godliness.html→www.rcpe.ac.uk/heritage/bathing-prescription-brief-history-treatment-water

Devon

→www.nbcnews.com/think/opinion/halloween-remember-witch-hunts-were-created-patriarchy-terrified-older-women-ncna1074236→www.theguardian.com/books/2018/apr/07/cursed-from-circe-to-clinton-why-women-are-cast-as-witches→www.historic-uk.com/CultureUK/Witches-in-Britain/→exetercivicsociety.org.uk/plaques/devon-witches/→www.devonlive.com/news/devon-news/dark-history-exeter-first-last-1609485→www.english-heritage.org.uk/learn/histories/eight-witchcraft-myths

Cornwall

→www.nationalarchives.gov.uk/education/resources/elizabeth-monarchy/→www.historyextra.com/period/tudor/edward-vi-forgotten-tudor-king-henry-son-legacy-death-when-how-did-he-die/→www.historic-uk.com/HistoryUK/HistoryofEngland/Lady-Jane-Grey/→www.smithsonianmag.com/history/myth-bloody-mary-180974221/→www.history.com/topics/european-history/mary-i→escholarship.org/content/qt0tk2n9p3/qt0tk2n9p3_noSplash_64709f8c2dafc2186f766441fc3884e6.pdf→ttu-ir.tdl.org/bitstream/handle/2346/58503/SCOTT-THESIS-2014.pdf→www.bbc.co.uk/bitesize/guides/zqt9xsg/revision/3#→www.rmg.co.uk/stories/topics/were-there-female-pirates→daily.jstor.org/women-were-pirates-too/→www.telegraph.co.uk/news/2021/02/16/statues-female-pirates-will-glamorise-crime-devon-villagers/→www.visitsouthdevon.co.uk/blog/read/2023/04/pirate-history-of-south-devon-b619→www.theguardian.com/artanddesign/2023/apr/04/woke-plank-pirate-ships-diversity-democracy-cornwall-exhibition→thepirateempire.blogspot.com/2017/10/lady-pirate-maryelizabeth-killigrew.html→historymuse.medium.com/women-of-the-sea-female-pirates-before-the-1700s-391dec8e6e39→www.historyofparliamentonline.org/volume/1558-1603/member/killigrew-john-i-1584→cornishbirdblog.com/the-notorious-women-of-the-killigrew-family/→foxlinks.com/john-killigrew-1508-1567/→www.westminster-abbey.org/abbey-commemorations/commemorations/killigrew-family→gw.geneanet.org/lard?lang=en&n=killigrew&oc=0&p=john→www.geni.com/people/Capt-John-Killigrew/6000000001531288654→en.wikipedia.org/wiki/John_Killigrew_(died_1605)

Oxfordshire

→childlawadvice.org.uk/information-pages/the-law-on-smacking-children→localhistories.org/a-history-of-corporal-punishment/→publications.parliament.uk/pa/ld200405/ldjudgmt/jd050224/will-1.htm→endcorporalpunishment.org/reports-on-every-state-and-territory/uk/→historicengland.org.uk/services-skills/education/educational-images/lockup-wheatley-7640→www.darkoxfordshire.co.uk/explore/the-wheatley-village-lock-up/→www.thejusticegap.com/history-holloway-war-years/→historicengland.org.uk/research/inclusive-heritage/womens-history/suffrage/hmp-holloway/→www.theguardian.com/news/2003/aug/14/guardianobituaries.thefarrigh→www.historic-uk.com/HistoryUK/HistoryofBritain/The-Art-of-Hanging/→crimereads.com/equality-at-the-gallows-the-hanged-women-of-england/→legalhistorymiscellany.com/2022/08/09/womens-executions-in-early-modern-england/→www.digitalpanopticon.org/Execution→www.parliament.uk/about/living-heritage/evolutionofparliament/houseofcommons/reformacts/overview/furtherreformacts/→commonslibrary.parliament.uk/1918-centenary-votes-for-some-women-and-all-men/→www.bbc.co.uk/news/magazine-17159966→commons.lib.jmu.edu/mhr/vol14/iss1/3/→victoriancity.wp.st-andrews.ac.uk/women-and-the-law-in-victorian-england/→digitalcommons.buffalostate.edu/cgi/viewcontent.cgi→www.bl.uk/romantics-and-victorians/articles/gender-roles-in-the-19th-century→navigator.health.org.uk/theme/contagious-diseases-act→www.oxfordmail.co.uk/news/3801377.set-free-last/→www.oxfordfreemen.org/what-is-a-freeman/admissions→www.oxfordhistory.org.uk/mayors/government/1_freeman.html

Warwick

→www.historydefined.net/ivar-the-boneless/→www.heritagedaily.com/2021/04/the-great-heathen-army-of-vikings-that-invaded-england/138660→www.reuters.com/article/us-rights-women-ageing-idUSKBN0N41RH20150413→www.tcd.ie/library/manuscripts/blog/2018/06/aethelflaed-an-anglo-saxon-queen-and-viking-nemesis→www.historic-uk.com/HistoryUK/HistoryofEngland/Aethelflaed-Lady-of-the-Mercians/→www.thebritishmonarchy.co.uk/post/%C3%A6thelfl%C3%A6d-lady-of-the-mercians→thewildpeak.wordpress.com/tag/aethelflaed/→hefenfelth.wordpress.com/2011/08/08/lady-aethelflaeds-defense-of-chester-c-907/→historytheinterestingbits.com/2018/06/12/aethelflaed-lady-of-the-mercians/→www.bbc.co.uk/sounds/play/m00045lg

West Midlands

↠historycompany.co.uk/2016/04/29/sister-dora-the-first-female-statue/↠www.expressandstar.com/news/Features/2021/10/18/doras-one-true-love-was-tending-to-the-sick/↠www.historywebsite.co.uk/articles/Walsall/sisterdora.htm↠hansard.parliament.uk/commons/2020-09-25/debates/D02DF3E1-DFA7-4736-B943-51824CFFB00F/PublicStatues↠pssauk.org/women/↠www.historiccoventry.co.uk/history/history.php↠www.expressandstar.com/news/Features/2021/04/03/the-birth-and-death-of-a-county-the-people-never-took-to-their-hearts↠hansard.parliament.uk/Commons/1982-03-23/debates/a89f97fe-2754-43ba-a351-1f02df1f65a7/WestMidlandsCountyCouncil(Abolition)↠ec.europa.eu/eurostat/documents/345175/7451602/nuts-map-UK.pdf

Worcestershire

↠www.soyinfocenter.com↠www.english-heritage.org.uk/learn/histories/the-english-civil-wars-history-and-stories/↠www.historyextra.com/period/stuart/incorrect-english-civil-war-term-phrase-what-correct/↠www.thescarboroughnews.co.uk/news/cavaliers-versus-roundheads-577750

Herefordshire

↠www.tht.org.uk/hiv-and-sexual-health/sexual-health/improving-your-sexual-health/public-sex-environments↠www.herefordtimes.com/news/15779509.hereford-so-needs-a-ring-road/↠www.herefordtimes.com/news/11111013.10-random-herefordshire-facts-you-may-not-know/↠www.bbc.co.uk/news/uk-england-hereford-worcester-56241833↠www.theguardian.com/politics/2003/nov/17/uk.gayrights↠oro.open.ac.uk/55535/3/55535%20SUBMITTED%20VERSION.pdf

Shropshire

↠historicengland.org.uk/research/inclusive-heritage/disability-history/1050-1485/from-bethlehem-to-bedlam↠www.ncbi.nlm.nih.gov/pmc/articles/PMC3480686/↠wellcomecollection.org/articles/ZN-ELxEAACMABO5a↠kamiearan.medium.com/the-characterization-of-hysteria-throughout-history-db05f3f3524a↠link.springer.com/content/pdf/10.14310/horm.2002.1737.pdf↠beyondforeignness.org/5765↠www.nature.com/articles/s41380-022-01720-6

Staffordshire

↠www.allure.com/story/julia-roberts-underarm-hair-notting-hill-1999-photos↠www.comparethemarket.com/meerkat-your-life/articles/the-pink-tax-how-women-are-charged-more-on-products-from-mortgages-to-moisturiser/↠www.unicef.org.uk/babyfriendly/still-talking-about-a-womans-right-to-breastfeed-in-public/↠www.theguardian.com/lifeandstyle/2019/feb/21/third-of-breastfeeding-mothers-forced-to-use-toilet-to-express-milk-at-work↠www.journals.uchicago.edu/doi/abs/10.1086/691698↠www.forbes.com/sites/kimelsesser/2021/02/03/tokyo-olympics-head-thinks-women-talk-too-much---research-says-they-dont/↠time.com/4837536/do-women-really-talk-more/↠www.washingtonpost.com/outlook/2021/02/18/men-interrupt-women-tokyo-olympics/↠www.bbc.com/future/article/20131112-do-women-talk-more-than-men↠www.washingtonpost.com/news/the-switch/wp/2017/06/13/a-top-uber-board-member-just-cracked-a-joke-about-women-at-the-worst-possible-time↠www.cmu.edu/news/stories/archives/2020/october/women-interrupted-debate.html↠www.managementtoday.co.uk/female-leaders-judged-differently/women-in-business/article/1728242↠web.stanford.edu/~eckert/PDF/zimmermanwest1975.pdf↠pure.mpg.de/rest/items/item_68785_7/component/file_506904/content↠pubmed.ncbi.nlm.nih.gov/35732238/↠www.ucc-today.com/journals/issue/launch-edition/article/boys-need-bins-campaign↠aroundthetoilet.wordpress.com/↠aroundthetoilet.files.wordpress.com/2018/05/around-the-toilet-report-final-1.pdf↠www.islingtontribune.co.uk/article/we-wont-stand-for-barbican-gender-neutral-loos-say-women↠www.mayoclinichealthsystem.org/hometown-health/speaking-of-health/is-urine-incontinence-normal-for-women ↠www.nytimes.com/2020/03/17/us/women-men-hand-washing-coronavirus.html

Derbyshire

↠commonslibrary.parliament.uk/research-briefings/cbp-8083/↠www.derbytelegraph.co.uk/news/nostalgia/amazing-things-derbyshire-has-given-221518↠www.thoughtco.com/history-of-sociology-3026638↠psycnet.apa.org/record/1985-14435-00↠www.smithsonianmag.com/science-nature/h

erbert-spencer-survival-of-the-fittest-180974756/→www.libertarianism.org/publications/essays/excursions/optimism-pessimism-case-herbert-spencer-part-7→www.ladymanners.derbyshire.sch.uk/about-us/history-of-the-school→places.wishful-thinking.org.uk/DBY/Bakewell/LadyManners.html→womeninsport.org/news/more-than-1-million-teenage-girls-fall-out-of-love-with-sport/→committees.parliament.uk/writtenevidence/117505/pdf/→www.statista.com/statistics/934564/number-of-sporting-activities-participants-in-england-by-gender/→theathletic.com/4169575/2022/07/06/england-in-talks-with-nike-over-changing-white-shorts-due-to-period-concerns/→www.hopkinsmedicine.org/health/conditions-and-diseases/endometriosi→www.local.gov.uk/parliament/briefings-and-responses/parliamentary-debate-government-support-leisure-centres→insight.cumbria.ac.uk/id/eprint/2540/1/Devine_SexSportAndMoney.pdf→researchonline.gcu.ac.uk/ws/portalfiles/portal/42219536/Osborne_C.A._Skillen_F._2020_Women_in_sports_history_the_more_things_change_the_more_they_stay_the_same.pdf→thesporting.blog/blog/the-10-most-popular-sports-in-the-uk→www.womenssporttrust.com/→publications.parliament.uk/pa/cm201415/cmselect/cmcumeds/513/5130 3.htm→www.theguardian.com/sport/2023/apr/07/girls-put-off-sport-by-clothing-requirements-tess-howard→payjustice.co.uk/blog/equal-pay-for-equal-work-at-wimbledon/

Greater Manchester

→museumofyouthculture.com/madchester/→faroutmagazine.co.uk/origins-of-madchester-movement/→yougov.co.uk/ratings/entertainment/popularity/all-time-tv-programmes/all→yougov.co.uk/ratings/entertainment/popularity/radio-stations/all→www.manchestereveningnews.co.uk/business/business-news/the-estate-where-splits-are-a-way-of-life-1125592→awpc.cattcenter.iastate.edu/directory/emmeline-pankhurst/→www.thehistorypress.co.uk/articles/the-pankhursts-politics-protest-and-passion/→www.politics.co.uk/blog/2018/02/08/the-sexual-assault-faced-by-the-suffragettes/→www.johndclare.net/Women2_DidSuffragettesHelp.htm

Cheshire

→onlinedoctor.lloydspharmacy.com/uk/sexual-health-advice/vajajay-wordplay
→saintsandheathens.wordpress.com/2013/09/30/rugby-hooligans-gentlemen

Liverpool

→www.liverpoolfc-newkit.co.uk/general-chat-forum/scouser-dictionary-for-a-confused-spaniard-t20409-30.html→www.bbc.co.uk/liverpool/content/articles/2005/01/11/voices_liverpoolaccent_feature.shtml→www.theliverpudlian.com/post/how-the-scouse-accent-is-viewed-by-the-public-in-a-yougov-poll-answered-by-british-adults-in-the-uk→www.babbel.com/en/magazine/british-accents-scouse→confidentials.com/liverpool/scouse-accent-is-uks-most-untrustworthy-and-unintelligent→www.gentside.co.uk/lifestyle/study-reveals-the-uk-s-least-trustworthy-accent_art6317.html→www.pprune.org/cabin-crew/300180-who-your-nicest-celebs.html→www.liverpoolecho.co.uk/news/liverpool-news/liverpool-most-listed-buildings-outside-7574497→www.liverpoolmuseums.org.uk/archivesheet3→academic.oup.com/manchester-scholarship-online/book/15382/chapter/169963112→gal-dem.com/toxteth-riots-1981/→www.theguardian.com/news/2004/jul/29/guardianobituaries.politics→www.bbc.co.uk/news/uk-16361170→forums.mercedesclub.org.uk/index.php?threads/do-liverpudlians-collect-hub-caps.17953/→accentbiasbritain.org/→www.thejusticegap.com/hillsborough-telling-truth-scum/→www.mirror.co.uk/sport/football/news/hillsborough-cover-up-former-editor-1321191→tfn.scot/news/hillsborough-campaigner-reveals-heartache-over-1200-cash-for-sons-death→www.liverpoolecho.co.uk/news/liverpool-news/margaret-aspinall-am-grateful-people-11243827

Lancashire

→www.independent.co.uk/news/long_reads/motorway-m6-roads-britain-anniversary-north-south-england-preston-a8090521.html→www.sabre-roads.org.uk/forum/viewtopic.php?t=40409→pathetic.org.uk/features/secret_history/1939%201948/→www.gov.uk/government/news/all-new-smart-motorways-scrapped→www.bbc.co.uk/news/business-59134013→www.infrastructure-intelligence.com/article/jun-2017/m6-toll-sold-australian-investment-group-ifm→www.roads.org.uk/blog/100-y

cars-road-numbers↠tribunemag.co.uk/2019/08/barbara-castle-transport-minister↠en.wikipedia.org/wiki/Reported_Road_Casualties_Great_Britain#cite_note-DfT2008Table2-↠www.bbc.co.uk/news/uk-politics-43925289↠www.bbc.co.uk/programmes/m001qnvj↠uk-podcasts.co.uk/podcast/desert-island-discs-archive-1986-1991/rt-hon-barbara-castle↠www.cottontown.org/Politics/Blackburn%20Members%20of%20Parliament/Pages/Barbara-Castle.aspx

Cumbria

↠weather-and-climate.com/region-averages-cumbria-gb,United-Kingdom-March/precipitation↠www.luxurylodges.com/news-and-blogs/10-facts-lake-district/↠www.scafellpike.org.uk/↠ramblingman.org.uk/articles/the-mountains-of-britain/↠weather-and-climate.com/region-averages-cumbria-gb,United-Kingdom-March/precipitation↠www.theguardian.com/business/2008/may/29/britishenergygroupbusiness.nuclear1↠www.wired.co.uk/article/inside-sellafield-nuclear-waste-decommissioning↠www.theguardian.com/environment/2022/dec/15/dismantling-sellafield-epic-task-shutting-down-decomissioned-nuclear-site↠metro.co.uk/2017/08/11/want-to-survive-nuclear-attack-this-map-shows-where-you-need-to-move-6845692/↠www.cv-library.co.uk/recruitment-insight/10-least-trusted-professions-uk/↠www.these-islands.co.uk/publications/i281/why_is_britain_called_britain.aspx↠www.historic-uk.com/HistoryUK/HistoryofBritain/Rule-Britannia↠www.bullionbypost.co.uk/index/gold-and-silver/who-is-britannia

Northumbria

↠englandsnortheast.co.uk/viking-age-northumbria/↠www.historyextra.com/period/tudor/battle-flodden-battlefield-scotland-scottish-invasion-guide-facts-dates/↠www.bbc.co.uk/scotland/education/sysm/scots/teachers/background.shtml↠www.visitnorthumberland.com/inspire-me/blogs/5-fascinating-facts-about-northumberland↠upload.wikimedia.org/wikipedia/commons/e/e5/Traffic_signs%3B_report_of_the_committee_on_traffic_signs_for_all-purpose_roads.pdf

Tyne & Wear

↠pubmed.ncbi.nlm.nih.gov/18690406/↠www.npr.org/sections/thesalt/2015/08/31/427735692/are-women-better-tasters-than-men↠medicine.yale.edu/news-article/accounting-for-taste/↠www.tandfonline.com/doi/abs/10.1080/07481180701356936↠www.bmj.com/content/358/bmj.j3445↠lordslibrary.parliament.uk/womens-health-outcomes-is-there-a-gender-gap/↠sitelines.newcastle.gov.uk/SMR/16617↠www.womenshealthmag.com/health/a19992955/why-guys-spit/

County Durham

↠www.phrases.org.uk/meanings/an-englishmans-home-is-his-castle.html↠wordhistories.net/2017/07/26/englishmans-home-castle-origin/↠www.adt.co.uk/blog/the-2022-adt-burglary-report↠www.durham.police.uk/News/News-Articles/2022/February/New-figures-praise-Durham-for-burglary-detection-rates.aspx↠www.cladcodecking.co.uk/blog/post/uk-burglary-statistics↠www.ons.gov.uk/peoplepopulationandcommunity/crimeandjustice/articles/overviewofburglaryandotherhouseholdtheft/englandandwales↠www.durhamworldheritagesite.com/↠whc.unesco.org/en/list/370/↠castlejcr.com/living-in/↠www.theguardian.com/money/2017/feb/11/welcome-rabbit-hutch-britain-land-ever-shrinking-home↠www.theguardian.com/uk-news/2020/aug/15/up-to-a-third-of-national-trust-historic-homes-have-slave-trade-links↠www.nationaltrust.org.uk/who-we-are/research/addressing-our-histories-of-colonialism-and-historic-slavery#rt-the-links-between-wealth-and-slavery-at-places-in-our-care↠www.lostheritage.org.uk/houses/lh_countydurham_coxhoehall.html↠thecountryseat.org.uk/2014/09/12/40-years-on-from-the-destruction-of-the-country-house-exhibition/↠houseandheritage.org/2018/06/18/the-1970s-the-future-of-englands-country-houses/

North Yorkshire

↠www.sarahwoodbury.com/the-wild-boar-in-britain/↠www.just-eat.co.uk/explore/most-loved-cuisines↠www.poultryworld.net/poultry/chicken-tikka-masala-voted-uks-most-popular-dish/↠www.yorkshirepost.co.uk/news/from-jelly-babies-to-fruit-gums-the-15-sweet-treats-that-yorkshire-gave-the-world-47840↠yougov.co.uk/ratings/consumer/popularity/british-dishes/all↠www.singgin.com/delicious-yorkshire-foods/

West Yorkshire
↠www.theguardian.com/world/2023/apr/02/only-surviving-fragment-of-slave-cloth-found-in-derbyshire-record-office↠britishtextilebiennial.co.uk/programme/the-penistone-cloth↠www.penpictorial.co.uk/histcloth.htm↠penistonearchive.co.uk/towns-and-villages/penistone/↠www.architecturaldigest.com/story/chintz-explained↠www.dilligrey.com/blogs/news/fine-print-the-origins-of-indian-chintz↠pseudoerasmus.com/2017/01/05/ca/↠soundideas.pugetsound.edu/cgi/viewcontent.cgi?article=1001&context=history_theses↠www.romanobritain.org/8-military/mil_soldiers_subligoria_.php↠blog.join-eby.com/article/when-was-underwear-invented/↠hu-ha.com/blogs/womens-health/the-evolution-of-women-s-underwear-the-good-the-bad-and-the-downright-painful↠www.cadolle.com/en/content/14-our-story↠www.theatlantic.com/entertainment/archive/2019/06/american-suffragists-bloomers-pants-history/591484/↠thepastandthecurious.com/episodes/underwear-chronicles-eight-amelia-bloomer/↠fashionhistory.fitnyc.edu/knickerbockers/↠www.vam.ac.uk/articles/a-brief-history-of-mens-underwear↠yourparade.com/blogs/underwear/who-invented-thong-underwear-why
East Riding of Yorkshire
↠www.bbc.co.uk/bitesize/topics/z82hsbk/articles/z34djxs↠warwick.ac.uk/fac/arts/classics/warwickclassicsnetwork/romancoventry/resources/prehistoricbritain/mesolithic/↠www.ucl.ac.uk/news/2019/apr/ancient-dna-shows-migrants-introduced-farming-britain-europ↠www.english-heritage.org.uk/learn/story-of-england/prehistory/↠www.gov.uk/government/statistics/agricultural-facts-england-regional-profiles/agricultural-facts-yorkshire-and-the-humber-region↠www.holmfirthhistory.org.uk/about/holne-holme-and-holmfirth-in-history/↠blogs.ucl.ac.uk/researchers-in-museums/2019/02/24/migration-event-when-did-the-first-humans-arrive-in-britain/↠historicengland.org.uk/images-books/publications/dssg-settlement-sites-1500/heag253-settlement-sites-to-1500-ssg/↠www.johndesmond.com/blog/design/history-meaning-fences/↠www.bbc.co.uk/programmes/articles/5SDjCt364rCWVY4FRcXxMyT/talk-of-the-town-how-where-you-live-got-its-name↠www.bl.uk/learning/timeline/item106122.html↠www.castlefordacademy.com/wp-content/uploads/2022/02/Feudal-system-guided-reading.pdf↠www.britainexpress.com/History/Feudalism_and_Medieval_life.htm
South Yorkshire
↠www.recyclingbins.co.uk/recycling-facts/↠www.fswaste.co.uk/history-of-glass-recycling↠www.gpi.org/glass-recycling-facts↠www.azobuild.com/article.aspx?ArticleID=8442↠www.suzannehowe.com/newsroom/think-men-still-empty-the-bins-what-a-load-of-rubbish↠www.telegraph.co.uk/news/newstopics/howaboutthat/4971565/Women-believe-men-should-take-out-bins-and-mow-lawns.html↠www.theguardian.com/notesandqueries/query/0,,-199674,00.html↠www.bbc.co.uk/news/uk-66866879↠www.letsrecycle.com/news/women-in-waste-sector-earn-more-than-men↠www.thetimes.co.uk/article/gender-pay-gap-female-staff-clean-up-in-a-dirty-business-9lf9lv7hn
Nottinghamshire
↠www.showhouse.co.uk/news/theresa-may-becomes-first-pm-to-speak-at-national-housing-summit/↠www.nottsheritagegateway.org.uk/events/ww1.htm↠www.highrisefirefighting.co.uk/history.html↠c20society.org.uk/book-reviews/homes-places-a-history-of-nottinghams-council-houses↠www.allcottassociates.co.uk/blog/building-survey-nottingham-crane-bungalow↠www.lentontimes.co.uk/back_issues/issue_1/issue_01_10.htm↠nottinghamhiddenhistoryteam.wordpress.com/2022/06/01/little-john-of-nottingham-the-10-tonne-chiming-bell↠en.wikipedia.org/wiki/Nottingham_Council_House↠www.bbc.co.uk/news/uk-england-nottinghamshire-51191509↠www.skyscrapercity.com/threads/nottingham-city-council-to-move-into-loxely-house.951068/
Lincolnshire
↠www.visitlincoln.com/blog/what-is-a-yellowbelly↠www.bbc.co.uk/lincolnshire/asop/people/what_is_a_yellowbelly.shtml↠www.cghjournal.org/article/S1542-3565(17)30323-3/fulltext↠www.cbi.eu/market-information/fresh-fruit-vegetables/united-kingdom/market-potential↠www.pridema

gazines.co.uk/lincolnshire/food-and-drink/farming-in-lincolnshire/08-2023↠www.grimsbytelegraph.co.uk/news/grimsby-news/grimsby-named-top-30-worst-8122072↠www.autocar.co.uk/car-news/advice-company-cars/what-are-tax-breaks-electric-company-cars↠www.carmagazine.co.uk/electric/benefits-of-electric-cars/↠www.energylivenews.com/2023/06/27/evs-cause-twice-the-road-damage-of-petrol-vehicles-study-reveals/↠discoverseafood.uk/places/grimsby/↠www.theguardian.com/cities/2018/jan/23/battle-grimsby-great-again↠unherd.com/2022/12/why-grimsby-was-left-behind/↠www.greaterlincolnshirelep.co.uk/funding-and-projects/uk-food-valley/clusters/seafood-processing-cluster/↠www.foodingredientsfirst.com/news/cabbage-based-protein-facility-to-propel-growth-of-new-plant-based-powerhouse.html

Leicestershire

↠www.tasteatlas.com/100-best-rated-cheeses-in-the-world↠www.leicsra.org.uk/articles/38-centre-of-england.html↠www.bbc.co.uk/news/uk-england-leicestershire-22890463↠yougov.co.uk/politics/articles/2237-cheddar-tops-cheese-poll↠www.youtube.com/watch?v=H83rLCivlF0

Rutland

↠www.historic-uk.com/HistoryMagazine/DestinationsUK/HistoricSitesinRutland/↠d3nkl3psvxxpe9.cloudfront.net/documents/YouGov_-_Superstitions.pdf↠www.lrwt.org.uk/rutland-water/about-rutland-water↠rutlandhistory.org/pdf/rutlandwater.pdf↠www.discover-rutland.co.uk/listing/rutland-water/nature-reserve↠normantonchurch.wedding/normanton-church/↠www.marriagerecords.me.uk/history-of-marriage/↠localhistories.org/a-history-of-marriage/↠www.historyextra.com/period/medieval/love-and-marriage-in-medieval-england/↠www.medievalists.net/2023/07/love-marriage-medieval/↠weddinghand.co.uk/wedding-horseshoe-tradition-symbolism/↠theweddingguide.co.uk/silver-sixpence-in-her-shoe/↠www.brideandgroomdirect.co.uk/blogs/news/10-fascinating-wedding-superstitions-and-traditions-explained

Cambridgeshire

↠www.upworthy.com/in-1889-a-british-newspaper-asked-women-why-they-were-spinsters-and-the-responses-were-savage↠academic.oup.com/ehr/article-abstract/CXXI/492/935/501574?redirectedFrom=fulltext↠www.harbourfamilylaw.co.uk/how-many-marriages-end-in-divorce-in-the-uk/↠www.relate.org.uk/sites/default/files/2022-09/separation-divorce-factsheet-jan2014.pdf↠www.dailymail.co.uk/news/article-3201497/Wish-weren-t-ten-divorce-hot-spots-Britain-sea-Blackpool-worst-place-live-want-happy-marriage.html↠www.cambridge-news.co.uk/news/local-news/peterborough-one-highest-divorce-rates-26312783↠vardags.com/family-law/the-most-common-reasons-for-divorce↠www.thelawsuperstore.co.uk/family/help-and-advice/common-reasons-for-divorce↠www.theguardian.com/uk/2005/mar/09/lucyward↠www.qredible.co.uk/b/common-reasons-divorce/↠www.mintel.com/press-centre/all-the-single-ladies-61-of-women-in-the-uk-are-happy-to-be-single-compared-to-49-of-men/

Norfolk

↠daily.jstor.org/science-baby-names/↠pubmed.ncbi.nlm.nih.gov/31275121/↠neurosciencenews.com/spatial-cognition-sexes-15576/↠www.sciencedirect.com/science/article/abs/pii/0193397394900051↠www.admiral.com/magazine/guides/car-insurance/cheaper-car-insurance-for-women↠www.theatlantic.com/magazine/archive/2014/05/the-confidence-gap/359815/↠www.dailymail.co.uk/sciencetech/article-10594845/Women-likely-blame-fail-men-failures-bad-luck.html↠www.julianwhite.uk/streets-of-norwich-opie-street↠www.invisibleworks.co.uk/hidden-history-opie-street/↠www.eveningnews24.co.uk/news/23109919.history-us-celebrates-norwich-abolitionist-amelia-opie/↠blog.mapbox.com/mapping-female-versus-male-street-names-b4654c1e00d5↠www.europeandatajournalism.eu/cp_data_news/the-gender-gap-in-europe-s-street-names-is-here-to-stay↠www.bbc.co.uk/news/magazine-17203823↠www.west-norfolk.gov.uk/info/20083/address_management/498/street_naming_conventions↠schoolsweek.co.uk/multi-academy-trusts-6-times-more-likely-to-be-named-after-men-than-women↠www.ethnicity-facts-figures.service.gov.uk/workforce-and-business/workforce-diversity/school-teacher-workforce/latest

Suffolk
↠inigo.com/almanac/what-is-suffolk-pink↠www.suffolklive.com/news/history/what-is-suffolk-pink-6552718↠msutoday.msu.edu/news/2019/how-toys-became-gendered↠www.lettoysbetoys.org.uk/whats-wrong-with-pink-and-blue/↠www.ncbi.nlm.nih.gov/pmc/articles/PMC8451877/↠www.semanticscholar.org/paper/Maternal-Behavior-and-Perceived-Sex-of-Infant↠www.jstor.org/stable/1128775↠merl.reading.ac.uk/explore/online-exhibitions/land-girls-womens-land-army-history↠www.womenslandarmy.co.uk/

Essex
↠www.theguardian.com/environment/2023/jul/04/thames-water-fined-33m-for-pumping-sewage-into-rivers↠www.theguardian.com/money/2023/may/20/the-whole-thing-stinks-uk-water-firms-to-pay-15bn-to-shareholders-as-customers-foot-sewage-bill

Hertfordshire
↠www.cambridgeassessment.org.uk/news/top-10-topics-studied-by-a-level-history-students/↠discovernewmarket.co.uk/secrets/devils-dyke-little-known-landmark/↠en.wikipedia.org/wiki/Devil%27s_Dyke,_Cambridgeshire#cite_note-Malim1997-3↠www.historic-uk.com/HistoryUK/HistoryofEngland/Boudica/↠www.historyhit.com/facts-about-boudicca/↠www.brainyquote.com/authors/tacitus-quotes↠www.history.co.uk/article/the-life-of-boudicca-the-warrior-queen-of-the-the-iceni↠www.historic-uk.com/HistoryUK/HistoryofEngland/Boudica-and-the-Slaughter-at-Colchester/↠www.roman-britain.co.uk/the-roman-conquest-of-britain/boudica-the-iceni-warrior-queen/boudica-and-the-fall-of-verulamium-st-albans/↠www.historyhit.com/locations/st-albans/.↠localhistories.org/a-history-of-st-albans/↠www.historic-uk.com/HistoryUK/HistoryofEngland/St-Alban-Christian-Martyr/↠www.fbrt.org.uk/wp-content/uploads/2020/06/The_Two_St_Albans.pdf↠aeon.co/essays/boudica-how-a-widowed-queen-became-a-rebellious-woman-warrior↠ralphhaussler.weebly.com/boudicca.html↠historyandarchaeologyonline.com/the-evidence-for-the-historical-boudica↠www.historyextra.com/period/roman/boudica-boudicca-boadicea-warrior-woman-celtic-who-what-fate-queen-roman-empire/

Bedfordshire
↠www.plumbworld.co.uk/blog/what-are-some-alternative-words-for-toilet-and-where-do-they-come-from↠www.heatandplumb.com/blog/skip-loo-origins-toilet-slang↠wordhistories.net/2020/01/12/wooden-hill-bedfordshire/↠www.phrases.org.uk/meanings/up-the-wooden-hill-to-bedfordshire.html↠www.wayofcats.com/blog/dear-pammy-why-do-cats-throw-up-in-the-worst-places/6013↠lifehacker.com/fish-dont-know-theyre-in-water-5821126

Buckinghamshire
↠www.visitbuckinghamshire.org/article/15-things-you-didnt-know-about-buckinghamshire↠www.laceygreenwindmill.org.uk/↠www.bakerswood.org/wildlife↠www.wildlifetrusts.org/wildlife-explorer/reptiles/slow-worm↠/midsomermurders.org/mainepisodeguide.htm↠www.buckinghamshirelive.com/whats-on/whats-on-news/midsomer-murders-midsomer-named-fifth-5302244↠www.femicidecensus.org/reports/↠www.oxfordmail.co.uk/news/19166486.latest-crime-statistics-reveal-risks-women-face/↠www.femicidecensus.org/wp-content/uploads/2020/11/Femicide-Census-10-year-report.pdf↠www.youtube.com/watch?v=wV-NcNwXqcA↠www.adambowie.com/blog/2022/04/ofcom-uk-podcast-survey-2022/↠news.northeastern.edu/2023/04/26/serial-killer-decline/↠www.discovermagazine.com/the-sciences/what-explains-the-decline-of-serial-killers↠www.theatlantic.com/magazine/archive/2019/10/are-serial-killers-more-common-than-we-think/596647/↠www.theguardian.com/books/booksblog/2014/jun/30/women-crime-fiction-real-anxieties-metaphorical↠unherd.com/2019/10/how-the-ripper-fired-up-my-feminism/↠www.theguardian.com/uk/2006/dec/13/suffolkmurders.gender↠www.bbc.co.uk/programmes/articles/5BQCFMQd3mPqj7YT4hlvdCL/true-crime-five-reasons-why-women-love-it

Printed in Great Britain
by Amazon

30505422R00169